WHITE HOUSE
Profile

*A social history of the White House,
its occupants and its festivities.*

by BESS FURMAN

Illustrated

THE BOBBS-MERRILL COMPANY, INC.
INDIANAPOLIS • *Publishers* • NEW YORK

TO ALL, PAST, PRESENT, AND FUTURE,
WHO HAVE LIVED IN, SLEPT IN, VISITED,
OR WHO HOPE SOMETIME TO VISIT
1600 PENNSYLVANIA AVENUE

CONTENTS

CONTENTS—*Continued*

LIST OF ILLUSTRATIONS

LIST OF ILLUSTRATIONS—*Continued*

PREFACE

THIS book resulted from twenty years of close contact with the ever-fascinating White House. Much curiosity is aroused in that length of time on the personalities of Presidents and their wives; the interplay of social and political history; what its masters and its mistresses did to the White House; and what the White House did to them. Here I attempt a sampling of these factors in the century-and-a-half flow of life through the most important house in the United States of America.

My personal knowledge, acquired through reporting for the Associated Press, for many publications as a free-lance writer and currently for the New York *Times*, includes the Hoover, Franklin Delano Roosevelt and Truman administrations and is summarized in my autobiography, *Washington By-line*.

My sources of information for the 130 previous years, to which I here acknowledge my deep debt, were:

Library of Congress: David C. Mearns, Assistant Librarian for American Collections, made available to me an unpublished bibliography of the Presidents and a 42-page listing by Ann Duncan Brown of White House sources. Robert Charles Gooch, Assistant Director there, sleuthed out for me rare early White House references in *Niles' Weekly Register*, and Grace H. Fuller aided in many ways.

The Manuscript Division made available to me the unpublished manuscript and notes of John G. Nicolay, Lincoln's secretary and biographer, who started to write a social history of the White House but did not complete it; the Division aided me with materials on many Presidents and First Ladies.

The Prints and Photographs Division aided me in my search for illustrations.

For the benefit of others interested in White House history, an uncut manuscript of this book, *White House Profile*, fully annotated on margin as to sources, is available at the Manuscript Division by special permission of Luther Evans, Librarian of Congress.

National Archives: A rich lode of unpublished White House his-

tory awaited my search at this repository, first made available to the
public in the time of the later Roosevelt. The Archives Index, Section
42, Public Buildings and Parks, pp. 150-153 led me to Deck 13-E, a
lucky little nook where Margareth Jorgeson and her small staff produced treasures. Sample items: Original 1800 documents detailing
the unfinished state of the White House when the Adamses moved
in; original architectural drawings of Mrs. Benjamin Harrison's varied
White House plans and tradesmen's estimates on her refurnishing.
Most valuable collection is a nine-foot shelf, 28 volumes, of White
House social records from the Theodore Roosevelt remodeling to the
First World War. Those kept by Archie Butt dovetail with his three
published volumes of letters on Roosevelt and Taft. (The White
House has no archives. When a President leaves, his papers are sealed
and go with him.)

The White House: What the White House lacks in papers, it
makes up in people. To Eleanor Roosevelt I owe most, but my debt
to Lou Henry Hoover and to Bess Truman is also deep. Mrs. James M.
Helm, social secretary to the Roosevelts and Trumans, who as Miss
Edith Benham had the same position with the Woodrow Wilsons, and
Adrian B. Tolley, head of the White House Social Bureau, helped me
with social history.

Mrs. Allen Campbell of Pasadena, California, who as Miss Mildred
Hall was secretary to Mrs. Hoover, wrote for me a summary of Mrs.
Hoover's White House changes, her contributions to its comfort and
her personal interests while there. I also learned much from Malvina
Thompson, Marguerite LeHand, Grace Tully and Reathel Odum.

Much firsthand information was also given me by Chief Ushers Ike
Hoover, Ray Muir and Howell Crim; Housekeepers Ava Long and
Henrietta Nesbitt; Colonel Edwin M. Starling of the Secret Service;
Director of Transportation E. W. (Doc) Smithers, who kept mileage
records and a scrapbook from T.R. to F.D.R., and White House physicians Dr. James Coupal (Coolidge), Dr. Joel T. Boone (Hoover)
and Dr. Ross McIntire (Roosevelt).

Living Links: Through Mrs. Helm of the White House, I met Mrs.
Arthur Haldane Doig, whose grandmother was the closest friend of
Betty Bliss, mistress of the White House in the Taylor administration;
whose mother, the former Anna Barnes, was closest friend and head
bridesmaid of Nellie Grant; and who herself came out with Helen
Taft. Her grandfather, Dr. Joseph Barnes, was Surgeon General of

the Army under five Presidents, Lincoln through Garfield. I had access to her wonderful collection of White House social mementoes, scrapbooks, and original letters from residents there, and she shared with me some of her memories, which include Betty Bliss Dandridge as a charming old lady in Virginia.

Arthur Krock, head of the Washington Bureau of the New York *Times,* from whom I have learned much about Presidents, introduced me to three men with important memories of any Presidents and their wives—Robert Lincoln O'Brien, once secretary to President Cleveland; Stephen Bonsal, born 1865, newspaper reporter, diplomat and writer; and Joseph Coy Green of the Board of Examiners for Foreign Service, Department of State.

To Kate Scott Brooks, niece of Mrs. Benjamin Harrison, and to her daughter Katherine, I am indebted for a closer acquaintance with that administration. Mrs. Brooks has known all First Ladies from Mrs. Hayes on.

My husband's parents, Mr. and Mrs. Robert B. Armstrong, gave me a clear close-up of the Theodore Roosevelt administration in which Mr. Armstrong was Assistant Secretary of the Treasury.

National Capital Parks: Governmentally, the White House is Reservation Number One of the National Capital Parks, National Park Service, Department of the Interior. Through the courtesy of Edward J. Kelly, Superintendent, I had access to its file of White House photographs.

Public Buildings Service: Commissioner W. E. Reynolds, in charge of the survey which resulted in the condemnation of the old White House, personally explained to me its construction hazards and furnished me with documentation.

Commission on the Renovation of the Executive Mansion: Major General Glen E. Edgerton, Executive Director in charge of the construction of the new White House, and White House Architect Lorenzo Winslow, Secretary to the Commission and in charge of design, have given me so much of their valuable time explaining the whole remarkable rebuilding process that I deeply regret that space limitations of this book preclude use of more detail. Mr. Winslow read the final chapter to check on its accuracy.

Shrines: Watt P. Marchman, Director of Research, the Hayes Foundation, sent me a wealth of photographic, photostatic and informational material from the Hayes Memorial Library, Fremont, Ohio.

The James Buchanan Memorial Association, Lancaster, Pennsylvania, presented me with *The Story of Wheatland* by Philip Shriver Klein, with its many delightful bits from old newspapers. I received descriptive booklets from the Harrison shrine at Indianapolis; the McKinley Memorial at Niles, Ohio; and Andrew Jackson's Hermitage. The Hoover Memorial Library sent me photographs of the Lou Henry Hoover room. I visited Thomas Jefferson's Monticello, the Monroe Law Office at Fredericksburg, the Roosevelt Library at Hyde Park and the Woodrow Wilson room in the Library of Congress.

From the American Antiquarian Society, Worcester, Massachusetts, I received permission to use the *New Letters of Abigail Adams*, copyrighted by them. Charles Scribner's Sons granted permission to quote extensively from *The First Forty Years of Washington Society* by Margaret Bayard Smith.

Many years ago, David Rankin Barbee, a specialist on the Lincoln administration, aroused my interest in Mary Lincoln. For this book, he gave me access to his unique file on Elizabeth Keckley and her book. Robert S. Pickens aroused my interest in Polk.

For special material on the Monroes my appreciation goes to Laurence G. Hoes, a Monroe descendant. I also appreciate the intimate knowledge of all First Ladies which was passed on to me by his mother, Rose Gouverneur Hoes, a life-long student of them.

For prolonged use of reference material I am indebted to Gladys Miller, Marguerite Hynson, Winifred Mallon, and Sara Lamport Azrael. My thanks goes to Margaret Martin for checking and alphabetizing the bibliography. I appreciate also the faithful work of the two typists of this book, Miriam Frank and Ruth Pirtle.

Putting 150 years between covers is primarily a matter of compression. For constructive criticism of my manuscript I am forever indebted to Elizabeth Bragdon of The Bobbs-Merrill Company; Anthony Netboy, my agent; Robert B. Armstrong, Jr., my husband; and Lucile Furman, my sister, who also furnished me with her summary of the Franklin D. Roosevelt years, done for the *Democratic Digest* right after his death.

BESS FURMAN

Washington, D. C.
July 21, 1951

WHITE HOUSE PROFILE

PRESIDENTS WITH THEIR TERMS

[NOTE.—The figures indicate the number of different persons who have served as President]

PRESIDENT	SERVICE
1 George Washington	Apr. 30, 1789–Mar. 3, 1797
2 John Adams	Mar. 4, 1797–Mar. 3, 1801
3 Thomas Jefferson	Mar. 4, 1801–Mar. 3, 1805
Do	Mar. 4, 1805–Mar. 3, 1809
4 James Madison	Mar. 4, 1809–Mar. 3, 1813
Do	Mar. 4, 1813–Mar. 3, 1817
5 James Monroe	Mar. 4, 1817–Mar. 3, 1825
6 John Quincy Adams	Mar. 4, 1825–Mar. 3, 1829
7 Andrew Jackson	Mar. 4, 1829–Mar. 3, 1833
Do	Mar. 4, 1833–Mar. 3, 1837
8 Martin Van Buren	Mar. 4, 1837–Mar. 3, 1841
9 William Henry Harrison[1]	Mar. 4, 1841–Apr. 4, 1841
10 John Tyler	Apr. 6, 1841–Mar. 3, 1845
11 James K. Polk	Mar. 4, 1845–Mar. 3, 1849
12 Zachary Taylor[1]	Mar. 5, 1849–July 9, 1850
13 Millard Fillmore	July 10, 1850–Mar. 3, 1853
14 Franklin Pierce	Mar. 4, 1853–Mar. 3, 1857
15 James Buchanan	Mar. 4, 1857–Mar. 3, 1861
16 Abraham Lincoln	Mar. 4, 1861–Mar. 3, 1865
Do[1]	Mar. 4, 1865–Apr. 15, 1865
17 Andrew Johnson	Apr. 15, 1865–Mar. 3, 1869
18 Ulysses S. Grant	Mar. 4, 1869–Mar. 3, 1873
Do	Mar. 4, 1873–Mar. 3, 1877
19 Rutherford B. Hayes	Mar. 4, 1877–Mar. 3, 1881
20 James A. Garfield[1]	Mar. 4, 1881–Sept. 19, 1881
21 Chester A. Arthur	Sept. 20, 1881–Mar. 3, 1885
22 Grover Cleveland[2]	Mar. 4, 1885–Mar. 3, 1889
23 Benjamin Harrison	Mar. 4, 1889–Mar. 3, 1893
Grover Cleveland[2]	Mar. 4, 1893–Mar. 3, 1897
24 William McKinley	Mar. 4, 1897–Mar. 3, 1901
Do[1]	Mar. 4, 1901–Sept. 14, 1901
25 Theodore Roosevelt	Sept. 14, 1901–Mar. 3, 1905
Do	Mar. 4, 1905–Mar. 3, 1909
26 William H. Taft	Mar. 4, 1909–Mar. 3, 1913
27 Woodrow Wilson	Mar. 4, 1913–Mar. 3, 1921
28 Warren G. Harding[1]	Mar. 4, 1921–Aug. 2, 1923
29 Calvin Coolidge	Aug. 3, 1923–Mar. 3, 1925
Do	Mar. 4, 1925–Mar. 3, 1929
30 Herbert C. Hoover	Mar. 4, 1929–Mar. 3, 1933
31 Franklin D. Roosevelt	Mar. 4, 1933–Jan. 20, 1941
Do	Jan. 20, 1941–Jan. 20, 1945
Do[1]	Jan. 20, 1945–Apr. 12, 1945
32 Harry S. Truman	Apr. 12, 1945–

[1] Died in office.   [2] Terms not consecutive.

I | *Off to a Good Start*

... JOHN ADAMS

IN NOVEMBER of the year 1800 Abigail Adams, First Lady of the Land, was in command of a notable entourage. With a coach, ten horses, eight servants and such final household effects as could not have been sent ahead by vessel she was bound from the Adams home in Quincy, Massachusetts, to the city of Washington, District of Columbia. She was taking the same trail the capital itself had taken, New York to Philadelphia and now to Washington.

She was then fifty-six years old. She had been wife of the President for more than three and a half years, after eight years as wife of the Vice President. She was, besides, a statesman in her own rights, vigorous in thought and action. Her journey to a city just opening up was a historical review.

Abigail Adams had capably run their Massachusetts farm while her husband helped get the republic started. She had reared five children—three boys, two girls. Going to Europe as a diplomat's wife, she had become an expert manager of large affairs with little funds. As business manager of the executive household she was versed in current prices, rates of exchange and invoices.

And as for politics, one of the criticisms used against Adams in his 1800 campaign for re-election was that she had "a degree of influence over the public conduct of her husband." Right now she was carrying forward her full share of a heavy and onerous public duty.

Much as they both hated to go to Washington, John and Abigail Adams were under strict instructions from their New England consciences to get the White House started off right.

17

Immediately upon his arrival in Washington, November 2, 1800, John had shown his deep sense of this historical duty by writing Abigail his prayer for the Executive Mansion: "I pray heaven to bestow the best of blessings on this house, and on all that shall hereafter inhabit it. May none but honest and wise men ever rule under this roof." It was President Franklin D. Roosevelt who finally had that prayer carved over the fireplace in the State Dining Room.

Abigail was facing her White House duties with as much devotion as John, but with, at that moment in history, a little less forbearance. He had realized more fully what he was facing, having driven down to Washington with coach and four at the close of Congress the previous June. The lease had run out at that time on the Executive Mansion in Philadelphia and President Adams had thriftily saved storage fees by seeing the national furniture under the White House roof, well boxed, of course. For John Adams had found the White House so far from being finished that he couldn't even spend the night there. He stayed at Tunnicliffe's Tavern on Capitol Hill. Abigail had gone directly home to Massachusetts. Now, on her way to Washington, she was still referring coldly to the White House as that "unknown and unseen abode."

How much more like home was Philadelphia. She stopped there on her southward journey. It was a short stay, filled with nostalgia. Mrs. Adams took rooms at the house which had been the Executive Mansion. It was now an inn. There in 1797 she had taken over from Martha Washington the stately "court" which they both considered in keeping with the dignity of the new nation. Many a grand reception and ball had she presided over, many a formal dinner had she held in that mansion where any traveler now could spend the night. Socially, no woman in the country was better schooled. Abigail had been the first American woman ever presented at the British court. She would not be setting up a new "court" if she could have remained in Philadelphia.

"Leaving a place is like burying a friend," she had said. "It is a very unpleasant thing to break up all establishments, and to move to a place so little at present, and probably for years to come, so ill calculated for the residence of such a body as Congress."

But deeper than this uttered complaint, gnawing at the heart of Abigail, was the political split which had become highly personal between her old friend Thomas Jefferson and her husband. In a way, the move to Washington in itself symbolized the rising triumph of Jefferson over Adams.

Years before, Abigail had said of Thomas Jefferson, "He is one of the choice ones of earth!"

When Jefferson was assigned to France and Adams to London, Abigail had met Jefferson's little daughter Maria, eight years old, on her arrival in Europe accompanied only by a Negro maid. Abigail had mothered Maria for two weeks until Jefferson could send a servant across the English channel for her. There was such an instantaneously strong attachment that the child clung to Abigail and had to be taken away by force. This scene seemed very far from Mrs. Adams now. Jefferson, with his French-fed ideas of democracy, was calling her husband a royalist. During the final session of Congress in Philadelphia, Jefferson and his Antifederalists, or Republicans, had hampered Adams at every turn. Abigail more than intimated that she suspected they had even prolonged their last tributes to Washington with time-consuming eulogies in order to filibuster her husband's program. And she was bitter that Jefferson as Vice President had not given her husband the support and loyalty which Adams as Vice President had given to Washington.

This country's first party cleavage had now become clear. John Adams headed the Federal party, which stood for a national government strong in all respects, in credit, court, armed forces, economy. It was the party of the industrial North, its principles forged mostly by Alexander Hamilton, strong admirer of the British system. Thomas Jefferson headed the Antifederalists or Republicans. His was a program of state and individual rights and of expansion to the westward. His was the party of the agrarian South. But the differences between them were deeper than this. They were an echo on this side of the ocean of the great forces sweeping Europe. Jefferson, while in France, had thrilled to the ideas which started the French Revolution.

So Jefferson was candidate for President against her husband, and Abigail was very bitter about the manner in which he had conducted his campaign in an election already over whose results were not yet known. "I have heard so many lies and falsehoods propagated to answer electioneering purposes, that I am disgusted with the world, and the chief of its inhabitants do not appear worth the trouble and pain they cost to save them from destruction," she had said.

But far more poignant than any political ills, or defalcation of friendship, was Abigail's immediate private grief. For in New York she had made an official trip serve a personal purpose, a final, fleeting visit to her brilliant, beloved, but doomed son Charles. He was an alcoholic. He had lost funds put in his charge by his brother, John Quincy, then serving abroad as a diplomat. He was down and out, given shelter only by the kindness of a friend. His father had cast him off. But Abigail couldn't. Her letter to her sister describing his condition revealed the full depths of her grief although it was penned in stoic New England phrases. Abigail said that she had known she was looking at him for the last time on this earth. Gazing upon his white face—his dropsy—she had tried to convince herself that since he was "bloated but not red," alcoholism was not his final ailment. She had to take what little comfort that thought gave her on her journey. The compulsions of politics were driving her on. In three weeks Charles Adams was dead.

The road south was long and tedious. There were stops to pull the coach out of the mud. Abigail had plenty of time for long thoughts on the perversity of men and politics. Much trouble might have been saved had the founding fathers only listened to the advice she had freely proffered, by way of her husband, even before the first code of laws had been drawn up.

"I suppose in Congress you think of everything relative to trade and commerce as well as other things," she then had written John. "But as I have desired to mention to you some things, I shall not omit them."

Among the things which she had not omitted to advocate were doing away with slavery; a more liberal plan for the education of the younger generation; an excise tax on spirituous liquors, "as too frequent use of spirits endangers the well-being of society"; and votes for women.

A trail-blazing feminist indeed was Abigail. Three months before the Declaration of Independence was formulated, she had put on paper the main arguments used by the Seneca Falls ladies when they paraphrased that document 72 years later in the interest of Equal Rights.

There were times when Abigail was irked indeed with the workings of masculine minds. This whole prolonged, involved move to Washington had always seemed sheer male madness to her. She was on her journey at this moment not because of anything remotely connected with common sense, but to make good on a gentleman's agreement

consummated ten years before at Thomas Jefferson's dinner table
when the capital was in New York.

John Adams had not been among the invited guests at that dinner. The Adams character did not lend itself to backstage conniv-
ings. As Vice President he would merely preside over the Senate
when the deal would come out into the open, to be publicly voted as
privately agreed on. But both he and Abigail were well aware of
every political nuance involved long before Thomas Jefferson set the
whole matter down for history under the title, "Note on Residence
Bill." In this case "residence" meant the permanent seat of government.

Congress in 1790 had been in a double deadlock which threatened
to wreck the Union almost before it got well started. The industrial
Northern states wanted their debts taken over by the federal government. The agrarian Southern states voted them down. The Northern states wanted the capital on the Delaware River at Philadelphia.
The Southern states wanted it on the Potomac River near Georgetown. John Adams wanted it to stay where it was, and so did Abigail.
Due to the exigencies of war, insurrection and pestilence, this country
already had had seven national capitals in swift succession, with Congress meeting in as many halls. There had been the Statehouse, Philadelphia; Congress House, Baltimore; Old Court House, York; Nassau
Hall, Princeton; State House, Annapolis; Old Court House, Trenton;
and Federal Hall, New York. No wonder there was determination
behind the plan to settle down.

Secretary of the Treasury Alexander Hamilton desperately wanted
the debts funded to save United States credit abroad. In his extrem-
ity he did not hesitate to ask a political enemy, Thomas Jefferson,
just back from his service as envoy to France, to arrange a compromise. The fact that Jefferson accomplished this important favor did
not deter Hamilton from hounding Jefferson out of his place in
Washington's cabinet. This might have contributed to the clarity
of Jefferson's account of the compromise, written years later.

"This fiscal maneuvre is well known by the name of the Assump-
tion," Jefferson stated. His very use of the word "maneuvre" re-
flected his later view that Hamilton had put over a slick trick. He
described the deadlock on the debts, then narrated:

"Hamilton was in despair. As I was going to the President's one day,
I met him on the street. He walked me backwards & forwards be-

fore the President's door for half an hour. He painted pathetically the temper into which the legislature had been wrought, and disgust of those who were called the Creditor states, the danger of the secession of their members and the separation of the States. He observed that the members of the administration ought to act in concert, that tho' this question was not of my department, yet a common duty should make a common concern, and that the question having been lost by a small majority only, it was probable that an appeal from me to the judgement and discretion of some of my friends, might effect a change in the vote, and that the machine of government, now suspended, might again be set in motion.

"I proposed to him to dine with me the next day, and I would invite another friend or two, bring them into conference together, and I thought it impossible that reasonable men, consulting together coolly, could fail, by some mutual sacrifices of opinion, to form a compromise which was to save the Union."

The deal had been, in the last analysis, a swap for a swamp. Statesmen and government workers would forever after pay for that bargain, in sweat if not in blood and tears. Miasmic and humid in summer, foggy in winter, was the capital city.

Aften ten years Abigail still hated to face the final consequence of this deal, the move to Washington. She still could not understand why "the gentlemen" could not have postponed their move until the city was ready. Nor could she see why after ten years the city had made so little progress.

The result of the 1800 election at last was known, so far as the Adams family was concerned. Defeat went right over the White House doorstep with Abigail. At a time when the Presidency went to the man having the highest number of electoral votes, the Vice Presidency to the man with the next highest, regardless of political party, John Adams was counted out. Thomas Jefferson and Aaron Burr, though running as President and Vice President respectively, had received the same number of votes. The choice as to which should be President, which Vice President, thus would have to be made by the House of Representatives.

Mrs. Adams' complete grasp of the political situation was amply proved by the letter she wrote to Thomas. "Well, my dear son," she started, "South Carolina has behaved as your father always said she would. The consequence to us personally is that we retire from public life."

View of the East front of the President's House, with the alteration of the Stair-case and Portico.

Benjamin H. Latrobe. 1807.

A copy of Benjamin Latrobe's 1807 architect's drawing, showing his and Thomas Jefferson's plan for North and South Porticos.

The Hannibal clock, brought from France by the Monroes.

The returns from South Carolina had been decisive in the very close election. It is to be noted that Mrs. Adams was watching them, and that in reporting the results she correctly counted herself in on her husband's career.

"For myself and family I have few regrets," she continued. "If I did not rise with dignity, I can at least fall with ease, which is the more difficult task."

Looking at the White House with the practiced eye of an official hostess and a thrifty New England housekeeper, Abigail penned eloquent missives to her sister and daughter. Her pointed and poignant sentences could have competed with Biblical lamentations.

"This House is twice as large as our meeting House," she said. "I believe the great Hall is as big. I am sure 'tis twice as long. Cut your coat according to your cloth. But this house is built for ages to come. The establishment necessary is a tax which cannot be borne by the present salary. Nobody can form an idea of it but those who come into it. I had much rather live in the house at Philadelphia. Not one room or chamber is finished of the whole. It is habitable by fires in every part, thirteen of which we are obliged to keep daily, or sleep in wet and dampness."

She gave the place its due. It had a good view. From her window she could see the sweep of the Potomac on which the vessels passed and repassed on their way to Alexandria.

But she saw also miles of trees between the White House and its nearest neighbors, but no choppers, no carters. Inside the great place there was no bell with which to summon a servant. Two things, Abigail said, "much distressed" her, "the one is bells, but the more important one is wood." Only nine cords had been delivered to the White House, and between six and seven had to be burned to dry up the walls of the house. And the roads were so bad wood could not be drawn. The vessel which carried Mrs. Adams' clothes had not arrived. The ladies were impatient for a drawing room. She had "no looking-glasses but dwarfs" for such a house, nor "a twentieth part enough lamps to light it." Many of her things had been stolen in the move, many more broken. More than half her tea china was missing. Her nearest shopping center, Georgetown, she said, "affords nothing." She also called it "the very dirtiest hole I ever saw for a place of any trade or respectability of inhabitants." Some of her visitors came three and four miles, and to return one visit was the work of a whole day. The principal stairs were not up. And as a final flourish, Abigail recorded, there was "not the least fence, yard, or other convenience without, and the great unfinished audience room I make a drying room of to hang the clothes in."

For that eminently practical solution of her laundry problem, reported solely by herself, Abigail Adams became better known to succeeding generations than for all her vigorous intellectual activity and social leadership.

Mrs. Adams had not exaggerated. Ample evidence of that still exists in the National Archives—an agreement between the District of Columbia and James Clarke for the completion of the President's house, made on November 15, 1800, the day before she moved into the White House. This document is here reproduced for the first time.

It is agreed this day between the Commissioners and James Clarke, that the said James Clarke shall undertake and complete all the work at the Presidents House within mentioned, at the price annexed to each particular article—The Necessary and back Stairs to be finished in one fortnight from this day, and the remainder of the work not exceeding one fortnight thereafter. The whole of the work to be done in a good, substantial, neat & workmanlike manner, and to be approved by the Superintendent of the Building. The Commissioners agree to pay to the said Clarke in consideration of his doing the said work, one third of the cost thereof in hand—one third when half the work shall be compleated & approved by the Superintendent, and the remaining third when the whole shall be finished and approved as above.

In witness whereof, we have put our hands and Seals this fifteenth day of Novr 1800.

Calculation of the following Work for the President's House.

Back Stairs

40 Noseings	@2/—	£ 4.0.0
120 Ballusters	@1/—	6.0.0
18 ft level handrail	@1/3 p ft	1.2.6
3 ft circular Ditto	@3/9	11.3
8 Ramps measuring 20 ft r——	6/	6.0.0
7 Knees	4/6	1.11.6
4 Doors to back Stairs— 6'6" by 2'9" = 71 feet	} 1/3	£ 1.8.9

BILL FOR THE COMPLETION OF THE
PRESIDENT'S HOUSE

It is agreed this day between the Commissioners and James Clarke, that the said James Clarke shall undertake and complete all the work at the President's House within mentioned, at the price annexed to each particular article. The Necessary and back Stairs to be finished in one fortnight from this day, and the remainder of the work not exceeding one fortnight thereafter. The whole of the work to be done in a good, substantial, neat & workman like manner, and to be approved by the Superintendent of the Building. The Commissioners agree to pay to the said Clarke in consideration of his doing the said work, ~~by payment~~ one third of the cost thereof in hand — one third when half the work shall be completed & approved by the Superintendent, and the remaining third when the whole shall be finished and approved as above

In witness whereof, we have put our hands and Seals this fifteenth day of Novr 1800

COSTS

Calculations of the following Work for the "Presidents' House.

Back Stairs

40 Nosings . . . . . @ 2/ £4.0.0
120 Ballusters ~ ~ ~ ~ @ 1/ 6.0.0
18 ft level handrail ~ @ 1/3 ft . . . 1.2.6
3 ft circular Ditto ~ ~ @ 3/9 ~ ~ ~ 11.3
8 Ramps measuring 20 ft in . 6/ . . . 6.0.0
7 Knees ~ . . . . 4/6 . . . 1.11.6
4 Doors to back Stairs - 6.6 by 2.9 }
 = 71 feet ~ ~ ~ } 1/3 ~ 4.8.9

Servants' Hall &c

2 Doors to oval Room 7.10 by 3.8 = 60 ft ~ 5.5.0
8 Do. to Closets ~ ~ 5.8 by 3.9 = 170 Do @ 1/3 10.12.6
8 Do. to pedestal past - 3.9 by 2.2 = 65 Do @ 1/3 4.1.3
1 Do. to Hall ~ ~ 8.6 by 4.2 = 35.6 @ 2/ 3.11.0
7 Necessary 10 feet by 4 ft - 3 holes & 2
    Doors - measuring 450 feet ~ ~ 6d ~ 11.5.0
The Window at the east end of the Presidents' House }
    measuring 82 ft ~ @ 7/6 8 ft } 30.0.0

Servants' Hall etc

2 Doors to oval Room . . .	7'10" by 3'8" = 60 ft		5.5.0
8 D° to Closets	5' 8" by 3'9" = 170 D° @1/3	.	10.12.6
8 D° to pedestal part . . .	3' 9" by 2'2" = 65 D° @1/3	.	4.1.3
1 D° to Hall	8' 6" by 4'2" = 35'6" @2/—	.	3.11.0

1 Necessary 10 feet by 4 ft.—3 holes & 2
    Doors—measuring 450 feet . . . . . @ . .   11.5.0
The window at the east end of the President's House ⎫   30.0.0
    Measuring 82 ft . . . . @7/6 p ft . . . . ⎭

$233.16   £87.8.9   £87.8.9

In spite of all this, the Adams household was duly functioning in time for the opening of Congress. John Adams held one weekly levee even before Abigail arrived. On the twenty-second of November, Adams, formally attired, in a coach with outriders, like George Washington before him, traveled up to the new Capitol and read his message to both houses, assembled in the Senate chamber. The House had 106 members, the Senate 32. President Adams in his message referred to the move of the capital and congratulated the people of the United States on the assembling of Congress at the permanent seat of their government. He also congratulated the Congress "on the prospect of a residence not to be changed."

Custom required that the entire Congress should personally make a return visit to the Presidential mansion. This presented quite a dilemma. As a new member of the House, Representative John Cotton Smith of Connecticut, pointed out, the only access was by a road "long and circuitous" to avoid the swamp that was Pennsylvania Avenue, and the mud was very deep even on the longer route.

"Fortunately a recruit of hackney coaches from Baltimore, by their seasonable arrival, enabled us to proceed in fine style, preceded by the sergeant at arms with the mace, on horseback," he recounted.

Thus was Adams' brief reign in the White House launched with flying colors and mace held high. That was before Thomas Jefferson's arrival in the city at the end of November.

The selfsame Sunday that Abigail arrived in Washington, another woman writer took up an also able pen. Like Abigail, she was newly arrived in the new capital. Like her, she had known politics in Philadelphia. But there the resemblance ceased. For this other newcomer was newly wed and saw the whole scene through the rose-colored glasses of a young bride. Moreover, she was a young Republican, though the daughter of a prominent Philadelphia Federalist. She thus was a member of the incoming, and not outgoing, party, and by her marriage was a highly placed member indeed.

Her name had been Margaret Bayard, but now she was Mrs. Samuel Harrison Smith. Her young husband had been secretary of the Philosophical Society in Philadelphia, of which Thomas Jefferson was president. The Philadelphia group had offered a prize for the best essay by one of its members on the best system of national education. Samuel Harrison Smith won it. Jefferson was so impressed by the essay that he took the young man under his political sponsorship and made the arrangement whereby Mr. Smith came to Washington to edit the Jeffersonian political organ, the *National Intelligencer*.

That was how it happened that on this particular mid-November Sunday Margaret Bayard Smith was writing first impressions of Washington utterly unlike those of Abigail Adams. She described the kindness of her neighbors, the beauty of the capital's setting, the cultural advantages already at hand in a teacher of French and drawing.

Though Margaret Bayard Smith's husband had known Jefferson in Philadelphia, Mrs. Smith had never met the Vice President until he dropped in one day to call on her husband. Mrs. Smith was thus unaware of the identity of her caller. Her account of the meeting told volumes about current politics.

She said that Jefferson had a voice "almost femininely soft and gentle," an "easy manner" and a "countenance beaming with benevolence." "I forgot that he was not a friend of my own, until on the opening of the door, Mr. Smith entered and introduced the stranger to me as *Mr. Jefferson*. I felt my cheeks burn and my heart throb and not a word more could I speak while he remained."

Mrs. Smith explained that while she had looked on Jefferson as "the champion of human rights" and "reformer of abuses," she had somehow retained her "previously conceived ideas of the coarseness and vulgarity of his appearance and manners.

"I was therefore equally awed and surprised, on discovering the stranger whose deportment was so dignified and gentlemanly, whose language was so refined, whose voice was so gentle, whose countenance was so benignant, to be no other than Thomas Jefferson."

Abigail Adams, as a proper Federalist, devoted the winter of 1800-1801 to setting up a dignified social salon in the Executive Mansion. Mrs. Adams believed in precedence as an outward symbol of respect to official position. Back in New York in 1790 she had recorded: "My station is always at the right hand of Mrs. Washington. I find it sometimes occupied, but on such occasions the President never fails to see that it is relinquished for me, and having removed ladies several times, they have now learned to rise up and give it to me."

Mrs. Washington and Mrs. Adams had thus presented a united front, often against criticism of courtly trappings. John Adams may have been jealous of Washington at times, but Mrs. Adams had only admiration for her predecessor. The move to the national capital brought Abigail closer geographically and in spirit to Martha Washington. One of her first callers was a messenger from Mount Vernon, bringing gifts and best wishes. Nothing could have pleased Mrs. Adams more.

With care and fidelity Abigail transplanted to the White House the customs they had worked out together in the preceding 12 years. Six rooms were habitable, and she made the most of them. The rose damask furniture which she and Mrs. Washington before her had used in the President's house in Philadelphia was arranged in the Oval Room upstairs. There Abigail set up her "drawing room," entertaining each week. There was held the New Year's reception of 1801, first full-scale social fete in the new mansion. John Adams, like George Washington, received in full dress—a suit of black velvet with silk stockings, silver knee and shoe buckles, white waistcoat, powdered hair, and gloves. He did not shake hands with his guests, but bowed to them as Washington had done.

The task of getting the social wheel going in Washington took longer than Abigail had planned. Instead of leaving in January, she found she could not tear herself away. She blamed it on ague and fever, caused by the dampness. She said there were "so many horrid Rivers to cross, and such Roads to traverse." But a letter written on February 7, 1801, revealed what really was holding her. It was the fascination of the Jefferson-Burr election contest on Capitol Hill. She would stay until after February 13, "the great important day which may in its consequences decide the fate of our country."

Abigail's letters paid some lip service to the boldness of Burr as against the visionary Jefferson, since her party was throwing its weight

to Burr. But her heart wasn't in it, and her letters showed she preferred Jefferson. Both Abigail and John Adams really feared for the
country if Aaron Burr won. Adams compared Burr's rise to "a balloon filled with inflammable gas," and said it surpassed Bonaparte's.

In spite of agues and damps Mrs. Adams was still carrying forward
the social program which must pace the Congressional session. For
her February 7 letter also said, "Today the Judges and many others,
with the heads of Departments and Ladies dine with me for the last
time."

No need to ask what the outgoing administration found to talk
about at that dinner! All eyes in the city and country around were
fastened on the election contest which had the incoming administration deadlocked up to less than a month before Inauguration Day.

In another part of the city Margaret Bayard Smith saw the Capitol Hill struggle with the same sense of a country's fate at stake.

"It was an awful crisis," Mrs. Smith wrote in her notebook as soon
as it was over. "The People who with such an overwhelming majority had declared their will would never peaceably have allowed the
man of their choice to be set aside, and the individual they had
chosen as Vice President to be put in his place. A Civil War must
have taken place, to be terminated in all human probability by a
rupture of the Union. Such consequences were at least calculated
on, and excited a deep and inflammatory interest." She added that
the citizens of Baltimore were with difficulty restrained from rushing
in with an armed force in behalf of Thomas Jefferson.

Mrs. Smith described Jefferson as a tranquil observer of the contest in which the two bodies of Congress met together, the Senators
serving "as witnesses," the Representatives as electors.

"The sitting was held with closed doors. It lasted the whole day,
the whole night." She told of how food was sent in, and beds for
the aged taken in, of how ballots were taken every hour and every
hour a messenger brought the results to the editor of the *National
Intelligencer*. "That night I never lay down or closed my eyes," said
the editor's wife.

Representative Joseph Hopper Nicholson of Maryland was carried
to the House through a snowstorm. His colleagues permitted him to
lie in a room next to the chamber, while his wife, kneeling beside him,
held up his head while guiding his hand to write his ballot.

However, it was Representative James A. Bayard of Delaware, Mrs.

Smith's first cousin and adopted brother, who finally deposited a blank ballot in the box on the thirty-sixth ballot, thus throwing the election to Jefferson. This act always was attributed to advice from Alexander Hamilton. But Margaret Bayard Smith also might have been a factor in the final result.

The political fight was over. Abigail Adams went back to Massachusetts, leaving John to tie up the loose ends. Her work would stand. No eight-year interruption by a genius named Jefferson could destroy the courtly social system in which Martha Washington and herself for 12 years had schooled many a younger woman. Among them were Mrs. Madison, Mrs. Monroe and Abigail's daughter-in-law Mrs. John Quincy Adams.

Seventeen years after she left the White House Abigail Adams still was defending her social regime there. On January 20, 1818, she wrote from Quincy to the editor of *Niles' Register* as follows:

Mr. Niles:
Upon taking up your register the other day a communication respecting drawing rooms attracted my attention. Your correspondent must have been misinformed when he states that there was any distinction of party made at the drawing rooms while I had the honor to preside there. Any gentlemen or lady, of either party, who chose to visit there were received with equal civility. And from your correspondent I have now for the first time learned that any person withdrew from political motives. The gentlemen of both houses of Congress received and accepted the invitations of the President to dine with him, and but one of the whole number ever so far forgot the character of a gentleman as to send an uncivil refusal.
I am, sir, your humble servant,
ABIGAIL ADAMS

Editor H. Niles, publishing this letter in his issue of January 31, replied in print to Mrs. Adams. The criticism of her drawing room had not appeared in his paper, but in another "published in the form and manner of the 'Weekly Register' in a different place." He described this publication as an attempted copy of scurrilous content which he saw only by accident and would not allow in his office. The article about Mrs. Adams' drawing room had been called to his attention, but he had "cast it aside" as repugnant to the principles under which he conducted his own paper.

"I could not believe that the public was in any way interested in the *domestic* arrangements of the president's *wife*," he wrote, emphasizing with italics. "Not being decisively instructed, I have only to hope that in publishing your letter I have met your wishes on the subject," he concluded his letter to Mrs. Adams. "The record of facts thereby made will much over-balance and out-live the calumny. Nay, when the calumny is forgotten, it will stand in evidence of your impartially polite attentions to all that were pleased to visit the 'Drawing room while you had the honor to preside there.'"

Mrs. Adams' drawing room did indeed go down in history—even to the point of an adequate detail as to how it looked. An inventory left by her successor, Thomas Jefferson, listed the drawing-room furniture installed by Abigail Adams in the Oval Room on the second floor of the White House, overlooking the south grounds. It consisted of 22 mahogany chairs with crimson damask bottoms, five crimson damask window curtains with cornice, and two mahogany sofas with crimson bottoms.

2 | *Master of the Mansion*

...JEFFERSON

THOMAS JEFFERSON'S dramatically democratic inauguration was authentically reported on the spot by Samuel Harrison Smith, editor of the *National Intelligencer*. His handling of this event went far beyond a routine reporting job. It was of the type which in a much later day resulted in Pulitzer prizes. Surely no reporter ever functioned with a sharper sense of history in the making.

Smith had secured from Thomas Jefferson an advance copy of the original script of his inaugural address, which was preserved from that time forth in the Smith family archives. In fact, Smith even had the speech in type in advance of the event. This made possible a journalistic scoop spectacular for that day and age. As the capacity crowd surged out of the Senate chamber after hearing Mr. Jefferson it was met with hawkers of the four-page *National Intelligencer* which displayed on page three the full text of the address that had just been heard. The headline was a bell note of journalistic triumph:

PRESIDENT'S SPEECH

THIS DAY

AT 12 O'CLOCK

Samuel Harrison Smith did not rest there. He accompanied the address with an editorial which began, "This day a new political era commences: the era of principle." Correctly he had called a major turn in history.

For his inauguration, Jefferson walked to the Capitol, as part of the parade of riflemen, artillery and pedestrians. After all, Mrs. Con-

33

rad's boardinghouse at C Street and New Jersey Avenue where Jefferson then lived was exactly one city block from the Capitol grounds.

In the light of this obvious situation the accounts in numerous books should have been more fair to John Adams. Always he was pictured as petulant and unreasonable for not staying to take part in Jefferson's induction. Believing as Adams did that a coach and outriders were the least to be expected of a President, his decision was understandable if not inevitable. In the political parlance of a far later day, it was preferable to "take a walk" than to share a walk with Jefferson. Adams might not even have been invited to stay. Jefferson was understandably angry with the Federalists for throwing their weight against him in the long election contest, and especially at Adams for busily filling governmental vacancies with Federalists up to his last day in the White House.

Margaret Bayard Smith glowingly recorded the inauguration:

"I have this morning witnessed one of the most interesting scenes a free people can ever witness. . . . I cannot describe the agitation I felt while I looked around on the various multitude and while I listened to an address containing principles the most correct, sentiments the most liberal, wishes the most benevolent, conveyed in the most appropriate and elegant language and in a manner mild as it was firm. . . . The Senate chamber was so crowded I believe not another creature could enter. On one side of the house the Senators sat, the other was resigned by the representatives to the ladies. . . . It has been conjectured by several gentlemen whom I've asked that there were near a thousand persons within the walls."

Those who heard Jefferson's low voice and those who read the speech later had plenty to ponder.

In sweeping sentences Jefferson described the country whose direction he was taking over as "a rising nation, spread over a wide and fruitful land, traversing all the seas with rich production of their industry, engaged in commerce with nations who feel power and forget right, advancing rapidly to destinies beyond the reach of mortal eye." He spoke of it as "a chosen country, with room enough for our descendants to the thousandth and thousandth generation." He said he was humble before the magnitude of his task. He sought to assuage the rancors of the past campaign. "We are all republicans; we are all federalists," he said.

He listed his "essential principles of government": equal and exact justice to all men; honest friendship with all nations, entangling alliances with none; the support of state governments in all their rights; preservation of the general government in constitutional vigor; jealous care of election rights; acquiescence in majority decisions; supremacy of the civil over the military; honest payment of debts; diffusion of information; freedom of religion, of the press, of speech and of the person, with right of trial by jury.

Having spoken as President, Thomas Jefferson returned to his self-chosen lowly lot at Mrs. Conrad's boardinghouse, at the very foot of a table for thirty.

"Even on the day of his inauguration when he entered the dining hall no other seat was offered him by the gentlemen," said Mrs. Smith. "Mrs. Brown [wife of Senator John Brown of Kentucky] from an impulse which she said she could not resist, offered him her seat but he smilingly declined it and took his usual place at the bottom of the table. She said she felt indignant for a moment and almost hated the leveling principle of democracy though her husband was a zealous democrat."

Here Mrs. Smith made one of her exceedingly rare adverse criticisms of Thomas Jefferson: "Certainly this was carrying equality rather too far."

President Jefferson continued to reside at the Capitol Hill boardinghouse until March 19. It must have taken that long to bring from his ever-amazing mountaintop home Monticello, near Charlottesville, Virginia, the household goods, staff of servants, ingenious gadgets and art objects which would enable him to live in the excellent style to which he was accustomed there.

Among the arriving Jeffersonian effects was a spectacular turnout of four full-blooded bays (newly purchased for him by his son-in-law, John Wayles Eppes, at a cost of $1,600) with coach and coachman. This equipage Jefferson maintained throughout his term of office, although he used it rarely. A superb horseman, he much preferred his daily rides on his saddle horse, "the magnificent Wildair."

With pride in the progress of a new nation Jefferson hung in his bedroom prints of Washington, Adams and himself. He installed there and in two other bedrooms three of his "machines to hang clothes on," described as similar to a turnstile. Its rotations brought the day's costumes out from the remoter recesses of the wardrobe.

Through the Jefferson years Dolley Madison delighted in displaying
this unique device to Washington visitors. Quite naturally Mrs.
Madison felt free to take guests on tours through the White House.
She was the wife of James Madison, the man Jefferson looked on as a
son. Madison was Jefferson's neighbor in Virginia, his collaborator
on countless documents elucidating the new political philosophy of
individual human rights, and his Secretary of State.

When Jefferson moved into the Executive Mansion it was with an
official declaration of continuing democratic processes—no drawing
rooms, no levees for the socially elect, no precedence; two mass celebrations—come one, come all—each year, on the Fourth of July and
on New Year's Day.

This edict was not acceptable to "the ladies" who had been so
pressing in their demands on Mrs. Adams for a drawing room. There
was even an organized movement against it. In a body the social
leaders of Washington went to the White House as though they had
been invited, and were allowed in. President Jefferson, returning
from his daily ride, walked into their midst in his riding boots and
was so affable and gracious that they never even voiced their griev-
ances and retired defeated.

His refusal to meet women on a "drawing room" basis did not mean
that Jefferson would eliminate them from the White House social
scene. On the contrary, he recognized their importance to his various
projects.

Jefferson always had on call perhaps the most famous hostess this
nation has ever produced, Mrs. James Madison. Either of his own
daughters would have graced the White House. But both the competent Martha—Mrs. Thomas Mann Randolph—and the beautiful
Maria—Mrs. John Wayles Eppes—were kept in Virginia by young
families. Jefferson considered the way of life available at rural Monticello far better than one which centered around city social affairs.
Family upbringing he rated high. So, while his sons-in-law, elected to
Congress, lived at the White House, his daughters kept the home
fires burning at Monticello.

Whenever a hostess was needed at the White House a messenger
would go forth with a note: "Thomas Jefferson begs Mrs. Madison
to take care of female friends expected——" If by any chance Mrs.
Madison were in the country, the President would call on the wife
of another member of his cabinet. His cabinet members and their
wives were often said to be "like one family." Jefferson would call

them together in a fatherly fashion and bespeak their co-operation. He did this on the subject of simplifying the social scene, explaining that Washington's first cabinet, to which he had belonged, had become so involved in large-scale social entertainment that the time they were compelled to devote to it proved a great burden.

By devoting only two days a year to the official scene and the populace en masse, Jefferson was able to make these events memorable spectacles. At one New Year's reception "citizens, cobblers, and tinkers" mingled with a particularly dramatic diplomatic corps. The western Indians had diplomatic representation in Jefferson's time. Osage chiefs in full regalia met the new Minister from Tunisia, Soliman Meley Meley, in rich tunic and scarlet doublet "splendidly embroidered in gold." With Meley Meley were his Creek interpreter and four somber "secretaries" with black beards and huge mustachios. Jefferson conversed with Meley Meley in Italian. The Tunisian minister was much interested in the Osages and took off his turban to show them that his head was shaved like theirs, with the exception of a tuft of hair on the crown.

Again at a Fourth of July celebration Jefferson was found by his guests "surrounded by five Cherokee chiefs" while the citizens of Washington and Georgetown "waited upon the President to make their devoirs." At these Fourth of July functions Jefferson initiated the Presidential custom of shaking hands instead of bowing. Large sideboards were covered with refreshments, cakes of various kinds. The "excellent band attached to the Marine Corps" played martial music. Year after year these midsummer receptions swelled until temporary tents and booths had to be scattered all over the White House grounds to take care of the crowds. With uncovered head the tall, slim Jefferson, gray hair bared, stood on the high steps of the White House receiving foreign ministers and citizens alike. This did not please the European diplomats. They said that Jefferson paid more attention to the aborigines from the West than to them.

From the start President Jefferson, a complex character, cleared his days in the White House for things he wanted to do, matters of infinite variety and intricate detail. One of the most absorbing of his hobbies was architecture, particularly the architecture of the White House. That huge and unfinished building might have been strange to Abigail Adams, but it wasn't to Thomas Jefferson. He had known it intimately for more than a decade.

Unknown to anyone, he had entered, incognito, the contest in

1792 to produce a plan for the President's House, for which he himself as George Washington's Secretary of State had written the advertisement. In all principal cities the offer had been published—"a premium of five hundred dollars or a medal of that value" to the winner. The prize had been no temptation to Jefferson, but an invitation to design a building he could not resist. As a youth he hadn't liked the Governor's Palace in Williamsburg and so made plans to remodel it. But he later decided to move the state capital to Richmond, which he had enough influence to do. As Ambassador to France he had been asked to find a French architect for the Richmond Capitol. Instead, he himself made the plan, a classic temple which preceded the classic revival in Europe by 20 years. On at least 15 fine old Virginia mansions, the homes of his friends, he already had, or later would, put his architectural imprint, purely as a personal favor.

So, succumbing to the inner urge, Jefferson drew up a design for the President's House. He made, in duplicate, a series of studies for a stately square building with dome and four porticoes, modeled on the famous Villa Rotonda near Vicenza. The original set of drawings he had entered in the contest under the initials "A.Z." The duplicate set he kept.

Perhaps he wondered when his ruse would be discovered. That didn't happen, however, until his great-grandson, Thomas Jefferson Coolidge, in making a careful collection of Jefferson's work, found the drawings. Soon it was also discovered that this set matched "line for line, distance for distance" A.Z.'s entry in the contest for the President's House, preserved in Baltimore.

However, George Washington and the city commissioners, the judges of the White House contest, had passed over Jefferson's classic design for that of James Hoban, who had been put in charge of the slow, discouraging task of erecting the building. Hoban's design often was compared to Leinster House in Dublin. Careful studies proved, however, that this resemblance was superficial. Actually Hoban had closely patterned the White House on a "Design for a Gentleman's House" published in *A Book of Architecture* by James Gibbs, a disciple of Christopher Wren.

When Jefferson set about improving the White House he did not consult his successful competitor, though Hoban was a permanent resident of Washington. Jefferson called in his architect friend, Benjamin Henry Latrobe, who had come to the capital to build some wharves shortly after Jefferson took office. In 1803 Jefferson appointed Latrobe surveyor of public buildings, a post he retained in the administration of James Madison.

Already at Monticello Jefferson had introduced his idea of long terraces, fronted by colonnades, on either side of the house to provide servants' quarters. Now he laid out a plan of similar colonnades for the White House, tailoring the building to its landscape. His sketches included stables, a saddle room, a coach house, icehouses and meat houses—even a henhouse fronted by classic columns. So Jefferson gave the White House the fundamental plan of terraces and colonnades, with Hoban's original ground plan in front of him. It was later found with his papers. On it Jefferson himself lightly sketched the initial idea for the South Portico, and he had Latrobe draw up the North Portico plan as part of a future-development scheme worked out in 1807. He drew also the designs for arranging the draperies at the White House windows, so detailed was his management of his ménage.

Using Thomas Claxton as purchasing agent, Jefferson canvassed the markets of the country for suitable furniture. He introduced chintz and dimity into the White House, whereas the previous occupants had clung to silks and brocades. With an eye always for the newest fashion he purchased the first gilt furniture. When Claxton wrote suggesting a pianoforte Jefferson replied that the funds were too low, and besides he had heard of a "new instrument called a claviole." Twenty-three rooms large and small were furnished to the last item by Thomas Jefferson.

When Congress convened, Jefferson initiated the custom, as more democratic, of sending up his annual message instead of appearing in person. He apparently was glad to keep the length of Pennsylvania Avenue between himself and Aaron Burr. Besides, he was no orator. He appeared to better advantage as autocrat of the dinner table.

As Minister to France, Jefferson had formed the habit of conducting his official business while acting as host. This custom he brought to high perfection in the White House. Thomas Jefferson was no keeper of a haphazard bachelor's hall. A connoisseur of the art of living, an epicurean extraordinary, he made his great gifts count in psychologically conditioning important people to his important purposes.

True, his invitations, printed in script type by Samuel H. Smith, always read, "Mr. Jefferson invites ____," instead of "The President invites ____," the form used by his two predecessors. But those who came to dine with Jefferson went away talking of his rare wines (he not only selected them himself, but also was an authority on their production); his remarkable viands (his large collection of French and Italian recipes was copied in his own neat hand); and his unique service.

Margaret Bayard Smith, of the Jefferson inner circle, best described his unique hospitality.

"It must be confessed that his domestic arrangements were full of contrivances, or *conveniences* as he called them, peculiarly his own and never met with in other houses. Too often the practical was sacrificed to the fanciful, as was evident to the most superficial observer, in the location and structure of his house at Monticello.

"Even in the President's House were introduced some of these favorite contrivances, many of them really useful and convenient. Among these, there was in his dining room an invention for introducing and removing the dinner without the opening and shutting of doors. A set of circular shelves were so contrived in the wall, that on touching a spring they turned into the room loaded with the dishes placed on them by the servants without the wall, and by the same process the removed dishes were conveyed out of the room.

"When he had any persons dining with him with which he wished to enjoy a free and unrestricted flow of conversation, the number of persons at table never exceeded four, and by each individual was placed a *dumb waiter*, containing everything necessary for the progress of the dinner from beginning to end, so as to make the attendance of servants entirely unnecessary, believing as he did that much of domestic and even public discord was produced by the mutilated and misconstructed repetition of free conversation at dinner tables."

Mrs. Smith said that President Jefferson assured distinguished travelers from countries where espionage was the custom, "You need not speak so low. We are alone and our walls have no ears."

When Alexander, Baron von Humboldt, the German scientist who taught that geography influences human beings, called on Jefferson after one of his South American expeditions, Jefferson entertained him tête à tête. When Humboldt remarked about the dumb-waiters Jefferson said that he used them when he had friends whose conversation he valued or with whom his talk was confidential. "Surely I was more gratified by this compliment than I would have been by the most costly and splendid banquet," said Baron von Humboldt.

Each day at four the President sat down at his round table with a carefully chosen company, never more than 14, to work out his formulated plans. The disgruntled diplomats who differed with him on etiquette said that he had a round table so that there could be no precedence. But Mrs. Smith had a different interpretation of the matter:

"One circumstance, though minute in itself, had certainly a great influence on the conversational power of Mr. Jefferson's guests. Instead of being arranged in straight parallel lines, where they could not see the countenance of those who sat at the same table, they circled a round, or oval, table where all could see the other's faces and feel the animating influence of looks as well as words.

"Let any dinner-giver try the experiment and he will certainly be convinced of the truth of this fact. A small, well assorted company, seated around a circular table, will ensure more social enjoyment than any of the appliances of wealth and splendor without these concomitants."

Describing Jefferson as host, Mrs. Smith told how he had brought a Mr. C., who up to that moment had been "a mere cypher," into an earnest and animated dinner-table conversation. Jefferson had turned the subject to improvement of agriculture, and said: "To you, Mr. C., we are indebted. No one more deserves the gratitude of his country." When all his guests, including Mr. C., looked astounded, President Jefferson continued, "Yes, Sir, the upland rice which you sent from Algiers, and which thus far succeeds, will, when generally adopted by the planters, prove an inestimable value to this country." Thereupon Mr. C. "took a large share in the conversation that ensued."

Mrs. Smith apparently was unaware that Thomas Jefferson at that moment was doing far more than putting a diffident guest at ease or making pleasant conversation. He was intent on the introduction of upland rice to this country because he believed it had great potentialities in the development of the Southern states. He was counting on Mr. and Mrs. Smith as publicists to mark well the words of Mr. C. and help to popularize his product.

Jefferson was versed in astronomy as well as agriculture and could discuss medicine and music as adeptly as mathematics. When Congress was in session his dinner invitations were limited to its members, others holding high office, and important foreign visitors. When Congress had gone home he called in old friends from Georgetown and Alexandria. The play of personalities about his table was meat and drink to him.

One of the liveliest subjects at his dinner table was the Lewis and Clark expedition. Even before he was Secretary of State, Jefferson had written George Rogers Clark, suggesting an expedition into the country beyond the Mississippi. As President he began immediately to push this idea. He was intent on the development of the West, whence came much of his political strength. He persuaded Congress to provide the funds and put at the head of the expedition his own secretary, Meriwether Lewis, and William Clark, younger brother of George Rogers Clark. He delegated Dolley Madison to lead a movement among the ladies whose stated purpose was "to provide everything which could possibly be needed on such a perilous journey." She depicted the dangers these men would face and collected handsomely.

To run his ménage Jefferson had a maître d'hôtel, Etienne Lemaire, who had served some of the best families abroad. He had an excellent French chef and the best-trained and highest-paid servants in the city. His White House Staff, numbering 14, was larger than the entire personnel of the State Department (which totaled nine), including the new Commissioner of Patents, Dr. William Thornton, original architect of the Capitol. When the President tallied up his first year's expenses on March 4, 1802, he found that his income did not cover the cost of his dinner parties, which he meticulously itemized as follows: $4,504.84 provisions; $2,003.71 groceries; $2,787.28 wines; and $2,675.84 for 14 servants. Jefferson himself always ordered the staple provisions from Alexandria, Georgetown or Richmond. And still his steward often paid $50 in a single day for meats and green groceries picked up at the local markets.

Any detail of gracious living was worth careful consideration by Thomas Jefferson. On a chart he kept track of the seasons when fresh vegetables would be available in the Washington market. His long list included several which came into common use generations later: broccoli, purchasable from April 7 to April 20; mushrooms, August 11 to October 19; endive, September 27 to February 29. On his return from service abroad Jefferson had introduced waffles from

Holland, macaroni from Italy and vanilla from Paris. He thereafter imported favorite foods from France—Parmesan cheese, figs, raisins, almonds, mustard, vinegars, oils, anchovies. His most varied and costly imports were wines. During his tenure in the White House he spent $10,855.90 on this item alone. In the campaign year of 1804 his wine bill was $2,668.94.

A number of American hostesses have been credited with introducing ice cream to this country. Jefferson's careful records indicate that the credit belongs to him. His recipe for ice cream was written in 18 careful steps. The very detail would indicate that he had gone into the matter thoroughly in France for the purpose of taking the process across the ocean. Included were such notations as "a layer of ice, a layer of salt for three layers," and "put it in moulds jostling it well down on the knee then put the molds into the same bucket of ice."

At one White House dinner visitors expressed amazement that the dessert had been "ice-cream brought to the table in the form of small balls, enclosed in cases of warm pastry"—obviously the forerunner of Baked Alaska. Jefferson's recipe book was handed down the generations to be printed at last in modernized version in Richmond, Virginia, in 1938.

When his two daughters, Martha and Maria, arrived with their children to spend the month of December 1802 at the White House there was a great round of festivities in Washington. Dolley Madison took them under her capable wing, and the White House coach with its beautiful bays went dashing about the town. The daughters stayed through the holidays and were present at the New Year's reception of 1803, standing near the President with Dolley Madison and her sister. During this visit one White House caller found the President on the floor playing with his grandchildren. Jefferson asked the man if he were a father and said, "If so, I need offer no apology."

Jefferson had a mockingbird which he had tamed and trained to sit on his shoulder and take food from his lips. It also hopped upstairs after him, step by step. The deep windows of the White House were filled with rare plants, his botanical experiments. He had a cabinet of rare beauty and singular shape which flew open at a touch to offer the things he needed when he studied late at night—a goblet of water, a decanter of wine, a plate of light cakes, a taper.

President Jefferson had plenty on his mind to keep him awake nights. He had to keep one jump ahead of active intrigue at home and abroad, a process which plunged him into the Louisiana Purchase.

Jefferson's first diplomatic appointment was a Minister to France. This early play for French favor was also settlement of an old score. Well he remembered how the British minister, George Hammond, in connivance with Alexander Hamilton, had checkmated his every diplomatic move when he had been Secretary of State under George Washington. At last Jefferson had exclaimed: "Hamilton is panic struck if we refuse our breach to every kick Great Britain may choose to give it." Now England was making herself more and more obnoxious by impressment of American seamen. Jefferson estimated that more than 2,000 had been seized from their ships.

But a matter came up which made Jefferson fear he would have to throw this country's weight to Britain against France. He had at last learned of the secret treaty of August 1800, under which Spain had been browbeaten into an agreement to cede Louisiana to France. With Napoleon on the rise this clearly meant that United States commerce on the Mississippi, permitted by Spain, would be cut off. Thoroughly alarmed, Jefferson started making overtures to England.

Never one to rely on a single method of achieving an end, Jefferson also empowered Minister Livingston in Paris to open negotiations to buy New Orleans and the mouth of the Mississippi. Then, to play both ends against the middle, he appointed James Monroe, almost as close a friend as Madison, to go to Paris and help Livingston in the negotiations. He furnished Monroe before sailing with an appointment in blank as Ambassador to England. If the French deal failed, the paper was to be filled in either with Monroe's name or Livingston's, whichever was less likely to be spurned by the British after the dealings with the French. An English alliance was then to be attempted.

Week after week Livingston tried to buy. Talleyrand, Napoleon's agent, blew hot and cold. But suddenly, seeing how hard it would be to defend Louisiana in the war with England, Talleyrand summoned Livingston on April 11, 1803, and offered the astonished minister all of Louisiana. Acceptance was not instant. After all, Livingston had authority to buy only New Orleans. But he did clinch the deal late at night on May 2, a few hours after his welcoming dinner to Monroe. The treaty was ratified by the Senate in October 1803, an event made more notable because John Quincy Adams, Senator from Massachusetts, made what James Madison called "a concise, nervous, manly, energetic and unequivocal eulogy of the measure" which was opposed by his own party. Madison predicted correctly that Adams would "certainly be denounced and excommunicated by his party." The denunciation came immediately, the excommunication later.

One argument against the purchase of Louisiana was that Jefferson should have conquered instead of purchased. Purchase was deemed "a mean and degrading mode of acquiring territory."

Jefferson's own qualms about the purchase centered on whether the central government had the power to do it. But never was a move more popular. The wave of public acclaim for Jefferson late in 1803 was ample to assure his re-election in 1804.

It was at this inauspicious moment that Great Britain, probably belatedly responding to Jefferson's momentary overtures of friendship in the crisis which preceded the purchase, sent a higher-ranking diplomat to Washington, Anthony Merry. He arrived in November 1803. But Jefferson was no longer interested in courting England. He had already sent Monroe from Paris to London, not to court favor, but to protest impressments. Had Minister Merry and his wife been as jolly as their name, they could hardly have found high favor at the White House.

But the mental attitude of the Merrys from the moment they set foot on American soil was enough to start trouble. Mrs. Merry immediately wrote a fellow voyager, Tom Moore, the Irish poet, how she had laughed every step of the way from Alexandria, where they landed, to Washington at the "coachie" sent for their conveyance. She cautioned Moore not to divulge this, as "trifles become *giants* in the mouths of Americans." She said that her husband repeatedly exclaimed, "Why this is a thousand times worse than the worst parts of Spain!" She wrote that the next day she would go to the Capitol, adding, "The Capitol—good heavens, what profanation! Here is a creek too—a dirty arm of the river—which they have dignified by calling it the Tiber."

Mr. Merry took umbrage at the manner in which Jefferson received his credentials. The most fanciful version of this scene, from a British source of course, was that Jefferson remained seated on a sofa, in dressing gown and slippers, and amused himself during the conversation by tossing up a slipper and catching it on a toe. If so, catching a slipper with a toe must be added to the infinitude of Jeffersonian accomplishments.

The Jefferson-Merry precedence controversy was set off when the British minister and his wife were among those bidden to dine at the President's round table. When the time came for the company to go in, Jefferson emphasized his long-held tenet of no precedence for diplomats by offering his arm as usual to Mrs. Madison instead of Mrs. Merry. Mrs. Madison's version was that she whispered to Jefferson to take Mrs. Merry, as she did not wish "to be pushed forward," but that Jefferson insisted on taking her in to dinner. The ensuing protests of the Merrys reverberated through Washington and world capitals in all the languages used in diplomacy.

Far from trying to quiet this clamor, Jefferson stirred it up further. Quite evidently he considered it good politics to be on the outs with the British as the campaign year came on. He called together his cabinet and secured their agreement to the issuance of a statement titled "Etiquette," spelling out his thesis of social equality, throwing it in the faces of the Merrys. "When brought together in society, all are perfectly equal, whether foreign or domestic, in or out of office," the statement declared. "No title being admitted here, those of foreigners give no precedence. Difference of grade among the diplomatic members gives no precedence." The document concluded with the agreement that to "maintain the principle of equality, or of pele-mele," cabinet officers in their own homes would have no rule of precedence other than "gentlemen in the mass giving precedence to ladies in the mass in passing from one apartment where they are assembled into another."

The controversy spread to Capitol Hill. After a floor debate the Senate voted to withdraw from foreign ministers a privilege which had hitherto been theirs, a chair on the right of the Vice President.

Among the many diplomatic communications going abroad on the subject was Jefferson's own account of the affair, sent to James Monroe in London in January 1804. The letter ran:

"Mr. Merry is with us, and we believe him to be personally as desirable a character as could have been sent us. But he is unluckily associated with one of an opposite in every point. She has already disturbed our harmony extremely. He began by claiming the first visit from the national Ministers. He corrected himself in this. But

a pretension to take precedence at dinner, etc. over all others is per-
severed in.

"We have told him that the principle of society, as well as of
government with us, is the equality of the individuals composing it;
that no man here would come to dinner where he was to be marked
with inferiority to any other; that we might as well attempt to force
our principle of equality at St. James's as he his principle of precedence here."

James Monroe was having a hard enough time in England without having this tempest added to his tribulations. In reprisal for the
rebuffs the Merrys experienced in Washington, the Monroes were
unmercifully snubbed in London. Not until they learned to be very
haughty indeed did the Monroes command proper recognition from
British officialdom.

Historians have habitually given light and humorous treatment to
the Mrs. Merry-versus-Mrs. Madison affair. Jefferson, to have taken
it so seriously, must have felt a premonition of international intrigue
connected with it. If so, his instinct was correct.

As early as January 1804 Merry had become chief repository of the
most vicious secrets of Jefferson's worst enemies. Conspirators against
the Union found a ready audience at the Merry residence on K
Street, close to Rock Creek. A former Ambassador to Spain, Merry
had in his political and social orbit the Marquis de Casa Yrujo, the
Spanish minister. But as time went on they intrigued more against
than with each other.

To Merry went two leading Federalists, Senator Timothy Pickering of Massachusetts and Senator Roger Griswold of Connecticut,
asking British aid in setting up a separate New England Republic.
The tide of secession sentiment rose in New England in direct ratio
to Jefferson's wooing of the West. Later in that campaign year of
1804 Merry received his first overtures from the indignant Aaron
Burr. Shoved off the Jefferson ticket by George Clinton, governor of
New York, Burr had sought the governorship, but had been thwarted
by the backstage manipulations of Alexander Hamilton. So Burr
challenged Hamilton to the duel which was fought on July 11, 1804.
Hamilton died the next day. Burr fled southward, pausing long
enough in Philadelphia to request, through an intermediary, British
financial aid from Anthony Merry for his scheme to separate the

Western states from the Union. In one year Merry had received two widely different dismemberment propositions from United States citizens holding high office. Burr later put up to Merry many spectacular schemes to make use of British resources, including the fleet, with a view to setting up a kingdom for himself. They all failed, but not for lack of interest on the part of Merry.

With all this business afoot the Merrys not only stood their social ground, but used every opportunity to hold the Jeffersons and the Madisons up to scorn. Mrs. Merry made fun of Dolley Madison's table, said it was "more like a harvest-home supper than the entertainment of a Secretary of State." Mrs. Madison pertly replied that abundance was preferable to elegance; customs formed taste; and as the profusion so repugnant to foreign customs arose from the abundance and prosperity of our country, she did not hesitate to sacrifice European delicacy for "the less elegant but more liberal fashion of Virginia."

While Jefferson was in summer residence at Monticello in 1804 his beautiful younger daughter Maria died there. Abigail Adams, remembering with tenderness the little girl she had mothered so many years before, broke the long silence between the two families. She wrote Jefferson a letter of condolence. Jefferson replied and asked Mrs. Adams the reasons for the estrangement. On his part, he said, he had but one grudge against Adams—"I did consider his last appointments as personally unkind; they were from my most ardent political enemies." Mrs. Adams aptly replied that her husband had only followed Washington's example in filling vacancies at the close of his term with men he considered able.

Matching frankness with his own, Abigail told Jefferson the two things which had rankled most with Adams—that Jefferson had remitted the fine of a man convicted of slandering Adams; and that he had removed their son John Quincy as district judge.

Jefferson's explanation on the first point apparently satisfied Abigail; but his statement that he had merely appointed a man who chanced to supersede her son brought from Abigail this comment: "a quibble, and as such I pass it." And in a few clear paragraphs she brought this remarkable correspondence to a close, wishing him well.

This exchange of letters, unknown to her husband until a month after it ended and then annotated by him with "no comment at this time," at least broke the ice between the two families. Undoubtedly

it helped to pave the way for the long-continued and friendly correspondence between John Adams and Thomas Jefferson in their later
years. A practical politician, Mrs. Adams also was trying to make
things easier for her son, whose fortunes again were in Washington—
and were not being aided by the Federalists. The two Massachusetts
Senators, Timothy Pickering, the Northern secessionist, and John
Quincy Adams, the stubborn patriot, inevitably would come to major
cleavage. This would have happened by ideology alone, even if
Pickering had not held an old grudge for being dismissed by Senator
Adams' father from his cabinet.

Often John Quincy Adams sat at Jefferson's dinner table, apparently critical and unbending, but coming closer and closer to the
Republican point of view. His diary described the White House
family scene in the winter of 1805 when Martha Randolph, to help
ease her father's pain at the death of Maria, spent the winter there
with her husband, six daughters and one son.

John Quincy Adams also told of the tall tales with which Jefferson
regaled himself and his guests.

"His itch for telling prodigies is unabated," said Adams after
one dinner. "Speaking of the cold, he said he had seen Fahrenheit's
thermometer, in Paris, at twenty degrees below zero; and that not
for a single day, but that for six weeks together it stood *thereabouts*.
'Never once in that time,' said he, 'so high as zero which is *fifty*
degrees below the freezing point.' Those were his own words. He
knows better than all this; but he loves to excite wonder."

Again John Quincy Adams recorded that the President had told
some of his customary stories at a dinner for Federalist members of
Congress, adding: "Among the rest, he said that before he went from
Virginia to France he had some ripe pears sewed up in two bags, and
that when he returned six years afterwards, he found them in a perfect
state of preservation—self candied."

Mrs. Merry made the advent of Martha Jefferson Randolph an
excuse for a revival of the year old controversy. She wrote Mrs.
Randolph, asking her whether she was visiting the White House
as the President's daughter or as the wife of a Virginia gentleman;
as in the former case Mrs. Merry would make the first call, but in the
latter, she would expect to receive it. Mrs. Randolph replied that
she was in Washington as the wife of a Virginia gentleman and as
such would expect the first call from the wife of the British minister,

as, according to the code of etiquette drawn up by Jefferson, all strangers in the capital should be called on by the residents.

Martha Jefferson Randolph did not care much at the time about calling or being called on. Her second son, James Madison Randolph, was born that winter in the White House. He was the eighth of her twelve children. Jefferson's daughter had been educated with titled French girls, had made her bow at the French court, but she was more the mother than the hostess or social leader in the White House.

When Aaron Burr nonchalantly returned to Washington to preside over the Senate until the end of his term he continued to keep in touch with Merry. This did not deter him from asking Jefferson for a place in his second cabinet, a request coldly refused. The Burr-Merry negotiations continued until May of 1806. Then a British prime minister about to aid Burr died, and one friendly to the United States succeeded him. Naturally his first official act was to recall Merry. The sailing orders came late in May 1806.

Jefferson might have become aware of the conspiracy, for as time went on there was a living link between the White House and the British Legation close to Rock Creek. To Washington had come a young and socially gifted French refugee, Jean Pierre Sioussant. He first found employment in the household of Minister Merry, where he could use his knowledge of the forms and ceremonies of the French court. Later Jefferson appointed him a doorkeeper at the White House, a position described as "an office of much greater dignity than that of a mere hall porter" in which he was "thoroughly acquainted with the customs of the house." Any doorkeeper at the White House who had served also in the legation of Minister Merry must have had information valuable to the President. Sioussant was to continue at the White House, increasingly entrusted with matters of utmost confidence, throughout the Madison administration.

Jefferson's second administration was more difficult than his first. Internationally he was balked in his efforts to get clear title to the Floridas. At home the Burr conspiracy went fantastically forward to the trial for treason at Richmond. Among his many machinations to reach Jefferson's ears were plans to conquer New Orleans and Mexico. Burr was said also to be contemplating infiltrating Washington with armed men to seize the President, Vice President and federal funds and make himself President. Jefferson called his cabinet into the White House for meeting after meeting to consider how to meet the stratagems devised by his former Vice President. On the subject of Burr he became implacable, calling his conspiracy "one of the most flagitious" in history, past or future.

His intense determination that Burr should be convicted only added to the cold hard triumph of his political enemy and fellow Virginian, Chief Justice John Marshall, who acquitted Burr on a legalistic interpretation of the treason law. The evidence which could have convicted Burr was absent. It was overseas, in the hands of foreign governments and in the personal knowledge of Anthony Merry and the Marquis de Casa Yrujo.

In Congress the New England Federalists opposed everything that Jefferson did. Sometimes they won enough support from the South and West to hamper his program. His son-in-law Thomas Randolph, living at the White House, once joined his kinsman John Randolph in an antiadministration vote. The Federalists also opposed the President in small and humiliating ways. He wanted to landscape the White House grounds, but Congress refused the appropriation. He had to be content with merely enclosing the property with a common stone wall. When Meriwether Lewis returned to the White House in 1806 he brought some grizzly bears from the West as trophies. Jefferson, always enthralled by wild animals—at Monticello he had taught 20 deer to eat Indian corn from his pockets—displayed the bears on the White House grounds. The Federalists thereupon dubbed the shrubless White House enclosure "The President's bear garden."

British impressments of sailors increased. As a weapon short of war Jefferson initiated the embargo. America would have no trade with British vessels. To them her ports would be closed. Looking about for those of like mind, Jefferson could hardly fail to take note of John Quincy Adams. Alone of public men, Adams had made a speech on the Senate floor saying he was ready for all acts short of war. Jefferson appointed Adams as a member of the committee which was to draft the Embargo Act.

This was the overt act for which Senator Thomas Pickering, the secret conspirator against the Union, was looking. He got John Quincy Adams ejected from the Federalist party by a large and angry majority vote. Never was a public man more maligned in his home state than Adams. This abuse was intensified when, in the extraordinary session in the fall of 1807, Adams voted with the majority which

enacted the embargo. Until his term ended in March 1809 he sat as
an outcast from his party.

In the White House, Jefferson and Latrobe had been fighting a
losing battle for funds enough to make the really major changes
needed there. At the close of Jefferson's first term Latrobe had
reported that a roof too heavy and too high had forced out both front
and back walls. These were secured with bands of iron, and a sheet-
iron roof was substituted for slate. Still the year 1808 found Latrobe
almost at the point of resigning, so fruitless had been his efforts to
secure an appropriation to finish the steps, gates, porter's lodge and
planting. At the Capitol he had discovered dry rot in the timbers
supporting the Senate chamber, so serious as to cause him to predict
it would "fall down in a year or two." He dourly reported this to
Jefferson, adding, "I have every reason to believe the President's
House is in the same shape."

That would have to be the worry of James Madison, over whom
Jefferson threw the Presidential mantle when confronted with a painful choice between his two best friends. To James Monroe Jefferson
that year wrote, "I have ever viewed Mr. Madison and yourself as the
two principal pillars of my happiness." Nevertheless, Monroe had
returned from England to compete for the Presidency. Jefferson had
pigeonholed the treaty with England which Monroe had so painstakingly negotiated. Monroe was in an independent mood. But Madison,
backed by Jefferson, won the election.

In that final month of February the General Assembly of Virginia
voted a resolution of highest praise to Jefferson: "We have you to
thank for the model of an administration conducted on the purest
principles of republicanism, for pomp and state set aside, patronage
discarded, internal taxes abolished . . . a vast fertile region added to
our country, far more extensive than her original proportions bringing
along with it the Mississippi and the port of Orleans." Jefferson,
replying, said, "It would have been a great consolation to have left the
nation under the assurance of a continued peace." Congress, led by
New England and New York members, had taken a final slap at him.
In a "sudden unaccountable revolution of opinion," as Jefferson told
it, Senate and House "in a kind of panic" had "voted the 4th of
March for removing the embargo and in such majority as gave all
reason to believe they would not agree either to war or noninter-
course."

Yet Jefferson left the capital city on a high crest of popularity. James Madison had urged him to sit in his coach while riding up to the Capitol for the inauguration ceremony. The outgoing President refused this honor and chose instead to ride as a plain citizen in the horseback cavalcade which followed the Presidential coach. "This day I return to the people," he told the committee who came to invite him to sit in a special chair, and with the people he sat in the Hall of Representatives while Madison made his low-voiced address. To everyone's surprise Jefferson also went with the crowds to the reception at Madison's house following the ceremony. This almost disrupted the day, which had been so planned that the citizenry would also make a farewell visit to Jefferson at the White House. He had to be told of this plan, intended as a surprise, so that he would go back to the White House to receive them. He was there presented with a written testimonial which included this sentence: "The world knows you as a philosopher and philanthropist; the American people know you as a patriot and statesman—we know you in addition to all this, as a *man*."

Astonishment increased when Jefferson attended the Inaugural Ball that night, arriving in advance of the President and Mrs. Madison.

"Am I too early?" he asked a friend. "You must tell me how to behave for it is more than forty years since I have been to a ball."

As when he had given his arm to Mrs. Madison, causing her name to become world-known in the Merry precedence controversy, Jefferson by his genial presence now lifted her up to the pinnacle of social success.

3 | *The One and Only Dolley*

... MADISON

DOLLEY P. MADISON brought to the White House a personality as yeasty and full-bodied as her rollicking first name. She had blossomed as Mrs. Madison from the long-retarded bud of a strict Quaker upbringing. At forty, and First Lady, Dolley was flamboyant. She was the leader of fashion, introducing the daring touch that won emulation. Her trade-mark was the beflowered and feathered turban with which she had supplanted the gray Quaker bonnet. Hers was a warmly outgoing personality. She loved life and kept it so rich in people and in projects that she dominated the Washington of the Madison administration.

Never should the spelling simplifiers or fanciers have tried to tamper with her name. It was inevitable that her own way would win out in the end, acknowledged as authentic, D-o-l-l-e-y. Thus it had been written when she was born. "Dolley" she herself had twice spelled it on the day she married Madison, an indisputable record which one day would come into the safekeeping of the Library of Congress.

Dolley had stolen away from the merriment in her sister's home, Harewood in Virginia, that September day in 1794 to write to her dearest friend, Mrs. Eliza Lee in London. Eliza like Dolley was dismissed from the Friends because of a non-Quaker husband. In that letter Dolley had poured out her heart. She had even told about the financial arrangements made for the son of her first husband in order to assuage the harsh criticisms of her second marriage by the Quakers in Philadelphia. The body of the letter she signed "Dolley Payne Todd." Then she added a postscript which ran: "Evening—Dolley

Madison! Alass! Alass!" Evidently the exclamation was more the happy sigh of a bride than regret for the religion she had left behind. For the letter had said she was giving her hand "to the man of all others I most admire" and also, "In this union I have everything which is soothing and grateful in prospect."

So it was "Dolley" at birth and in marriage. It was "Dolley" when her portrait was painted, and "Dolley" eventually would be carved on her tombstone. Yet biographers made her Dorothy, Dorothea, or Dolly if informally inclined. This had gone so far in her own lifetime that she once was asked to say which of these names was hers. Her reply was "Dolley." It is rather noteworthy that the ablest women writers who were her White House intimates took no liberties. They respectfully referred to her as "Mrs. Madison"; or—in all seriousness—as "her majesty," democratically spelled in small letters; or as "Lady Presidentess" in capitals.

The true picture of James and Dolley Madison was not in the much quoted chuckling comment of Washington Irving: "Mrs. Madison is a fine, portly, buxom dame, who has a smile and a pleasant word for everybody. Her sisters, Mrs. Cutts and Mrs. Washington, are like to merry wives of Windsor, but as to Jeemy Madison—ah, poor Jeemy!—he is but a withered little apple-John." And there was much more below the surface than was evident to Mrs. William Seaton, who observed: "Her frank cordiality to all guests is in contrast to the manner of the President who is very formal, reserved, and precise, though not wanting in a certain dignity. Being so low of stature, he was in imminent danger of being confounded with the plebeian crowd, and was pushed and jostled like a common citizen—but not so her ladyship! The towering feathers and excessive throng pointed her station wherever she moved."

James Madison was five feet four inches tall. Dolley was several inches taller, and statuesque. But they looked on each other with eyes of mutual devotion, symbolized by intermingled locks of hair set in gold. Dolley referred to James as "my darling little husband." He addressed her as "my beloved." When for brief times they were separated, if only the distance between Montpelier and Washington, they wrote each other ardent love letters. Madison said that an hour's conversation with his wife refreshed him like a long walk. She found him tremendously enjoyable, as did others whom he knew well enough to talk to without constraint.

Madison was far from being the dry and scholarly character he appeared to be in his public life and writings. He was described in private life as "an incessant humorist" who "set his table guests daily into roars of laughter." When he spoke of this country's past history, with anecdote and epigram, "his every sentence was worth writing down." One close friend considered it inconceivable that "this entertaining, interesting and communicative personage, had a single stranger or indifferent person been present, would have been mute and cold." He could therefore take the more pride in his effervescent wife and her sweeping social conquests.

The direction of the entire Executive Mansion was turned over by Madison to his wife even before they entered the White House. He had directed Benjamin Latrobe, when bound for Philadelphia in February to buy furniture, to take his instructions from Mrs. Madison and render his accounts to her. Together Dolley and Latrobe assembled a stage setting singularly suitable to her outstanding role as First Lady before she ever threw open the doors in her first "drawing room."

The old crimson damask furniture in the Ladies' Drawing Room at the White House had for some years been a matter of disparaging comment by women guests. It had served the nation for two decades and was no longer presentable. New sofas and high-backed chairs upholstered in yellow damask were purchased, with matching yellow damask window hangings. More mirrors were hung on the walls. The fireplace was "ornamented with a gorgeous 'rising sun' in yellow damask." Before this elaborate central spot Dolley, often garbed in blending buff velvet or yellow satin, or in contrasting crimson, held court. There she could advance her husband's political causes tremendously by tendering to some key person the seat of greatest honor closest to the fire.

The costs of this 1809 refurbishing were not unreasonable. The first appropriation made in May was for $5,000, and others brought the total up to around $11,000. Included in Mrs. Madison's purchases were a piano, a guitar, china, silver and mirrors.

To have proper forms and precedence observed in all matters, Mrs. Madison elevated Thomas Jefferson's doorman, Jean Pierre Sioussant, a onetime factotum of Minister Anthony Merry and Mrs. Merry, to the position of Master of Ceremonies. He increasingly enjoyed Mrs. Madison's confidence, taking over the conduct of many of her personal affairs.

On May 31, 1809, almost three months after she entered the White House, Mrs. Madison at last was ready to give the first of the "drawing rooms" which she thereafter held each Wednesday when in residence. No written invitations were issued, none was needed. Wednesday night at the White House was well understood in Washington—it was the wheel on which life turned. Week after week the same people went to display the latest fashion, to make the deal for the next day's move on Capitol Hill, to pull the strings for appointments, to exhibit their musical and conversational talents and to conduct their courtships. The popularity of the White House on Wednesday night for the young blades brought forth the rhyme:

"Tom Tingey, Tom Turner, Tom Elwell, Tom Digges,
  All go to the palace to eat up the figs."

Dolley's was called "the" drawing room—others just had parties. Lions of the evening would be the newsiest notables from other countries and other cities, or the outstanding orators in the latest debate in Congress, or, as the country was drawn into war, the top generals. Members of both Houses and both parties were expected to attend. The cabinet of course would be there, and the other higher officials of government. The diplomats paid their respects. And the White House was open to Washingtonians who moved in the same "old families" circle as the Madisons did and to any guests they might bring. For a new feminine resident, however, it was not considered etiquette to appear publicly at Mrs. Madison's drawing room without having been first "presented to her majesty" in private.

Dolley herself presided at the White House table, with one of her husband's cabinet, usually the Secretary of State, opposite. President Madison insisted on occupying a chair at the middle of the table, a choice accepted as eminently sensible by his guests since it "relieved him from the trouble of serving guests, drinking wine, etc." The Madison cuisine quite naturally followed the Jefferson pattern—many French dishes, rare wines, ice creams and macaroons. According to descriptions by Mrs. Madison's guests, there was also an array of after-dinner titbits; dessert plates were removed, and "almonds, raisins, pecan-nuts, apples, pears, etc." were brought on.

In addition to her drawing rooms and dinner parties Dolley had "dove parties" for the cabinet wives when their husbands were in consultation with President Madison. She was also the chief center of interest at ship launchings, civic celebrations and fund-raising events for charities. And she called on all who called on her. From his own purse, for $1,500, President Madison bought from a firm in Philadelphia a coach and harness for four horses. Unlike the equipage of Jefferson, this coach would be constantly on the go as Mrs. Madison performed her social duty.

She was a good housewife too. One of her first White House purchases was a "Yardwood Washing Machine." She rose very early every morning and had her household machinery running smoothly before her first relative or latest guest stirred. Wherever she lived there were semipermanent relatives and long-staying guests. The children that they brought along were more than welcome. Mrs. Madison would say, "Come, sweet one, and let us be tidied up," and then she'd whisk out a clean pinafore from her storeroom stock.

Far from being another Abigail Adams, astute as any man and given to arguing things out, Dolley left the issues to her erudite husband. But she won political victories in the drawing room and at the dining table. She saw James Madison through many a tight situation by smoothing down his enemies and playing up to their wives. This naturally required a common-sense grasp of practical strategy in which she was the equal of any man of her times, including Madison.

"You know I am not much of a politician," Dolley had once written her husband in an unusual fit of self-analysis. "But I am extremely anxious to hear (so far as you think proper) what is going forward with the Cabinet. I believe you would not desire your wife to be the active partisan, nor will there be the slightest danger while she is conscious of her want of talents, and the diffidence in expressing those opinions, always imperfectly understood by her sex."

An approach as politic as that naturally netted Mrs. Madison ample knowledge of what went forward with the cabinet. So she was able as the President's wife to warn her sister in Maine when it was time for her husband to get his ships in, as there would be a war coming on. Mrs. Madison's announcements habitually antedated the event, as when she said, "I wrote you the embargo would take place three or four days before it did, dear Anna."

Jefferson had left Madison in charge of a great and growing nation with one most pressing problem, the freedom of the seas. The rival blockades of warring Britain and France, declared in 1806 and 1807 respectively, were a terrific obstacle to economic advancement. Trade was the lifeblood of a nation so new. The incessant seizure of ships and seamen kept American indignation at the boiling point.

Madison's term started off with hopeful indications of better relations between the two nations. British Minister Merry had been succeeded in 1806 by David Montague Erskine, decidedly friendly toward the United States. Left over from the Jefferson administration was the affair of the *Chesapeake,* the U. S. ship fired on and captured by the British *Leopard.* Madison was demanding the court-martial of the British admiral who had attacked the *Chesapeake.* Minister Erskine went to Madison and offered easement of the British blockade if he would withdraw his *Chesapeake* demands. Madison accepted, and issued a proclamation to that effect. Whereupon, a thousand ships left American ports in the belief the blockade had ended. Then came one of the most peculiar diplomatic incidents in all American history.

Suddenly the British government repudiated the Erskine agreement and recalled its minister, sending in his stead Francis James Jackson, a widely hated diplomat, known as "Copenhagen Jackson" because he had ordered the bombardment of that hapless city when his demand for the surrender of the Danish fleet had met with refusal. Jackson was received politely by the President of the United States. When he presented his credentials Mrs. Madison sent in to him a tray of punch and little cakes, her business-hour hospitality. And when he dined at the White House he was accorded the honor of handing Mrs. Madison in to dinner.

But no surface civility could long survive in the circumstances. Jackson had been sent to bully Madison into conceding that he had known that Erskine, in offering to end the blockade, exceeded his authority. The British government, moreover, had instructed its envoy to wring from Madison an admission that his publication of the proclamation was done to compel it to stand behind the unauthorized act of its agent. Jackson was to tell the United States government that the embargo would be lifted only on prohibition of all trade between the United States and France. Privately the British government instructed Jackson not to make any settlement, and if the United States made offers, he was to refer them to his government and await further instructions.

As soon as even part of Jackson's purposes were known, through his first interview with the Secretary of State, Robert Smith of Maryland, the British minister was told to put all of his propositions in writing. This was not only because Madison distrusted Jackson, but because he was also none too sure of Smith. The latter and his brother, Senator Samuel Smith, whose interests were in shipping, already were murmuring against Madison's firm policy on England. So Madison took over as his own Secretary of State, leaving Smith as a mere figurehead.

Jackson protested, but finally put in writing his charge that the American government knew Erskine was exceeding his powers. Madison replied that when a government disavowed the act of its own agent, the government affected was owed the explanation. Jackson repeated in writing that Madison had known the exact nature of Erskine's instructions. Madison replied that before proceeding further Jackson must show exactly what his own powers were. For the third time Jackson reiterated his charges. Madison coldly informed him no further communications would be received from him. Minister Jackson had been dismissed by the government to which he was accredited.

Madison's enemies, the Federalists, rallied around the repudiated British diplomat and showered him with social honors. He was feted in Baltimore and in New York. In Boston, heart of the Federalist territory, he was given a tremendous ovation at a great public dinner in his honor. That New England statesman and secret secessionist, Senator Timothy Pickering, raised his glass high and offered the toast: "The world's last hope—Britain's fast-anchored isle!"

After Jackson went back to England he carried on a conspiratorial correspondence with Timothy Pickering. In a letter from London, dated April 24, 1811, he explained the appointment of his successor, Augustus J. Foster, as follows:

"He goes therefore as well to satisfy the claims of the United States to a Minister of the same rank as their own as to act as a sort of political conductor to attract the lightning that may issue from the crowds round the capital and the *white house* at Washington. I hope that he will convey the flashes harmless into the Potomac, or, if not, into one of the powder magazines that abound in that neighborhood."

This was the earliest written record of a bit of nomenclature that would crop up again in the Madison period. Many historians have

The White House as rebuilt by President James Monroe.

The White House during the Abraham Lincoln administration.

A print from *Harper's Weekly* showing a presidential reception in the East Room just preceding the

set down that the Executive Mansion was never called the White House until after the Madison administration. Research has conclusively proved this to be untrue. Instead, it was called "the white house" colloquially from the first, because of the way its newly quarried sandstone, then described as "dazzlingly white," stood out from the surrounding green of the trees and red brick of neighboring houses. The New England secessionists who hated Madison picked up the term and used it much as a far later group would say "That Man" in referring to Franklin D. Roosevelt.

The Congressional overturn of 1810 demonstrated the temper of the common people, particularly in the new West. They had had enough of British bullying. More than half the older members of the House, the pacifists, lost their seats. Elected were the War Hawks. Their leaders were Henry Clay of Kentucky and John Calhoun of western South Carolina. Clay, who had filled a Senate vacancy for a time, was elected Speaker his first day in the House.

Dolley Madison lost no time in taking over this alien flock with invitations to the White House. Her extra endeavors caused her to make one of her rare complaints. "We have new members in abundance with their wives and daughters," she said. "I never felt the entertainment of company oppressive until now." Young Henry Clay soon became Mrs. Madison's great favorite. He was at her elbow at the drawing rooms, and she accorded him the honor of taking snuff from her box.

Whether or not she got the nuances of issues, Dolley Madison grasped the plain fact that the War Hawks were the political power of the future. If Madison was to have a second term, he must be won to their views. This promptly became her personal course of political action.

Madison also saw that he must strengthen his hand. Jefferson acted as intermediary to patch up the President's old friendship with Monroe, and Madison dismissed the self-seeking Smith and appointed Monroe Secretary of State.

Mrs. Monroe, a woman of distinction from her many years of residence abroad, entered the social scene with a splash. Four years earlier, on her arrival from England, she had immediately introduced the fashion of pantalets for little girls, the model being her young daughter Maria. A visiting Virginian, Judge St. George Tucker, could not wait to get home from Washington to tell his wife to obtain a similar costume for their "darling Fancilea." In a letter to her he thus described the new fashion: "She [Maria Monroe] was dressed in a short frock that reached about half way between her knees and ankles—under which she displayed a pair of loose pantaloons, wide enough for the foot to pass through with ease, frilled around with the same stuff of her frock and pantaloons."

Now Mrs. Monroe herself set the style of not looking like a grandmother. A contemporary description ran: "Mrs. Monroe paints very much, and has besides an appearance of youth which would induce a stranger to suppose her age to be thirty; in lieu of which she introduces them to her *granddaughter*, eighteen or nineteen years old, and to her own daughter, Mrs. Hay of Richmond." This fashion also was not slow in catching on, with the result that at Dolley Madison's drawing rooms, "Ladies of fifty years of age were decked with lace and ribbons, wreaths of roses and gold leaves in their false hair, wreaths of jasmine across their bosom, and no kerchiefs!" Most beautiful of all was Madame Patterson Bonaparte of Baltimore, "divorced wife and widow of Jerome Bonaparte, King of Westphalia." Madame Bonaparte, heroine of the most spectacular international romance of her day, had undertaken personal supervision of the education of Dolley's son, Payne Todd, at a Catholic school in Baltimore, so that when he was fully grown he might make a proper appearance at the French court.

As the election year 1812 opened, Mrs. Madison's drawing rooms were at their height. That they were having a profound effect on the culture of the capital, and indeed on the equality of womankind, was recognized by that keen observer, Margaret Bayard Smith.

"The drawing room—that center of attraction—affords opportunity of seeing all those whom fashion, fame, beauty, wealth or talent have rendered celebrated. It has this winter been generally much crowded, seldom has the company been less than two or three hundred, and generally more. I cannot tell you what an interest is imparted to this assembly by the entrance of some celebrated person."

She mentioned the latest lion, Captain Oliver H. Perry, who had just been given command of six vessels built on Lake Erie. She then analyzed a capital custom, originating with Dolley, which was bringing women more social freedom:

"I think the manners here are different from those in other places. At the drawing room, at our parties, few ladies ever sit. Our rooms are always so crowded that few more could find a place. The consequence is that ladies and gentlemen stand and walk about the rooms in mingled groups, which certainly produces more ease, freedom and equality than in these rooms where the ladies sit and wait for the gentlemen to approach and converse."

Equality in the White House led to equality at the Capitol, Mrs. Smith revealed. "The women here are taking a station in society which is not known elsewhere. On every public occasion, a lunch, an oration, in the court, in the representatives hall as well as the drawing room, they are treated with marked consideration." The House of Representatives, she observed, had become "a lounging place of both sexes where acquaintance is as easily made as at public amusements." Mrs. Madison and a "train of ladies" had even visited the Supreme Court to hear the arguments.

This felicitous picture was suddenly wiped out by a complete boycott of Dolley Madison's drawing rooms. It was a long story, not to be known in full for some generations. Dolley suffered this blow just when she was marrying off her widowed sister Lucy, who made her home in the White House, to Judge Thomas Todd of Kentucky—the first wedding ever held in the White House. She wrote her sister Anna Cutts in Maine, on March 20, 1812, about her grief at losing her sister and in the same letter made a frank report of social disaster.

"The federals [are] affronted to a man," she said. "Not one of the two houses of Congress will enter Madison's door since the communications of Henry except Livingston who considers himself attached by his appointment."

The "communications of Henry" came into the national picture in February and March of 1812 because two international rogues happened to meet on board the *New Galen* of Boston bound home from London. One was Major John Henry, an Irishman who had made a spying trip for the British in the spring of 1809 under the orders of Sir James Craig, Governor General of Canada. The other was a French adventurer, wanted by police in all ports. His true name was Soubiran, but he was using the title Count Edward de Crillon.

The two voyagers got to telling each other their adventures. The count was tremendously excited when Major Henry confided to him,

"I was about to succeed in dividing the five states of the north—in separating them from the American Union—when the affair of the *Chesapeake* occurred." The count said he had been struck with the idea that he would be welcomed back to France if he were able to reveal this flagrant example of British perfidy. Upon arriving in Boston, his memoirs stated, he had written the French minister in Washington, M. Serurier, about "the treasure of which I was repository." Immediately he "got a flattering letter" and was invited to bring Henry to Washington. On his arrival the count "was presented to the President and the Ministers," and, he added, "The French Legation became my hotel."

The "hotel" was Octagon House, leased that winter to the French. Life there was rich enough to satisfy any adventurer; indeed it had the whole town talking. Though he lived but a few blocks distant, the French minister visited the White House in a coach described as "a rolling ball of burnished gold" and "gilt to the edge of the wheels." On it were two footmen with brass hats, gilt-braided skirts and splendid swords. When M. Serurier emerged from this turnout, he himself was "weighted with gold lace." Certainly the count and his revelations were impressively introduced to the White House when they came with M. Serurier.

The French minister's version of the story, sent back to the home government in dispatch after dispatch, differed in a few details from that of the count. Serurier's explanation of De Crillon's presence at the Legation was "As he has been received and dined at the President's, and by all the Ministers, I have thought that, in order not to discredit the offer he made to the administration, I should occasionally receive him myself." Undoubtedly one reason why the French minister was taken in by this count without credentials was the credible content of the Henry papers for which this government, on recommendation of Madison and Monroe, paid $50,000.

For Madison they had solved the mystery of the British about-face when Erskine had been recalled and Jackson substituted. As Erskine and Madison negotiated to lift the blockade and insure peace, the dispatches of Henry had convinced the home government that New England was practically theirs and the Madison government about to fall. John Henry had conducted a public-opinion sampling from Quebec to Boston, sending back reports of disaffection; then, going into Boston, he had reported the Massachusetts legislature ready to set up a separate government and to receive proposals from Great Britain. His trip took three months.

Henry's final dispatch spelled failure of the mission, ending bitterly, "If Mr. Erskine be sanctioned in all he has conceded by his Majesty's ministers, it is unnecessary for me, as indeed it would be unavailing, to make any attempt to carry into effect the original purposes of my mission." Henry was back in Montreal by June 1, 1809, trying to collect the 1,000-pounds-a-year position which Sir James Craig had promised him. But the job had been given to another man, and Major Henry went off to England to seek payment for his mission. Failing to collect, he had returned early in 1812 to this country in a mood to have vengeance on Sir James Craig.

Madison's message to Congress on the Henry papers pointed out that "in the midst of amicable professions and negotiations on the part of its public minister, a secret agent of that government was employed in certain states, more especially the seat of government in Massachusetts, in fomenting disaffection to the constituted authority of the nation," and hoping eventually "in concert with a British force, to destroy the union and form the eastern part thereof into a political connexion with Great Britain."

New England secessionists were indeed trying to block every move made by Madison. They wanted to split the Union and again become a colony of England. Their aim was aid to Britain and not to the United States. They were no shrinking underground, but a vocal majority in sectional public opinion. Preachers openly thundered against democracy from the pulpit. And they were using "the white house," spelled with small letters, as the symbol and target of their spleen.

On March 18, 1812, Abijiah Bigelow, member of the House from Massachusetts, wrote a letter to his wife. In a passage referring to President Madison he said, "Many think he has been most grossly imposed upon by Henry. There is much trouble at the *white house* [sic] as we call it, I mean the President's."

This was all so logical to Madison he could not foresee that he would become a laughingstock for lack of any other proof than the word of two rascals who had not given him one single name of a federalist conspirator. And having collected the $50,000, they both disappeared across the seas, the count "dogging Henry's footsteps" because he had got only $1,000 before Henry disappeared. The count, as was his custom, sent messages ahead of himself—this time to the French police: "There will arrive on the coasts of France an agent of England, Major Henry, about 36 years old, blonde, about 5 feet 9 inches in height who must be put under surveillance and severely confined. He knows how to take all colors, and is sent to commit the most frightful crime." But it was the count who was arrested on arrival.

The recently arrived British minister, Augustus J. Foster—the Jackson vacancy had not been filled for two years—protested that any such plot was unknown to him. He asked the American people to consider the character of Henry and suspend judgment. But instead of suspending judgment Congress turned on Madison, even deserting his wife's drawing room.

Before the next week, however, this pathetic picture was suddenly reversed. Mrs. Madison's drawing rooms boomed to the point where she had to hold two in the same week. To her sister she wrote:

"The Vice President lies dangerously ill, and electioneering for his office goes on beyond description—the world seems to be running mad what with one thing and another. The Federalists, as I told you, were all affronted with Madison—refused to dine with him or even come to the house. But they have changed. Last night and the night before, our rooms were crowded with Republicans, and such a rallying of our party has alarmed them to return. They came in a large body last night also, and are continually calling; even D.B.W. (who is a fine fellow) came last night. The old and the young turned out together. The war business goes on slowly, but I fear it will be sure. Where are your husband's vessels? and why does not he get them in? Congress will be here until May, and perhaps longer."

This letter in itself was not sufficient explanation for so sweeping a change in the political situation that even Representative Daniel B. Webster, chief antiwar orator, had been "alarmed to return" to the White House. But another letter written by Dolley at the same time completely clarified the situation. It was to the U. S. Ambassador to France, Joel Barlow, and his wife. To these U. S. representatives overseas Mrs. Madison spoke freely:

"Before this you know of our Embargo to be followed by War!! Yes, that terrible event is at hand, I fear: our appointments for the purpose are mostly made, and the recruiting business goes on with alacrity. The major-generals are Henry Dearborn, Thomas Pinckney, Joseph Bloomfield, J. Winchester, William Polk, William Hull, etc. You will have an account of our political opinion in all its shades by this vessel. We anticipate some little contention among ourselves on the death of the Vice-President whose physicians give out that he cannot live until morning. The sentiment is in favor of John Langdon as his successor. Congress will remain in session, perhaps until July; if not full power to declare war will be vested in the President."

This letter was unmistakable evidence that in the week following the boycott the sudden illness of the Vice President had brought the coming election sharply into focus. An accord that there would be war had been arrived at between James Madison and Mrs. Madison's protégé, Henry Clay, Speaker of the House and leader of the War Hawks; and Clay would throw his strength to Madison in the election. Only from Clay could Dolley have such certain information on what Congress would be doing.

Dolley carried on a running correspondence with Mrs. Joel Barlow, mostly about clothes she wanted her to buy for her in Paris. Regardless of the British and French blockades, Dolley had to have her latest furbelows. In her letter telling of the impending war she informed the Barlows that the duty on her latest consignment of fabrics, headdresses, flowers and feathers, gloves and stockings had been 2,000 dollars. Still she was expecting more finery by the *U.S.S. Hornet*, which for a time was thought lost.

Mrs. Barlow, replying to the grave letter she had received from Mrs. Madison, told her that the *Hornet* would be sailing in a few days and would bring this country a treaty of commerce. This seemed to promise easement of the French restrictions, and President Madison hoped for word by the *Hornet* of similar British concessions which would bring last-minute reprieve from war.

Instead, the *Hornet*, reaching these shores early in May 1812, brought news that the British had stiffened their stand and would not rescind the blockade decrees even if the French revoked theirs. Even Monroe was now determined on war. The war message was sent to Congress by President Madison on June 1. War was declared on June 18. Over in England the offensive orders in council had just been repealed, but the news couldn't travel fast enough.

In the Congressional caucus that June the War Hawks supported

Madison for President, Elbridge Gerry for Vice President. As a protest against the "Virginia dynasty," Republicans in the New York legislature nominated DeWitt Clinton, nephew of the deceased Vice President. A convention of Federalists then endorsed DeWitt Clinton as a peace candidate. The West—the War Hawks—won the election for Madison. The five new states cast their entire 38 votes for him. In the original states the vote was 90 for Madison, 89 for Clinton. Many years later when James G. Blaine, famed analyst of elections, would make a thorough study of all the ramifications of this contest, Dolley Madison would get the political credit that she deserved. Said Blaine: "She saved the administration of her husband, held him back from the extreme of Jeffersonianism and enabled him to escape the terrible dilemma of the war of 1812. But for her DeWitt Clinton would have been chosen President in 1812."

Month after month the War of 1812 went badly. It was evident that Madison would have to make sweeping changes in his cabinet. Yet he hesitated over replacing even the weak Secretaries of the War and Navy departments until disasters on land and sea forced his hand.

On the ocean this country was hopelessly outnumbered, but captured some ships. The only real naval victories were on the lakes, notably that of Oliver Hazard Perry—one of Mrs. Madison's social lions—on Lake Erie. General William Hull's entire army was captured at Detroit. The defeat was wiped out in the same territory by the successful campaign of General William Henry Harrison in October 1812.

No one knew better than Dolley Madison the importance of dramatizing the victor. When General Harrison came into Washington to consult with his superiors early in 1813, President Madison thought he had gone right out again. But Dolley informed him that the general would be at her drawing room that night.

"General Harrison should be thirty or forty miles on his way west by now," insisted Madison.

"He must be here for I laid my command on him and he is too gallant a man to disobey me," said Dolley.

"We shall soon see whose orders he obeys," replied her husband.

The door opened. In walked General Harrison.

The chronicler of this family incident, grandniece Lucia Cutts, concluded, "The lady smiled her triumph over the most successful general of that day and the President of the United States."

The worst and most inexcusable calamity to befall during the War of 1812 was the burning of Washington. It had been predicted in a dramatic fashion by one of those Federalist preachers who thundered against Madison and his war.

This was preached in the Capitol, where church services were often held, by the Reverend Mr. Breckinridge. His subject was Sabbath observance, and Mrs. James Madison was in his audience. He condemned "the dinner parties given at the *white house*," then, addressing himself to the members of Congress, accused them of "violating the day by laws they had made, particularly the carrying of mail on the Sabbath."

The Reverend Mr. Breckinridge then thundered at the Sabbath breakers. "It is the government that will be punished, and, as with Nineveh of old, it will not be the habitations of the people, but your temples and your palaces that will be burned to the ground."

"His predictions were verified," said Mrs. Smith, who heard the sermon. "The Capitol, the President's House, and every building belonging to the government was destroyed, and that by fire."

When British ships arrived at the mouth of the Patuxent Madison's cabinet held a meeting at which an adequate defense plan for the city was drawn up and ordered. This plan never was carried out even in the slightest detail, for the reason that the Secretary of War believed that Baltimore, not Washington, would be attacked. As the British debarked and advanced amid Maryland skirmishes the situation already had become hopeless. Orders were given for the state papers to be taken to hiding places in Maryland and Virginia. The alarmed residents scattered.

Mrs. Smith wrote excited pages about her flight:

"We were roused on Tuesday night by a loud knocking. On opening the door Willie Bradly called to us, 'The enemy is advancing, our own troops are giving way on all sides and are retreating to the city. Go, for God's sake go!' He spoke in a voice of agony and then flew to his horse and was out of sight in a moment. We immediately rose, the carriage and horse were soon ready, we loaded a wagon with what goods remained, and about 3 o'clock left our house with all our servants."

But Dolley Madison held her ground almost to the hour the British entered Washington in the evening of August 24, 1814. While the rest of Washington was fleeing, Dolley, deserted by the guards who should have protected the White House, was writing an event-by-event account to her sister. It was a document as historic as any of the papers that she preserved for her husband. Some excerpts:

August 23—"My husband left me yesterday morning to join General Winder . . . beseeching me to take care of myself and of the cabinet papers, public and private. . . . I have pressed as many cabinet papers in one trunk as to fill one carriage. . . . I am determined not to go myself until I see Mr. Madison safe. . . .

August 24—"Since sunrise, I have been turning my spy-glass in every direction . . . hoping to discover the approach of my dear husband . . . but alas! I can descry only groups of the military, wandering . . . as if there was lack of arms or lack of spirit to fight for their own fireside. . . .

"Two messengers, covered with dust, come to bid me fly—but here I mean to wait for him—Our kind friend Mr. Carroll has come to hasten my departure and is in a very bad humor with me because I insist on waiting until the large picture of General Washington is secured, and it requires to be unscrewed from the wall. This process is found too tedious for these perilous moments; I have ordered the frame to be broken and the canvas taken out. It is done, and the precious portrait placed in the hands of two gentlemen of New York for safe keeping."

Thus was saved for the White House the 1800 portrait of General Washington, partly painted by Stuart and finished by Winstanley with John Adams' son-in-law, Colonel William Stephens Smith, posing for the unfinished limbs and body. But there was long a bitter dispute as to the manner of its saving. Dolley's letter that day showed that Jean Pierre Sioussant remained as her faithful aide, offering to spike the cannon at the gate and lay a train of powder which would "blow up the British should they enter the house." Certainly he helped save the portrait.

But the persistent legend that Sioussant cut the portrait from the frame with a penknife in order to get it down in time—a fiction repeated as late as in a book dedicated to Franklin D. Roosevelt—was proved untrue by later evidence. When the portrait was found and restored, the canvas had never been cut.

All through the night which followed Mrs. Madison's eventual flight, the skies of Washington were lurid with the flames of burning buildings. The Capitol, the Navy Yard buildings, the White House, the bridges, the Departments—all were burned. On Thursday came the hurricane which "blew down houses, tore down trees, and spread terror around." Men told of being blown from their horses as they were drenched with rain. The fires were quenched.

The President and Mrs. Madison, somehow reunited, returned to the city after three days of panicky wanderings on both sides of the Potomac. Mrs. Madison's description of this scene was: "Such destruction—such confusion! The fleet in full view and in the act of robbing Alexandria! The citizens expecting *another visit*—and at night the rockets were seen flying near us."

Mrs. Smith told the extent of the devastation:

"In the President's House not an inch, but it's crak'd and blacken'd walls remain'd. That scene, which when last I visited it, was so splendid, throng'd with the great, the gay, the ambitious placemen, and patriotic heros was now nothing but ashes . . . alas, yes, and this is human grandeur! How fragile, how transitory! Who would have thought that this mass so solid, so magnificent, so grand, which seem'd built for generations to come, should by the hands of a few men and in the space of a few hours be thus irreparably destroy'd. Oh vanity of human hopes!"

The Madisons lived for a few days in the home of Mrs. Madison's sister, Mrs. Cutts. Then they were offered Octagon House, just vacated by the French minister, a fitting background for affairs of state. They lived there for a year. The city of Philadelphia invited the national government back there, but Madison chose to stick it out in Washington. A brick structure was being erected on Capitol Hill for temporary use by the Congress until the Capitol could be rebuilt. The Departments moved into private houses. The slow work of rebuilding got started. Hoban again was put in charge of the White House construction, Latrobe of the Capitol.

A week after the burning President Madison issued a proclamation calling on the people to rally in defense of the country. He then called Congress into special session to consider "the threatened attack on New Orleans and the embarrassing condition of the finances." He obtained the resignation of Secretary of War John Armstrong and made James Monroe his Secretary of War as well as of State. Monroe pledged his personal credit to get the militia of the Western states to the defense of New Orleans. This enabled General Andrew Jackson to achieve the spectacular victory there which postdated the war.

While the war dragged on toward its end, the New England Federalists, who had hampered it from the start—withholding capital, refusing state militias, beating down war appropriations in Congress—made a play for actual secession. The Hartford Convention was called, supposedly for this purpose. It adopted demands to Congress that no war should be declared except by a two-thirds vote of both houses, and that no blockade could be imposed for more than 60 days. The three commissioners sent to Congress with these demands heard of the victory of New Orleans on their way to the capital. They never finished their journey, but turned around and went home, to raucous Republican laughter. The Hartford Convention ended the Federalist party.

Again communications had been too slow to prevent bloodshed. Peace had been concluded as a Christmas present to the world on December 24, 1814. Jackson won his victory in January 1815. The two events were celebrated simultaneously for a week in Washington in February.

On Saturday February 11 rockets were fired for the evacuation of New Orleans amid wild rejoicing. On the thirteenth, the people started celebrating the first peace rumors. On the fourteenth a special messenger arrived in Washington, bringing the Treaty of Ghent in its metal box. On the fifteenth Mrs. Madison had her drawing room, all Georgetown was illuminated, the cabinet held a night session and joy reigned supreme. So did Dolley. There were those who said she was the most popular person in all America that night. The President being closeted with his cabinet, she did the honors of Octagon House, which was jammed with members of Congress of both parties, diplomats, citizenry, felicitating her and each other.

One of her guests wrote:

"The most conspicuous object in the room, observed of all observers, was Mrs. Madison herself, then in the meridian of life and queenly beauty. She was in her person, for the moment, the representative of the feelings of him who was in grave consultation with his official advisers. No one could doubt, who beheld the radiance of joy which lighted up her countenance and diffused its beam all around that all uncertainty was at an end, and the government of the country had in very truth 'passed from gloom to glory'. With a grace all her own, to her visitors she reciprocated heartfelt congratulations upon the glorious and happy change in the aspect of public affairs; dispensing with liberal hand to every individual in the large assembly the proverbial hospitalities of that house."

The treaty was signed by President Madison on February 17, 1815, in the tower room just over the entrance, his study. The table on which the treaty was ratified, circular, with wedge-shaped drawers, would be re-established there after a century and a quarter, as part of a minor patriotic shrine. The next night the peace celebration was completed with the firing of cannons and the sending up of rockets and illuminations far into the night.

Regardless of the carpings of detractors then and later, it was peace with honor, made by five of this country's strong statesmen. Without armistice, the peace commissioners had been negotiating at Ghent, Belgium, since August 1814. The first overtures had been made even earlier, instigated by John Quincy Adams, U. S. Minister to Russia. That country had offered to mediate. Although this offer was not accepted, the two countries agreed to negotiate, and Adams was made one of the commissioners. The others were Henry Clay, James Bayard, Jonathan Russell and Albert Gallatin.

When the parley had first started, Adams reported, the British commissioners were haughty and demanding. But the U. S. delegates, while conceding that no mention had to be made in the treaty of impressments, which had ceased, gave way in no major matter. Said John Quincy Adams, "Everything for which the United States had engaged in the contest was either directly or tacitly conceded." There could have been no better or more honest judge of this matter. He had been the first public man to offer stiff resistance to British impressments, had suffered most in public calumny in his own state.

With the peace commission to Ghent went Dolley Madison's son Payne Todd, who had been educated for just such a moment. Handsome, elegant-mannered, tutored in French, he was the idol of the moment. He was called "the American Prince." Henry Clay and John Quincy Adams watched from a gallery as Payne Todd, accepted on a level with royalty, danced with a princess. But already Payne was showing the traits which would bring his mother grief and penury in her old age. He drank to excess, went on wild exploits, stayed overlong in Paris. Mrs. Madison wrote anxious letters to Mrs. Gallatin, who accompanied the party, trying to ascertain even the whereabouts of her son Payne, who did not write to her.

A visit from General Jackson in the autumn of 1815 caused great commotion—"Dinners, plays, balls throughout the District." The question of the social standing of Jackson's wife Rachel was satisfactorily answered then, but would rise again. Mrs. Seaton made a report on this matter: "Immediately on Mrs. Jackson's arrival a dilemma was presented, and a grand debate ensued as to whether the ladies would visit her. Colonel Reid and Dr. Goodlet, the friends of years of General Jackson, having settled the question of propriety satisfactorily, all doubts were laid aside. I have seen a good deal of General Jackson and his wife." She described Mrs. Jackson as "a totally uninformed woman in mind and manners, but extremely civil in her way," adding, "I suppose there have never been in the city so many plain women, in every sense of the word, as are now here among the families of official personages."

Again the Madisons moved, this time to the corner house of the Seven Buildings, Pennsylvania Avenue and Nineteenth Street, to finish out the term. A report to Congress on the government-owned furniture in this place at the close of Madison's term showed how makeshift had been its appointments. There were no carpets—the floor had been covered with green and blue baize. Chairs, tables and bedsteads were a worn-out oddly assorted collection. There were but two mirrors in the house. Two pier tables and one ordinary sideboard were worth taking into the new White House. Glass, earthenware, china and linen were remnants. Gone were the great chandeliers, the "elegant girandoles with glass clusters" listed in Jefferson's inventory.

But the First Lady was resourceful. Even in such surroundings, with the aid of her own belongings, Dolley Madison had been able to stage spectacular parties. A guest at a Wednesday drawing room in the spring of 1816 gave this description: "The decorations were magnificent, and the building was brilliantly illuminated from garret to cellar, much of the light being made by pine torches held in the hands of trained slaves." The Chief Justice of the Supreme Court and all the Associate Justices attended in their gowns. Four of the leading generals of the War of 1812 also were present—Brown, Gaines, Ripley and Scott—in military full dress. The peace commissioners of Ghent were present—Bayard, Clay, Gallatin and Russell. The diplomats attended, wearing their decorations. Cabinet and Congress and citizenry attended. As for Dolley—

"Mrs. Madison appeared in a toilet of rose-colored satin and white velvet train, which swept the floor for several yards. The train was lined with lavender satin and edged with a ruching of lace. She wore a gold girdle and gold necklace and bracelets. This costume was completed by a turban of white velvet, trimmed with white ostrich tips, and a gold embroidered crown." The new British minister, Charles Bagot, said, "She looked every inch a Queen."

4 | *On a Footing of Form and Ceremony*

... M O N R O E ,

J O H N   Q U I N C Y   A D A M S

JAMES MONROE went into the White House with a major piece of long-standing and delicate diplomatic business on hand. When he had helped wind up the Louisiana Purchase in 1803, it was with the understanding that the Floridas had been included in the deal, having been clearly ceded by Spain to France. But Spain continued to occupy this territory. For 14 years Monroe had been trying to get clear title to the area for the United States. Needing the sharp qualities and staying powers of a Yankee trader in this matter, Monroe reached across the ocean and brought back John Quincy Adams, then Minister to Great Britain, as his Secretary of State.

Monroe had a strong, if quiet, sense of showmanship and of the fitness of things. He realized that a duplication of European formality would strengthen his hand with Europe's diplomats. The new White House gave logical opportunity for a break with the past. To begin with, it required the sort of furnishings which would be correct background for social formality. No longer would the diplomats visit the President familiarly, just dropping in to call or have tea, as they had done in the days of Jefferson and Madison. Monroe determined to place them, as he himself expressed it, "upon much the same footing as the American Ministers were placed in European courts, upon a footing of form and ceremony." He served notice on the diplomatic corps that if they sought personal audiences, he would grant them and receive them in form, but that he did not expect a foreign minister to come to the White House without invitation.

With the President taking such an attitude, Mrs. Monroe obviously had to eschew the free and easy ways of Dolley Madison, even had she been inclined to follow them. From long attendance at Dolley's court she had already decided that the pace Mrs. Madison set—always at home to all, calling on all who called on her—was far too fatiguing. When her attitude gradually became apparent to the social leaders of Washington, Mrs. Monroe was in for a long and bitter battle.

In choosing Adams for the State Department, President Monroe took into consideration the national as well as the international situation. New England and New York had long protested "the Virginia supremacy" which had been maintained by using the State Department as the steppingstone to the Presidency. Those wise old counselors, Jefferson and Madison, agreed with Monroe that national unity now demanded that a Northern man be chosen. So Monroe passed over politically powerful Henry Clay, Speaker of the House, openly ambitious for the line-of-succession portfolio and actively resentful when he didn't get it.

Monroe first felt the sting of Clay's antagonism on Inauguration Day, March 4, 1817. The Speaker refused the use of the House Chamber in the new and temporary brick Capitol fronting the Capitol Plaza at its northeast corner for the swearing-in ceremony. Clay said that the floor was not strong enough to hold the crowds. And so an outdoor ceremony was held on an elevated portico in front of this building.

The sun smiled on Monroe and the crowd, 7,000 or 8,000, ladies as well as gentlemen. To them the new President talked unity—the American people were "one great family with a common interest." He talked national defense—there must be "security against foreign danger." He said: "We must support our rights or lose our character, and with it perhaps our liberties. National honor is national property of the highest value. It ought therefore to be cherished."

That spring and summer the White House was not yet ready for occupancy. For the inaugural reception and all preliminary official entertaining the Monroes had to use their handsome home on I Street, later preserved for history by the Arts Club of Washington.

Diplomatic negotiations were at a standstill until Secretary of State Adams could reach the city in September.

Monroe took advantage of the enforced lull in the capital city to translate his inaugural address into action. For the promotion of national unity he made a personal inspection tour of the national defenses. This trip lasted three and a half months and took him to 13 states. If he had planned it for the purpose of building up personal strength so that his official acts would be able to withstand the heckling that they would undergo from Clay, he could not possibly have made a more effective move. That title "Era of Good Feeling" which came to be applied to the Monroe administration was not acquired through happenstance. Monroe really worked for it.

He steered his course straight through the territory which once had been the stronghold of the Federalists, that party which had committed hari-kari on the sword of secession. Monroe wanted New England to know that all was forgiven and that a united America now was ready to forge ahead. He realized that in his own person was symbolized a potent appeal to the Northeast. He had been the youngest member of the Old Congress. He had fought in the Revolution, had been wounded in the battle of Trenton. To stir men's memories and to link the nation's present and future with the virile ideals of the founding fathers, he wore again the hat and cockade of Revolutionary fashion, and with it "old blue and buff"—a plain blue coat and buff underdress.

The cumulative effect of the President's tour already was recognized. The Boston *Chronicle and Patriot* said, "People now meet in the same room who could scarcely before pass on the same street." And the Boston *Centinel* coined the phrase "Era of Good Feeling."

Monroe went on through Vermont, swung back to Buffalo, Detroit, Zanesville, Ohio, and Pittsburgh, to reach Washington on September 18. He found a White House still smelling of fresh paint, and hurried to the Monroe estate in near-by Loudoun County, Virginia, to spend a few days with his family. Mrs. Monroe had spent the summer in the cottage on the estate where the magnificent home, Oak Hill, was soon to be built by the White House architect, Hoban, on plans made by Jefferson.

A year later Monroe made a swing through the South, taking in Augusta, Nashville, Louisville and Lexington, a total of 5,000 miles. The last three months of 1817 were spent by the Monroes in refurnishing the White House sufficiently to permit its reopening for the New Year's reception of 1818. Due to long diplomatic experience abroad, their standards were high. From the homes of nobility made poor by the French Revolution Monroe had purchased exquisite furniture to bring back to this country. Since it was obviously impossible otherwise to get the mansion fittingly equipped in time for official entertaining, Monroe sold the government his best furniture, household linen, dishes and silver. Federal appraisers set the prices which Monroe would receive. The government bought the silver plate by weight, figuring the price to the fourth of a cent. Four casseroles brought $402.97½; a bread basket $74.81¼; two soup ladles, $9.56¼. The bill totaled $9,071.22½. This included the major pieces of furniture for the official dining room, two bedrooms and a good start on two drawing rooms. The public rooms were to be made more impressive with elaborate furniture and bric-a-brac ordered by Monroe from France (where he had twice served as minister).

Gossip and controversy about the refurnishing of the President's house was rife that autumn. Under the caption "French Influence" *Niles' Register* commented in November: "A good deal of noise has been made in the papers about certain 'Furniture' imported from France for the president's house. It turns out as we expected—the 'furniture' consists exclusively of porcelain, mirror plates and carpets and a few such small articles as are not manufactured in the United States." Taking Monroe's part against continued criticism, Mr. Niles even listed a series of articles which the British government had just bought for His Highness the Prince Regent, for Carleton House. Five items totaled $110,976.46. Mr. Niles termed them all "trinkets and gee-gaws, a mere show."

Strangely enough, he hit upon one of the very items which Monroe had purchased. The British government had bought for the Prince a "plateau and dessert ornaments" at $20,986.34. Monroe had purchased for the White House a *surtout de table*, a mirror plateau covering a space 13½ feet long and two feet wide, with elaborate matching candelabra and fruit baskets. It was destined to be the centerpiece for White House state dinners from that time forward. The set was designed by the best Parisian artisans, of carved and gilded bronze, featuring figures of Bacchus and Bacchantes. Sixteen small figures around the mirror plateau held wreaths in outstretched hands. Into these wreaths either 32 candles or 32 small vases carrying flowers or vines could be placed. The government secured a great bargain in this elaborate table decoration. It cost 6,000 francs, and the manufacturer said he "lost by it near 2,000 francs," so it was one fourth off actual cost.

What the government saved on the *surtout*, however, was more than swallowed up in the extra cost of the Oval Drawing Room furniture. For this room—the Blue Room of the far future—Monroe had ordered mahogany. But Russell and La Farge, the Havre firm through which he obtained the White House furniture, was unable to fill the order. "Mahogany is not generally admitted in the furniture of a Saloon, even at private gentlemen's houses," these dealers admonished Monroe. They informed him they were substituting gilt "made by the first Ebeniste in Paris of the name of Bellanger," upholstered in "silks bought by Cartier fils," in "crimson 50 per cent dearer than other colors." On the bill of lading this furniture was described as "a set of drawing-room furniture of gilded wood carved with branched olive leaves and covered with a heavy satin material of delicate crimson color, with a pattern of laurel leaves in two tones of gold."

For this room an Aubusson green velvet carpet, centered by the arms of the United States of America and "with a beautiful border" was ordered. But since it had to be specially made, all in one piece, an area of 76 square ells, it did not arrive in time for the opening reception.

The bric-a-brac bought by Monroe at this time was of the sturdy and surviving sort. Any claim which the White House ever would have to antiques would be in these works of art which arrived in America in the autumn of 1817. Statesmen all down the years would come to know them like old friends. The clock, carved and gilded, representing Minerva leaning on a shield which carried the face and works (2,000 francs), would be a latter-day ornament to the Blue Room mantel. And that other clock representing Hannibal after the battle of Cannae (900 francs) would strike a stately note on the mantel in the Green Room. A pair of bronze candelabra with female forms standing on a square base (1,400 francs) would come to rest, in the Theodore Roosevelt restoration, on a marble pier table in the downstairs corridor. There were also porcelain vases, gilt mirrors and great silver dishes good for all the White House years, and innumerable other objects fated for oblivion. From the effects of George Washington at Mount Vernon, Monroe purchased three busts—one of Washington himself, one of Christopher Columbus and one of Americus Vespucius.

All in all, Monroe assembled a royal background. As part of his general move toward stateliness the President even had contemplated "a uniform dress adopted for the heads of Departments and officers of government." That idea, apparently, did not get far.

The protocol which President Monroe established for the diplomats was set down early in the administration by Secretary of State Adams, who recorded in his diary:

"The former Presidents, particularly Jefferson and Madison, have admitted to a certain extent social visits from the foreign ministers. Mr. Monroe, upon principle, has precluded that sort of intercourse and receives them only: 1, at private audience requested by them; 2, at the drawing room; 3, at diplomatic dinners, once or twice a winter."

At his private audiences with the ministers, usually arranged to hand over some written message of formal courtesy from other heads of state, Adams noted, "the President observed the usual forms practiced by European sovereigns on such occasions.

"He receives them standing, dressed in a half-military uniform or a full suit of black. The Ministers are in full Court dress. He stands in the center of the drawing room, and I accompany them, keeping the right hand. On receiving the letter, the President hands it, unopened, to me. The English Prince Regent had the same practice with Lord Castlereagh."

Adams mentioned that the President had a stock formal answer to these presentations, that "the United States takes great interest in everything that concerns the happiness of their sovereign." And there the audience ended.

A bit of regality when the circumstances demanded was not a pose with the Monroes. Elizabeth Monroe had secured the release of Madame de Lafayette from La Force prison, and indeed from the very shadow of the guillotine, by using the official carriage of the United States Legation and assuming the voice of authority when she went to the prison to call on her.

Monroe's elder daughter Eliza had a link with thrones both real and lasting. At the school of Madame Campan, Eliza had become a close friend of Hortense Beauharnais, daughter of the Empress Josephine by her first husband, who was killed in the Reign of Terror. Hortense grew up to marry Napoleon's brother, Louis Bonaparte. Napoleon made this couple king and queen of Holland, and their son would become Napoleon III. But in 1816, the year Monroe was elected President, Hortense became an exile in Germany, due to the Battle of Waterloo. As queen and ex-queen, she corresponded with Eliza Monroe, who had married George Hay, prosecutor of Aaron Burr, and had named their daughter Hortense for her old friend. Indeed, Eliza felt the pull of childhood conditioning so strongly that she spent the last years of her life in Paris and there was buried in a cemetery only a few miles from the one in which Hortense was buried.

The elder Monroes also felt the drama of the Napoleonic court. Preserved for posterity was the suit in which Minister Monroe had been presented at the time of the Louisiana Purchase. It was of black cut velvet, with pressed steel buttons and hand-embroidered vest of cream-colored satin. It was worn with sword and sash. So excellent were the materials in this garment that the colors still remain fresh a century and a half later. Five of Mrs. Monroe's formal gowns worn at foreign courts and as mistress of the White House were similarly saved, museum pieces all. These dresses would be the inspiration for the collection of costumes of the mistresses of the Executive Mansion on display in the Smithsonian Institution. A Monroe descendant, Mrs. Rose Gouverneur Hoes, conceived the collection a century later and made of its assemblage a patriotic avocation for many years.

Considering their elder daughter a great social asset, the Monroes arranged for her and her husband to move from Richmond into the White House. Mrs. Hay was to be her mother's assistant; Mr. Hay was to serve as a sort of administrative assistant to the President. Monroe had also two secretaries—one, his brother Joseph Jones Monroe; the other, Samuel Lawrence Gouverneur, Mrs. Monroe's nephew. The other daughter, Maria, who had introduced the pantalets, was now fourteen and ready to share in the social life of the mansion, which soon became the scene of a cousinly courtship between her and young Gouverneur.

Margaret Bayard Smith was bitter that even she, who had been on intimate terms with both the Jefferson and Madison families, had no special standing with the Monroes as the First Family.

"Although they have lived 7 years in W. both Mr. and Mrs. Monroe are perfect strangers not only to me but to all the citizens," she said.

This remark went down in history far too literally, some authors flatly stating that Mrs. Monroe was an invalid recluse. She was indeed quite often ill. But she moved through Washington society with a stately grace. This was amply proved by records of the time. Indeed, Mrs. Smith's own niece and house guest, Miss Mary Kirkpatrick, had written home as recently as December 1816, "With Mrs. Monroe I am really in love. If I was a Washingtonian you might say I worshipped the rising sun—but as I am not you will believe my adoration sincere. She is charming and very beautiful." What Mrs. Smith really was saying in her much-quoted sentence was that Mrs. Monroe and her husband had withdrawn behind the White House walls in the manner of perfect strangers.

The two leading foreign ministers, Charles Bagot of Great Britain and Hyde de Neuville of France, fell in with the new scheme of things to the extent of requesting that their wives be allowed to call on Mrs. Monroe. They objected, however, to falling in with the multitude at the New Year's reception which would reopen the White House. Monroe took this matter up at a cabinet meeting. It was agreed that the diplomats should be received at 11:30 in the morning, the general public at noon.

Of this important event in White House annals the *National Intelligencer* said:

"The President's House, for the first time since its re-aerification, was thrown open for the general reception of visitors. It was thronged from 12 to 3 o'clock by an unusually large concourse of ladies and gentlemen, among whom were to be found the Senators, Representatives, Heads of Departments, Foreign Ministers, and many of our distinguished citizens, residents, and strangers. It was gratifying once more to salute the President of the United States with the compliments of the season in his appropriate residence, and the continuance of this Republican custom has given, as far as we have heard, very general satisfaction. The Marine Corps turned out on the occasion and made a very fine appearance."

The grand opening of the White House was a signal for the eruption of the precedence controversy which had been seething below the surface for months. The first official complaint came from the Senate. The president pro tempore, Senator John Gaillard of South Carolina, and a colleague called on the Secretary of State to announce the discovery of an old rule, originally drawn by Senator Aaron Burr, which decreed that the Senators should be first callers only on the President; all others should call on the Senators first. Secretary of State Adams dryly replied that he had served five years in the Senate and had never heard of any such rule, but to the contrary "at the commencement of every session had invariably paid the first visit to all the heads of Departments."

Two weeks later Mrs. Adams was called in by Mrs. Monroe. It was for the purpose of telling her that the ladies of Washington were up in arms, a matter which Secretary Adams deemed to be of sufficient importance to record in his diary.

"All the ladies arriving as strangers, it seems, expect to be visited by the wives of the heads of Departments and even by the President's wife. Mrs. Madison subjected herself to this torture, which she felt very severely, but from which, having begun the practice, she never found the opportunity to recede."

At this first conference on the subject of social precedence Mrs. Monroe and Mrs. Adams formed an offensive-defensive alliance. Mrs. Monroe would neither pay nor return calls. Mrs. Adams would return all visits, but would pay first visits to none. Two more courageous and firm-minded women could not have been found. Their agreement set a lasting social pattern.

The going was not made smoother by the fact that the President's daughter, Eliza Hay, also had her own precedence controversy. She held that the ladies of the diplomatic corps should call on her first. This they would not do, so she declared a personal boycott on the whole diplomatic corps. This situation first came to a crisis in December 1818 when the French minister asked Adams to use his good offices to induce the President and Mrs. Monroe to attend a ball he was giving to celebrate the evacuation of France by the allied troops. When Monroe had ascertained that no former President had gone to a foreign minister's house, he declined, but left it up to Mrs. Monroe whether she would go. Mrs. Monroe said she did not think it proper for her to go where it was not proper for her husband to go. President Monroe then said he would request his daughter to attend.

Adams was delegated to pass this information on to the French minister, who, Adams said, "was apparently much mortified but suppressed his feelings within bounds of decency." Mrs. Hay was no better pleased.

"Her object [said Adams] was to desire me to inform Mr. Hyde de Neuville that she would at the request of her father, though it was much against her own will, go to the ball next Monday, but it was upon conditions: first, that it should leave her position with the ladies of the foreign Ministers precisely where it was; that she would afterwards neither visit them, nor receive visits from them, nor accept any invitations to their parties; second, that no rank or station should be assigned to her at the ball—no pretense of distinguishing her as the President's daughter; that at supper she would find her place somewhere among the Commodore's wives, but must have no particular distinction shown her; third, that Mr. de Neuville might write to his own government anything that he pleased on the subject, but that if an account of the ball was to be published in the newspapers here, her name should not be mentioned as having been present."

So the diplomats, who had refused official éclat to Eliza by refusing to call on her first, had to take Eliza as proxy for her parents and with no gain in éclat. And the unrelenting Eliza would neither invite the diplomats nor permit them to send presents when her sister Maria was married in February 1820 to her cousin, Samuel Lawrence Gouverneur. Maria was the first daughter of a President to be married in the White House.

White House dinners to the diplomats were also a great problem. When other cabinet officers protested the presence of the Secretary of State only, Adams told Monroe to leave him out and invite diplomats only rather than crowd them to the bottom of the table with cabinet officers and their wives. This Monroe did, and "all the gossips of the District drew conclusions," Adams said.

At the height of this prolonged social struggle, in December 1819, the drawing rooms of both Mrs. Monroe and Mrs. Adams were completely boycotted by the social leaders of the capital.

That month a Congressional delegation made a formal visit to the

President to complain that Secretary of State Adams refused to pay them the first visit. Monroe called Adams in. Adams, with his diary as backing, reported it was the same complaint made to him and answered by him two years before. But the pressure on the President was so strong that he called a cabinet meeting on December 20, 1819, for the sole purpose of considering social calling. The upshot was that Adams was instructed to write two state papers on calling, one addressed to the President of the United States and the other to the Vice-President for the information of the Senate. Diplomatically indeed Adams stated his great respect for the Senate, reiterating at the same time the position taken by himself and his wife—they would call when called upon.

However, all members of the Monroe administration, the Secretary of State set forth, were "free to pursue the course of conduct dictated by their sense of propriety respectively." Thus one of the greatest of American freedoms was declared. The precedence controversy was settled. The pride of the Senators was salved. Mrs. William W. Seaton, wife of one of the two editors of the *Intelligencer*, called it a "curious document" which proved Adams to be "more of a bookworm than a man of the world." But the social leaders needed the prestige of the White House more than the White House needed their prestige. They returned to Mrs. Monroe's weekly salons, which became so crowded that extra constables had to be employed to keep order in the yard before the carriages drove up. And Mrs. Adams' parties were conceded to equal, if not surpass, those of the wives of the British and French ministers.

The Monroe social discipline in its stiffly dignified White House setting may not have pleased the residents, but it did pay off on the diplomatic front. The British and French, accustomed to using social front to awe lesser nations, found themselves equaled at their own game. They ceased to regard the officials of this country as a collection of colonials and began to respect them as representatives of a great nation. This changed attitude became evident as a series of diplomatic successes led to the enunciation of the Monroe Doctrine, which served notice on the world that the whole of the Western Hemisphere was no longer open to colonization.

East Florida was a nagging trouble spot, base for raids against the border settlements. Secretary of State Adams diligently pressed for a bloodless acquisition by purchase. So wary was the Spanish minister,

Luis de Onis, that the French minister, Hyde de Neuville, served as mediator whenever negotiations deadlocked. At one point Adams became so exasperated he told De Neuville he would "give him a certificate he was a faithful liege to the King of Spain." De Neuville answered that Onis "would give him a counter certificate he was an honest American."

Suddenly in May 1818 the highly volatile personality of Andrew Jackson became the chief factor in this situation. A few months earlier Monroe had considered sending Jackson as Minister to Russia. But he mentioned the matter to Jefferson on a trip to Monticello. "Why, good God! he would breed you a quarrel before he had been there a month!" Jefferson had exclaimed. So Jackson was left at home to breed a quarrel which served him as an issue in three successive Presidential campaigns.

Monroe sent General Jackson to South Georgia to repel a raiding party of Seminole Indians. Jackson chased the Seminoles back across the border into Florida, took and manned a fort, executed two British subjects, Armbrister and Arbuthnot, who were with the Seminoles, took Pensacola from the Spanish and there remained in occupation.

President Monroe and all the cabinet except Adams said that Jackson had exceeded his authority and deserved reprimand. The British and Spanish governments were furious and sent their ministers to Secretary Adams at all hours, demanding redress. The cabinet was in daily session on the subject.

The solid statesmanship of John Quincy Adams was equal to this crisis. He argued that the issue was not Jackson but the prestige of the United States, which must now be firmly asserted. The President, having put Jackson in charge of the expedition against the Seminoles, must back his action in Florida. Adams worked out in legal detail the principle that everything which Jackson had done was defensive and, as such, was neither war against Spain nor violation of the Constitution. He held that the British executions were justified on the conclusive evidence that the two Englishmen were spies inciting the Seminoles. This point of view he was able to fight through to acceptance by President Monroe; by the British minister, who dropped the cases of Armbrister and Arbuthnot; and by the Spanish minister, who ceased to threaten war and on February 22, 1819, signed a treaty to sell the Floridas for $5,000,000.

"It was perhaps the most important day of my life," Adams wrote the night the treaty was signed. "Let no idle and unfounded exultation take possession of my mind."

But Adams certainly deserved the credit for keeping the peace. The British Prime Minister, Lord Castlereagh, said the Jackson expedition would have meant war "if the Ministry had but held up a finger."

The heated controversy as to whether Missouri should be admitted as a slave state raged concurrently with the Florida question. All Washington went to hear the violent debates in which the antislavery faction was led by Rufus King, the proslavery by John Randolph, and Henry Clay won his title as the Great Compromiser. Mrs. Seaton reported the galleries "crowded with colored persons, almost to the exclusion of whites," adding "they know it is a question of servitude or freedom and imagine the result will immediately affect their condition." With eyes wide open Monroe signed the compromise adopted on March 1, 1820, admitting Missouri as a slave state but prohibiting further slavery above Mason and Dixon's line. He had prophetically set down a month earlier that the majority in votes and in physical force would eventually be on the side of the free states, and either their will would prevail or the Union would be dissolved. He added he would not make his own personal decision on the subject until compelled by events to do so.

The Florida purchase and the Missouri Compromise downed all opposition to Monroe's re-election in 1820, only one elector voting against him, the diarist Senator William Plumer of New Hampshire, a rugged individualist who insisted on voting for John Quincy Adams. Immediately, three members of his cabinet, Adams, Secretary of State, John C. Calhoun, Secretary of War, and W. H. Crawford, Secretary of the Treasury, began a campaign to succeed him.

Outside the cabinet two other powerful men were competing, Speaker Henry Clay and General Andrew Jackson. All five candidates were Jeffersonian Republicans, as was Monroe, who declared a hands-off policy on the succession and so managed to keep his own program moving forward.

With the aid of Adams, Monroe had been playing a slow, sure game on the South American front, where independence followed the uprisings led by Simón Bolívar. Monroe and Adams had been opposed at every turn by the impetuous Clay, who made immediate recognition of the new republics his pet political issue. Monroe's careful timing paid off in 1822 when he was able to receive diplomats from South America without creating more troubles in Europe. The new situation in South America, coupled with a surprising and sternly rebuffed ukase from the Czar of Russia claiming that his Alaska extended into this country's Oregon, started Adams thinking in terms of the Monroe Doctrine. While Adams as Secretary of State was in a large measure the architect of this doctrine, credit for its promulgation was Monroe's. The Monroe Doctrine was part of the President's routine annual message to Congress on December 2, 1823: "The American continents by the free and independent condition which they have assumed and maintain, are henceforth not to be considered as subjects for future colonization by any European powers. . . . We should consider any attempt on their part to extend their system to any portion of this hemisphere as dangerous to our peace and safety. . . ." This pronouncement was the greatest triumph of Monroe and in itself gave him a high place among American statesmen. He might have been able to accomplish it without receiving the European ministers stiffly. But undoubtedly his quiet dignity was a short cut to his desire of achieving a high-ranking place for this republic, able to declare and enforce a world policy.

The strict social discipline which Monroe had initiated at the beginning of his stay in the White House also stood him in good stead in the election year 1824. How he kept himself aloof in that bitter campaign was brought out in Adams' diary. Knowing what the answer would be, yet not wishing to slight Monroe, Adams invited him to the party which he and Mrs. Adams were giving in honor of General Jackson on January 8, 1824, the anniversary of the battle of New Orleans. Jackson was then Senator from Tennessee.

Monroe thought Adams' invitation over and then replied that when Crawford had been in Virginia the previous summer, even when he was ill at the home of the governor, he, Monroe, had "pointedly avoided meeting him," and that if he should depart from his rule of not visiting private houses, it might be thought he was "countenancing one of the candidates for the next Presidency while he had so cautiously abstained from giving even seeming countenance to another."

By all accounts, including Adams' own, the ball was one of the historic social successes of Washington. Said Adams, "About 1000 persons attended. General Jackson came about eight o'clock and retired after supper. The crowd was great, and the house could scarcely contain the company." From the society writers came pictures of Mrs. Adams, elegantly dressed, with headdress and plumes tastefully arranged; and of the Adams' three sons, with their sweethearts, dancing under festoons with which they themselves had decorated the Adams home on F Street. George Washington Adams and John Quincy Adams, Jr., were in their early twenties, Charles Francis Adams was sixteen.

Before the election it was evident that Crawford, a political opportunist, darling of Washington's social set and instigator of no small part of the earlier precedence fracas, might throw his strength to Jackson. And friends of Clay, fearful of Jackson's rising star, made tentative overtures to Adams, but no bargain was made.

Resourceful Louisa Adams thought up a way to campaign for her husband. Margaret Bayard Smith, an ardent Crawford advocate, not only recorded it, but also went her one better. Wrote Mrs. Smith: "Society is now divided into separate battalions as it were. Mrs. Adams collected a large party and went one night to the theater, Mrs. Calhoun another, so it was thought by our friends that Mrs. Crawford should go too, to show our strength." Mrs. Smith went on to say that she had intended only to take the ladies, but Senator Martin Van Buren of New York and a colleague rallied for them members of Congress as escorts, so they made an imposing display.

But no amount of wifely loyalty could counteract the colorful Jackson, whose wife was considered no help to his cause.

The vote of the electoral college, counted on February 9, 1825, was: Andrew Jackson, 94; John Quincy Adams, 84; W. H. Crawford, 41; Henry Clay, 37. This threw the election into the House of Representatives, where the final vote was taken that same day. Crawford's friends crowded the galleries, hoping for a deadlock in which he could win. Clay, being lowest on the list, was ruled out and turned his votes over to Adams. The first vote by states was unexpectedly decisive. John Quincy Adams had a majority of the states, 13, Jackson seven, Crawford, four. John C. Calhoun then was elected Vice-President.

Adams had advised his friends in the House to vote for Jackson for Vice President, giving as his reason, "I thought the place suited to him and he suited to the place." In his diary he told why. "The Vice Presidency was a station in which the General could hang no one, and need quarrel with no one." But Jackson did not have that spot in mind for himself. He started to run for the Presidency again the moment he saw Henry Clay's name as a member of Adams' cabinet, as Secretary of State. Adams thus was forced to spend his whole term running for re-election. Moreover, Vice President Calhoun helped Jackson campaign against President Adams.

Jackson's method was a bitter and unremitting personal attack on John Quincy Adams. His first charge was that there had been a nefarious pre-election collusion between Adams and Clay. When Adams disproved this charge, Jackson only shouted "bargain and corruption" the louder. Jackson then delved deep into Adams' past to resurrect all possible unpleasantness, including his old split with the New England Federalists. False charges were trumped up on Adams' mission to Russia. For three and a half years Jackson actively campaigned for the Presidency, devoting to it his entire time, speaking at banquets in all major cities and building up a gigantic personal following. Jackson's was the politically winning "smear" technique at its worst, but he was also exponent of a constructive democracy which the people understood. Eventually Jackson got in return a personally devastating dose of smear, but not at the hands of John Quincy Adams.

In this extended campaign Crawford, who had opposed every move of the Monroe administration from within, and Martin Van Buren, a sharply rising political star from New York, joined Jackson and Calhoun to form the Democrat-Republicans, later the Democrats. The followers of Adams and Clay, believers in a strong central government, called themselves National Republicans and later merged into the Whigs.

Monroe's administration ended as it had begun—with a great burst of pageantry. This time the occasion was the visit of his old friend and hero, General Lafayette. Fetes in Boston, Philadelphia and Baltimore, all attended by Secretary of State Adams, preceded the round of ovation in Washington.

All through December 1824 and into 1825 Lafayette was honored in Washington. The climax was the banquet of the night of January 1, 1825, followed by a crowded New Year's reception at the White House. Even President Monroe went to Williamson's Hotel, where about 150 members of the two Houses and 30 officers of government tossed down 16 toasts in honor of Lafayette, and Henry Clay made a speech about Bolívar and the cause of South America. Clay sat next to Adams, made cordial overtures which soon became a tacit political alliance against the great popular movement led by Jackson.

In the closing weeks of his administration President Monroe confided to Adams a matter which had long been weighing heavily on his mind. He had appealed to Congress, by special message in 1818, to put the White House in official charge of a custodian. Samuel Lane, Commissioner of Public Buildings, was made responsible. A total of $50,000 was put into Lane's hands to pay for refurnishing the White House. Lane died a year and a half before Monroe's term ended with $20,000 unaccounted for. Congress made an investigation, and one member raised a hue and cry about the money which had been paid Monroe for his furniture. Monroe, to whom the government had owed great sums for years due to his services abroad, dug down into his own pocket once again and bought back his furniture. Adams' comment was: "I read this day the President's memoir upon the transactions relating to the appropriation for furniture for the President's house. It enters into details of a very humiliating character, and which ought never to have been, or to be, required of him." Adams resolved to keep his own accounts straight. Little did he realize the limitless possibilities of Congress in humiliating Presidents.

Again the inauguration pattern was changed. On March 4, 1825, the President-elect in one carriage was followed up Capitol Hill by the retiring President in another. The swearing-in ceremony again was held indoors—in the House Chamber of the restored Capitol, where Adams was fated to die 24 years later with his political boots on. In his inaugural address Adams outlined a broad program of national public works which he intended to push with federal funds. A man of original ideas, he had formulated domestic plans as far-reaching as he already had initiated in the diplomatic field. The difference was that his foreign policy was steered through to political completion by the quietly expert James Monroe, who knew when to act and when to wait. But Adams, who kept all his principles on parade and wouldn't give an inch in any of them, was balked completely by the Jackson party in Congress. The Jacksonians said that Adams' public-works plan was taking power from the states. On that issue they captured a majority in Congress in the elections of 1826. In the White House the frustrated President became almost a recluse, passing sleepless nights and taking long walks before the dawn.

Courtesy of Mrs. Arthur Haldane Doig

Facsimile of the cover of the 18-page illustrated supplement of the *New York Graphic* commemorating the wedding of Nellie Grant.

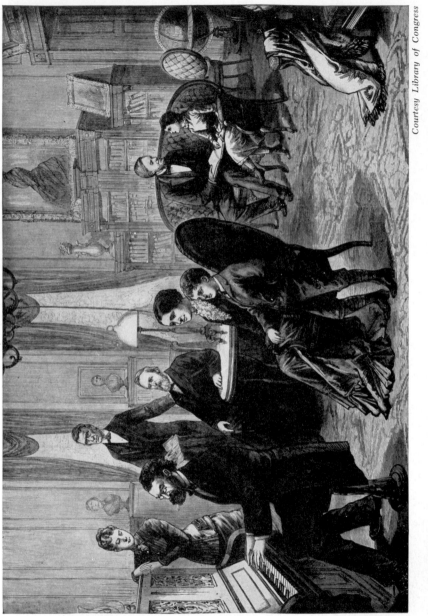

A sedate social evening with the President and Mrs. Rutherford B. Hayes as sketched in April, 1880.

President Adams urged a national university. With a loan from his own private funds he helped the Columbian University get started which George Washington had visualized and remembered in his will and which later became George Washington University. Adams had aimed to use federal funds to further agriculture, science and the arts. This interest found expression only in the planting of a vast array of trees and shrubs on the White House grounds; and in indoor White House experiments in raising silkworms, shared in by Mrs. Adams. He wanted to start a great national observatory. All he could do was to put a telescope up on the White House roof and look at the stars.

But Adams' cabinet was loyal, his administration excellent, and during the entire four years he had a smooth-running official regime. In summer he rose early, took a swim in the near-by Potomac, put in a long and arduous official day and finished with a round of billiards with his college-age sons. In winter he rose early, took long walks in the starlight, put in a long and arduous official day and practiced a bit at billiards.

After the New Year's reception of 1826 the subject of getting the White House properly furnished was brought up again, this time by a well-meaning Congressman, General Stephen Van Rensselaer of New York. Adams recorded that the general had come to speak to him "of the long eastern lower hall of the President's house which remains unfurnished"—that East Room again.

"The crowd of New Year's day overflowed into it and it was seen in its nakedness by many members of Congress," said Adams. "Van Rensselaer has since offered a resolution in the House proposing a committee to enquire and report upon the propriety of finishing and furnishing the public buildings. He is chairman of the committee and enquired what I thought would be the cost of furnishing the eastern hall."

Mrs. Adams was called into the conferences, and the upshot was that Adams furnished the committee with three documents: (1) an inventory of the worn-out and useless furniture in the house; (2) an estimate from two upholsterers of the probable cost of furnishing the East Room, one setting the amount at $16,000, the other at $20,000; (3) a list of the items already purchased by the Adams family for the White House, not required by Congress but furnished for the purpose of showing a thrifty spending pattern.

It was the third list which was Adams' undoing. His enemies in Congress pounced on it and found four items suited to their forensics: "billiard table $50"; "cues $5"; "billiard balls $6"; and "chessmen $23.50." The resultant furor was later summarized by Representative Edward Everett of Adams' home state, who defended him on the floor of the House:

"A portentous outcry arose. The matter was taken up with all the energy of the press: the President was denounced as a corruptor of the youth of the country; the articles themselves were declared to be parts of a splendid gaming establishment; the administration was represented as a set (not merely politically but morally) of desperadoes and debauchees and the President's house was the scene of their orgies."

Adams paid the government from his own pocket for the billiard table and also for a mirror which his wife had ordered for the ladies. And when Congress at last got around to voting $25,000 to furnish the East Room, Adams was so standoffish he used only $6,000.

The complete inventory of the White House furniture late in the Adams administration revealed a strange admixture of the very grand with the extremely shabby. The withdrawal of Monroe's own furniture when he bought it back meant taking out of storage the second-hand stuff hastily purchased for Mrs. Madison at various auctions after the fire. In the public rooms the Monroe purchases from France still gave a predominant air of grandeur. But even these were interspersed with such items as "one pair mantel lamps old and damaged" and "five footstools, one broken." And in the imposing Oval Drawing Room were listed "one mahogany crimson cloth sofa (cover damaged) and fourteen ditto armchairs (covers damaged)." That extra-expensive crimson cloth foisted on the Monroes by their French dealers hadn't worn well.

In the private rooms upstairs the furniture which belonged to the White House was in a sad state. Three rooms were completely unfurnished, a fourth contained only a few storage items.

James Hoban was urging the building of a north portico, lack of which on the principal front he called "a material defect, making the extension appear too great for the elevation." Charles Bulfinch, sent by Van Rensselaer to look over the grounds, reported of the exterior wings used for carriage houses and cow barns, "The appearance is certainly not in conformity with the style of the house, and is such as no gentleman of moderate property would permit as his own residence." He also reported "unsightly sheds built against the enclosing wall near the Treasury office, twelve of them, put up by indulgence, by those clerks in that and the State Department who reside at a distance, for the purpose of sheltering their horses."

Each summer the Adams family remained at the White House until after the traditional Fourth of July reception to the public, then went to their Massachusetts home. So it was that Adams was on duty in Washington on July 4, 1826, fiftieth anniversary of the signing of the Declaration of Independence, and the death day of two of its signers, John Adams and Thomas Jefferson. The President learned of Jefferson's death before he found out that his father also was gone. He hastened home to Massachusetts.

By November 1828 Adams' defeat by Andrew Jackson was a foregone conclusion. The electoral college vote was 178 for Jackson, and 83 for Adams. Calhoun again was elected Vice President. Adams felt thoroughly repudiated.

Mrs. Adams had met all the political attacks with equanimity, and her drawing rooms were ever popular. She had worked out the philosophy for the wife in public life—and her sum total would be 40 years of it—never "to attach the idea of disgrace" to any of the vicissitudes of serving country. Her theory was: "Popular governments are peculiarly liable to factions, to cabals, to intrigue, to the juggling tricks of party, and the people may often be deceived for a time—but they will never be deceived long."

So she gave her gayest party—threw open the East Room to dancing for the first time—in mid-December 1828, right after her husband was defeated by Andrew Jackson, the man whom Adams had saved from reprimand and to whose prestige Mrs. Adams had greatly added by giving that party in his honor.

But no amount of brave front could counteract the mood of John Quincy Adams, who not only thought his career unjustly ended, but also was smarting under the years of petty, exasperating and uncalled-for attacks, which had come to crescendo in the 1828 campaign. So he did no glossing over when he sat down at his White House desk on December 30, 1828, to answer an awesome-looking letter which was a campaign aftermath. Ten leading former Federalists of Boston and three sons of deceased Federalist leaders had joined in a letter calling

Adams to account for a statement he had made 20 years before, in 1808, which had been republished by his opponents just before the election. In the statement Adams had said of "certain leaders of the Federalists" that "their object was, and had been for several years, a dissolution of the Union and the establishment of a separate confederation," a matter which he knew "from unequivocal evidence although not proveable in a court of law."

The 13 Bostonians now called on President John Quincy Adams to prove his 20-year-old statement. Adams' reply was a masterpiece of telling sarcasm. He suggested that they had closer sources of evidence than he did, noting that two of them had been members of the Hartford Convention and one was the son of its president. He then reiterated that in 1803-1804 "the secession project had gone to the length of fixing on a military leader for its execution."

Then Adams, in a few brilliant sentences, set forth his views on secession. These words, written in the White House, were in their way as significant as the Emancipation Proclamation written there later, for Adams was destined to champion these principles in the House of Representatives for two decades.

"My principles do not admit the right of the people, still less of the legislature of any one state in the Union to secede at pleasure from the Union. No provision is made for the exercise of this right, either by the Federal or any of the State constitutions. The act of exercising it presupposes a departure from the principle of compact and a resort to that of force.

"If there be such a right, it is the right of an individual to commit suicide—the right of an inhabitant of a populous city to set fire to his own dwelling house. These are my views."

He told these leading Bostonians—H. G. Otis, Henry Cabot, John Lowell and William Prescott were among the signers—that they had no official status, and that he would give his proofs when, as and if he chose. But he did not choose, at their instigation, to hurt innocent relatives of men living or deceased.

Adams certainly was able to document his case. He soon did it to the extent of 222 printed pages which were published a half century later by his grandson, Henry Adams, in a book titled *New England Federalism* which contained also the correspondence of Timothy Pickering, secessionist leader. Henry Adams told why John Quincy

Adams had never published this work—he had decided the public good would not be furthered "by reviving the memory of Northern schemes of resistance to the national authority at a time when the Union was staggering under the shock of similar projects in South Carolina and Georgia."

The exit of the Adams administration from January to March 1829 was a slow and painful process, pointed up from February 11 on by the presence of President-elect Jackson in Washington.

On January 1 Adams wrote in his diary, "The year begins in gloom. My wife had a sleepless and painful night. The dawn was overcast, and, as I began to write, my shaded lamp went out, self-extinguished. It was only for lack of oil; and the notice of so trivial an incident may serve but to mark the present temper of my mind." Yet he and Mrs. Adams rose and faced the traditional New Year's reception, which was "crowded beyond all former example." All officialdom was on the way out, farewelling each other, and diplomats and townspeople were farewelling all officialdom.

With their great sense of public duty, the President and Mrs. Adams also would have been quite willing to share in the inauguration ceremonies for Jackson. But Jackson paid no visit to Adams, sent him no direct communication. The newspapers commented on it. Through an intermediary Jackson sent word to Adams that he did not wish to inconvenience him, but he would like to receive his visitors at the White House on Inauguration Day—his hotel wasn't large enough to hold them. Adams sent back word that the White House would be ready for him.

On his own Inauguration Day, John Quincy Adams had let President Monroe remain in the White House for a farewell reception on March 4, and he himself had attended it; the Madisons had accorded Jefferson the same courtesy. Now Adams, who had taken a house far out on Meridian Hill, was left with no downtown place to receive his friends. So on March 4 he simply withdrew to Meridian Hill. He had been precluded from Jackson's induction as his father had been from Jefferson's.

But on his last day in the White House, March 3, 1829, there was no lack of drama. The editors of the *National Intelligencer* had somehow got hold of the text of the attack on Adams by the 13 Bostonians and his reply to them—and chose that day on which to print this startling correspondence. It took up a fourth of the paper, and the editors explained they had to omit the entire proceedings of Congress in order to do it.

The editorial column in which this explanation was made was headed by an item which Adams himself had sent to the editor with the request that it be printed. It read:

"The Citizens of the District of Columbia, and others, friends of Mr. Adams, who might be disposed, conformable to the usage hitherto, to pay him a friendly visit after the Inauguration of the President-elect on Wednesday, the 4th inst. are requested by Mr. Adams to dispense with that formality, which the distance of his residence from the Capitol would render inconvenient to them. He thanks them all for the kindness which they have constantly extended to him, and prays them to accept the assurance of his best wishes for their health and happiness."

An era indeed had ended as only an Adams could end it.

5 | *The People Take Over*

. . . JACKSON

AN EARLY prophet of trouble ahead in the Jackson administration was Margaret Bayard Smith, who by now was a dominating power in Washington's social and cultural life. Always one to put a knowing finger on the throbbing of the public pulse, she put New Year's Day, 1829, to the useful task of recording for posterity the talk of the town.

"Tonight General Eaton, the bosom friend and almost adopted son of General Jackson is to be married to a lady whose reputation her previous connection with him both before and after her husband's death has totally destroyed."

This was Mrs. Smith's delicate way of conveying the fact that Senator John Eaton of Tennessee was marrying his pretty and vivacious mistress, Margaret O'Neale Timberlake.

"She has never been admitted into good society, is very handsome and of not an inspiring character and violent temper," Mrs. Smith went on. Being one of Washington's inner circle, Mrs. Smith probably was acquainted with the tale that when Mrs. Monroe was First Lady she had sent Mrs. Timberlake a note requesting her not to come to the White House drawing rooms.

"She is, it is said, irresistible and carries whatever point she sets her mind on. . . ." Mrs. Smith's pen had caught precisely the point at issue. The White House from which she had been excluded was the goal of Peggy O'Neale, the tavern keeper's daughter who had been petted by her father's patrons—statesmen all—but shunned by their wives.

99

"The General's personal and political friends are very much disturbed about it; his enemies laugh and divert themselves with the idea of what a suitable lady in waiting Mrs. Eaton will make to Mrs. Jackson, and repeat the old adage, 'birds of a feather will flock together.' The ladies declare they will not go to the wedding, and if they can help it will not let their husbands go."

Mrs. Smith added that at the New Year's Eve party which she had attended the night before, even the Jacksonians were joking about Mrs. Jackson's smoking a pipe. If Mrs. Smith erred in any way, it was in understatement.

Andrew Jackson and John Eaton as the two Senators from Tennessee had lived in Franklin House, the tavern run by Peggy Eaton's father. Jackson became very fond of the pretty Peggy and wrote to his wife Rachel how well he liked to hear Mrs. Timberlake play and sing. Peggy's husband, John Timberlake, a ship's purser, spent most of his time at sea on posts secured for him by the patronage of Senator Eaton. But Timberlake was always getting his accounts mixed up—and Senator Eaton would have to make up the deficits. Peggy's father, too, got into financial straits. Senator Eaton bought O'Neale's hotel and held it until he could sell it to John Gadsby. Eaton set the O'Neale family up in an exclusive boardinghouse where he was star boarder. It was from that headquarters that he conducted the Jackson campaign when he was not in Tennessee. John Eaton wrote Jackson's campaign biography and much of his campaign literature.

Suddenly in the midst of political overturn, word reached Washington from the far-off Mediterranean that John Timberlake was dead—a suicide. Senator Eaton was in an unsavory situation. From the Hermitage, Andrew Jackson wrote him to marry Mrs. Eaton at once or leave her parents' roof.

Even as Mrs. Smith wrote of these nuptials Rachel Jackson, of whom she so lightly and slightingly spoke, had lain for a week in her Tennessee grave. Rachel was killed by slander, so her neighbors said, and so her husband implicitly believed. And since it was the political campaign which had generated that slander, Jackson laid Rachel's death directly at the door of Henry Clay and John Quincy Adams, in that order. He believed he had evidence of Clay having been at work digging up the gossip of the distant past.

When Andrew Jackson and Mrs. Rachel Donelson Robards were married in 1791, both believed that Robards had obtained a divorce for desertion. But he merely had obtained permission from the Virginia legislature, which handled divorce cases in those days, to sue for divorce in Kentucky. In 1793 Robards did sue in Kentucky, naming Jackson, to whom Rachel had been married for two years—and won his case. The stunned Jacksons quietly went through a second marriage ceremony to legalize a union on which unexpected doubt had been cast.

Tennessee had long since brushed this whole matter aside as an inconsequential incident of frontier life. The home state was as proud of Rachel as of the tough old soldier who now had become the symbol of a new and vociferous democracy. Rachel's good character and philanthropy were well known. She was always surrounded by young relatives whom she and Andrew were helping to a good start in a good world. Rachel's nephews were given college educations, her nieces social advantages and big weddings. One nephew, Andrew Jackson, Jr., was legally adopted. Another, Andrew Jackson Donelson, who married Rachel's niece, Emily Donelson, was Jackson's trusted secretary.

When giving his young men good advice on the choice of wife, Andrew Jackson said: "Recollect the industry of your dear aunt, and with what economy she watched over what I made, and how we waded through the vast expense of the mass of company we had. Nothing but her care and industry could have saved me from ruin."

In Tennessee, Rachel had nothing to fear except that Andrew Jackson would go on the military or political march again. She wrote one of her nieces, "In the thirty years of our wedded life he has not spent one-fourth of his days under his own roof. The rest of the time away, travelling, holding court, or at the capital of his country, or in camp, or fighting its battles, or treating with the Indians—mercy knows what not."

Andrew Jackson had built for Rachel a church close to the Hermitage. She had one prayer so important to her that she wanted a whole church to say it in—that Andrew Jackson would settle down and live happily at home, as he had repeatedly told her he would.

"I had rather be a doorkeeper in the house of God than live in that palace in Washington," she said.

In her youth Rachel had been beautiful. But at sixty-one she was pudgy. She puffed sometimes as she went about her work. On the only two visits she had ever made to Washington, in 1817 and again just before the House election in 1824, the well-entrenched fashionables of the capital had taken pains to convey to her their strong sense of superiority. There was always an undercurrent of gossip too—that old story about her delayed divorce from Robards.

But for her husband's sake Rachel bravely faced the First Lady role. She went into Nashville and bought an inauguration gown of white satin and all the rest of a rich White House wardrobe. She also received lavish gifts. One was a lace veil from the ladies of Cincinnati, Ohio, on which the name "Jackson" was spelled out, each letter in a different pattern of lace, with 24 stars for each of the 24 states above the name. She had planned to wear it on Inauguration Day.

The locally accepted tale of Rachel's death was that while in Nashville having fittings for the inaugural gown she overheard a conversation which revealed to her campaign canards which Jackson had kept from her—that she and her husband had been intimate prior to their marriage, and that she was not his equal socially and would be a great detriment to him as President. From that day forward she slumped into melancholy and on December 17, 1828, had a serious heart attack. A tremendous farewell banquet and ball had been arranged for the Jacksons at Nashville Inn for December 23. It was never held. Rachel died December 22 and was buried at the Hermitage the day before Christmas in her white satin inaugural gown. Ten thousand people, twice the population of Nashville, attended the outdoor funeral. After tortured weeks Andrew Jackson penned her epitaph, one of those pithy Jacksonian sentences which would have endured even had it not been engraved upon a tomb: "A being so gentle and virtuous, slander might wound but could not dishonor."

Back in Washington, Mrs. Smith sharply changed her tune so far as Rachel Jackson was concerned.

"Oh what a gloom is cast over the triumph of General Jackson by the death of a wife fondly and excessively loved," she said, "of a wife who, it is said, could control the violence of his temper, soothe the exacerbations of feelings always keenly sensitive and excessively irritable, who healed by her kindness wounds inflicted by his violence, and by her universal charity and benevolence conciliated public opinion."

Mrs. Smith also had compassion for the outgoing administration, remarking, "Every one of the public men who will retire on the Fourth of March will return to private life with blasted hopes, injured health, impaired or ruined fortunes, embittered tempers, and probably a total inability to enjoy the rest of their lives."

But she was giving no quarter to Peggy Eaton.

"Public opinion will not allow General Eaton holding a place which would bring his wife into society," she said.

What Mrs. Smith had failed to reckon with was that the bitter Andrew Jackson brought public opinion with him when he arrived in the stricken capital city wearing a ten-inch crepe mourning band for Rachel. One of his first and firmest choices for his cabinet was John Eaton of Tennessee, Peggy's husband, as Secretary of War.

The stand which Jackson took and held regardless of the wreckage was that Mrs. Eaton was a victim of slander, just as Rachel had been, and that any affront to her was an affront to Rachel and therefore to him.

The large Jackson entourage had temporary headquarters at the new National Hotel run by John Gadsby, who had closed the old Franklin House. At the northeast corner of Pennsylvania Avenue and Sixth Street, N. W., the National was conveniently close to the Capitol.

Just as Jefferson had done on a similar popular overturn, Jackson chose to walk to the Capitol for his inauguration. He turned down two handsome equipages offered by his adoring public, a superb coach drawn by eight white horses, gift of Philadelphia, and a carriage made of hickory wood, sent by Baltimore. He discarded the "Plan of Parade" already printed.

In his inauguration address, delivered on the north portico in a tone so low that few heard, Andrew Jackson openly declared his principle of "rotation in office," the party patronage system. He said he would undertake the "task of reform, which shall require, particularly, the correction of those abuses which have brought the patronage of the Federal government into conflict with the freedom of elections, and the counteraction of those causes which have disturbed the rightful course of appointments, and have placed, or continued power, in unfaithful or incompetent hands."

The *National Intelligencer* pounced on this paragraph the next day and made an editorial effort to appeal to Jackson not to do what he had said. But Jackson was not taking admonitions from Editor

William W. Seaton. He was giving them out through Duff Green's *Telegraph*. And the *Telegraph's* constant clamor was to turn the rascals out.

President Jackson made his trip back down the avenue, from Capitol to White House, on the horse that had been held for him on the Capitol grounds. His dashing figure stood out in the midst of a motley cavalcade. At journey's end he was swept into what undoubtedly was the wildest scene ever staged in the Executive Mansion. Mrs. Smith's account of it, the best of many written at the time, left little doubt it was due to lack of police protection.

Mrs. Smith said she had waited for about two hours to be able to get into the White House and then:

"The Majesty of the People had disappeared, and a rabble, a mob, of boys, negroes, women, children, scrabbling, fighting, romping, what a pity, what a pity! No arrangements had been made, no police officers placed on duty, and the whole house had been inundated by the rabble mob. We came too late. The President, after having been *literally* nearly pressed to death and almost suffocated and torn to pieces by the people in their eagerness to shake hands with Old Hickory, had retreated through the back way or south front and had escaped to his lodgings at Gadsby's. Cut glass and china to the amount of several thousand dollars had been broken in the struggle to get the refreshments. Punch and other articles had been carried out in tubs and buckets. But had it been in hogsheads it would have been insufficient ice creams and cakes and lemonade for 20,000 people, for it was said that number was there, though I think the estimate exaggerated.

"Ladies fainted, men were seen with bloody noses and such a scene of confusion took place as is impossible to describe—those who got in could not get out by the door again but had to scramble out the windows. At one time the President who had retreated and retreated until he was pressed against the wall could only be secured by a number of gentlemen forming round him and making a kind of barrier of their bodies. . . . The noisy and disorderly rabble in the President's House brought to my mind descriptions I had read of the mobs at Versailles."

Obviously Mrs. Smith had changed a good deal since the days when she had been one of the expounders of Jeffersonian democracy. She now was the wife of the President of the Washington Branch of the

Bank of the United States, an institution on which Jackson would declare war to the death as soon as he had a few other issues settled, first of them Peggy Eaton.

Mrs. Smith did not fail to record that on Inauguration Day Mrs. Eaton had been publicly shunned by all the rest of the cabinet wives at all public functions, including the Inaugural Ball, not attended by Jackson but by the young people of his household. At the ball even Jackson's niece and hostess, Emily Donelson, and her cousin and White House companion, Mary Eastin, had ignored Mrs. Eaton.

Then followed a strange two years in which not only all Washington society but all national politics was permeated by seething controversies over a woman who loved the limelight thus focused on her. As this fracas proceeded from climax to climax President Jackson was busy turning the rascals out—though not to the extent at first expected. He also was learning about the White House the hard way.

The place was full of emotional crosscurrents as well as being topheavy with expenses. Into the White House had moved not only Rachel's nephew and niece, the Donelsons, and Emily's cousin, Mary Eastin, but also Major Eaton's brother-in-law, William B. Lewis, an early Jackson-for-President plumper. Jackson had made Major Lewis a sort of superintendent of household accounts, a fact which may have accounted for the coinage of the term "Kitchen Cabinet," in which he held the top portfolio. The other initial members of that body were three able editors—Duff Green; Isaac Hill, who had run a Jackson paper in New Hampshire; and Amos Kendall, who had run one in Kentucky. Jack and Emily Donelson were irked at Lewis because he kept trying to compel Emily to accept Peggy Eaton. Duff Green charged that Lewis was trying to set himself up as the one and only news channel from the President. And various generals charged that he was trying to run his brother-in-law's War Department.

The master of the Hermitage took constructive charge of the White House. The long-neglected East Room became a stately show place. It had been papered by Adams in a "fine lemon color." Its four fireplaces were now finished with black marble mantels. Over them were hung four great mirrors, costing $2,000. Three handsome 18-candle gilt-and-cut-glass chandeliers were suspended from the ceiling at a cost of $1,875. Under each chandelier was set a round table, described as "of beautiful workmanship, with Italian black and gold slabs." On the center table was a lamp supported by female figures; on the end tables were gilt astral lamps. Stationed about the walls were four pier tables, also with Italian slabs and richly bronzed and gilded. On each pier table was a lamp and a pair of French china vases corresponding to the decorations of the mantel. The floor was covered with 500 yards of Brussels carpet, fawn, blue and yellow, with a red border, at a cost of $1,058.25. Curtains of blue and yellow moreen were held up by gilded eagles, and around the cornice a line of gilded stars was emblazoned. Over the semicircle of the door were gilded ornamental rays and 24 stars, emblematic of the states. Fine paintings were placed on the walls. Sofas and chairs were covered with the blue damask satin. In all, Jackson spent almost $10,000 for the furnishing of the East Room. The White House drawing room no longer would be called a "squeeze." It had become a promenade. And such were the current customs that Jackson ordered for the state parlors 20 spittoons which cost $12.50.

There was no place in a Jacksonian household for empty upstairs chambers such as Adams had inventoried, nor did Jackson have inhibitions about obtaining White House appropriations from Congress. In his two terms he spent $45,000 on White House furniture, silver, china and cut glass, always of the best. From the Hermitage he brought his best-trained slaves, so that the ground floor of the White House teemed with life, as did its ceremonial rooms and upper chambers. For a chef he kept Michael Anthony Guista, hired by John Quincy Adams in Amsterdam in 1814 and regretfully relinquished by him when he left the White House.

Jackson lost no time in starting construction on the North Portico which had been contemplated for many years. Just before leaving the Mansion, President Monroe had completed the gracious, curving South Portico on the plan of Jefferson. Though this South Portico had been conceived as the ceremonial entrance of a house facing the Potomac River, custom already had made it a back door. Pennsylvania Avenue was the only one of L'Enfant's great thoroughfares cut through. Down Pennsylvania Avenue the people came. Andrew Jackson sensibly built his ceremonial entrance accordingly, a move which had the effect of reversing the original plan of the White House.

All the old outbuildings, which were in the semblance of wings, Jackson had repaired. And close to the southwest corner of the mansion he planted magnolia trees in memory of his wife Rachel, trees which still blossom in beauty after more than a century.

President Jackson also erected a racing stable, where he kept thoroughbreds which he entered on near-by tracks under the name of his nephew and secretary, Andrew Jackson Donelson. The rest of the country might continue to call him "Old Hickory," but the capital, taking note of all this splendor and also of some of his more high-handed actions, called him "King Andrew." And Peggy Eaton, who furnished motivation for his most spectacular acts, was called Bellona, Goddess of War.

Jackson waged three major campaigns in the Eaton affair. First came the campaign against the clergy. Two leading preachers—one in Philadelphia, the other pastor of Jackson's own church in the capital—became convinced it was their duty to protect the President from a designing woman. To their charges against Mrs. Eaton, made in writing, the President responded with page on page of refutation. This brought on still more scandalous oral charges against her character, to the effect that Mrs. Eaton, prior to her marriage to the then Senator, had had a miscarriage in a pregnancy which could not be attributed to her then husband Mr. Timberlake because of his long absence on the high seas. Jackson called the two preachers into a cabinet meeting, where he confounded them with date discrepancies in their tale. The cloth retired, discomfited.

The second campaign was a disciplinary one against Rachel's niece Emily, whom Jackson loved like a daughter and who refused to accept Mrs. Eaton. All Washington breathlessly watched that drama. Emily would not talk to Mrs. Eaton when she came into the White House, queening it over the Presidential drawing rooms. Neither would Emily call on Peggy, but she did call on Peggy's next-door neighbor, who unfortunately lived in a house owned by the Eatons. Mrs. Eaton was so furious when the White House carriage came into the neighborhood and failed to stop at her door that she gave notice to her neighbor to move out, though the lease would not expire for many months. When Emily became ill on a river excursion, she haughtily refused the smelling salts offered by Mrs. Eaton. Peggy took her injured feelings to the President, who promised to send Emily back to Tennessee if she didn't change her ways. Mrs. Eaton trumped up a situation in which she could go tattling on Emily again—and Jackson did send Mrs. Donelson home, her husband choosing to go with her.

There was a short period in which Peggy Eaton flaunted her White House ascendancy and was called "Unofficial First Lady." One gentleman guest at a dinner of state described the scene: "Fifty guests, one hundred candles and lamps, silver plate of every description, and for a queen, Peggy O'Neale, led in by Mr. Vaughan (the British minister) as head of the Diplomatic Corps, and sitting between him and the President."

The third campaign, and the most significant, was waged in the cabinet and in the "Kitchen Cabinet." Chief champion of Mrs. Eaton was Secretary of State Martin Van Buren, who had nothing to lose socially, being a widower, and everything to gain politically. In his exceedingly active Presidential aspirations Van Buren was supported by Peggy's husband and by William T. Berry, the Postmaster General.

Cabinet members who came out openly against Mrs. Eaton were Secretary of the Treasury S. D. Ingham, Secretary of the Navy John Branch and Attorney General John Macpherson Berrien. All three gave large evening parties to which Mrs. Eaton was not invited, and word went out that their wives had induced the wife of the Dutch minister to start a similar move in the diplomatic corps. Whereupon Andrew Jackson called the three gentlemen to the White House.

He read them a prepared statement, the purport of which was that if they continued to exclude Mrs. Eaton they had better withdraw from the cabinet. By this time, however, developments on the political front had made obvious the fact that their official days were numbered more because they were friends of Calhoun than because they were enemies of Mrs. Eaton.

Early in his administration President Andrew Jackson had cooled toward Vice President John C. Calhoun, and on a basic issue—nullification. Jackson was more than willing that a whole series of events should accentuate this schism. He openly resented the fact that Mrs. Calhoun stayed in South Carolina rather than countenance Peggy Eaton. When Calhoun maneuvered him into a position at which he would seem to sanction at a Jefferson Day dinner a series of toasts verging on nullification and secession, Andrew Jackson rose and broke up Calhoun's party with the toast, "Our Federal Union: It must be preserved."

Another old Presidential contender, William H. Crawford, saw the widening breach between Jackson and Calhoun and was inspired to

add to it. Jackson had allied himself with Calhoun because he believed that Calhoun, as Secretary of War in the Monroe cabinet, had
been his one strong backer on the Seminole invasion. Crawford
revealed to Jackson that in the secret councils of the Monroe cabinet
Calhoun had opposed this move and had even stood for publicly
censuring Jackson. So had Crawford, but that wasn't the way he told
it to Jackson.

The President pounced on this old cabinet controversy as though
it were a matter of the most current and vital importance. He demanded an explanation from Calhoun. He demanded from ex-
President Monroe additional details. Both Calhoun and Crawford
sought out Adams to try to get more data to bolster their competing
arguments. Column after column on the subject seethed through the
Washington newspapers, captioned simply "The Controversy."

By the peculiar osmosis of politics the Eaton affair and the Calhoun
affair were one. Van Buren, ostensibly Peggy's champion, really was
maneuvering to make a clean sweep of Calhoun and his friends to
clear the way for his own candidacy.

The first head to fall was in the "Kitchen Cabinet." Duff Green,
pro-Calhoun editor of the administration's *Telegraph*, suddenly found
himself on the outside. Jackson brought in Francis P. Blair of Kentucky to start a new administration organ, the Washington *Globe*.

This made things interesting for the reading public, since Duff
Green, having been so lately a member of the Jackson inner circle,
was qualified to give vivid detail to his interpretation of events. A
bold man was he, putting "By Duff Green" in big type over the
entire contents of his paper. He pictured a wily Van Buren pulling
every possible string to make himself President, using as his chief
tool Major Lewis, whom Green described as "the brother-in-law of
the Secretary of War who has long hung upon the skirts of the President and aspires to be considered the keeper of his secrets, and the
secret spring controlling his political actions." Duff Green charged
Major Lewis with having fed to the New York *Standard* the following
item. "We have little doubt that Mr. Ingham will resign as Secretary
of the Treasury and will be succeeded by the Hon. Lewis McLane,
now Minister to England." In refutation of this statement Duff
Green had it from Ingham himself that he had no intention of
resigning.

Duff Green also pounced on wraithlike Amos Kendall, Jackson's gifted ghost writer. "Who are Amos Kendall and Francis P. Blair that they should assume the President belongs to them?" he demanded. "It is my duty to speak out and I will do it, against Major Eaton, Major Lewis, Amos Kendall and Mr. Van Buren."

Although Secretary Ingham did not yet know it, he really was going to resign—so were all the rest of the cabinet—and Minister McLane was going to take Ingham's place because Secretary of State Van Buren wanted to go to London as Minister to England. On a horseback ride with President Jackson the Secretary of State artfully dangled this scheme—a complete change of cabinet such as happens in European countries, with the President's friends taken care of in other places. The idea was that Eaton should again become Senator from Tennessee by appointment to the first possible vacancy.

The way Eaton later told this story in his revised biography of Andrew Jackson was:

"By a series of skillful maneuvers the President shelved three members of his cabinet—Ingham, Branch and Berrien—who were Calhoun's friends and political allies. A dissolution of the Cabinet was the expedient decided upon. . . . The obnoxious three were asked for their resignations, which of course were tendered. The dissolution, its causes and consequences, and the many scandals it gave rise to, of which we cannot here speak, were the newspaper topic of the whole summer."

Eaton's own contribution to the immediate controversy had been a couple of challenges to duels with former cabinet colleagues which were never fought; and also an able and cogent monograph entitled, "A Candid Appeal to the American Public." Taking pen in hand to defend his own wife by the pamphlet method, as he had defended Rachel Jackson during her husband's campaign, Eaton began:

"In civilized society, a man's house is his castle, and the circle of his family a sanctuary never to be violated. He who drags before the public its helpless inmates, and subjects them to rude assaults, deserves to be considered worse than a barbarian. Against those who commit such a sacrilege, and shun honorable accountability, the public will justify an appeal."

With Eaton out of public life and bound for his home in Tennessee, this pamphlet was received with some sympathy in Washington.

The scandal died down. But Peggy also proved to be flamboyant in Tennessee. That state would not send Eaton back to the Senate, and Jackson, having found a face-saving way out of the original impasse, dropped him as an issue. But he kept him on as a responsibility, making him governor of Florida and, later, Minister to Madrid. Social Washington was not pleased to learn that pretty and vivacious Mrs. Eaton was well received at court and became a great favorite of the queen of Spain.

In the move he had made for Van Buren, President Jackson also was balked. Under the tight rein of Vice President John C. Calhoun, the Senate refused to confirm Van Buren's recess appointment, and Jackson had to bring him back from England. Calhoun thereby defeated his own purposes, for Jackson saw to it that Van Buren's return to these shores was not as a rejected diplomat but as a triumphant candidate for the Vice Presidency. The first national political convention ever held in this country was called by the Democrats in 1832, on the initiation of Jackson, for the sole purpose of nominating Martin Van Buren as Vice President.

To be teamed with Andrew Jackson was of course tantamount to election. As early as March 1830 John Quincy Adams, commenting on Jackson's extraordinary popularity, had bitterly said, "He may be re-elected not only once, but twice or thrice."

Calhoun swiftly made other plans. Down in South Carolina medals were struck: "John C. Calhoun, First President of the Southern Confederacy." He resigned as Vice President, a step never taken before or since. With more control over his state than Jackson had had over his in attempting to give a seat to Eaton, Calhoun got the governorship for Senator Robert Y. Hayne and sent himself to Hayne's seat in the Senate. The doctrine of nullification he had simmered down to "Any single state may nullify any act of Congress which it deems unconstitutional" and also "Any state of the Union may secede whenever it likes."

Said Andrew Jackson, "If this thing goes on our country will be like a bag of meal with both ends open. Pick it up in the middle or endwise, it will run out." Jackson laid plans to use force if South Carolina got out of line and, having thus disposed in his own mind of Calhoun and nullification, squared off for the battle with Whig candidate Henry Clay and the United States Bank.

On the election issue that the bank represented entrenched privilege and must be brought within bounds, Jackson won over Clay in the 1832 Presidential campaign with a bigger majority than he had had four years before. Seeing four more years of Jacksonian supremacy ahead, Calhoun caused a convention to be called in South Carolina which voted nullification of the tariff. Jackson issued a proclamation that he would send troops in to see to it that the customs were collected, and privately sent word to Calhoun that he was in danger of being hanged for treason. Clay then came up with one of his famous compromises, an easing off on the tariff which permitted both sides to claim victory. Jackson settled down to finish off Clay on the bank issue. By shifting Secretaries of the Treasury until he arrived at Roger B. Taney, who was completely co-operative, Jackson withdrew federal funds from the United States Bank and scattered them through state banks. Before his term had ended he had paid off the public debt.

After his first big cabinet overturn Jackson never hesitated to make changes which would further his program. The tally for his score in two terms of office was: four Secretaries of State, five Secretaries of the Treasury, three Secretaries of War, three Secretaries of the Navy, three Attorney Generals and two Postmaster Generals.

Jackson's opponents held that he had little understanding of the democratic movement that bore his name, and that he supported it principally because it supported him. But in the public debate over the bank issue he clearly brought out the tenets which had made him powerful. The simple people believed him when he said, "Every man is equally entitled to protection by law. . . . When laws undertake to make the rich richer and the potent more powerful, the humbler members of society, the farmers, mechanics and laborers who have neither the time nor the means of securing like favors for themselves, have a right to complain of the injustice of their government."

When the Senate voted a resolution of censure of Jackson for withdrawing the federal funds from the bank, it took him three years to get it expunged from the record—but expunged it was.

Jackson's political life continued to be tempestuous throughout the four years which followed his ultrasimple second inauguration. It was a stormy day, and he had been ill of his old malady, hemorrhages. So there was only a brief ceremony in the House Chamber—he wouldn't have been happy in the Senate with Calhoun and Clay there. There was no public reception such as the one which nearly wrecked the White House four years before. And his young folk represented him at the two Inaugural balls.

Socially the Jackson administration had passed through its age of adolescence and had entered upon a serene adulthood. Emily Donelson was again the gracious hostess, with a young family about her. Three children were born to Emily in the White House, a record to date. Andrew Jackson, Jr., had brought to the White House his small dark-eyed bride, Sarah York Jackson of Philadelphia. She and her husband went back and forth between Washington and Tennessee, quiet Sarah serving alternately as mistress of the Hermitage and assistant hostess to Emily. Sarah's first-born, a girl, arrived at the Hermitage and was named Rachel.

A typical home scene in the White House in Jackson's second administration was thus described by a writer of that time:

"A blazing fire on the grate; four or five ladies sewing around it; five or six children playing about, regardless of documents or work baskets. At the farther end of the room, the President in his armchair, wearing a long loose coat and smoking a long reed pipe, with a bowl of red clay; combining the dignity of the patriarch, monarch, and Indian chief."

The White House invitation on a large-scale basis made its debut. Besides holding general levees, President Jackson staged invitation receptions, attended by as many as 1,000 people. For his invited guests a lavish supper was spread on a great horseshoe table in the State Dining Room, described as "covered with every good and glittering thing that French skill could devise, and at either end a monster salmon in waves of meat jelly."

Amid all his battlings President Jackson somehow found time to further the improvement of the capital city. He did not succeed in getting his million-dollar bridge built across the Potomac with a new suburb, "Jackson City," at the end of it. But he did get macadam spread the length of Pennsylvania Avenue. He decided an old dispute as to where the Treasury Building would be placed and got the building started. And when he left the White House his portrait was placed in the city hall as the result of a popular dollar subscription "as a mark of gratitude" for his active interest in behalf of the citizenry.

Before he returned to the Hermitage he won one more election, that of Martin Van Buren, the fourth successive time that he had carried off the popular vote in the Presidential sweepstakes.

The last three months in the White House were greatly saddened by the death of Emily 'Donelson from quick consumption. She had gone home to the Hermitage in the vain hope of building back her health. Sarah York Jackson was hostess at the few public events of the final winter.

When the time came to go, Andrew Jackson made his most lingering farewells at Blair House. His sentimental side was shown in the letter he wrote to Mrs. Blair: "I cannot leave the city without presenting you my grateful thanks for the kindnesses you have extended me and my family whilst here. When sick you visited us and extended to me and our dear little ones all the comforts within your power." Jackson told her that as a memento of all this, he was giving her "a heifer used by me since my second election . . ." adding, "She will bring you in mind my fondness for good milk, and how I was gratified in this fondness from your liberal land."

His embattled side was shown at the final meeting of the "Kitchen Cabinet" in Francis P. Blair's study, with Jackson, it would be deduced from the foregoing, quaffing a glass of milk. When they asked Jackson if he had any regrets about his Presidency, he made his famous reply that he had two of them—he was sorry he hadn't shot Clay or hung Calhoun.

6 | Gallant Politicians and Young Hostesses

... VAN BUREN, WILLIAM HENRY HARRISON, TYLER

MARTIN VAN BUREN had been master of the White House for less than a fortnight when this country's first great depression struck an astounded populace. Banks failed. Railroad, townsite and colonization schemes collapsed. Bitterly the bankers blamed Andrew Jackson's campaign against them for the debacle. They stimulated an angry outcry against Van Buren, demanding a special session of Congress for the recharter of the U. S. Bank.

In this crisis Martin Van Buren, the politician who had been called "The Fox," "The Weasel," "The Sweet Little Fellow," "The Political Grimalkin," "The Follower in the Footsteps" and constantly and especially "The Little Magician," rose to statesmanship. He determined on meeting the banking crisis by entirely divorcing the federal funds from the private banking system. This would be done by setting up a Federal Treasury with subtreasuries. Thus private enterprise would be freed from federal pressures; and the federal government could remain financially sound if panic should strike again.

No politician as astute as he was could have failed to know that in making this choice he was jeopardizing his chance for a second term. He was estranging all the "pet banks" over the country into which Jackson had put public funds, as well as the powerful "moneyed interests" of the old U. S. Bank, which had been credited with buying up Congressmen right and left.

Van Buren's first canny move was to play for time until part of the panic storm should subside. Under pressure he did call the special session of Congress, but he called it for September to prolong the cooling-off period.

He himself occupied the interim by creating a man-about-town atmosphere in the White House. The Executive Mansion took on an exclusive rather than a democratic air. He sold at auction such White House furniture as he considered worn out or unsuited to the place, obtaining thereby $5,680. He then proceeded to spend about $25,000 on a cleaning and refurnishing program, a reasonable enough sum as compared with the $45,000 Andrew Jackson had spent in two terms.

Soon Van Buren was becoming famed for his perfectly appointed small dinners, served to a select group of statesmen, political foes as well as friends. For Van Buren enjoyed the exchange of political repartee on social occasions. He was the *bon vivant*, polished and imperturbable.

His four sons were completely a part of this life. Van Buren's wife had died 19 years before, when his youngest son Smith was born. So Van Buren had trained his boys in the niceties of social graces and the intricacies of politics. In the White House he immediately made Abraham, the eldest son, his private secretary, with Martin, Jr., as alternate. His third son John, who had accompanied him to England when he went there as minister, returned on a visit during his father's Presidency and was royally received by Queen Victoria. The British court journal published a dinner-guest list which ran, "Prince Nicholas Esterhazy; Prince Windisch Gratz; John Van Buren, son of the President of the United States; the Lord Chancellor and Lady Cottenham . . . ," and this started the Whig papers to gibing at "Our Prince John." For Smith Van Buren, his youngest son, the President entertained at elaborate parties. They had to be good to match those given for the very young of official Washington and social Georgetown by the aged Russian minister, Count Bodisco.

In porches which he had "permanently enclosed, curtained, mirrored, carpeted, and pictured," the count hung red-and-gold swings. Tables there were piled high with games and toys and sacks of little satin bags marked "Bon Bons" in gilt letters. In the dressing rooms were whole boxes of white gloves and yards of all colors of ribbons and maids to aid in fitting them on pretty little girls. Parlors and ballrooms on three floors were thrown open to games and dancing. One gay and pretty little girl who went to the Bodisco parties, Harriet Williams, was chosen Queen of the May at the select school run by Miss English in Georgetown. This election was countermanded by the faculty on the grounds that Miss Williams was not up in her grades. She also was not from one of the first families. The head mistress evidently had not read the tea leaves, for Count Bodisco almost immediately married the beautiful fourteen-year-old Harriet, and she ruled for many years as the veritable queen of Washington society.

As one of the leaders of the "Harriet for May Queen" movement, Jessie Benton, daughter of the Missouri Senator, was chosen a maid of honor at the wedding. Years later as Mrs. John C. Frémont, wife of the general, she described this high moment of her early youth: "The President, Mr. Van Buren, was there. All the officials, of all kinds. All the Diplomatic Corps, in full dress—Army and Navy Officers in full uniform, and a crowd of ladies in full morning dress." This audience, she said, waited on one side of folding doors, while on the other:

"Bodisco with his paper still in hand, directed each couple into proper position. The bride and himself to face the folding doors. To his left, Henry Fox, British Minister—a withered, cynical, silent gray old man in scarlet and gold court suit—his rough gray eyebrows frowned over his half-shut eyes and his whole attitude a protest— while by him was a smiling rosy little blonde of thirteen, sister of the bride. To the right of the bride was Senator James Buchanan, former Minister to Russia, tall and of fine presence and quite a type of Saxon coloring and freshness despite his silvered head, and with him myself—aged fourteen. . . . Of the eight couples, only two were of equal youth, Smith Van Buren, the President's youngest son, and Kemble Paulding, also under twenty, whose father was Secretary of the Navy —these had been given two pretty cousins of the bride."

The wedding party was completed by Senator Henry Clay, who was to give the bride away, and a bishop in full canonicals. Said the narrator of this scene, "When we were arranged quite to his taste, in a horseshoe curve, the glistening white dresses and young faces and flowers thrown into higher relief by the age and court dress of the men, Bodisco gave a last reviewing look, then ordered the doors to be rolled back."

A few nights later, Jessie Benton said, Count Bodisco presented his tableau again, this time at the White House, where Martin Van Buren entertained the entire wedding party at one of his faultless dinners. Naturally the affair was the talk of the capital and set a trend—the enthronement of extreme youth at the tiptop of the social scene. Gray-haired statesmen tossed their best epigrams into the ears of pretty little girls.

The political tides were still against Van Buren when his special session got into swing in September 1837. From the Hermitage Andrew Jackson wrote frequent letters of understanding and encouragement: "I see a few of our *prodigal political sons* have gone astray and are fighting with the opposition" and "You, sir, have a right to be satisfied with the results of the called session of Congress. The Divorce bill will pass at the next session. The people will demand it."

That November, Van Buren was repudiated in the elections of his home state of New York, where his name had been supreme.

The New York tornado may not have taken Washington in its first sweep, but it was headed straight for the White House. Its vortex was the rise of the first of the great backstage political bosses, Thurlow Weed. Working against Van Buren's administration with such able aides as Governor William H. Seward and Horace Greeley, Weed played all the political tricks that Van Buren had taught his home state, and added a few ingenious twists.

In mid-October 1837 widowed Dolley Madison returned to Washington to live in the former home of her sister, which her husband had bought and left to her. It was less than a block from the White House on the east side of Lafayette Park. Her coming caused a great stir among the old-timers. Said John Quincy Adams, "I had not seen her since March 1809. The depredations of time are not so perceptible in her personal appearance as might have been expected."

Dolley gave her own reaction: "I seem suddenly to have awakened after a dream of twenty years to find myself surrounded by strangers." One of her early hosts was Memucum Hunt, Minister Plenipotentiary from Texas, now recognized as an independent state.

One caller gave Mrs. Madison a résumé of the intervening years which ran: "Ah, Madam, the city is no longer what it was when you were mistress of the White House. Your successors have been sickly, tame, spiritless and indifferent. The mansion you made so charming and attractive is now almost inaccessible. The present incumbent has no female relative to preside over it and seems so much absorbed in party politics he will scarcely open the house to those who wish to see it."

This was exactly the sort of an appeal to put Dolley Madison into action. She immediately had in mind a "female relative"—one of her own—to preside over the White House. Up from South Carolina came Angelica Singleton to be introduced to Abraham Van Buren. Soon Abraham was paying court to Angelica at the home of Senator William C. Preston of South Carolina, another relative of Angelica's. When Congress adjourned in 1838 Miss Singleton returned to South Carolina with the Prestons, and there, at her father's house, Angelica and Abraham were married in November. Their wedding trip was home to the White House, where Angelica made her initial appearance as hostess at the New Year's reception of 1839. The newspaper accounts of that reception noted that "a constant current set from the President's house to the modest mansion of the much-respected lady of ex-President Madison." Thus was started a Washington custom which prevailed for the rest of Mrs. Madison's lifetime. Officialdom paid its respects on her each New Year's day right after calling on the President of the United States.

President Van Buren sent Angelica's uncle, Andrew Singleton, as Minister to Great Britain. In the spring of 1839 Angelica and Abraham Van Buren went abroad to visit him, and while there enjoyed the greatest social triumph. They were presented at both the British and the French courts, and Mrs. Van Buren had her portrait painted in her court costume of white silk, with a scarf thrown loosely about beautiful shoulders and the traditional three feathers in her jeweled headdress.

Altogether, Angelica fitted as perfectly into her White House role as she did into the royal-blue velvet gown which became quite the handsomest in the White House costume collection in Smithsonian museum. Hoops had definitely come into fashion, and they billowed out the ten-yard skirt which fell from Angelica's tiny waist.

Soon sadness marred this perfect picture. Angelica's first baby, a girl, born in the White House, lived only two hours. Angelica's mother was staying with her and helped her bear the disappointment. But Dolley Madison also was wanted, and Dolley hurried back from a Virginia visit to solace her young relative.

Martin Van Buren put through his "Divorce bill," quieted a

Canadian border uprising and otherwise showed himself to be an able President. But up in Albany, Thurlow Weed tirelessly maneuvered for the same sort of landslide against Van Buren that Van Buren had maneuvered against John Quincy Adams. A full year before the nominating convention Weed settled on his candidate—it would be General William Henry Harrison, an "Old Tippecanoe" who would have a popular appeal like "Old Hickory" of the battle of New Orleans. The Vice-Presidential place Weed first offered to Daniel Webster, who turned it down with the remark that he thought he'd be the Presidential nominee. So Weed put his wing over the Vice-Presidential candidacy of John Tyler of Virginia, on the correct theory that Tyler would win slave votes and Harrison would win votes against slavery.

Henry Clay undoubtedly had not only first right to the Whig nomination but also the votes to put it over. But Clay was eliminated in advance of the convention by a device known as the "Triangular Correspondence." Weed had the Whigs write to each other saying, "Do all you can for Mr. Clay in your district, for I am sorry to say he has no strength in this."

From the old anti-Adams campaign run by Van Buren 12 years previously there was still one more below-the-belt tactic to be borrowed—the old billiard-table-and-cue routine. But instead of singling out a White House billiard table for moral horror, the Whigs hit on some old gold-plated spoons which had been part of the White House table service since the time of Monroe. This symbol of effetism they would finish off with the finger bowls which Van Buren actually had purchased. Representative William Ogle of Pennsylvania, often a guest at Van Buren's small private parties, was the Whig chosen as spokesman. He was a famous orator and had the House roaring at repartee when he delivered an address which came to be known far and wide as the "Gold Spoon Speech." It was a lengthy address—in fact, of precisely the length to make a substantial and hate-inspiring campaign pamphlet. Ogle presented—page after page, with repetitions and sums twice added—all the records of purchases of White House furnishings from the time of Monroe down—and he laid them all in a veritable extravaganza of extravagance at Van Buren's door. The President at that time was being backed by a much-maligned political group called the Locofocos. He also traveled in the same social set with the actress Fanny Kemble. That Ogle rang all the changes was evident from a few much-quoted excerpts:

"How delightful it must be to a real genuine Loco Foco to eat his pate de foie gras, dinde desosse and salade a la volaille from a silver plate with a golden knife and fork. And how exquisite to sip with a golden spoon his soupe a la Reine from a silver tureen.

"What will honest Loco Focos say to Mr. Van Buren for spending the People's cash in foreign Fanny Kemble green finger cups, in which to wash his pretty, tapering, soft, white lily fingers?"

The Van Buren press struck back with charges of uncouthness against Whig candidate William Henry Harrison. Said the Baltimore *American*: "Give him a barrel of hard cider and settle a pension of two thousand a year on him, and my word for it, he will sit the remainder of his days in a log cabin." Thurlow Weed hit on that paragraph with glee, and soon the "Log Cabin and Hard Cider" campaign was on, the wonder of a century—the whole country singing log-cabin doggerel, shouting log-cabin ditties and, like naughty small boys, picking up the catcall, "Van, Van, is a used-up man."

As a matter of fact, William Henry Harrison was as much the Virginia aristocrat as his running mate John Tyler, and the log-cabin connotation was strictly a political stage prop. Tyler's father had followed Harrison's father as speaker of the Virginia House of Delegates. The $20,000 mansion Harrison built in early Vincennes, from which to conduct his lordly rule of Indiana territory, was counterpart of a fine Virginia home. In it his well-educated and aristocratic wife, Anna Symmes Harrison, daughter of a New Jersey judge, and the large Harrison family—they had ten children—lived as luxuriously as their Virginia cousins, if more adventurously. Harrison's subsequent Ohio home was also more than substantial. But a log-cabin symbol Weed had decreed, and it carried the country for Harrison and Tyler. Van Buren won only seven of the 27 states.

Van Buren cherished among his papers a clipping which told of how imperturbably he met defeat. He stepped out of church and was met by a party messenger. "The news today, sir, gives the Whigs ten thousand majority in New York and a small majority in Pennsylvania."

Not a muscle in Mr. Van Buren's countenance changed. "Then

General Harrison is your next President," he said with his usual courtly bow.

From Andrew Jackson at the Hermitage came vigorous if slightly word-tangled solace: "I still hope there is sufficient virtue in the unbought people of this nation to stay the perjury, bribery, fraud and imposition on the people by the vilest system of slander that ever before has existed even in the most corrupt days of ancient Rome."

Martin Van Buren was not so impervious to personal hurt as he sometimes seemed. After the election Senator Preston, in whose home Van Buren's son had courted Angelica, got the cold shoulder at the White House—and ruefully admitted he deserved it. Said the Senator: "I was goose enough during the recent canvass to make myself a party in one of my Virginia speeches to the absurd gold-spoon story—I was heartily ashamed the moment I had done it and have been so ever since."

Van Buren's last big fete in the White House was the New Year's reception of 1841, at which Angelica received with him.

Genial old General Harrison called at the White House as soon as he arrived in Washington on February 9, his sixty-eighth birthday. President Van Buren and his entire cabinet returned the call at Gadsby's Hotel. The general then went down into Virginia to visit his daughter until inauguration week. On Inauguration Day, since it was not yet the custom for a defeated President to share in the ceremonies, Martin Van Buren was seen calmly walking the streets of Washington, a spectator to the spectacular but shivery Log Cabin Parade.

Van Buren would have bowed out with a vote of thanks from the corporation of Washington had it not been for William W. Seaton, now mayor of the city as well as editor of the *National Intelligencer*. Seaton refused to sign this resolution, saying that since it seemed to be in praise of Van Buren's official acts, his signature would not be in unison with his avowed opinion.

Mayor Seaton had at the time as house guest incoming President William Henry Harrison, who had found that he could get no rest at any hotel because of his log-cabin campaign popularity. The big project at the Seaton home was to try to make Harrison key his already written inaugural address, full of classical allusions, to the log-cabin legend. Daniel Webster, who was Harrison's appointee as Secretary of State, spearheaded this task. Arriving late one night at the dinner table, so Seaton loved to tell in later years, Webster said, "Excuse my tardiness, but I have been able to dispose of two Roman Emperors and a pro-Consul, which should be sufficient excuse."

This story quite naturally grew with the telling until Mrs. Seaton was credited with repeating Webster's remark as "I have killed seventeen Roman pro consuls as dead as smelts!" The Harrison speech when delivered showed little evidence of Webster's tailoring, and was more ancient Athens than current America.

Mrs. Harrison was not present at the inaugural. At sixty-three she had heartily wished that the general's friends had left him alone. She had not been well that winter and was not able to make the long stage trip from Ohio to Washington in February. She promised to go in May and sent in her stead her daughter-in-law, Jane Findlay Harrison, widow of the President's second son and namesake, to serve as White House hostess. With Jane went her two small sons and her mother, Mrs. James Findlay. One Harrison biographer said that the President's daughter, Anna Tuthill Taylor, came up from her Virginia home to assist Jane. However, the scanty social notes of the time merely recorded, "Today, President Harrison received the ladies. There was a large and splendid assemblage." And "The Lady of the White House was the President's daughter-in-law, an attractive young widow."

President Harrison considered himself as head of the household, even doing his own marketing in the early morning for a short while. The avalanche of office seekers made that impossible, and he turned the running of the White House over to his steward.

Harrison's entire cabinet had been chosen before he took office. Clay had refused the position of Secretary of State, expecting to be the backstage dictator. He pressed so strongly for one appointment that President Harrison had to say, "Mr. Clay, you forget that I am the President." And when Clay had the temerity to send to Harrison a "confidential letter" urging a special session of Congress and even enclosing the wording of the message to call it, President Harrison promptly replied in writing, "You are too impetuous. Much as I rely upon your judgment, there are others I must consult." At the usual summer recess Clay left Washington in a huff.

When the cabinet converged on the President, demanding more vacancies to be filled, he rose in anger and swore he'd be no party to dismissals without cause. He had Secretary of State Webster send around an official notice to department heads that they were to dispense with party patronage. The cabinet members got a ruling from the Attorney General that they had a right to review Presidential appointments. This made Harrison so determined to make his own that he personally walked to Octagon House on a wet and slushy day to offer a diplomatic post to Colonel John Tayloe. And still the office seekers overran the White House, loading the President down with their petitions.

William Henry Harrison succumbed to a severe cold on March 27, which worsened into pneumonia. His fever brought delirium in which he was described as still bedeviled by the problems of patronage— "It is wrong—I won't consent—'tis unjust—these applications, will they never cease?" On April 4 he died. John Tyler had to be summoned from his home at Williamsburg, Virginia, the first Vice President ever to succeed to the chief office.

William Henry Harrison was the first President to lie in state in the East Room. The whole city was dressed in mourning, with business places as well as the White House swathed in black.

Elaborate were the funeral services of April 7. Two of the President's swords were placed on the flower-decorated bier. At one side of it sat President Tyler and the cabinet, ex-President John Quincy Adams and former cabinet members; on the other side sat Harrison's family and household. The foreign ministers and their suites were present in full diplomatic costume. The procession was two miles long and was estimated to number 10,000 persons, including several military companies. Harrison's body was placed in the public vault to wait its interment at his Ohio home.

Many statesmen of the time, ex-President John Quincy Adams among them, took the stand that Tyler was only an "Acting President." But Tyler soon brushed that aside with proof that the Constitution gave full title as well as full powers to the Vice President on the death of the President.

Three years before Tyler entered the White House his capable wife, Letitia, who had carried the chief responsibility of the rearing of their seven children, suffered an almost completely disabling stroke of paralysis. Tyler once wrote one of his daughters, "I could not hold up for you a better pattern for your imitation than is constantly presented to you by your dear mother. You never saw her course marked with precipitation, but on the contrary, everything is brought before

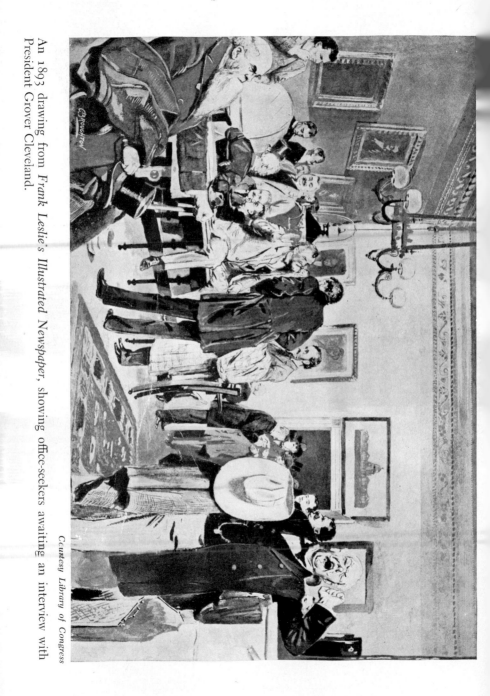

An 1893 drawing from *Frank Leslie's Illustrated Newspaper*, showing office-seekers awaiting an interview with President Grover Cleveland.

A sketch of an Easter Egg Rolling in the Cleveland administration.

the tribunal of her judgement, and all her actions are founded in prudence."

Letitia's course was running out. She appeared in public at the White House only once, in January 1842 at the marriage of her youngest daughter, Elizabeth, to William Waller of Williamsburg. That East Room wedding brought out cabinet officers, diplomats and Washington society, including Dolley Madison. Mrs. Tyler was described as wearing "a quiet gown of faultless taste," her face "shaded by the soft lace of her cap." Not until after Mrs. Tyler died in September 1842 did her daughter and namesake, Letitia Temple, who was constantly at her mother's bedside, have time to serve as her father's hostess.

This honor for the first year and a half of Tyler's term devolved on the President's daughter-in-law, Mrs. Robert Tyler, whose husband served as the President's secretary. No one could possibly have savored the role more than she. Born Priscilla Cooper of Philadelphia, she was the daughter of the great tragedian, Thomas Apthorpe Cooper, and of the brilliant Mary Fairlie Cooper. Of her father, Washington Irving said that no actor in England could equal his Macbeth. And Irving called her mother "the fascinating Fairlie" and made her the "Sophy Sparkle" of his *Salmagundi Papers*. As a young girl Priscilla had played the role of Virginia to her father's Virginius. To his line, "Send her to me, Servia," she entered with "Well, father, what's your will?" When she played this daughterly bit in Washington the applause was so great the play was halted. Priscilla also remembered "a miserable engagement of a few rainy nights" playing Lady Randolph in a Washington theater.

It was small wonder that Priscilla Tyler was almost overwhelmed with the sense of how much stranger was fact than phantasy. To her sister she wrote:

"Here am I, nee Priscilla Cooper, actually living in, and what is more, presiding at—the White House! I look at myself, like the little old woman, and exclaim, 'Can this be I?'

"And the most extraordinary thing is that I feel I had been used to living here always, and receive the cabinet ministers, the diplomatic corps, the heads of army and navy, etc., etc., with a facility which astonishes me. . . . I am complimented on every side; my hidden virtues are coming out.

"I have had some lovely dresses made, which fit me to perfection—one pearl-colored silk that will set you crazy. . . .

"The greatest trouble I anticipate is in paying visits. There was doubt at first whether I must visit in person or send cards; but I asked Mrs. Madison's advice upon the subject and she says, return all my visits by all means. So three days in the week I am to spend three hours in the day driving from one street to another in this city of magnificent distances. . . .

"I see so many great men and so constantly that I cannot appreciate the blessing! The fact is, when you meet them in everyday life, you forget they are great men at all, and just find them the most charming companions in the world, talking the most delightful nonsense, especially the almost awful-looking Mr. Webster, who entertains me with the most charming gossip."

Yet in the White House, as elsewhere, a young mother having to be an official hostess had her difficulties.

"My first state dinner is over; oh! such a long one, our first dinner in the state dining room. I was the only lady at the table. . . . I tried to be cheerful as possible, though I felt miserable all the time, as my baby was crying, and I received message after message to come to the nursery."

Happier was the White House party given by Priscilla for her eldest daughter, Mary Fairlie Tyler. Dressed as a fairy, a diamond star on her forehead, a silver wand in her hand, Mary as Queen Titania stood at the door of the East Room, welcoming the young elite of Washington. Dolley Madison's grandniece, Adele Cutts, even then getting the training which would make her a social queen, came as a flower girl to that masquerade.

Then there was the state dinner and ball given for the Prince de Joinville, third son of Louis Philippe, a youth of twenty-three. Priscilla was the hostess, and the ball was opened by the prince with the President's daughter Elizabeth Tyler as partner.

To one of the early Tyler receptions came two of the great literary figures of the time, Washington Irving, who had just been appointed Minister to Spain, and his friend, Charles Dickens, on his first triumphal tour to this country. The lengthy description which Dickens wrote of this levee included a compliment to Priscilla: "In the smaller drawing-room, the center of a circle of company, were the

President and his daughter-in-law who acted as the lady of the mansion: and a very interesting, graceful and accomplished lady too."

Charles Dickens also contributed to this country a daytime description of the White House of the early 1840s. He said the President's mansion was "like an English club-house, both within and without." He pronounced the ornamental grounds and garden walks about it "agreeable to the eye," but with "that uncomfortable air of having been made yesterday."

He and the official who took him in charge to present him to President Tyler—presumably one of the staff of the British legation—"thrice rang a bell, which nobody answered." Then they entered, as into any other public building, and "walked without further ceremony through the rooms on the ground floor, as divers other gentlemen (mostly with their hats on and with their hands in their pockets) were doing very leisurely. . . .

"After glancing at these loungers, who were scattered over a pretty drawing-room, opening upon a terrace which commanded a beautiful prospect of the river and the adjacent country, and who were sauntering too about a larger state-room called the Eastern Drawing-room, we went upstairs into another chamber, where were certain visitors, waiting for audiences. . . ."

Charles Dickens and his escort did not have to wait their turn, but soon were taken by a messenger into another room "of smaller dimensions where, at a business-like table covered with papers, sat the President' himself." Said Dickens: "He looked somewhat worn and anxious, and well he might, being at war with everybody—but the expression of his face was mild and pleasant, and his manner was remarkably unaffected, gentlemanly and agreeable. I thought in his whole carriage and demeanor he became his station singularly well."

Coming from the agrarian South, Tyler did not agree with the Northern financiers who had conducted the entire election with the idea of re-establishing the United States Bank. He vetoed two bank bills in succession, both pushed through the Congress by his former political ally, Henry Clay. At this, Clay organized a dinner party at which it was arranged that the entire cabinet resign at intervals on Saturday, September 11, 1831. Daniel Webster would have no part of this proceeding and left the party as soon as he got an inkling of what was afoot. As Tyler's son and secretary Robert Tyler, who handled the resignations, told it later, the plan was to have the last resignation take place at 5 P.M. The next day, Sunday, Congress did not meet, and both Houses were scheduled to adjourn the special session on Monday at 2 P.M.

Said Robert Tyler, "It was deemed by the conspirators that the President would be utterly unable to form a cabinet before the adjournment, and therefore that he would be compelled to resign because of an impossibility to conduct the administration." In 24 hours' time President Tyler had a new cabinet formed. It was made up, he said, "of the best materials, all original Jackson men."

The bank vetoes brought a public demonstration in front of the White House which resulted in the city government putting on the White House its first regular night police. Tyler was so unpopular that he was called "the President without a party," and he himself said that the path of his duty was made more plain by the light of burning effigies.

However, he calmly proceeded to the negotiation of the Northwest-boundary treaty with Great Britain. Lord Ashburton came over from London and rented a mansion across Lafayette Square from the White House, at 1525 H Street, and Daniel Webster moved into the mansion at 1611 H Street. Webster and Ashburton spent their days and nights together during the long and involved negotiations, and President Tyler took a hand to smooth out many an apparent impasse. The treaty was concluded August 9, 1842. Webster, uncomfortable at being at odds with the Whigs, then resigned, and Tyler appointed a Secretary of State who would be sympathetic with his secret plan of concluding a treaty of annexation with Texas. Since a treaty would require only a two-thirds vote of the Senate, he would be able to by-pass the House of Representatives and that embattled foe of further slave territory, John Quincy Adams. President Tyler, however, always insisted his championship of the addition of Texas was not sectional, but for the good of the United States as a whole, involving a monopoly on cotton which would give this country a tremendous economic advantage over Great Britain.

Hugh S. Legare as Secretary of State had just got well started on the Texas negotiations when he suddenly died. Tyler then appointed Abel P. Upshur, who had the annexation treaty almost to the point of signature when he was one of four statesmen killed by the explosion of the new-type gun, the Peacemaker, on the experimental ship, the *Princeton*. At that time—February 28, 1844—Tyler even had two thirds of the Senate quietly pledged to vote for the annexation of Texas.

The *Princeton* catastrophe altered Tyler's course in more than one way. A large official party had gone down the Potomac for the tests, which had been apparently successful. On the return trip the Secretary of the Navy called for one more firing of the Peacemaker—and he was one of those killed. So was David Gardiner, a former New York state senator famed for his beautiful and accomplished daughters. Gardiner Island, off Long Island, was their ancestral home. At the moment of the explosion President Tyler was on the lower deck, talking to the ladies—among them Julia Gardiner—and so escaped. Dolley Madison was one of the heroines of the hour, ably nursing the wounded. A state funeral was held for the four *Princeton* victims in the East Room. While they were sharing this tragedy, a swift courtship began between the President and Miss Gardiner. In June they were married in her New York home, and the final eight months of Tyler's term were made glamorous by a youthful and beautiful First Lady.

Julia Tyler was an unusual young woman. At Naples and at Paris at the court of Louis Philippe she and her sister had been sensations. In 1840 she was the toast of this country, called "The Rose of Long Island"—a colored lithograph was even struck off depicting her charms. It was the forerunner of the class advertisements, Julia being shown on her way to purchase at Rogert and McCamey's. As First Lady she put on such a social show as this country had never seen before—"The lovely lady Presidentress is attended on reception-days by twelve maids of honor, six on either side, dressed all alike. . . ." "Her serene loveliness receives upon a raised platform wearing a headdress formed of bugles and resembling a crown. . . ." "She received seated—her large armchair on a slightly raised platform in front of the windows opening to the circular piazza looking on the river."

Whatever Julia Tyler did was prompted by hero worship of her husband, the chief motivation of the rest of her life. She understood political issues and identified herself completely with her husband's aims and ambitions, particularly with regard to the annexation of Texas.

After Upshur's death Tyler appointed an acting Secretary of State who could have concluded the Texas annexation treaty. But one of Tyler's trusted political lieutenants, to whom he owed much, completely overstepped his authority by offering the portfolio of Secretary of State to Calhoun in Tyler's name. Tyler went through with the appointment as a lesser evil than estranging his friend and making Calhoun his enemy. But he knew that Calhoun, with his strong nullification views, would stir up antislavery animosity against the annexation of Texas. Tyler's two-thirds majority vanished. The ratification treaty failed in the Senate.

But Tyler adroitly managed to make Texas the chief campaign issue that fall. By jockeying through friends in the Democratic party he was able to block the nomination of anti-Texas Martin Van Buren and force the candidacy of pro-Texas James K. Polk of Tennessee. Clay was the Whig candidate, on an anti-Texas platform. Tyler headed a splinter party, holding the balance of power. When old Andrew Jackson came out yelling for Texas, Tyler knew his cause was saved and permitted Jackson to negotiate him into the withdrawal of his candidacy and the merger of his party with the Democrats. Polk won the election. Tyler then sent Andrew Jackson Donelson to Texas as the diplomat to finish up the negotiation.

When Congress reassembled in December, Tyler's bride wrote:

"The president's message has made a prodigious sensation. Senator McDuffie says it is the finest that ever, in any time, proceeded from the White House. The style is the president's own, peculiar and beautiful and of the truest simplicity. The whole cabinet yield it merited admiration. Oh! if it will only have the effect of admitting Texas!"

In the measured manner that Congress grinds such things out, it did. The House passed a resolution that Texas should be extended statehood in the same manner as had been done to other states. In the Senate powerful Senator Benton of Missouri, who had strong Presidential aspirations, chose to be a prima donna and forced the adoption of a measure which would create a commission to decide how Texas was to be admitted.

At this juncture, February 1845, Julia Tyler gave a grand ball in the White House to which 2,000 came, causing Tyler to make his famous jest: "They cannot now say I am a President without a party." One of the distinguished guests at this ball was that other leading figure in a May-January wedding, the Countess Bodisco.

Good feeling set in, and on Capitol Hill a compromise was effected whereby President Tyler would be empowered to take his choice between the Senate and House methods of dealing with the Texas question. He immediately admitted Texas. Julia was radiant because her husband gave her "the immortal gold pen" with which he signed the bill; and she wore it around her neck as a pendant on a gold chain all through the Polk inauguration ceremonies. Julia had earned it by a master social move which put across a long-pending political deal at a psychological moment.

The Tyler farewells were most felicitous. A deputation of citizens waited on them on the afternoon of March 3, with farewell speeches which drew from Tyler, so his wife recorded, a masterpiece of oratory. Then the entire company went with them to their hotel. Julia Tyler lived to see one of her sons, Lyon Gardiner Tyler, become president of William and Mary College, the alma mater of his father and his grandfather. And Lyon Gardiner Tyler lived to see old Williamsburg restored by the Rockefellers. He also devoted no small portion of his life to writing the history of his father's Presidency. He said that with a single issue, Texas, John Tyler killed four political giants—Henry Clay, Martin Van Buren, Thomas Benton and Francis P. Blair. Blair, he said, was "toppled off the tripod of the *Globe*."

7 | *The Hard-Working Polks*

JAMES K. POLK, a short President with a great program, slogged doggedly through inaugural ceremonies conducted in a downpour. Behind him on the Capitol portico stood a bedraggled officialdom. On the theory that the day would be fair, orders had been issued that no carriages should enter the Capitol grounds. So diplomats as well as common people had to make their way in the rain from side gate to the semishelter of the portico. Plumed hats were soggy, elaborate uniforms damp. The people on the plaza below scarcely saw the President. Old John Quincy Adams dryly commented that Polk's inaugural address was delivered "to a large assemblage of umbrellas."

Had the day been ideal, Polk could hardly have held his hearers enthralled. He read his address. He was no such orator as his opponent Henry Clay, who so recently had double-talked himself out of the Presidency by the narrowest margin. Clay had not made himself clear to many Northerners as to exactly how firmly he would resist the annexation of Texas, and so they voted with the abolitionist Liberty party, costing Clay New York and Pennsylvania. Polk had a right to feel that oratory was beside the point at this moment in history. He had an era to end, the era of expansion. He had to finish rolling the great blanket of the United States across plain and mountain, and tuck it in all along the Pacific Ocean. And he was allowing himself four years, no more, to do it in.

Proudly on the inaugural platform behind him stood his tall and handsome wife, dark-haired Sarah Childress Polk. In her hands she faithfully held the most useless accessory she could have had on a cold and rainy day. It was a fan, presented to her for the purpose of becoming a historic relic of the moment when Chief Justice Taney administered the oath to her husband. Its ivory sticks were elaborately carved. Its silken spread was imprinted on one side with portraits of the 11 Presidents from Washington to Polk, each inscribed with name and dates of the term of office. Polk, at forty-nine, was the youngest to have entered the office. Sarah was eight years his junior. Sarah Polk would preserve the fan until her dying day, more than half a century later.

The Capitol scene typified to Mrs. Polk a triumphant political comeback for her husband. For 14 years a Representative from Tennessee, he closed that career as the Speaker of the House who steered through to success Andrew Jackson's program of smashing the United States Bank. He had then gone home to hold the Tennessee governorship for the Democratic party, but after serving a single term he was twice defeated. Polk had entered the 1844 race aspiring only to the Vice Presidency. When a chance for the Presidential nomination had amazingly opened he was ready with a quietly built but efficient personal machine. He also had the potent blessing of Andrew Jackson. The Whigs, secure in the fame of Clay, had set up the war cry, "Who is James K. Polk?" To which the Democrats replied, "Young Hickory"— and won. So there Polk stood, ready to augment United States acreage and trim down the tariff in a dedicated spirit of personal austerity. Mrs. Polk had a quiet confidence in her ability to further his program. A strict Calvinist upbringing made her the ideal helpmeet for the nose-to-the-grindstone Polk.

Probably the greatest concession Mrs. Polk ever made to political exigencies was an appearance that night at the Inaugural Ball at Carusi Hall. Even then she held aloof from worldly pleasures. As she herself told the story in later years, the dancing ceased on the arrival of the Presidential party. The band played "Hail to the Chief," and there was a general reception. Mrs. Polk recalled that she wore "a mazarine blue velvet dress with a deeply fringed cape." From childhood—she was the daughter of a well-to-do merchant—Sarah Childress Polk had dressed in rich and expensive fabrics and in high fashion, avoiding, however, any flamboyance of line or color. Murmurs of admiration and approval greeted her appearance at the Inaugural Ball. Introductions and handshaking over, the Polks left the ball, and, it may be presumed, dancing was resumed.

In order to concentrate completely on territorial expansion and tariff reduction President Polk from his first day in office renounced any idea of re-election. Indeed, he went much further. Andrew Jackson, who certainly had had enlightening experience along this line, advised Polk to exclude from his cabinet "all aspirants to the presidency, or vice." Polk took this counsel literally, and reduced it to writing, as of Inauguration Day. The form letter he sent to his cabinet was certainly one of the most remarkable documents ever circulated by any President. It read:

"Sir:

"The principles and policy which will be observed and maintained during my administration are embodied in the Resolutions adopted by the Democratic National Convention of Delegates, assembled at Baltimore in May last, and in my Inaugural Address this day delivered to my fellow citizens.

"In making up my Cabinet I desire to select gentlemen who agree with me in opinion, and who will cordially co-operate with me in carrying out these principles and policy.

"In my official action I will myself take no part between gentlemen of the Democratic party who may become aspirants or candidates to succeed me in the Presidential office, and shall desire that no member of my Cabinet shall do so. Individual preferences it is not expected or desired to limit or restrain. It is official interference by the dispensation of public patronage or otherwise that I desire to guard against. Should any member of my Cabinet become a candidate or an aspirant to the Presidency or Vice Presidency of the United States, it will be expected that upon the happening of such an event that he will retire from the Cabinet.

"I disapprove the practice which has sometimes prevailed of Cabinet officers absenting themselves for long periods of time from the seat of Government, and leaving the management of their Departments to Chief Clerks, or less responsible persons. I expect myself to remain constantly at Washington, unless it may be an occasional necessary absence and then for a short time. It is by conforming to this rule that the President and his Cabinet can have any assurance that abuses will be prevented and that the subordinate executive officers connected with them respectively will faithfully perform their duty.

"If, Sir, you concur with me in these opinions and views, I shall be pleased to have your assistance as a member of my Cabinet; and now tender you the office of _____ and invite you to take charge of the Department. .

"I shall be pleased to receive your answer at your earliest convenience."

President Polk lived up to the peculiar pledges made in this document. He kept his hands off the succession. His absences were indeed few. When he had been in the White House a year and a half he took a four-day excursion to Fortress Monroe. In May 1847 he permitted himself a visit to the campus of his alma mater, the University of North Carolina, he and Mrs. Polk being feted en route at Richmond. Later that same spring he spent a month in a good-will tour of Northeastern states. And during his last summer in office he spent a few days in the Pennsylvania mountains for the sake of his health.

Mrs. Polk also started her White House regime in a steady and sedate tempo. The gossip columnists had been stirring things up a bit, but she quickly quieted them. Their rumors were to the effect that the Tylers had left the White House in a sorry state; and that the Polks would have to embark on a large-scale and expensive renovation.

But soon the New York *Journal of Commerce* was describing how Mrs. Polk had dispelled the dreams of tradesmen seeking to aid in setting up her new establishment:

"A couple of upholsterers who went from this city to procure so much of the job as falls within their department came back with very reduced expectations. They were referred to the President's lady, who gave them a courteous interview of three-quarters of an hour, but told them only the public rooms would require repairs, for if the private apartments had been satisfactory to Mrs. Tyler, they would be so to herself."

In one adroit stroke Mrs. Polk had disclaimed any gold-spoon extravagance for the administration; had given youthful Mrs. Tyler a vote of confidence where it counted most, in her own home city; and had rebuked a gibe at the dignity of the White House. Whatever repairs she thought necessary were quietly procured and little noted, and the White House took on the ordered look which betokens a superior housekeeper in complete control.

Mrs. Polk, moreover, had leisure in which to give regular help to her husband. He found little time in which to scan newspapers, yet it was necessary for him to know what editors were saying about his administration and the general drift of public opinion. He therefore had the papers delivered to Mrs. Polk, requesting that she mark such articles as it was desirable for him to read. This stimulating task she performed with pleasure. Carefully folding the papers with the marked places outside, she piled them beside his chair, so that whenever he had a few moments he could read without loss of time.

Polk held the principle that the people were entitled to the President's time for private interviews and public receptions. He received callers each morning till noon, mostly office seekers of whom he chronically complained most bitterly in his diary. And two evenings each week he and Mrs. Polk held public receptions. One of his diary notations ran:

"At eight o'clock received visitors informally in the parlour. Forty or fifty persons, ladies and gentlemen called—among them the Russian Minister, the Secretary of State and the Secretary of the Navy, and several members of Congress. These informal evenings twice a week (on Tuesdays and Fridays) are very pleasant and afford me moreover an opportunity to devote the other evenings of the week to business."

However a contemporary chronicler, noting that Polk burned his light far into the night, said, "It was known that he was in the habit of cutting off from his sleep the hours lost, to make up the amount of time which he felt belonged to the nation."

Washington society was not long in learning that the gay ways of the young Tylers were indeed gone. Mrs. Polk banned dancing and the serving of wine or spirituous liquors of any kind. She decreed that refreshments at public receptions were beneath the dignity of the White House. A strait-laced press sang her praises until the whole nation gave her full credit for being the paragon that Polk and Presbyterianism had made of her. She never saw a horse race, nor played cards. An incident of the trip which had brought her to Washington as First Lady showed the strength of her principles. The steamer on which the Polks were going up the Ohio was blown ashore by a terrific storm near Louisville one Saturday night. On Sunday morning a band came aboard, intending to amuse the stranded party by playing during the day. When Mrs. Polk heard the music she asked that it be stopped, as being unseemly on the Sabbath day. The band picked up and went home. Polk merely made the quiet comment, "Sarah directs all domestic affairs, and she thinks that is domestic."

Polk's own idea of any amusement was that it was a waste of time. In his diligently kept diary he recounted that "the young ladies of the household with Mrs. Polk's assent" had arranged that "a juggler or sleight of hand performer should visit the executive mansion and exhibit before a select company." Called down from a good night's work to see the show, Polk pronounced it "innocent in itself but time unprofitably spent." The "young ladies" were Mrs. Polk's two nieces, whom Polk always referred to in a formal fashion, usually as "Miss Rucker" and "Miss Hayes."

Polk refused to accept any costly gifts and decreed for the whole household the same Spartan attitude. Mrs. Polk even refused bouquets grown in the federal conservatory attached to the Patent Office rather than seem to enjoy a special privilege. Yet for all their strict ways the Polks had a good time in the White House and were popular with the people of Washington.

Another magician had made an easy atmosphere around the Polks— Dolley Madison. While it was impossible to change their staid demeanor, nevertheless Dolley humanized the Polks. She herself was a waltz-loving, card-playing old woman who still took snuff from a platina box. Senator William C. Preston set down in his journal, "Two years before her death, I was in a whist party with her, when Mr. John Quincy Adams was her partner and Lord Ashburton mine. Each of the three was over seventy years of age." This was understatement. All three were crowding eighty. But Dolley kept up her gay spirits and social prestige in spite of a bothersome eye affliction and a son whose extravagances reduced her to such penury that she had to pawn her silverware.

With Mrs. Polk, Dolley Madison shared her mighty memories, made vivid by original portraits bearing the signatures of famous artists and by many other rich relics of past splendors. Mrs. Polk accorded Mrs. Madison highest honors at White House receptions. An account of the first Polk levee gave the pattern followed throughout the administration·

"The President and his lady received the numerous visitors in the most courteous manner, and after the company had generally assembled, he took the arm of Mrs. Madison and went into the East Room followed by the Vice-President and Mrs. Polk. The Cabinet Ministers followed, and then, intermixed, were Navy and Military officers, foreign Ministers, Senators, Members of Congress. It was one of the most interesting incidents of the evening to see Mrs. Madison promenade the East Room with the appearance of almost youthful agility."

Naturally Dolley found in the busy President a supporter of her plan to sell to the nation her husband's historic papers. If she could only get the bill pushed through Congress, he would sign it. Already Congress had accorded her the highest honor ever given a President's widow. She had been voted a lifetime seat on the floor of the House. But the bill which would permit her to end her days in ease was bogged down, and she was getting nearer and nearer the end of her resources. She began to lay plans for selling her portraits.

"Young Hickory" soon shuffled off his nickname. Polk was no rubber stamp. By December of his first year Polk had completed all the legal details of the annexation of Texas and was giving the deepest thought to more worlds to conquer. The disputed southern boundary of that state was the obvious place to expect an incident of enemy aggression which would cause Congress to declare, and the public to support, a war. Later Abraham Lincoln, a one-time Representative, challenged Polk to show one spot where American blood had been shed on American soil.

From the White House Polk strove to manage the Mexican War—psychological, diplomatic, economic and military campaigns. His mind explored every avenue which "might bring about an honorable and a speedy peace." By that he meant the acquisition of all Mexican territory lying between Texas and the Pacific Ocean.

On the psychological front he sent a "confidential circular" to all United States consuls abroad, instructing them in "the causes of the war and the view of the government" for their use in diplomatic conversations. He decreed that volunteers should be "from each State and Territory, so as to make each feel an interest in the war." He called in Bishop Hughes of the Catholic Church in New York and secured his co-operation in a counterpropaganda campaign. Polk explained to the Bishop that a false idea had been industriously circulated in Mexico that the United States' object was to overthrow their religion and rob their churches, a canard which he thought would cause "desperate resistance" by the Mexicans. The President asked Bishop Hughes if some of the United States priests who spoke Spanish could "accompany our army as chaplains and visit Mexico in advance of the army for the purpose of giving assurance to the Catholic clergy in Mexico that church property would be secure and religion protected." This was done.

Polk also instructed his generals in a "divide and conquer" technique. They were to make use of "all elements of social, political and personal and local discord" to "reach the interest, passions, or principles of some of the parties and thereby to conciliate their goodwill and make them cooperate with us." Mexican states were to be encouraged "to declare their independence of the central government of Mexico, and either to become our allies or assume a neutral attitude."

On the economic front Polk stood ready at all times to pay the Mexican government many millions for her lands. Diplomatically, he was ready to negotiate peace if he could get what he wanted. Indeed, he was so eager that he compelled Secretary of State Buchanan to send a State Department representative, Nicholas P. Trist, son-in-law of Martha Jefferson Randolph, into General Winfield Scott's camp near Mexico City to start such negotiations at the very moment when Scott was working up to the decisive military engagement of the war.

Polk's military methods would have been unbelievable had he not recorded them himself in his diary. There he complained bitterly that General Zachary Taylor, on the Rio Grande, failed to send him sufficiently detailed field information on which to base the campaign. He railed at Taylor's using wagons when he ought to be using pack mules. He berated both Taylor and Scott as blunderers. Both were Whigs, and he attributed to them dark plottings as Presidential aspirants. He planned to put over both their heads power-hungry Senator Thomas Benton of Missouri. But Congress would not set up any new pinnacle post. On the California front both Lieutenant Colonel John C. Frémont and Colonel Stephen W. Kearny thought themselves empowered to take military charge and to set up a civil government. By the time Polk definitely tipped the scales on Kearny's side it was too late for Frémont to get out gracefully. Mrs. Frémont, once the beautiful bridesmaid of the Countess Bodisco wedding, visited Polk, to no avail. He evaded any commitment, and when Kearny had Frémont court-martialed Polk upheld the verdict of insubordination even though it would mean the enmity of Senator Benton.

White House levees increased in attendance and quickened in interest during the Mexican War. Sometimes Polk would give the latest news from the battle fronts. Sometimes Mrs. Polk would hush all conversation for a report from some young officer on leave because of injuries.

When General Scott prevented Trist from putting out peace feelers, President Polk made Buchanan recall Trist. Word reached Trist at the precise moment when Scott won his victory and Trist could move forward with peace negotiations. Breathing forth maledictions on President Polk and all his cabinet, Trist went ahead and negotiated the peace. It was a good treaty, following closely the original instructions of Polk for certain territories as war indemnity and the rest for a purchase price, $15,000,000. Polk saw no reason for not accepting the treaty, even though he had repudiated Trist. The President was much put out when Secretary of State Buchanan, who after all had also been flouted by an underling, argued against that course. Polk set down in his diary his belief that Buchanan's true reason was that he was a candidate for President and did not wish to estrange voters who favored the conquest of all Mexico. Polk added, "No candidate for the Presidency ought ever to remain in the Cabinet. He is an unsafe advisor."

Polk had Trist brought home under escort, a virtual prisoner, and confronted Buchanan with a direct question as to his Presidential aspirations and received a denial. But he sent Trist's treaty to the Senate, where after considerable debate it was ratified by a narrow margin on March 10, 1848.

Through the Mexican War, Polk added 525,000 square miles of territory to the United States, which would become the states of California, Nevada and Utah, most of Arizona and New Mexico and parts of Colorado and Wyoming. With the previous Oregon settlement Polk brought his grand total to more than 800,000 square miles. The war he waged had given combat experience to Ulysses S. Grant, William T. Sherman, Robert E. Lee and Thomas (Stonewall) Jackson.

To make the war's end truly historic President Polk had Mexico's assent to the treaty delivered to him on July 4, 1848—the same day he laid the cornerstone of Washington Monument, with both Dolley Madison and Mrs. Alexander Hamilton in honor seats. Dolley, who so recently had been at wit's end financially, was in fine fettle, receiving congratulations as chairman of the committee which was raising the funds for the monument. Through a stroke of fate she had also raised some funds for herself.

One night in the second week of May 1848 fire broke out in Dolley Madison's house. She was rescued from an upper floor at four o'clock in the morning, but not before she had seen to it that the trunk containing her husband's papers was safely carried down the stairs by a servant. On May 20 Congress, brought to its senses by this near-destruction of the historic documents, passed a bill to buy them and on May 31 voted an appropriation of $25,000. This sum was safeguarded for Mrs. Madison in trust, with Secretary of State Buchanan as one of three trustees. So Dolley was enabled to redeem some silver forks late in July. She tossed off the kind of party she loved best—a boat trip down the Potomac to Piney Point for a sizable group of friends. She reported herself as "deriving benefit and pleasure from her indulgence."

No longer need she wear that rusty old black gown and turban to White House receptions. She had a beautiful new outfit made of white satin.

When Henry Clay came back to Washington early in 1848 he was cordially received at the White House. Clay made the gay and gallant comment that whatever difference of opinion he might have heard from over the land about her husband's administration, he had heard only praise for Mrs. Polk's administration.

John Quincy Adams died in February, stricken on the floor of the House of Representatives and cared for in a little adjacent room the two days he lingered. The entire cabinet met at the White House on Saturday, February 26, to go with President Polk to the funeral services in the House Chamber. Mrs. Polk, Mrs. Madison and Mrs. Dallas, wife of the Vice President, sat together in the gallery.

Polk gave himself no respite when the war ended. Instead he thought of himself as shouldering more and more burdens. In August 1848 he remarked that he had not been three miles from his office in 18 months. In September he complained that so many members of his cabinet had been out of town he had not been able to hold a full council for more than a month. "I have conducted the government without their aid," he wrote in his diary. "Indeed, I have become so familiar with the duties and workings of the government, not only upon general principles but in most of its minute details, that I find but little difficulty in doing this. It is only occasionally that a great measure or a new question arises upon which I need the aid and advice of my cabinet." A few weeks later he wrote, "No President who performs his duty faithfully and conscientiously can have any leisure. I prefer to supervise the whole operations of the government rather than entrust the public business to subordinates."

Polk's policy of concentrating on Presidential duties and refusing to take part in the campaign, fully as much as the slavery question, lost the Democrats the 1848 election when Lewis Cass ran against General Zachary Taylor.

During the Polks' last winter in the White House gas illumination was installed, a long and tedious process. Contrary to general advice, Mrs. Polk insisted on keeping the reception hall as it was, "with its elegant chandelier for the use of candles." As she was fond of relating in later years, on the first reception night on which the gas lights were in use, "lo, the brilliant jets vanished and the company was left in darkness." But not completely. There was "one room still lustrous with many points of light—the reception room where the wax candles were shedding their soft radiance." Mrs. Polk was greatly complimented for her foresight and sagacity.

The new era was crowding on the heels of the old. In January 1848 gold had been discovered in California. In December the Secretary of War brought several nuggets to a cabinet meeting. They were to be sent to the Philadelphia mint to be made into coins commemorating the year. On January 20, 1849, a cabinet meeting was held to consider a special problem presented by the gold rush. Letters were read from the commander of the Pacific squadron, and from the Army paymaster in California, depicting "desertions from the squadron and the army to go in pursuit of gold to be such as to destroy all efficient services in both arms of the service." Polk saw deeper than this difficulty. He burned with zeal to make California a state and establish law and order there. On this project he worked unremittingly through his last weeks in office.

On February 9 the Polks held their last routine White House reception. It was the last White House reception for Dolley Madison, too. She was described that night as "seated on a raised platform, attired in white satin, with the habitual turban of fringed satin of the same shade twined about her head . . . the gown cut décoletté." Eyewitnesses were ready to take oath that Dolley's arms and shoulders were still beautiful at eighty-two. In his diary that night Polk stated that he had shaken ·hands unceasingly with well-wishers for more than three hours, adding, "Towards the close of the evening I passed through the crowded rooms with the venerable Mrs. Madison on my arm." The hour then was nearly midnight.

Mrs. Polk's last months in the White House were happily spent planning the purchase of Polk Place, in the heart of Nashville, for their retirement. So that Mrs. Polk need never suffer from poverty as Mrs. Madison had suffered, Polk made a will which would keep the place intact for her through her lifetime. Mrs. Madison permitted the Polks to have copies made of all the Stuart originals in her house. The President and Mrs. Polk had their own White House portraits painted by Healy. They also yielded to Mathew B. Brady and sat together for a daguerreotype. Many other White House mementoes would make Polk Place a private museum.

On March 1, 1849, the Polks held a large dinner for the President-elect, General Zachary Taylor, inviting leaders of both political parties. Conversation must have been strained, for Polk's term was ending in a great furor—the fight over the admission of California to the Union. The "balance of power" between slave states and free had for many years been carefully preserved by the admission of states in pairs, one slave state, one free. There were now 15 slave states, 15 free states. From the new territory acquired by Polk, California and New Mexico were up for admittance to the Union. But Northern anti-slavery forces had gained political strength and proposed to force through Congress the Wilmot Proviso, which would forbid slavery under any territorial government. Polk, an advocate of the self-determination of states, was resolved to veto any bill containing the Wilmot Proviso. He feared that California, if not admitted as a state, would set itself up as an independent nation.

The battle raged on toward the session's end. Polk's diary detailing his last long dramatic day in office reveals an incomparable portrait of a self-adjudged paragon. Again and again he emphasized the meticulous manner in which he was tying up all the odds and ends of his administration.

"The cabinet dispersed and I disposed of all the business on my table down to the minutest detail and at the close of day left a clear table for my successor," he added.

After he had spent several hours signing his name to the last routine Army and Navy promotions he and Mrs. Polk and her two nieces left the White House at sundown of Saturday, March 3, for a suite in the Willard Hotel. Mrs. Polk's four-year task was ended.

President Polk, however, took his entire cabinet up to the Capitol, where he would sign the last-minute bills. They walked into one of the worst week-end, session-end snarls in history. Polk described it development by development, with himself as hero. California statehood had been attached as a rider to the general-appropriations bill which would keep the government functioning. To this the House attempted to add the Wilmot Proviso. Polk, in constant conference with his cabinet in the Vice President's chamber close to the Senate chamber, said he would veto the bill if this happened. About midnight he learned that the House had switched to a phrasing which did not mention slavery—it would continue in force the laws of Mexico. Polk called this the Wilmot Proviso in another form, Mexican law having banned slavery. Southern members of both Houses swarmed in on him, urging veto. Polk had to send word to the House Democrats to quit circulating a veto petition, "for the President could not perform a high constitutional duty of this kind upon petition." But he added they should "rest easy" as "I was prepared with a veto message in my pocket."

At this point President Polk saw himself as a great historic figure. Against the advice of a majority of his cabinet, who thought the new phrasing was a convenient "out" on the subject of slavery and who couldn't see how Washington would run without the appropriations, Polk sat down and rewrote his Wilmot Proviso veto to cover the Mexican laws.

"It was a moment of high responsibility, perhaps the highest of my official term," he said.

Already embattled legislators were saying that since it was long past midnight of March 3 Polk's term of office was over. He replied that he had not been inaugurated for a four-year term until noon of March 4. And besides, if his term was over, so was that of the whole House and one third of the Senate, both still in session. In the early hours of the morning Polk returned to his hotel for a few hours' sleep, leaving them deadlocked.

But the veto message in his pocket never became history. There was no occasion for its use. At six in the morning he was roused by a joint committee of House and Senate, reporting the results of the all-night battle. The appropriations bill had been passed without its rider giving statehood to California and New Mexico. It was just an appropriations bill, which he signed. There also was a bill extending the United States revenue laws to these two "states" which had dramatically been denied organization and representation. Polk signed that one too, and Congress adjourned at seven o'clock on a Sunday morning. All the little details of Polk's administration had indeed been done. Left behind, however, was the big battle over California's statehood.

That Sunday morning the President and Mrs. Polk made their farewell appearance at the First Presbyterian Church on Four and a Half Street where they had worshiped throughout all their years in Washington.

On Monday March 5 he not only rode up Capitol Hill beside the new President, Zachary Taylor, to the inauguration ceremonies, but also rode back to the White House sitting beside Taylor. Polk's appraisal of his successor, set down that day in his diary, ran:

"General Taylor is I have no doubt a well-meaning old man. He is, however, uneducated, exceedingly ignorant of public affairs, and, I should judge, of very ordinary capacity. He will be in the hands of others and must rely wholly upon his Cabinet to administer the government."

A roundabout trip home proved to be a great physical strain on Polk after his hard-working years in the White House. Welcoming delegations woke him early in the mornings. He was forced into parades hours long through streets of cheering citizenry. Lavish meals were piled on lavish meals until his upset digestion cried out for plain food and his weary body for rest. In New Orleans, Polk was confronted with sumptuous dishes cooked in French style, fish of every variety and every variety of light wines. Said Polk: "As soon as an opportunity offered, I asked a servant in a low tone if he could give me a piece of cornbread and boiled ham." He canceled the rest of the public events and rushed home. But he could not regain his strength and died on June 15, 1849, at the age of fifty-three. Dolley Madison survived him by almost a month, dying on July 12. It was President Taylor who attended her funeral services, elaborate as for any President.

In Nashville, Tennessee, Sarah Polk was such a widow as Dolley

Madison had been in Washington. Hers was the first priority on New Year's calls, the whole Tennessee legislature coming in a body. No convention met in Nashville but sent its highest officers to Polk Place to see Mrs. Polk's historic mementoes. Parades stopped and saluted her husband's tomb on the grounds. And through the years she cherished her husband's papers as Mrs. Madison had done.

8 | *Languishing Ladies and Miss Lane*

...TAYLOR, FILLMORE, PIERCE, BUCHANAN

IN SENECA FALLS, New York, in 1848, the year of the Zachary Taylor campaign, a few brave ladies led by Lucretia Mott and Elizabeth Cady Stanton issued a new Declaration of Independence, dealing at length with equal rights for women. These pioneer feminists lashed out against the then current concept that woman was the weaker, indeed the invalid, sex. Idealized at that time was the woman who fainted at the slightest pretext. To foster a healthier womankind the Seneca Falls ladies went in for dress reform and mild physical culture. Throughout the 1850s the women's-rights movement increased in strength and in the shrillness of its demand for votes for women.

But the White House took no cognizance of the women's-suffrage campaign. Its First Ladies clung tenaciously to the cloistered and languishing pattern. In those hero-worshiping years between the Mexican and Civil wars, White House wives were self-submerged almost to the point of obliteration.

Margaret Mackall Smith Taylor, a woman of proud Maryland lineage who was also related to leading families of Virginia, did not wish her sixty-four-year-old husband to run for the Presidency. She was an aging invalid, worn out with the rigors of moving from military post to military post while rearing a family. She argued that General Taylor had already done enough for his country and should be allowed to spend his closing years in peace. She even charged that the movement for his nomination was a plot to deprive her of his society and to shorten his life by unnecessary burdens. There was, of course, no plot; still, she was quite a prophet.

Zachary Taylor himself revealed to what length his wife had gone in her opposition. During an eventful trip to the nation's capital to take over his post he amused audiences by telling how his wife "had made a nightly prayer for several months that Henry Clay might be elected President in his place."

Clay was the Whig leader whom Taylor had defeated for the nomination. Clay had earned the honor a dozen times over. But the Whig party again chose the sure-fire vote-getting pattern with which it had triumphed in the log-cabin campaign—a popular old general to head the ticket; a younger man from a different section of the country as Vice-Presidential candidate. This time it was Taylor—"Old Rough and Ready"—who then lived at Baton Rouge, Louisiana, and Millard Fillmore of Buffalo, New York. Defeated by this combination was a Democratic ticket headed by Lewis Cass, with General William Orlando Butler as Vice-Presidential candidate.

Mrs. Taylor did not go to Washington with her husband. When she did finally take up her residence in the White House, it was as a social recluse. Only the old Maryland and Virginia families who had been friends of her girlhood had access to her. In gossipy Washington fantastic stories sprang up about the First Lady who refused that role. One of the most persistent, entirely untrue, was that the family kept her from appearing in public because she smoked a pipe. When Zachary Taylor's letters were printed more than a half century later, a foreword stated with regard to his wife: "Many absurd and cruel stories were printed about Mrs. Taylor's character, habits, and daily life, passed up by her descendants with silent contempt, and perhaps for that reason accepted as true, in part at least, by the public."

However, Mrs. Taylor's record was set straight by a remarkable character witness, none other than Mrs. Jefferson Davis, who knew Mrs. Taylor well as First Lady of the Land a decade before she herself became First Lady of the Confederacy. Mrs. Davis' praise of Mrs. Taylor was the more noteworthy in that she was Jefferson Davis' second wife, whereas Mrs. Taylor's second daughter, Sarah Knox Taylor, had been the first Mrs. Jefferson Davis. This Miss Taylor did not use the name of Sarah, but signed her letters "Knox."

So strongly had Zachary Taylor opposed her marriage to Jefferson

Davis that Knox was married at the home of an aunt instead of in her own. Mrs. Taylor, however, had upheld Knox in her choice. The union was idyllic but brief indeed. Sarah Knox Taylor Davis died of typhoid fever three months after her marriage. Years later, during the siege of Monterey, chance threw Taylor and his erstwhile repudiated son-in-law together and the two arrived at a basis of mutual admiration and friendship. One account said they "embraced each other and wept tears of reconciliation upon the battlefield." When Taylor went into the White House, Jefferson Davis of Mississippi had become an influential Senator. Immediately he and his second wife were accorded a family footing in the Executive Mansion.

So it was that Mrs. Jefferson Davis was able to refute the darkling tales about Mrs. Zachary Taylor. Said Mrs. Davis:

"I always found the most pleasant part of my visit to the White House to be passed in Mrs. Taylor's bright pretty room where the invalid, full of interest in the passing show in which she had not the strength to take her part, talked most agreeably and kindly to the many friends admitted to her presence. She always appeared at the family dinners to which a few friends were unceremoniously bidden, of which many charming ones were given during General Taylor's administration, and ably bore her share in the conversation at the table.

"The President at one of these dinners at which I was present, after telling an anecdote of his army life in which his wife had taken part, turned to Jefferson Davis and said, 'You know my wife was as much of a soldier as I was.' His every look and tone bespoke respect, esteem, and love."

In the formal rooms of the White House on all public occasions Mrs. Taylor's twenty-two-year-old daughter, the happily named Mrs. Betty Bliss, carried forward the official-hostess role with a zest and poise which won public acclaim.

The press of that time pictured a folksy regime in the White House. The war horse which had carried Taylor through many campaigns, "Old Whitey," cropped grass on the White House lawn. Of a summer evening, when the Marine Band played on the south grounds, as had long been a capital custom, President Taylor was often seen "strolling over the lawn among the company, ready to shake hands with anyone who chose to introduce himself."

Following some repairs and refurbishing, the White House was reopened to the public early in November. The East Room was described by a visitor as "newly carpeted and redecorated and illuminated by gas jets from splendid chandeliers." To this first Taylor levee a delegation of six Osage Indians added color.

New Year's 1850 brought the usual big public reception. The diplomatic corps, after having been first received by the President, clustered about him as he shook hands with the populace. Again Taylor's gift of friendliness to the common man was emphasized. One account said the President "had a few words of greeting for every individual, and his kindness and ease of manner prevented any stiffness among his guests, who seemed fully disposed to imitate the frank bearing of their host."

Taylor's temperate make-up recoiled from the avid expansionism of Polk, who had put Cuba next on the list for acquisition. He issued a proclamation to quell a proposed military expedition to that island led by exiled Cubans.

Chief contribution of Taylor to foreign policy was the Clayton-Bulwer Treaty of 1850, which clarified the powers of the two most interested nations, Great Britain and the United States, with regard to the proposed canal across Nicaragua to shorten the sea route to California. While the canal was not built, this treaty checked British expansion in Central America and established a principle of free access to all nations on payment of tolls. However, most of the President's attention had to be centered on this nation's most bitter and clamorous problem, slavery.

One of the most spectacular sessions of Congress ever held was that which occupied more than half of the entire time spent by Zachary Taylor in the White House. The debates extended through nine months, 273 days, many of them stretching far into the night in veritable tornadoes of oratory. There was no decisive majority in either House of Congress. But the antislavery forces, backed by the vast vote potential of the recent immigrants brought in by the Northern free-labor system, were rising fast.

The principal point at issue was that which had made President Polk's administration end in a sleepless night. Should California be admitted as a free state—she had by this time drawn up a constitution prohibiting slavery—and upset the long-held "balance of power?"

In that tumultuous session Fate was a great tragedian dramatically writing off the chief characters in a play which had been on the Senate boards for many a year. The dying John C. Calhoun direly threatened secession with his last breath. Too weak to read his last scathing speech attacking the North and depicting the wrongs of the South, he listened while a fellow Senator read it. The aged Daniel Webster, replying to Calhoun, rose to new oratorical heights in a speech urging the preservation of the Union at any cost. And Henry Clay pulled the last rabbit from his tall political hat—the compromise of 1850, although the actual bills passed were written by Stephen A. Douglas. Four of its five separate acts concerned slavery. California, with its slavery-prohibiting constitution, was to be admitted as a free state. The territories of New Mexico and Utah were to have self-determination as to slavery. The slave trade was prohibited in the District of Columbia. And, as a concession to the South, the Fugitive Slave Act of 1793 was amended to make its enforcement effective.

As the presiding officer over this debate, handsome Millard Fillmore was described as a "model for all time," holding the scales "with such judicial nicety and unfailing courtesy that no one could tell which policy he approved." A Washington visitor of the time remarked, "Vice President Fillmore looks more of a President than Taylor." The ultrajudicious presiding officer was fated to become President before the debate over which he wielded the gavel would end in the final vote for compromise.

Taylor in the White House opposed Clay's compromise because it would lead to disunion. A slaveholding Southerner, he nevertheless declared himself as interested first in the welfare of the whole country, saying: "Attachment to the Union of the States should be habitually fostered in every American heart. Dissolution would be the greatest calamity" and "Disunion is treason."

However, General Taylor began to enjoy the political battle as he got deeper into it. And when he staged a spectacular reception on March 4, 1850, to celebrate the anniversary of his entrance into the White House, it was widely interpreted as a bid for a second term. This impression was strengthened when Taylor accepted an invitation to sit on the platform at a big Independence Day celebration at the site of Washington Monument, the cornerstone of which had been laid by Polk two years before.

A newspaper account of this event said:

"When the orator of the day quoted from a letter of Hamilton to Washington, protesting against his refusing to serve a second term, President Taylor, who sat on the left of the orator, roused from his listless attitude as if desirous of catching every word. Perhaps General Taylor was thinking what would be his conduct in a similar emergency."

Second-term talk was cut short immediately by the sudden illness of the President. Five days after his appearance at the Monument celebration, he was dead. One contemporary writer stated that on his return to the White House he "feasted on cherries and iced milk against the protestations of Dr. Wotherspoon, who was his guest" and "soon afterward he was seized with a violent attack of cholera morbus." A later author called it typhoid fever. A third hazarded a guess it might have been coronary thrombosis.

Mrs. Taylor had remained so sequestered in the White House that her very existence was news at the time of her husband's death. Senator Jefferson Davis was a member of the large and demonstrative family gathered around the deathbed. His wife left to history an intimate picture of the widowed Mrs. Zachary Taylor. Said Mrs. Davis:

"When General Taylor died, I saw her endure all the torture of a state funeral. Mrs. Taylor was worn to a shadow, and lay without uttering a sound, but trembled silently from head to foot as one band after another blared the funeral music of the different organizations, and the heavy guns boomed in quick succession to announce the final parting."

Laura C. Holloway, early biographer of Presidents' wives, recorded: "From the time Mrs. Taylor left the White House, she never alluded to her residence there, except as connected with the death of her husband." Mrs. Taylor died two years after her husband at the home of her son in Louisiana.

In Chicago two weeks after Taylor's death a former one-term Congressman named Abraham Lincoln delivered a eulogy at City Hall:

"The Presidency, even to the most experienced politicians, is no bed of roses; and General Taylor, like others, found thorns within it. No human being can fill that station and escape censure. Still, I hope and believe, when General Taylor's official conduct shall come to be viewed in the calm light of history, he will be found to have deserved as little [censure] as any who have preceded him. . . . I fear the one great question of the day is not now likely to be partially acquiesced in by the different sections of the Union as it would have been could General Taylor have been spared to us."

Biographers of much later date backed up Lincoln's judgment by declaring that Taylor in his statesmanlike attitude on the slavery question showed unmistakably greater sagacity than the experienced statesmen who distrusted his judgment. Certainly the signature of Millard Fillmore on the Fugitive Slave Act spelled the death of the Whig party, although it was also credited with holding off the Civil War for ten years.

Millard Fillmore, like John Tyler, was sworn in, not by the Chief Justice of the United States, but by old Judge William Cranch, Chief Justice of the Circuit Court of the District of Columbia. For 54 years William Cranch, the favorite nephew of Abigail Adams, held the judicial appointment which she had secured for him while she was in the White House.

Tall, auburn-haired Mrs. Fillmore was not in Washington at the time of this brief ceremony in the House of Representatives. Because she was not robust, she had remained in Buffalo during her husband's entire service as Vice President and did not join him until October 1850. Yet so devoted were this couple that they wrote letters to each other every day when apart. And Fillmore often said he consulted his wife on all important matters.

Millard Fillmore was sometimes called a "wife-made man." Born on the New York frontier, cradled in a sap trough hollowed out for the making of maple syrup, he was untaught until late adolescence. In his autobiography, written for the Buffalo Historical Society which he founded, he told how at the age of eighteen he for the first time "heard a sentence parsed and had an opportunity to study geography with a map."

Said Fillmore, "I pursued much of my study with, and perhaps was unconsciously stimulated by the companionship of, a young lady whom I afterward married."

Rose Gouveneur Hoes, a tireless researcher into the lives of the Presidents' wives, put the situation more clearly. She said that Abigail Powers, of a learned family proud of its lineage, turned to teaching school to help support the family, her father having died. "Abigail Powers met Millard Fillmore, who was one of her pupils, and being a few years his senior, she was able to round out his character."

Fillmore was handsome and courtly of manner. He did not drink nor use tobacco. He had excellent health and steady nerves. He once said that the only night's sleep he ever lost in his life was when he was suddenly confronted with the fact that he would have to take over the Presidency.

On Taylor's death his whole cabinet resigned and left Washington, since Taylor and Fillmore had been of different schools of Whig thought. "Radical" Whigs, led by William H. Seward, who opposed the Fugitive Slave Act on the ground that it abrogated a "higher law" than the Constitution, had dominated the Taylor cabinet. Fillmore belonged to the conservative wing, called "Silver Grays" because of the preponderance of older men among them. Daniel Webster was their ideal. Fillmore quickly made Webster his Secretary of State. Both Fillmore and Webster had weathered the tempest of the slavery debate and knew the full force of the Southern threat of secession. So when at last the Fugitive Slave Law phase of the Clay compromise was passed by Congress in September 1850, Millard Fillmore signed it.

"None knew more than Fillmore himself that if he signed the Fugitive Slave Law it would be the death blow of his personal popularity in the North and that the great portion of his political friends would be alienated forever," said his biographer, William Elliot Griffis. "Indeed, his wife told him so and made it clear to him. Nevertheless, when he saw his duty to the whole country all thoughts of self-interest were like a feather in the scale."

The President's explanation was that, had he not signed, the Southern states would have seceded, and the North was not yet strong enough to win a civil war. Fillmore said that his had been a choice between terrible evils—to inflict suffering which he hoped might be temporary, or to precipitate an era of bloodshed with the destruction of the country as a possible result.

The Northern outcry was immediate and vociferous. John Greenleaf Whittier was among those writing stirring verses. Travel along the "Underground Railway," the slave-smuggling system from the South to Canada, was accelerated. Free Negroes in the North, fearful of being taken for fugitives, fled across the northern border into

Canada by thousands. One hundred members of the Baptist Church in Fillmore's home town of Buffalo crossed the Niagara River into Canada. But with the serene air of a healthy man who had performed his duty Millard Fillmore continued his zestful career in the White House. His course was one of improvement, physical and cultural, of the White House, the city of Washington and international relations.

With Taylor's sudden death the unhealthy condition of the White House became a subject of public comment. The Georgetown *Advocate* printed a statement that the cellars of the White House were "exceedingly damp at all times" and that "the malaria from the Potomac, without an intervening object to break its effect, came up full upon the south side in all its unabated, unbroken power." In the Baltimore *Patriot* appeared this item: "President Fillmore, by advice of his physicians, has taken apartments in Georgetown in consequence of the unhealthy condition of the White House."

A letter written by Fillmore to Salmon P. Chase during the very month after Taylor's death was ample evidence of the groundlessness of this rumor. Fillmore, thanking Chase for a gift of wine, said: "Like yourself, I am chiefly a water drinker, but it will nevertheless be received by me with great pleasure and as soon as the removal of the habiliments of mourning from the White House will permit the entertainment of my friends, it will be as you request, submitted to their criticism."

However, the adverse publicity on the White House may have aided the Fillmores in obtaining from Congress an appropriation large enough to make noteworthy improvements. A contemporaneous account ran:

"The old black cook who had served many years at the White House was greatly upset when a range of small hotel size was brought to his quarters. He had managed to prepare a fine State dinner for thirty-six people every Thursday in a huge fireplace, with cranes, hooks, pots, pans, kettles and skillets; but he could not manage the draughts of the range, and it ended in a journey of the President to the Patent Office to inspect the model and restore peace to the kitchen."

Book-loving Mrs. Fillmore, unable to find even a dictionary or a Bible in the White House, secured from Congress an appropriation earmarked for a library, and a Fillmore letter showed that the books were purchased in New York by the librarian of the War Department.

President Fillmore had his son Powers as his secretary. Mrs. Fillmore, who had little heart for society, due to ill health and the recent death of her sister, had her talented daughter Mary Abigail as her assistant hostess. At eighteen Mary Abigail spoke French fluently, played the harp, piano and guitar. This young girl was sole social representative of the family outside the White House. Mrs. Fillmore, for all her vigor of mind, subscribed to the current theories of woman's place being in the home. Had she been in robust health, she still would have considered any public role unseemly. This was shown when, as wife of the Vice President, she had met with "silent laughter" (her own expression) an official invitation to be present with the mayor of Buffalo at a grand opening of the Canadian railroad at Hamilton, Ontario.

Soon the Fillmores had made a home of the big old White House. One Saturday night, shortly before Christmas 1850, the exuberant President was writing to his law partner, Solomon G. Haven, in Buffalo:

"The busy week is nearly ended, the last letter read—but not answered—and the last office-seeker politely bowed out of the room, and I seize the precious moment simply to say that I am anxious that you and Mrs. Haven should come and make us a visit this winter. Do come!—come directly to the White House. We have one spare room in this temple of inconveniences, neatly fitted up—and just the thing for you and Mrs. H."

The Havens came, and it was Mrs. Haven who later described the heart of the Fillmore home, the upstairs Oval Room:

"Here Miss Fillmore had her own piano and harp, and here Mrs. Fillmore, surrounded by her books, spent the greater part of her time, and in this room the family received their informal visitors. The President had but little time to give to this library, but he usually succeeded in leaving the executive chamber at 10:30 at night, and spending a pleasant hour in the library with his family."

Mrs. Fillmore insisted on carrying her share of White House social duties even though an ankle permanently injured in a fall several years before made hours of standing acutely painful. Sometimes she

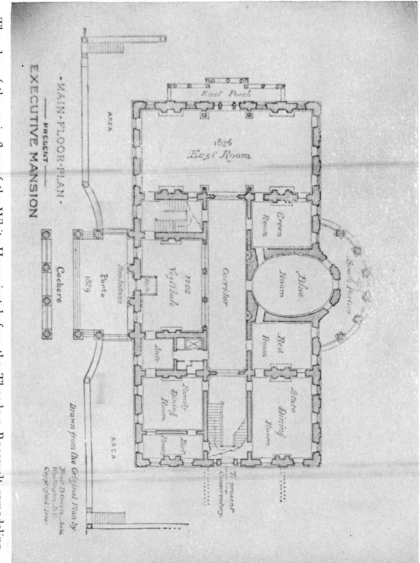

The plan of the main floor of the White House just before the Theodore Roosevelt remodeling.

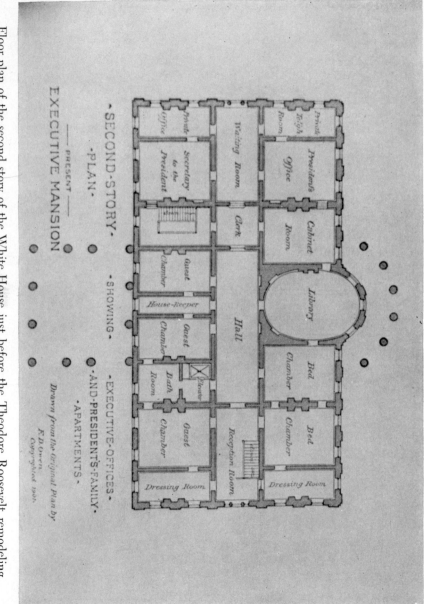

Floor plan of the second story of the White House just before the Theodore Roosevelt remodeling.

- SECOND-STORY -
- PLAN -
—— PRESENT ——
EXECUTIVE MANSION

- SHOWING -
- EXECUTIVE-OFFICES -
- AND-PRESIDENT'S-FAMILY -
- APARTMENTS -

Drawn from the original plan by
F. D. Owen,
Copyrighted 1901.

Private
High
Room

Private
Office

Secretary
to the
President

Waiting Room

President's
Office

Clerk

Cabinet
Room

Guest
Chamber

House-Keeper

Library

Hall

Guest
Chamber

Guest
Chamber
Bath
Room

Closet

Bed
Chamber

Bed
Chamber

Reception Room

Guest
Chamber

Dressing Room

Dressing Room

rested all day in bed so as to be able to bear this strain. The Fillmores held a reception each Tuesday morning and a levee each Friday evening when Congress was in session. They had a large dinner on Thursday evenings in the "Congressional dining room" and small ones on Saturdays in the Private Dining Room.

Millard Fillmore knew that he had little chance of re-election. He had broken with the Whig boss, Thurlow Weed, and with that party's outstanding leader, William H. Seward. Through his own Congressman, Fillmore sent an open letter to the Whig Convention of 1852, withdrawing his name.

The delegates at Baltimore did not consider this withdrawal conclusive and briskly balloted on Fillmore's name, along with those of Webster and General Winfield Scott. On the fifty-third ballot the Whigs again endorsed an old formula which had lost its magic, a venerable general at the head of the ticket. Scott, vain and pompous, was unable even to hold the leaders of his own party, who indeed were disappearing along with the party itself. Henry Clay died at the close of the convention, Daniel Webster at the close of the campaign.

The Democrats, after days of deadlock, nominated a dark horse, Franklin Pierce of New Hampshire, with William R. King, then president pro tempore of the Senate, as his running mate.

Millard Fillmore set a record in courtesy to an incoming President of an opposing political party. William Makepeace Thackeray was in Washington delivering his lectures on English humorists, and Washington Irving came in for the literary feast. President Fillmore took President-elect Franklin Pierce with him to Thackeray's lecture. Both Pierce and Irving accompanied Fillmore on a trip down the Potomac on the *Vixen* to view the *Ericsson*, a steamship which was considered a great advancement in navigation. The Fillmores not only entertained Pierce and the two literary lions at dinner and at a public reception, but also remained at the White House to help Franklin Pierce receive after the inauguration ceremonies. Thackeray and Irving were present. It was later stated that Mrs. Fillmore caught her death of cold standing with Thackeray and Irving on the wind-swept portico of the Capitol while Franklin Pierce took the oath of office and delivered his inaugural address. The Fillmores had planned a trip abroad, but Mrs. Fillmore never left Washington. As that month ended she died at Willard's Hotel in the suite used by Pierce before entering the White House.

It was an inauguration with a heavy undercurrent of sadness and was held without some of its leading characters. Mrs. Pierce, utterly abandoned in her bereavement at the loss of the last of her three sons, stopped off in Baltimore and did not continue to near-by Washington until after the inauguration. Her first son had died in infancy; her second at the age of four of typhus. Two months before the inauguration she and her husband had seen their adored son Benjamin, aged eleven, mangled and killed in a railroad wreck from which they both escaped unhurt. The tragedy darkened the next four years for the convivial Pierce as well as engulfed in deepest depression his already morose wife. Vice President King never reached Washington to assume his duties. He took the oath of office in Cuba, where he had gone to recuperate from an illness. He was able to return to his Alabama home, but died there on April 17.

Jane Appleton Pierce, beautiful in an ethereal, fine-featured fashion, was so much the clinging vine that she had for ten years choked off her husband's political career. She had hated Washington when she went there as a bride, the wife of a young Congressman. When a withering Washington June made her take to her bed she wrote to relatives: "Oh, how I wish he was out of political life! How much better it would be for him on every account!" Between the lines those who knew Pierce could read her agony at the fact that Franklin Pierce was an alcoholic. Any bout with drink ended in his having too much.

After the birth of Benjamin she succeeded in persuading her husband to retire to the life of a circuit lawyer in Concord, New Hampshire. There he was easily the leading citizen of the state, also president of the Temperance Society. He was famed for his eloquence. And he added to his laurels by service as a Mexican War general. Indeed, he began to be mentioned as a Vice-Presidential possibility. Then a deadlock developed among the four leading candidates for the Presidential nomination, Lewis Cass, James Buchanan, William O. Butler and Stephen A. Douglas. Unyieldingly they killed one another off politically. Fellow generals of the Mexican War got the consent of Pierce to push him forward.

Jane Appleton Pierce and her husband, on a visit to her old home in Massachusetts, had just finished a quiet afternoon visit to the cemetery when a messenger on horseback met them with news that Pierce was the Presidential nominee. Mrs. Pierce fainted dead away.

When their son died before they even entered the White House, Mrs. Pierce thought it the judgment of God.

Mrs. Pierce took into the White House, to serve as hostess in her stead, Mrs. Abby Kent Means, her long-time friend and the second wife of her uncle. It was in the home of Mrs. Means at Amherst, Massachusetts, that Jane Means Appleton and Franklin Pierce had been married. The very presence of Mrs. Means in the White House 19 years after that event was a measure of the tenacity with which Jane Pierce clung to her intellectual Puritan Massachusetts background. Pierce was the son of a New Hampshire governor and a young political prodigy in his own right when he was married. Yet he was considered to have benefited his station greatly by a union with a close relative of the Means family of Amherst, the Masons of Portsmouth and the Lawrences of Boston. Mrs. Pierce was the daughter of a former president of Bowdoin College, the beloved alma mater where Pierce had met his closest friend and later his campaign biographer, Nathaniel Hawthorne.

Both Pierce and Hawthorne chose as life partners ailing young women, but their approaches to the problem were entirely different. Hawthorne loved Sophia Peabody, the artist among the three famous Peabody sisters of Salem, who had been taught from childhood that she was too frail ever to marry and have children. Hawthorne, then living in a darkened house with a recluse mother and unmarried sisters, put up a successful battle for sanity. He took his Sophia on long walks and built up her health and morale to the point where her chronic headaches vanished. Thus he got a home of his own and she became a normal wife and mother. But Jane Pierce suffered from tuberculosis, and her husband had no such imaginative grasp of the problem as Hawthorne. His attitude toward her was ever commiseration, devotion, indulgence.

While President Pierce, aided by Mrs. Means as his official hostess, carried forward a sparse social program in the formal rooms of the White House, Mrs. Pierce stayed in the family quarters. Distinguished guests found her at the family table, an intelligent listener. When Nathaniel Hawthorne came to accept an appointment to a diplomatic post abroad she went down the Potomac to Mount Vernon with him. She had her New England relatives as house guests. She finally took over her duties as official hostess on New Year's Day, 1855, a year and ten months after her husband took office, when she appeared at his side at the big annual reception. However, she still depended on Mrs. Means as an aid, and the home of Mrs. Jefferson Davis, wife of the Secretary of War, was much more the gay center of Washington society than was the White House.

Even Mrs. Cassius Clay, wife of the Kentucky Senator, a close enough friend of the White House family to take occasional drives with Mrs. Pierce in her carriage, considered the Pierce state dinners too stiff and formal. She spoke of the gold spoons bought by Monroe so long ago and invariably used at these affairs; and of the "remarkable bouquets made at government greenhouses":

"They were stiff and formal things, as big around as a breakfast plate, and invariably composed of a half-dozen wired japonicas ornamented with a pretentious cape of marvelously-wrought lace-paper. At every plate, at every state dinner, lay one of these memorable rigid bouquets."

Franklin Pierce spent a great deal of time outside the Executive Mansion. He visited the Departments weekly, winning the reputation of being an able administrator of governmental affairs. He also went to concerts regularly, unaccompanied by Mrs. Pierce. Often his Secretary of State appeared with him.

An excellent example of how the fortunes of the White House itself rose and fell with the political prestige of the Presidents residing there was furnished in the Pierce administration. At its start Pierce was a President with a mandate from the people—he had carried every Northern state but Vermont and Massachusetts, in addition to the traditionally Democratic South. He had no difficulty in getting from Congress $25,000 with which to repair and refurbish the White House, although the four preceding Presidents had been granted much less. He installed the first furnace, had the place painted outside and in and purchased for the East Room a carpet that weighed a ton. His political power then declined so rapidly that at the 1854 Congressional election his party had lost every Northern state but New Hampshire and California. A member of his party attempted to aid the overburdened Pierce by moving a slight enlargement in the White House staff, including a steward to be responsible for White House furniture and equipment, and a furnaceman. This venture failed after a House member sarcastically moved an amendment for a $500 appropriation for "one lady of the bed chamber."

Pierce's swift fall from popularity in the North was due to his championship of the Kansas-Nebraska Bill, which provided that those territories should become states under self-determination as to slavery. This was contrary to the terms of the Missouri Compromise, which had barred future slave states north of the parallel of 36° 30'. The result of the Kansas-Nebraska Bill was border warfare under "squatter sovereignty" as the South sought to make Kansas a slave state to balance an admittedly free Nebraska. The fight for control of the land caused the coinage of the term "Bloody Kansas." Pierce further incurred the ire of the abolitionists by personally taking charge of the return of a slave, Anthony Burns, from Boston to Virginia under the Fugitive Slave Act.

The end of the administration found Mrs. Pierce presiding at weekly state dinners, seldom absent from her husband's side at his receptions and, so one observer recorded, "punctually public at her own Friday receptions, although at times suffering greatly."

The end of the administration found Franklin Pierce older-looking, more subdued and struggling, but without rancor, to maintain his party leadership. He let his name go up for re-election with a statement of strategy to party leaders which ran:

"General Pierce, while he is a candidate for renomination, is not the antagonist of any other candidate. He desires nomination only when the convention at Cincinnati considers that he is the best and most available candidate. . . . In Pennsylvania he is the friend of Mr. Buchanan and Mr. Dallas. In Virginia, he treats Mr. Hunter and Mr. White as like entitled to his confidence and esteem."

Mr. Buchanan got the nomination. President Pierce not only helped him win the election, but also moved out to the home of his Secretary of State so that the White House could be cleaned up for his successor. After appearing in the Buchanan inauguaration the Pierces returned to Concord.

After a succession of three devotees of the secluded life the White House was ready for a young and healthy hostess, the niece of James Buchanan, Miss Harriet Lane. But Harriet Lane was far more than that. She was a personality hand-picked and meticulously trained for the role of a princess—no less.

James Buchanan, sixty-five years old and a bachelor, had been an obvious candidate for President for 12 years before he was at last elected. It was rumored prior to his inauguration that he would marry the widow of James K. Polk and bring her back to the White House. He had been most gallant to Sarah Polk when he served as her husband's Secretary of State. But Buchanan had in mind for his regime far more social brilliance than could ever have been achieved by the staid Mrs. Polk. Presiding over his household he wanted youth and beauty, all the social graces, high fashion, keen intelligence and circumspect speech. More than a decade of deferred hope had given him time to produce such a paragon.

Harriet Lane at nine years of age was the youngest of four orphaned children left to Buchanan's guardianship. He provided for good homes among other relatives for the three older. But Harriet he took into his own Lancaster, Pennsylvania, home, Wheatland, still preserved as a historic shrine. It was presided over by Miss Hetty Parker as housekeeper. Buchanan reared his little niece as though she were his own daughter. He chose her schools carefully—a few years in the hometown schools; then with her sister Mary to a Charlestown, Virginia, boarding school; and—for finishing—the famous old Georgetown, D. C., convent. Never was he too busy as a Senator, as Secretary of State or diplomat, to write her weekly letters of detailed advice. When she was away at school he kept her keyed up to leading her classes and calmed her down when her ideas seemed to him too ambitious.

A biographer who had read this voluminous correspondence said: "There is rarely to be met, in any literature of real life with which I am acquainted, a more interesting and instructive picture of a man's care for a woman's education, manners, deportment, and inner character than is to be traced in Buchanan's letters to his niece."

Buchanan had at first feared that she would be "spoiled outright" by going to London while he was minister, but soon she persuaded him to let her join him there. In 1855 she thus was writing to her sister, Mary Baker, letters as colorful as ever went from London to San Francisco.

All London was "mad with excitement and enthusiasm" at the visit of the Emperor and Empress of France. Said Harriet of the Empress Eugénie, "I had a long talk with Her Majesty who was most gracious and affable. She is very striking, elegant and graceful. She wore a green silk, flounced to the waist with seven or eight flounces, white lace mantle, and white grape bonnet and feathers. We go to the palace tonight——"

Harriet airily told of having been at one of Queen Victoria's drawing rooms, in "a pink silk petticoat, overskirts of pink tulle, puffed and trimmed with apple blossoms, train of pink silk." She added: "Her Majesty was very gracious to me as also was the Prince. On Wednesday next, there is to be a state ball at Buckingham Palace, and we shall, of course, attend."

Buchanan too was a success at the British court. He was more than six feet tall, of distinguished appearance, and was the more noticeable because of a personal peculiarity. A Whig writer, describing Buchanan, said: "He carried his head slightly to one side like a poll-parrot." His nephew, J. Buchanan Henry, who served him as secretary, said, "His eyes were blue, intelligent and kindly, with the peculiarity that one was far and the other near sighted, which resulted in a slight habitual inclination of the head to one side." A society reporter, describing his approach to one of the grande dames of the day, tossed off the phrase, "his wonderful head nearer his shoulders than ever, his miraculous eye cocked with unwonted precision of aim." At any rate, he was a person immediately noticed in any group, even one including royalty, and he was credited with being one of the best conversationalists on either side of the Atlantic.

With regal scenes fresh in their minds James Buchanan and Harriet Lane went into the White House on March 4, 1857. Journalists of the day were quick to note the changed atmosphere of the mansion. One account ran:

"During the late Administration the President's house had assumed a sombre, melancholy aspect, in consequence of the heavy dispensations of Providence which have fallen on Mrs. Pierce. Her efforts to entertain were forced and gave only pain to those who attended her receptions. Everything seemed to partake of her own serious melancholy and mournful feelings, and every echo of the merry laugh had died from the walls. But Miss Lane has enticed that echo back and again all is joy and gladness in the Executive Mansion."

Again the White House receptions were described as gorgeous displays of finery. Chestnut-haired, clear of complexion and full-figured, Harriet Lane was the ideal person to set the Victorian fashions. Everybody wore low necks and lace berthas, voluminous skirts and elaborate headdresses because she did.

Again the White House took on the air of a European court. Indeed, titled travelers habitually made it a stopping place. Buchanan took the attitude that they all came as his personal friends, due to his long residences abroad as minister to the Russian and British courts. From his private purse he paid all expenses incident to these visits, no matter how elaborate the arrangements. He was moderately wealthy, having made enough money as a lawyer by the age of forty to finance his subsequent political career.

Years later, in a Southern prison, Jefferson Davis said, "The White House under the administration of Buchanan approached more nearly to my idea of a Republican court than the President's house has ever done before since the days of Washington."

The breach between North and South had begun to be a social chasm. Over it Harriet Lane glided on the tightrope of faultless social etiquette, balancing with the parasol of discretion. A contemporary described her: "Always courteous, always in place. Silent whenever it was possible to be silent, watchful and careful, she made no enemies, was betrayed into no entangling alliances, and was involved in no contretemps of any kind." It was a performance the more brilliant because her every social move was for James Buchanan's political purposes. And politics were by no means going well for President Buchanan.

By the time Buchanan took office Kansas was in such an embattled state that he needed a Supreme Court decision to strengthen the Kansas-Nebraska Bill. Kansas had two warring governments: the territorial government set up by Pierce, which was backed by those who were trying to make it a slave state; and the "Topeka government" organized by the antislavery forces. The territorial government held that the settlers had a right to bring in their slaves as property. The Topeka government held that the slaves became free the minute they entered territory not yet slave.

This difference of opinion caused frontier fights, and the territorial governor was charging the Topeka government with atrocities. He was also demanding that federal troops be sent in to restore order. This step President-elect Buchanan, who hated abolitionists, was only too ready to take as soon as he was in office and equipped with a Supreme Court decision which would definitely say that slaves were still slaves in Kansas. He was aware of the fact that Chief Justice Taney was about to hand down this opinion in the case of Dred Scott, a transported Negro. He was confident the decision would "settle all these questions and eventually restore harmony among the

States." In his inaugural address he therefore urged that the Dred Scott decision should be cheerfully observed by all good citizens. Two days later the decision was announced.

But it only caused more controversy. Stephen A. Douglas, the "Little Giant" of Illinois, was the only leader in his own party whom Buchanan had not consulted in forming his cabinet. Senator Douglas started a spectacular struggle for the control of the Democratic party. His had been the doctrine of "squatter sovereignty." He chose to consider the Dred Scott decision antagonistic to that doctrine and, the day it was handed down, served notice that the next day he would in the Senate "define his position on the Kansas question."

The news of such open opposition to a new administration ran swiftly through the town. An account of this oratorical event ran: "Every Senator was in his seat; every past or present dignitary who could claim a right to 'the floor' was there, and the galleries were packed with spectators, Mrs. Douglas prominent among the fairer portion of them." While Douglas referred with "studied courtesy" to President Buchanan, his speech was a repudiation of the Dred Scott decision. Douglas argued that after masters had taken their slaves into a territory they must take their chances on their being set free by a vote of the majority of the people when the territory became a state. It was said that at the conclusion of the speech a Southern Senator sarcastically congratulated a Northern Republican on Douglas' having joined the Republican party.

From that day on Miss Harriet Lane carried on a quiet but bitter prestige war with beautiful Mrs. Douglas, grandniece of Dolley Madison. At balls and theater parties where Addie Cutts Douglas had a front box, so did Harriet Lane. One such occasion was the triumphant Washington debut of Adelina Patti. Mrs. Douglas held brilliant parties in keenest competition with the social events at the White House. In this social war Miss Lane was the predestined winner, not because hers was the role of First Lady of the Land, but because she had the social backing of the Southern aristocracy into which Adele Cutts had been born. But Mrs. Douglas had the pleasure of seeing her husband outmaneuver Buchanan at every turn.

Although he credited his niece with ability to understand all political questions, Buchanan was bitter about the increasing political activity of women. He blamed them for keeping the slavery question stirred up.

The Buchanan regime was good for the White House itself. Buchanan had its interior renovated and repaired and many improvements made in the grounds, including the building of a red-brick barn. He also had an "elegant conservatory" built adjoining the White House on the west side. Twenty thousand dollars were spent for new furniture, and portraits of five past Presidents were purchased at $1,000 each.

Still President Buchanan considered the mansion unfit for occupancy in the summer months because of the malarial swamps close at hand. President Pierce had had a long siege of malaria. Buchanan and Miss Lane, aside from short trips to spas, spent their summers in a comfortable house on high ground, built for the superintendent at Soldiers' Home. That Buchanan had in mind building a similar permanent retreat for himself and later Presidents may have been indicated by an article which appeared in the public prints during his first summer in the White House. It read in part:

"After a few years, the edifice used as the Presidential Mansion will be abandoned as a private residence, and appropriated only to executive business and public reception.

"The President will be allowed as he ought to be, a private residence, free from the intrusion either of curiosity or business.

"A tasteful, elegant and convenient mansion, in a salubrious part of the city, is proposed to be built for the President's private residence. No one should be allowed to visit him there, upon any business matter, or without an invitation. From nine or ten till four o'clock he will then as at present attend to business at the executive office. The President would certainly be the better enabled to discharge his duties to the country under such an arrangement, than while perplexed and annoyed at all hours, by the crowd of licensed beggars and borers."

Nothing came of this trial balloon.

President Buchanan's engraved invitations, five by seven inches in size, admitted their recipients to dinners described as "superb in manner and style." At large receptions, however, a newspaper noted, guests had to leave "through the great front window, between which and the pavement a temporary bridge has been constructed."

The Buchanan administration reached its social zenith in the year 1860, the same year that it crashed politically. In May the

Japanese diplomatic staff, first delegation from that country, arrived in Washington, an entourage of 60 persons. The Japanese ministers bowed low to Miss Lane and the ladies of the cabinet—the only American women they considered of high enough rank to meet personally. They brought rich gifts to the President, Miss Lane and the Executive Mansion itself—"saddles beautifully embroidered and embossed in gold and silver, bed curtains and screens, two princely swords, kimonos, lacquered ware, writing cases, and a superb tea set inlaid with pearls and gold and valued at $3,000." A handsome cabinet then presented was deemed still worthy of a place in the Green Room 42 years later when Theodore Roosevelt staged a major White House restoration.

The Prince de Joinville, third son of Louis Philippe of France, who at the age of twenty-three had added to the glamour of the Tyler White House, returned again in compliment to Buchanan and his niece.

In October 1860 came the Prince of Wales, later King Edward VII, son of Queen Victoria, traveling incognito as Baron Renfrew, with a large suite. President Buchanan entertained him lavishly at the White House. Queen Victoria wrote President Buchanan a personal letter of thanks for his entertainment of her son, and both she and the prince sent gifts to the President and his niece. Miss Lane's was a set of engravings of the royal family. Gossip had it later that England stayed neutral during the Civil War instead of recognizing the Confederacy because of the royal family's friendship for Buchanan and his niece. It was also said that others counted this no great gain, contending that Great Britain might just as well have been an open enemy as to be busy with her ships in secret aid of the Southern cause.

During that fateful year President Buchanan received one political blow after another. A committee of the House of Representatives, headed by Representative John Covode of Buchanan's home state, started on March 5 a general investigation of the actions of the President.

"I defy all investigation," said the President in a hot message to Congress. "Nothing but the basest perjury can sully my good name." The whole proceeding, he said, was unconstitutional and degrading to the Presidential office.

Then came the wide-open split of the Democratic party. The

Democratic convention at Charleston, South Carolina, in April ended with the cotton states walking out without the adoption of a platform or the selection of a candidate. Stephen A. Douglas, the high man, could muster only 145½ votes, with 202 necessary for nomination under the two-thirds rule. The convention reconvened in Baltimore in June. There, after the South had again walked out, Douglas was nominated. That same day dissenting delegates, declaring themselves to be the true Democrats, held their own convention in Baltimore and nominated John C. Breckinridge of Kentucky. In Chicago the Republicans nominated Abraham Lincoln.

Buchanan's whole cabinet resigned. General Cass quit because Fort Sumter wasn't reinforced. Secretary of the Treasury Cobb went because he believed in the secession of his home state, Georgia. Secretary of War Floyd withdrew under protest after endless arguments over his failure to send more troops to the federal forts in Charleston Harbor. President Buchanan also found irregularity in his accounts, and there was a charge that he had sold old U. S. muskets southward. Both Cobb and Floyd later joined the Confederacy. The rest all went at Buchanan's request because he thought that by choosing the right men he might possibly pull the country together again. Entering as Attorney General was Edwin M. Stanton, destined to be a controversial figure in national life for many a year.

Even after six Southern states in quick succession had followed South Carolina out of the Union, President Buchanan still hoped for peaceful settlement. South Carolina, secession-minded ever since Jackson's time, had withdrawn right after Lincoln's election. When a bipartisan Congressional committee failed to agree on a proposed compromise on slavery at the close of 1860, Florida seceded on January 7, 1861; Mississippi on January 9; Alabama, January 11; Georgia, January 19; Louisiana, January 25; and Texas on February 5. When South Carolina, at the year's end, had sent three commissioners to talk to Buchanan, he had received them—to gain time "for passion to subside and for reason to resume her sway." And when the border state of Virginia sent ex-President Tyler up to propose a Peace Convention, so Buchanan held, "it became the duty of the President to render her all the aid in his power in a cause so holy."

The Peace Convention met in Washington on February 4, 1861. With John Tyler came his wife, Julia, to listen to the doings of the convention. Inevitably she was again the belle. Old friends told her she was as beautiful at forty as she had been at twenty-four. There was a big reception on which she reported to her mother in New York: "I paraded the room with the handsomest man there, Governor Morehead of Kentucky." The Tylers visited the White House. President Buchanan spent an evening with them. Buchanan's niece came to call on Mrs. Tyler. Thus Miss Lane came to know a prior White House mistress in her own mold, as years later she was also to meet the third in a notable tradition of young success, Frances Folsom Cleveland.

The Peace Convention continued throughout the month of February, when it was too late to hope for any favorable action of Congress on anything it might decide. By the scant majority of nine to eight states the Convention voted a proposition close to the so-called "Crittenden Compromise," which was that the South would surrender its right to take slaves into all the territories if the North would recognize this right in territories south of the Missouri Compromise line. Congress did find time to vote this down.

As the February days went by, adding to the nation's peril, President Buchanan's life was made miserable by General Scott on the one hand and ex-President Tyler on the other. Scott wanted to parade troops through Washington as evidence the city was being guarded against seizure by the secessionists, whose leaders were still sitting in Congress. Tyler wished to keep an appearance of peace while the Convention lasted, and Buchanan promised him no troops would be called out. Scott forced his first parade on February 22, honoring, of course, George Washington. Inauguration Day found Buchanan permitting under protest the big military parade insisted on by General Scott as protection to the new President against an assassination plot.

Buchanan said he had assurances based on full investigation that there was no plan to kill Lincoln, but "the General was so convinced of the reality of the plot nothing would shake his faith."

Buchanan also remarked that throughout their long "progress in the same carriage" to the inauguration ceremonies at the Capitol and back to the White House, Lincoln "was far from evincing the slightest apprehension of danger." Buchanan's admirers thought that he was the brave man that day, one of them remarking, "The presence of the outgoing side by side in the open barouche with the incoming president dispelled all fears of a day of war. Under the circumstances, this ride of Buchanan with Lincoln was a courageous act of official courtesy."

9 | *Saddest of Them All*

. . . LINCOLN

ABRAHAM LINCOLN went into the White House on the first great power tide of the Republican party. This new political alignment, which included the radical Whigs, the antislavery Democrats and various splinter parties, had held its first national convention in 1856 with opposition to the spread of slavery as its paramount principle. However, it was considered a purely sectional party until the Democratic split of 1860 gave it a national victory. So divided was the country that Abraham Lincoln won his office with only 40 per cent of the popular vote. Southerners spoke of him as a "sectional President."

Wishing to achieve as broad a base of popular support as possible for his administration, Lincoln in his own mind had chosen a majority of his cabinet on the night of the election, November 6, as he sat with the telegraphers in the Springfield, Illinois, office, closed that night to everybody but him. On the theory that the men who had been his strongest opponents at the Chicago nominating convention would have the largest political following, the newly elected President decided to take four of them into his cabinet. They were: William H. Seward of New York; Salmon P. Chase of Ohio; Edward Bates of Missouri; and Simon Cameron of Pennsylvania.

Obviously only a man long self-disciplined to a vast forbearance would have invited four bitter rivals into his political inner circle. Abraham Lincoln's training in this rare virtue had come in part through years of marriage to the tempestuous Mary Lincoln. She was highly nervous and had severe headaches. As her outbreaks of violence increased down the years Abraham Lincoln became the more com-

170

miserative. But no amount of loving-kindness could save Mary Lincoln. She suffered from a mental disease which became progressively worse as life dealt her the same bitter shocks which others had to suffer in a time of civil war.

Under normal conditions a Kentucky Todd would have been the type likely to succeed in the White House. Some inkling of what a proud family Mrs. Lincoln came from might be gleaned from her husband's humorous remark long told around Springfield: "One 'd' is enough for God but not for the Todds." Mrs. Lincoln came from the same blue-grass section and from the same social background as Henry Clay. In her childhood she had adored Clay. Through his long-continued but ever-frustrated candidacy for the Presidency she had fed her young imagination on dreams of living in the White House. When her husband had been first elected to Congress, she was quoted as saying: "He is to be President of the United States some day; if I had not thought so I never would have married him, for you can see he is not pretty. But look at him! Doesn't he look as if he would make a magnificent President?"

Mary Lincoln, moreover, was trained correctly for the drawing room of her day. She spent four years in an exclusive Lexington, Kentucky, school where only French was spoken. There she learned all the accepted social graces. School was followed by a three-year social whirl in Springfield, Illinois, where her sister had married the governor's son.

Mrs. Lincoln also had some notable natural endowments. She had a driving ambition. She had a flair for spirited and quotable conversation and a gift of mimicry. Politics was native to her blood. And she had a passion for pretty clothes. Her husband's nomination had been a signal for a big shopping trip to New York. She did not then realize that all the beauties cluttering about Miss Harriet Lane were buying their clothes in Paris in keenest competition with the belles of the European courts.

When the time came for the Lincolns to leave Springfield for Washington, Mary Lincoln—according to a tale given credence by the Lincoln historian, Carl Sandburg—was having one of her "spells." This story was traced back to Henry Villard, reporter on the Lincoln special train for the New York *Herald*, a friendly paper. Villard said that he was told by a man who had been sent to fetch the belated Presidential family that he had found a strange scene at the hotel where they were staying—Mrs. Lincoln had thrown herself on the floor and was refusing to budge until her husband would promise her that a certain man would be appointed to a federal post. This story further ran that Lincoln, with his eldest son, Robert, at last had to leave without her, and that Mrs. Lincoln with the two little boys, William and Thomas (called Tad), joined the train at Indianapolis. Sandburg indicates that this emotional upset might have caused Lincoln to make then "one of the most poignantly moving and melancholy speeches of his career." In saying good-by to Springfield forever he mentioned his second son, Edward, who had died at the age of four.

Mrs. Lincoln's niece, Katherine Helm, in her book about her aunt, told the Todd side of this story: "Eight o'clock in the morning being an inconvenient hour, Mrs. Lincoln had decided to take a later train and join the Presidential party at Indianapolis where they were to stay all night." She added that Mary Lincoln stood on the platform waving her husband off in the midst of a party of Todd relatives, four of whom went with her from Springfield to Washington as inauguration guests—a sister, two nieces and a cousin.

No account of a disrupted leave-taking at Springfield was given by John G. Nicolay, who went to Washington in the party of the President-elect to serve as Lincoln's private secretary. He recorded that the Lincolns all boarded the special train together at Springfield. If Nicolay in this case was discreetly putting the best face on a strained situation created by the hysterical Mrs. Lincoln, he himself later added to the evidence that there were times when her husband regarded her as less a wife than a problem child.

The Lincolns' trip to Washington was equally disturbed toward its end when the President-elect, warned of attempts to be made on his life in Baltimore, was persuaded to leave the special train at Harrisburg, Pennsylvania, and go into Washington ahead of it the night before. Mrs. Lincoln was described by one author as arriving in the capital the next morning distraught at the separation from her husband.

However, Katherine Helm said that Mary Lincoln and her relatives had left the Presidential train in New York, where she stayed until March 2 "with a party of eighteen or twenty relatives and friends," thus reaching Washington barely in time for the inauguration ceremonies. Whatever the correct version of Mary Lincoln's trip from

Springfield, such confusions would ever follow her mercurial course among established official plans.

Immediately she encountered in Washington an antagonistic attitude which was no hallucination. The city teemed with South-North hatred. She was a Southern woman, but the wife of the Northern man who typified social revolution. His very arrival signaled the end of Southern social supremacy. Lincoln, easygoing, humorous, sure of his salty values, was not perturbed, and met ex-President Tyler and his wife and President Buchanan and his niece with poise. But Mrs. Lincoln soon suffered under the aristocratic airs of the Washington social leaders.

One of the chief social weapons of the entrenched aristocracy was dress. Short, plump, child-faced Mrs. Lincoln almost immediately realized that her clothes could not compete with those of the women she had met. To the Lincoln rooms in Willard's Hotel she summoned a modiste who had been recommended to her, Elizabeth Keckley, a remarkable Negro woman who thereafter would play a bizarre role in her life. Mrs. Lincoln told Mrs. Keckley that she had spilled coffee on the gown she had intended to wear at her first White House reception, set for March 8. She would have to have another made in haste. However, Mrs. Keckley was not set at the task until the day after the inauguration, when she was called to the White House in competition with three other seamstresses and was low bidder. The President's wife told Lizzie Keckley that the number of dresses she would be hired to make would depend on how little she charged. Mrs. Lincoln had Lizzie Keckley make her "fifteen or sixteen dresses" that first spring in the White House.

"I must dress in costly materials," said Mrs. Lincoln to Mrs. Keckley. "The people scrutinize every article that I wear with critical curiosity. The very fact of having grown up in the West subjects me to more searching observation."

William O. Stoddard, who was brought into the White House office staff to sign land patents and who took on the handling of Mrs. Lincoln's mail, remarked that Mrs. Lincoln was no match for the Southern social leaders. Said Stoddard:

"There is no denying the attractiveness of Southern society, the charm of manner, the attainments, the capacities of the leaders of both sexes. Its women were a power here, as much almost as were its statesmen; and those of them who remain are slow to yield their own supremacy, or to place themselves in relation to the changed order of things."

Records left by some of these powerful women themselves tell of the "competitive expenditure," "very reckless gayety," "rivalry and vanity" which had "lifted the Capital to the very apex of its social glory" immediately preceding the Civil War. Because ladies wore enormous hoops, their heads "looked like small handles to huge bells." Their hair, worn with broad bandeaux and braids, was "loaded with garlands of flowers." An evening's floral garniture included head wreaths with trailing vines at the back, bouquets to be fastened to the gloves at the wrists and wreaths to festoon the double skirts. American-made goods were not of high enough quality for these ladies, and gloves, hats, fans, handkerchiefs and rich dress patterns had to be purchased in Paris. The men in the diplomatic service, even the bachelors, were pressed into duty as shoppers for fine laces, shawls, flounces and undersleeves, flowers and bonnets.

Dress for social display had thus been built up psychologically to the point where it was a devil as devastating for women as drink was for men. And so it really proved to be with Mary Lincoln. While she lived in the White House two aberrations were increasingly marked in her—pinching pennies and a grand-scale purchasing of clothes. Each fed on the other. When conscience smote for the sums spent on clothes, Mrs. Lincoln soothed it by small economies.

Mrs. Keckley's first creation for Mrs. Lincoln was a "rose-colored moire-antique" which the First Lady wore "with pearl necklace, pearl ear-rings, pearl bracelets, and red roses in her hair." Lizzie helped her dress that night for her first White House reception.

"I was surprized at her grace and composure," said Mrs. Keckley. "I had heard so much in current and malicious report of her low life, of her ignorance and vulgarity, that I expected to be embarrassed.

"Report was wrong. No queen, accustomed to the uses of royalty all her life, could have comported herself with more calmness and dignity."

The society reporters also approved. Just the same, the next editions of the newspapers did not hesitate to state that absence of "familiar Southern faces of distinguished men and beautiful and accomplished women" had created a "lamentable vacuum" and had made the reception "almost a purely provincial assemblage." High-ranking Army and Navy officers also were absent, and the fashionable circles of old-family Washington itself were "but slimly represented."

Mrs. Lincoln's reaction was to buy more clothes. She never seemed to be able to enwrap herself sufficiently to insulate herself from the condescensions and social cuts of the Washington elite.

Her character, now queenly, now shrewish, puzzled the White House staff. Said Stoddard, "It was not easy to understand at first why a lady who could one day be so kindly, so considerate, so generous, so thoughtful and hopeful, could, upon another day, appear so unreasonable, so irritable, so despondent, so even niggardly, and so prone to see the dark, the wrong side of men and women and events."

Mrs. Lincoln dispensed with the White House steward and herself took over all the minutiae of running the establishment. Stoddard put it flatly: "Mrs. Lincoln is absolute mistress of all that part of the White House inside of the vestibule on the first floor, and of all the upper floor west of the folding doors across the hall at the head of the stairs."

Robert had returned to college, but the two little boys, Willie, a lad with poetic talent, and Tad, mischievous and with a speech defect due to a cleft palate, romped through the White House upstairs, downstairs, conservatory and attic at will. The Lincolns were indulgent parents.

Abraham Lincoln took over the east end of the second floor of the White House, used by most of the Presidents of the 1800s as offices. There for four years and a few fateful weeks he struggled with the troubled times. His was the task of improvising military strategy, foreign policy, domestic policy, political techniques as led or forced by events. His was the role of keeping a remarkable assortment of political and military prima donnas moving toward a goal. In the high-ceilinged, rectangular White House rooms he somehow found the stamina to see his administration through. He stood at tall south windows, looking across the near by Potomac at the neighboring Virginia shore, which soon claimed to be a foreign land, and thought out his next moves. All night long, at times, when the affairs of the Union were at their worst, he paced his office floor. Daily his great feet tramped up and down the cramped little private stairway toward the west end of the White House as he went on his frequent trips to the War Department across Executive Avenue. There he got the latest news by telegraph and sent long telegrams to his commanders. Soon his personality permeated the whole mansion, and his imprint was on it to stay. Three quarters of a century later Mrs. Franklin D. Roosevelt told her press conference that if any ghost walked in the White House it was that of Abraham Lincoln.

Of an infinitude of word pictures of Lincoln, probably none came closer to an introduction to him than his own brief, factual recital. He wrote:

"If any personal description of me is thought desirable, it may be said, I am, in height, six feet, four inches, nearly; lean in flesh, weight an average of one hundred and eighty pounds; dark complexion, with coarse black hair and grey eyes—no other marks or brands recollected."

Lincoln had to have his little jokes. Of the hordes of office seekers who come pestering every President, he remarked that getting rid of them was like "trying to shovel a bushel of fleas across a barn floor." When pressed by the multiplicity of inconsequential requests which beset the Chief Executive, he said he could as easily bail the Potomac out with a teaspoon as deal with all the details brought to him. Life with him was enlivened by laughter.

The crisis immediately upon Lincoln as he opened his administration was the worsening situation at Fort Sumter in Charleston Harbor, South Carolina. Major Robert Anderson, exceeding authority given him by President Buchanan, had entrenched himself there to hold federal property from seizure by the Confederation. Could more provisions be got to him? Lincoln held two cabinet meetings on the subject before a scant majority of his advisers would say it was worthwhile even to try to save the fort.

At this juncture Secretary of State Seward, who still considered himself the rightful head of the Republican party, sent Lincoln an amazing memorandum in which he practically offered to take over the Presidency himself. Seward, author of the South-baiting phrase "There is a higher law than the Constitution" in reference to fugitive slaves, now was thoroughly frightened at what the slavery issue was doing to the country. "CHANGE THE QUESTION BEFORE THE PUBLIC FROM ONE UPON SLAVERY, OR ABOUT SLAVERY, for a question upon

UNION OR DISUNION," Seward advised Lincoln. His proposition was to start a world war in which the secession of a few states would be forgotten. "I would demand explanations from Spain and France, categorically, at once," said Seward. "I would seek explanations from Great Britain and Russia, and send agents into Canada, Mexico, and Central America to rouse a vigorous continental spirit of independence on this continent against European intervention. And, if satisfactory explanations are not received from Spain and France, would convene Congress and declare war against them." This document flatly stated that the Lincoln administration had neither a domestic nor a foreign policy and should declare both immediately. It was a highly insubordinate statement.

Lincoln, slowly studying this document, saw in it the hand of New York's venerable political boss, Thurlow Weed, for whom Seward was widely regarded as a "front man." Lincoln wanted to hold Seward, Weed and their influential following. So he sent to Seward a carefully worded reply, saying that Seward himself had helped formulate both the domestic and foreign policy and that he, Lincoln, whose sole responsibility both were, hoped to continue to benefit from his advisers.

The secessionist attack on Sumter suddenly struck on April 12, 1861. The supplies sent by Lincoln had not yet reached the fort. War was an actuality. Northern sentiment solidified behind Lincoln. Secretary of State Seward swung into line under Lincoln and stayed there. "The President is the best of us all," said Seward.

Thurlow Weed also became a lasting Lincoln asset. Weed was a globe-trotter. He had crossed the ocean a dozen times and had large numbers of influential friends in Europe. Lincoln sent him to England as a good-will emissary to make informal moves to keep England from recognizing the Confederacy. Minister Charles Francis Adams, son of John Quincy, was at work on the same task officially—and his brilliant son Henry wrote pro-Union articles for English newspapers.

In completing his cabinet Lincoln had appointed as Postmaster General Montgomery Blair of Maryland, son of old Francis P. Blair of President Jackson's "Kitchen Cabinet." Once more Blair House, across the avenue, was a White House neighbor, again available, in the mind of the elder Blair, for such extracurricular political activities as might be better taken up there than at the White House. By no means as extinct politically as President Tyler had once thought him, Francis P. Blair was soon deep in backstage strategy. His first role in this capacity was to act as go-between in the proposed tender of the command of the Union Army to General Robert E. Lee.

This move was the more logical because Montgomery Blair's daughter Elizabeth, who lived next door to Blair House in a house built for her by her father just before the Civil War, had married Robert E. Lee's cousin and childhood intimate, Captain Samuel Phillips Lee of the United States Navy. Phillips Lee was on the high seas, reputedly dispatched to a far corner of the earth by Buchanan's Southern-sympathizing Secretary of War so that he could not entice three outstanding Virginia cousins, including Robert Edward, into the service of the Union Army. With handsome Phillips Lee ruled out of the equation, his wife's grandfather, old Francis P. Blair, took over the diplomatic negotiations. He stood on firm ground as a go-between, for he was also kin, in a peculiar sort of way, to the Lincolns. Francis P. Blair was a double cousin to the stepmother who had reared Mary Lincoln. Both Blair and the second Mrs. Todd were first cousins to John C. Breckinridge, one of the two Democrats that Lincoln defeated for the Presidency.

From Arlington House across Long Bridge, Robert E. Lee was summoned by the elder Blair on the morning of April 18. In the small front study of Blair House Lee was "sounded out" as to whether he would accept the Union command. But Robert E. Lee had already decided to cast his lot with his native state, Virginia, which along with Arkansas, Tennessee and North Carolina had seceded at Lincoln's first call for troops to put down the rebellion. Soon Lee was galloping at the head of rebel hosts. His wife, the only surviving child of George Washington Parke Custis, grandson of Martha Washington, was driven from her ancestral home, Arlington, in May. In desperate haste Mrs. Lee had to move southward with the heirlooms she had inherited from Mount Vernon. Among them was the bed in which Washington had died.

Disobeying orders, Captain Phillips Lee came steaming back to Washington, eager for the fray. Without a moment's hesitation he declared for the Union, saying, "When I find the word Virginia in my Commission I will join the Confederacy." President Lincoln promoted him to rear admiral and put him in command of the naval force blockading Virginia and North Carolina. Brilliant thereafter was his war career.

A biographer of the Lee family propounded the puzzle of why these two cousins, Robert Edward and Samuel Phillips, both lofty-minded inheritors of the same ideas, family traditions and social environment, when brought face to face with the same question should make opposing decisions.

The Robert E. Lee estate, handsome old Arlington Mansion and its hilltop acres, had to be the first enemy property seized, not because its owner had taken top place in enemy ranks, but because Arlington strategically commanded the Federal City.

The White House, like many another American mansion, held a family pitted against its kinfolk across the border. Abraham Lincoln offered a major's commission to Ben Hardin Helm, who had married Mrs. Lincoln's half-sister Emilie. Helm was a guest at the White House that April. While thinking the offer over, Helm went out and visited old friends from West Point, where he had been graduated, and ran into Robert E. Lee. Talking with Lee, Helm decided for the South. When the lines at last were drawn, Mrs. Lincoln, whose twice-married father sired 16 children, had a full brother, three half-brothers and three brothers-in-law wearing the Confederate gray.

With so many Southern relatives Mrs. Lincoln was berated as a Southern sympathizer, was even called a Confederate spy. One of Stoddard's duties was tossing letters containing these charges into the wastebasket before they reached Mrs. Lincoln. But she knew about them just the same. She requested Stoddard to read even letters from her sister before he brought them to her. Said Stoddard, "Read! Read! You know why she wishes you to inspect her letters. The President's wife is venomously accused of being at heart a traitor, and of being in communication with the Confederate authorities."

From the first, Fate itself seemed determined that the White House should feel the full force of the war. Colonel Elmer E. Ellsworth, commander of the crack, colorful Chicago Zouaves who had been chosen to ride the Lincoln special train into Washington as a bodyguard, was killed in June while tearing the Confederate flag from the roof of Marshall House, a tavern in near-by Alexandria, Virginia. His body was brought to the White House, where he had been like one of the family, and lay in state in the East Room. It was viewed by thousands. In a flag-draped casket it was taken on a hearse drawn by four white horses, with military escort, to the depot to be returned to Illinois.

Just across Lafayette Park from the White House lived Mrs. Rose O'Neal Greenhow, leader of Washington society, aunt of Mrs. Stephen A. Douglas. She was a Marylander, widow of a Virginian. Tad Lincoln played with her little girl. Secretary of State Seward and many other leading men and women were her constant callers. A Southern sympathizer, she was able to keep the enemy apprised of every Union move until she was at last put into the Old Capital Prison, a proved spy.

The war went anything but well for Lincoln. General Winfield Scott, General in Chief of the Army since 1841, was much too old to be effective. As a native of Virginia, he had been promoting promising young Southerners for many years. Quite naturally the best of his officer material accepted commands below Mason and Dixon's line. So Scott had to put inexperienced officers, too rapidly promoted, in command of raw troops. His first choice, Brigadier General Irvin McDowell, was defeated at Bull Run in July 1861.

This sobering debacle started Lincoln himself on an intensive study of military tactics. Only two days after Bull Run, Nicolay said, Lincoln wrote a memorandum suggesting three principal war objectives: the already planned attack on Richmond; a movement from Cincinnati on Cumberland Gap and East Tennessee; and an expedition from Cairo, Illinois, against Memphis. Nicolay noted that the second of these objectives, unremittingly urged by Lincoln, did not seem important to the military committees of Congress or to his own commanding generals. To quote Nicolay, "He devoted every spare minute to the study of such military books and leading principles of the art of war as would aid him in problems that must necessarily come to himself for final decision." He added that Lincoln later was called by experts "the ablest strategist of the war." Other experts accorded that honor to Robert E. Lee.

Stoddard gave Lincoln credit for contributing also to Civil War naval strategy. He told of a queer model of a fighting vessel being brought into the White House offices. "Mr. Lincoln made a careful study of what was said to resemble a cheese-box on a raft," said Stoddard. "He ordered a board of Naval officers to get together and examine it. Then he turned himself into a Naval officer and met with the board. There were adverse opinions from several other old salts, but Mr. Lincoln said he was like the fat girl when she put on her stocking—she thought there was something in it, and so did he, and the building of the *Monitor* was ordered."

General Scott next placed in active command General George B. McClellan, only thirty-five years old, whom Scott had speedily promoted from a mere captaincy to the rank of major general. McClellan proved to be an organizing genius who could train and parade an army and throw up impressive-looking earthworks all around Washington. But it took Lincoln 17 months to learn that McClellan would never bring himself to the point of real battle in full-scale warfare. Nicolay summarized the McClellan character in a sentence: "His hope of victory was always overawed by his fear of defeat." So McClellan kept insisting on more and more troops, draining strength from the more active armies in the West. It was McClellan's massive inertia which made a national catchword of the phrase reiterated day after day in the telegraphic dispatches, "All quiet on the Potomac." And so a discouraging 1861 merged into an equally discouraging 1862. Mr. Lincoln changed his Secretary of War, accepting Cameron's resignation and appointing Edwin M. Stanton.

Early in her second White House year Mrs. Lincoln decided that, with a war on, she would dispense with official dinners and merge all the official receptions into one. Since previous White House receptions had been held on the basis that Washington society could come if it so chose, Mrs. Lincoln feared too large an attendance at this affair. She hit on the plan of sending out engraved invitations and thereby drew down a very avalanche of protest and condemnation. Those who received no cards were furious. Stoddard did his best to explain to the press corps of Washington, omitted from the invitations, that it was a "rigidly official affair—a consolidated reception" to include cabinet, Supreme Court, heads of departments, diplomatic corps, members of Congress, generals and admirals and governors of states. However, Stoddard noted, the newspapers were crammed with discussions of "Mrs. Lincoln's Party," and "one illustrated weekly printed a full column of mournful verses, supposed to be sung by a wounded volunteer in the hospital, 'My Lady President's Ball.' " A last-minute stretching of the invitation list to include some of unofficial Washington, and also the press, failed to end the "storm of absurd disapprobation," and Stoddard, at the close of this reception, said in summary, "It is no ball, no party, nothing but a jam."

Elizabeth Keckley recalled that she listened to the Marine Band music at that party from the bedside of Willie, who was ill. In fact, both of the little boys were, and their father had taken turns with their mother in staying up nights and giving them medicine. They had even talked of calling off the party, but the doctor had told them there was no reason for alarm. Tad improved, but Willie died of typhoid fever on February 20, 1862. To Nicolay the grief-stricken Abraham Lincoln said, "My boy is gone, he is actually gone!" and burst into tears. And to Mrs. Keckley, who helped to dress Willie, he said, "It is hard, hard to have him die." Mrs. Lincoln was in such grief that she was unable to attend the funeral. Mrs. Keckley said that after Willie's death Mary Lincoln never again entered the room in which he died or the Green Room, in which he was embalmed. The White House was swathed in mourning for days.

Mrs. Lincoln banned flowers from the White House because Willie had loved them. That summer she cut off the Marine Band concerts on the White House south grounds, to which the public had grown accustomed. She said she could not stand the sound of gay music because of her loss. This sort of sentiment had been thought appealing in Mrs. Pierce, but not in Mrs. Lincoln. The newspapers even printed a Southern woman's caustic comment that Mrs. Lincoln at least had the privilege of seeing her son die, instead of having to send him out to be shot on a battlefield.

It was already evident to Lincoln, that summer of 1862, that he could not save the Union short of freeing the slaves. The anti-slavery forces of the North would not keep on fighting with any lesser objective. It was also mandatory as a matter of foreign policy. England might have actively espoused the cause of the South in the hope of adding a cotton colony, had the rank and file of her citizenry been able to stomach slavery. Lincoln kept up an active propaganda barrage in England on this subject, himself writing open letters to workmen and sending overseas this country's ablest platform speakers, including Henry Ward Beecher. When in August he informed his cabinet of his decision to issue an Emancipation Proclamation, Secretary Seward advised him to wait for a victory, and Lincoln quickly conceded this would be excellent psychological tactics.

So Lincoln kept on waiting. He seemingly could not relinquish the hope that a general who looked so good on the parade ground as McClellan would one day go into real action. Instead McClellan kept dashing about in a dither of self-importance, speaking more and more disdainfully about Abraham Lincoln. His troops adored him, and the country accepted him at his own measure, calling him "Little Napoleon." Perhaps his ineffectiveness in executing military movements was due in part to his interest in political maneuvers calculated to pick up the pieces of the smashed Democratic party. General McClellan was to be the next Democratic candidate for President, in opposition to Abraham Lincoln. Secretly Lincoln's backers met by night and formed the Union League Club of America, termed by one of its charter members, "the most perfect party skeleton ever put together for utter efficiency of political machine work." Its province was to see that the re-election of Lincoln was "securely won beforehand."

Even Willie's death did not long halt Mrs. Lincoln's shopping trips to New York City. In September 1862 she had Lizzie Keckley follow her to the Metropolitan Hotel there, and they both went on to Boston, where Robert was in school. In both cities Mrs. Keckley solicited for the "Contraband Relief Association," to aid the throngs of destitute freed Negroes in Washington, which Lizzie organized and to which Mrs. Lincoln gave $200.

The fine points of mourning dress were absorbing to the First Lady. In one letter ordering materials, she wrote:

"I want you to select me the *very finest* and blackest and lightest long crepe veil, and bordered as they bring them. Please get me the finest that can be obtained. Want a *very, very* fine black crepe veil, round corners and folds around. Want one of very fine black silknet— with folds around for summer—round at corners and short. . . . I liked the undersleeves and collars. Please have me *two more*, white and black collars mixed, with cuffs to match. . . . I want the genteelest and tastiest you can find and have made."

That same September saw Lee moving into Maryland. Lincoln chose to consider the drawn battle of September 17 at Antietam as a Union victory, and on September 22, 1862, he issued a preliminary proclamation, serving notice that he would by proclamation free the slaves on January 1, 1863. McClellan did not follow up the slight advantage he had shown in this battle, but camped at Antietam for two weeks. President Lincoln, visiting that field on October 1, looked over the great ranks of the army of the Potomac and bitterly termed it "McClellan's body guard." And McClellan's bodyguard it remained until Lincoln finally ordered General McClellan dismissed on November 5.

Lincoln and Secretary of War Stanton tried out a series of generals, never picking a real winner until General Ulysses S. Grant rose out of the West. When the inland battles at last were won, Secretary Nicolay noted, they had followed the exact lines which Abraham Lincoln had mapped right after Bull Run. And Grant still had to take Richmond, which old General Scott had thought the first and easiest objective.

Had Lincoln been aiming for psychological impact, he could have chosen no better day for issuing his Emancipation Proclamation than New Year's. That was the day on which all Presidents, having shaken hands with all the diplomats of all the countries and all Washington officialdom besides, threw open the White House doors and let the common folks pour through. Lincoln shook so many hands on January 1, 1863, that he held his own hand still for several minutes to steady it before signing his name to the Proclamation. The Proclamation, as he had foreseen, gave great impetus to the Union cause at home and abroad. A historic painting of the scene in which Lincoln read its text to his cabinet, painted by Francis B. Carpenter in the White House, toured the West in the 1864 campaign and helped to re-elect Lincoln.

Soon after the Emancipation Proclamation a Washington correspondent, Mary Clemmer Ames, wrote for her papers a series of articles on "Emancipation in the District—Stories of the Late Slaves." One of her prize subjects was Elizabeth Keckley, who, as a matter of fact, had not been emancipated by the proclamation but had bought her own freedom years before. However, Lizzie was unquestionably a slave success story. At the height of her popularity as a modiste Elizabeth Keckley had 20 seamstresses working under her. She also had classes, teaching a new system of cutting and fitting which included the draping of dress forms. She made a small fortune, too, which she eventually lost in a stamp-canceling-machine scheme.

Mary Ames spared no adjectives. She described Mrs. Keckley as "a stately, stylish woman, cheek tawny, features regular . . . a face strong with intellect and heart." "It is Lizzie who fashions those splendid costumes of Mrs. Lincoln, whose artistic elegance have been so highly praised during the last winter," said this author. "Stately carriages stand before her door, whose haughty owners sit before Lizzie docile as lambs, whilst she tells them what to wear. Lizzie is an artist, and has such a genius for making women look pretty that no one thinks of disputing her decrees."

Mary Clemmer Ames had no such admiring phrases for Mary Lincoln. Of Mrs. Lincoln she wrote:

"While her sister-women scraped lint, sewed bandages and put on nurses' caps, and gave their all to country and to death, the wife of the President spent her time in rolling to and from Washington and New York, intent on extravagant purchases for herself and the White House. Mrs. Lincoln seemed to have nothing to do but 'shop' and the reports of her lavish bargains, in the newspapers, were vulgar and sensational in the extreme. The wives and daughters of other Presidents had managed to dress as elegant women, without the process of so doing becoming prominent to the public. But not a new dress or jewel was bought by Mrs. Lincoln that did not find its way into the newspapers.

"The Capital had become one vast hospital. The reluctant river every hour laid at the feet of the city its precious freight of lacerated men. The wharves were lined with the dying and the dead. One ceaseless procession of ambulances moved to and fro. Our streets resounded with the shrieks of the sufferers which they bore. Churches, halls and houses were turned into hospitals. Every railroad train that entered the city bore fresh troops to the Nation's rescue, and fresh mourners seeking their dead, who had died in its defense. Through it all, Mrs. Lincoln 'shopped.'

"At the White House a lonely man, sorrowful at heart and weighed down by mighty burdens, bearing the Nation's fate upon his shoulders, lived and toiled and suffered alone. His wife, during all the summer, was at the hotels of fashionable watering-places. Conduct comparatively blameless in happier times became culpable under such exigencies and in such shadow.

"Jarred, from the beginning, by Mrs. Lincoln's life, the Nation, under its heavy stress of sorrow, seemed goaded at last to exasperation. Letters of rebuke, of expostulation, of anathema even, addressed to her, personally, came in on her from every direction. Not a day that did not bring to her many such communications, denouncing her mode of life, her conduct, and calling on her to fulfill the obligations and meet the opportunities of her high station.

"But just as if there were no monstrous national debt, no rivers of blood flowing, she seemed chiefly intent upon pleasure, personal flattery, and adulation; upon extravagant dress and ceaseless self-gratification.

"The men who fed her weakness for their own political ends were sure of her favor. Thus, while daily disgracing the State by her own example, she still sought to meddle in its affairs. Woe to Mr. Lincoln if he did not appoint her favorites. Prodigal in personal expenditure, she brought shame on the President's House by petty economies which had never disgraced it before. Had the milk of its dairy been sent to the hospitals, she would have received golden praise. But the whole city felt scandalized to have it haggled over and peddled from the back door of the White House. State dinners could have been dispensed with, without a word of blame, had their cost been consecrated to the soldiers' service, but when it was made apparent that they were omitted from personal penuriousness and a desire to devote their cost to personal gratification, the public censure knew no bounds."

From inside the White House, William Stoddard gave testimony that Mary Lincoln was a regular hospital visitor and gave generously from White House stores. He was of the opinion Mrs. Lincoln would have received less criticism if she had cultivated the press more.

"If she were worldly wise, she would carry newspaper reporters, from two to five, of both sexes, every time she went and she would have them take shorthand notes of what she says to the sick soldiers and what the sick soldiers say to her. Then she would bring the writers back to the White House, and give them some cake—and coffee, and show them the conservatory. By keeping up such a process until every correspondent is dealt with, say twice, she could somewhat sweeten the contents of many journals and of the secretary's waste basket."

For a second summer Mary Lincoln refused to let the Marine Band hold concerts on the White House south lawn. Her niece Katherine held that the First Lady also was inwardly grieving, not only for Willie, but at the other losses which befell the Todds. All three of her Confederate half-brothers were killed in the war. And Ben Helm, the brilliant young brother-in-law whom Lincoln had wanted for the Union, was killed in Alabama. His widow, Emilie, mother of Katherine, returning from the funeral with her little girl, was told when she reached Fortress Monroe that she could not proceed to her parents' home in Kentucky without taking an oath of allegiance to the United States. Emilie refused, saying it would be treason to her dead husband. The officer in charge wired President Lincoln asking what to do. Lincoln wired back, "Send her to me." The sisters sorrowed together, but did not dare discuss the war.

Emilie Helm and Abraham Lincoln talked about their mutual grave concern over Mary Lincoln's mental health. But only to her diary did Emilie confide that Mary had come into her room one night and told her that Willie came to her nightly, sometimes bringing his brother Eddie, and twice he had brought their own youngest brother, Alec Todd, recently killed. Wrote Emilie, "It is unnatural and abnormal, and it frightens me."

The two children playing together in the White House, Tad Lincoln and his little girl cousin, also furnished a sidelight of civil war. Tad proudly displayed a photograph of his father, saying, "This is the President." She replied, "No, that is not the President, Mr. Davis is the President." Tad shouted back, "Hurrah for Abe Lincoln!" She countered, "Hurrah for Jefferson Davis!" Lincoln, listening, quizzically said, "Well, Tad, you know who is your President and I am your little cousin's Uncle Lincoln."

Emilie stayed only a week, refusing President Lincoln's invitation to spend the summer with them at Soldiers' Home.

The Committee on the Conduct of the War, which had been organized by Congress with a truculent abolitionist, Benjamin F. Wade of Ohio, as chairman, held a secret session to weigh the renewed gossip charging disloyalty which her sister's visit had brought upon Mrs. Lincoln. Suddenly Abraham Lincoln's tall figure appeared at the foot of the committee table as though he were an apparition. He made a short formal declaration: "I, Abraham Lincoln, President of the United States, appear of my own volition before this committee of the Senate to say that I, of my own knowledge, know that it is untrue that any of my family hold treasonable communication with the enemy." The shaken committee members dropped the subject forever.

That autumn of 1863 a dynamic newspaper woman, Jane Grey Swisshelm, returned to Washington from the Midwest. A rampant abolitionist and lone-wolf campaigner for women's rights, Jane had made a double-crusade mission to Washington in 1850. She wrote off the suffragists as ineffectual sentimentalists and turned her own vast energies into practical campaigns. In the heat of the 1850 slavery debate she had sailed into the Senate press gallery simply to prove that a newspaperwoman could sit there. She was right. In her footsteps followed the brilliant women journalists of Civil War and Reconstruction days—Mary Clemmer Ames, Emily Edson Briggs, whose letters were signed "Olivia," and many others.

To the surprise of all Jane Swisshelm became the ardent champion of Mrs. Lincoln. At first she had refused even to attend a Lincoln reception, giving her reasons: "He had proved an obstructionist as well as an abolitionist and I felt no respect for him; while his wife was everywhere spoken of as a Southern woman with Southern sympathies—a conspirator against the Union."

Said Mrs. Swisshelm:

"I watched the President and Mrs. Lincoln receive. His sad, earnest, honest face was irresistible in its plea for confidence, and Mrs. Lincoln's manner was so simple and motherly, so unlike that of all Southern women I had seen, that I doubted the tales I had heard. Her head was not that of a conspirator. She would be incapable of successful deceit, and whatever her purposes were, they must be known to all who knew her. . . . I recognized Mrs. Lincoln as a loyal, liberty-loving woman, more staunch even than her husband in opposition to the Rebellion and its cause, and as my very dear friend for life."

Jane Swisshelm rushed into print with her changed opinion of Mrs. Lincoln, raising the conflicting hue and cry about her all over again. *Leslie's Weekly* gave the controversy, pro and con. On the day of Mrs. Lincoln's funeral in 1882 Jane Grey Swisshelm was still asking in print for a fairer evaluation of Mrs. Lincoln's place in history. She credited Mrs. Lincoln with "an intimate knowledge of political issues, past and present, and an intuitive perception of their bearings."

Mrs. Lincoln had little regard for most of the men chosen by her husband as leaders. She characterized McClellan as a "humbug," Grant as a "butcher." Senator Andrew Johnson, the Tennessee Democrat who had the spectacular courage to stick to the Union, was to Mrs. Lincoln "a demagogue." She considered Seward a schemer, bent on outwitting her husband. She had tilts with arrogant and ambitious Secretary of War Stanton. But her most bitter and continuing warfare was carried on against Lincoln's Secretary of the Treasury, Salmon P. Chase of Ohio. Chase certainly had Presidential ambitions, and he was spurred on by his brilliant and beautiful daughter and official hostess, Kate Chase Sprague. All through Buchanan's time Kate Chase had been supreme. Then she enhanced her prestige by marriage to the very wealthy Rhode Island governor, William Sprague, who became a United States Senator.

The more radical antislavery forces, who already were demanding

The elaborate Tiffany screen which President Chester A. Arthur had built across the White House foyer to insure privacy for his family.

The White House foyer as remodeled by President Theodore Roosevelt.

The Red Room decorative scheme which was changed by the Theodore Roosevelt remodeling of the White House.

the vote for the Negro as soon as the war was won, got out a statement saying that Lincoln could never be re-elected and declaring for Chase. In this group was the one political leader who did have Mrs. Lincoln's complete approval, Senator Charles Sumner of Massachusetts. So great was Mrs. Lincoln's hatred of Kate Sprague that she determined to invite neither the Secretary of the Treasury nor his daughter and son-in-law to the cabinet dinner when White House official entertaining was resumed in January of the campaign year, 1864.

Secretary John G. Nicolay, whose duty it was to seat official dinner guests according to the protocol furnished him by the Department of State, noted the highly significant omission and "ordered Rhode Island and Ohio to be included in the list." Whereupon, Nicolay noted, "there arose such a rampage as the House hasn't seen for a year." He added, "having compelled Her S. Majesty to invite the Spragues, I was taboo." Mrs. Lincoln then determined to bar Nicolay from the dinner, but he simply withheld his expert services in its organization until she capitulated.

Mrs. Lincoln was terrified lest her husband should fail to be reelected. "If he should be defeated," she told Elizabeth Keckley, "I do not know what would become of us all. To me, to him, there is more at stake in this election than he dreams of." When the puzzled Mrs. Keckley queried her as to her meaning, Mrs. Lincoln confessed, "I have contracted large debts of which he knows nothing and which he will be unable to pay if he is defeated." Mrs. Keckley said that Mrs. Lincoln estimated her debts at about $27,000, "the principal portion at Stewart's in New York." The President's wife added, "Mr. Lincoln has but little idea of the expense of a woman's wardrobe. He glances at my rich dresses, and is happy in the belief that the few hundred dollars I obtain from him supply all my wants." "And Mr. Lincoln does not even suspect how much you owe?" asked Mrs. Keckley. "God, no! and I would not have him suspect," was the answer. "If he knew his wife was involved to the extent she is, the knowledge would drive him mad. . . . If he is re-elected, I can keep him in ignorance of my affairs; but if he is defeated, then the bills will be sent in and he will know all."

Again Mrs. Lincoln told Mrs. Keckley, "The Republican politicians must pay my debts. Hundreds of them are getting immensely rich off the patronage of my husband and it is but fair that they should help me out of my embarrassment." This was an idea that she would never relinquish, and on which she took action during her husband's campaign for re-election. Isaac Newton, appointed to head the Agricultural Bureau when it was set up in 1862, said that Mrs. Lincoln wept and wailed and beseeched him to help her pay her debts on which she had put a too conservative estimate. There later came to light evidence that Mrs. Lincoln owed about twice what she said she did. Her rich accouterments gave rise to persistent rumors she was taking rake-offs on Army contracts. Few indeed knew that Mrs. Lincoln just said "Charge it" when she shopped.

The Union League Club secured Lincoln's second nomination by staging an early convention, June 7, 1864, before the Chase forces had a chance to consolidate their strength. The Republicans that year called their convention the Union Convention, and the preservation of the Union was their platform. To emphasize the Union idea, when Lincoln refused to pick a running mate, they chose a Democrat from a secession state, Andrew Johnson of Tennessee, as Vice-Presidential candidate. The presence of Chase in the cabinet after his open attempt to take the Presidency from his chief soon became galling to both, and Lincoln accepted Chase's resignation. However, before the year was out Lincoln appointed Salmon P. Chase Chief Justice of the United States. His daughter Kate was not pleased with this most lofty post on the Supreme Bench. It did not carry with it the social setting of the White House, and so she continued her campaign for her father as President.

The Democrats held a very late convention, delaying until August, when they nominated General George B. McClellan on the first ballot. Theirs was a peace platform—"that immediate effort be made for cessation of hostilities."

The Lincoln family spent that summer at Soldiers' Home as usual—although to look at a map of Washington and its vicinity it would seem as though they were determined to go right out Seventh Street and meet trouble. Closer and closer came the war to the capital, until it was almost on the doorstep at Soldiers' Home. One day early in July the President and Mrs. Lincoln, with a large official party, drove the short distance to Fort Stevens to see how the Union troops were faring. A sharp skirmish with the Confederate advance took place then and there. Lincoln's lanky figure and tall hat were a tempting target. A bullet whizzed in from the Confederate lines, killing an army surgeon less than a yard from President Lincoln. This incident lived on in story, partly because of another character in the scene. The young officer who yelled at the President, "Get down, you fool!" chanced to be the son of a famous father who would one day make the name even more famous, Lieutenant Colonel Oliver Wendell Holmes.

A few weeks before the November 8 election the long-deferred military successes began to come. Lincoln could, and did, await election night with confidence. When the returns were decisive, he said to those gathered around him, "It is no pleasure to me to triumph over anyone, but I give thanks to the Almighty for this evidence of the people's resolution to stand by free government and the rights of humanity."

The masterpiece of Lincoln's second inaugural address—"With malice toward none, with charity for all, with firmness in the right as God gives us to see the right, let us strive to finish the work we are in"—was somewhat dimmed for high officialdom by the unseemly conduct of Vice President Johnson, still weak from typhoid fever, who took too deep a draught shortly before he was sworn in. Lincoln and others were quick to start in circulation the word-of-mouth assurance that such conduct was not in character for Andrew Johnson.

That Inauguration Night, a Saturday, the President and Mrs. Lincoln received at the White House 15,000 people in a four-hour reception. And on Monday night Mrs. Lincoln, in a $2,000 dress, shimmering white silk and lace, with elaborate fan and headdress, paraded the Patent Office, scene of the Inaugural Ball, on the arm of Senator Sumner. It was her night of triumph over Kate Chase. Young Robert Todd Lincoln's Inaugural Ball partner was the Iowa Senator's daughter, pretty Mary Harlan, who would become his wife a few years later. Mary Harlan Lincoln would live to be well past ninety years, visited from time to time in her Georgetown home by a Democratic First Lady, Mrs. Franklin D. Roosevelt. Mary Harlan was a great favorite with Mary Lincoln. To the younger woman Mrs. Lincoln poured out her philosophy: "You should go out every day and enjoy yourself—trouble comes soon enough, my dear child"; and "I know full well by experience, power and high position do not ensure a bed of roses."

As the Union armies fought on toward victory in late March and early April of 1865 events around the Lincolns heightened the proportions of climax in a great drama, all plot threads clear, all characters converging.

On Thursday, March 23, President and Mrs. Lincoln with a large official party boarded the *River Queen*, bound, at the invitation of General Grant, to his headquarters at City Point, Virginia, to which their son Robert Lincoln was now attached. In the Lincoln party were Mary Harlan and her parents. Lizzie Keckley was there too, combining the duty of dressing Mrs. Lincoln with the pleasure of visiting old friends, newly emancipated, in the state where she was born. Generals Phil Sheridan and William Tecumseh Sherman, as well as General and Mrs. Ulysses S. Grant, were on and off the *River Queen*. Started ostensibly for a vacation trip to give the President a brief respite after his long years of war, and from the locustlike horde of pardon seekers beseiging the White House, the *River Queen* steamed straight toward the spot where peace terms would be promulgated. Petersburg was evacuated by the Confederates and Richmond fell while the *River Queen* lay off City Point.

The erratic Mrs. Lincoln returned to Washington for a week end and missed her husband's dramatic entry into a still-blazing Richmond on the morning of April 4. Lincoln and his companion, Rear Admiral David D. Porter, went there on the *River Queen*, until they had to transfer to a smaller boat and finally to a barge rowed by 12 sailors. Ten of these sailors formed a guard as Lincoln and Porter walked all the way—about a mile and a half—to the mansion which Jefferson Davis had occupied as President of the Confederacy. It had been Lincoln's hope personally to grant Davis an honorable peace. But Davis had fled southward with his staff in a special train, in the vain belief that he could find a capital where he could continue the Confederacy.

On the City Point excursion the shocked wives of high-ranking officers, including Mrs. Ulysses S. Grant, were witnesses to a series of Mary Lincoln's jealous emotional outbursts. Mrs. Lincoln heard that a young officer's wife had been given special permission by the President to stay at the front. The President's wife flew into a rage, interpreting this routine act as a mark of her husband's favor. Again, in the course of a field inspection one of the Army wives on horseback found herself riding beside the President. Mrs. Lincoln, ensconced in a carriage with Mrs. Grant, gave vent to her spleen: "What does this woman mean by riding by the side of the President? Does she suppose that he wants her by the side of him?" When Mrs. Grant tried to turn the incident off with soothing words Mrs. Lincoln turned on her with "I suppose you think you'll get to the White House yourself, don't you?"

In Washington conspirators, led by the handsome actor John Wilkes Booth, eagerly awaited the return of Abraham Lincoln to Washington. The *River Queen* docked on Palm Sunday, April 9, the week end of Lee's surrender to Grant at Appomattox. A theater party was planned for the night of Good Friday, April 14, as part of a triumphant celebration of the peace. It was also a return of hospitality from the Lincolns to the Grants. However, the Grants withdrew at the last possible minute, saying that they were anxious to get home and see their children. Grant had no taste for such fanfare, and after the City Point trip Mrs. Grant felt too rebuffed to wish to spend an evening in a theater box beside Mrs. Lincoln.

That Good Friday night the conspirators struck. Booth, so swagger that he gained admission to the Lincoln box by saying he was a Senator, shot the President as he sat with Mrs. Lincoln at Ford's Theatre, enjoying Laura Keene in the play *Our American Cousin*. The assassin escaped by leaping to the stage and dashing out the stage exit. In the Seward home on Lafayette Square his accomplices simultaneously attacked Seward, coming so close to killing him that he never really regained the look of the living, although he lived on for years.

The fatally wounded Lincoln was carried to a house across the street from Ford's Theatre, where his frantic wife called on him to speak one word, begged him to let her die with him, fainted, and when revived covered his face with kisses as surgeons counted his fading pulse. At last the physicians persuaded her to sit in an adjoining room, where the word was brought to her: "It is all over. The President is no more." Mrs. James Dixon, wife of the Senator from Connecticut, one of four women called to share with Mrs. Lincoln her awful vigil, described Mrs. Lincoln's return to the White House. The doctor's orders were that she must be put to bed immediately. "She refused to go into any of the rooms she had previously occupied," said Mrs. Dixon. " 'Not there! Oh, not there!' she said—and so we took her to the one she had arranged for the President for a summer home to write in."

Mrs. Dixon said that as she herself started to go downstairs she met the cortege bringing the remains of the murdered President "which were taken into the great State Bedroom wrapped in the American Flag."

For five weeks Mary Lincoln lay in that White House room in the throes of her grief, watched over by the faithful Mrs. Keckley and little Tad. The great pageantry of the state funeral in the East Room came and went, and she did not emerge. The Lincoln funeral train, bearing the huge casket of the great man, with the small coffin of his son Willie at his feet, went on its majestic way, honored at Baltimore, Harrisburg, Philadelphia, New York, Albany, Buffalo, Michigan City, Indianapolis and Chicago before it finally reached Springfield. Thousands on thousands of people filed past Lincoln in death who had never seen him in life. Springfield citizens were planning a regal last resting place for Lincoln. His widow roused herself from her lethargy long enough to send a message forbidding the citizens of Springfield to inter him in a public place where she would not wish to lie beside him.

As Mrs. Lincoln lingered in her upstairs room souvenir hunters, who for many weeks had been packing off anything loose about the White House in the same spirit that they took shells from the Civil War battlefields, had a heyday. Wrote eyewitness Mary Clemmer Ames:

"The rabble ranged through it at will. Silver and dining ware were carried off and have never been recovered. It was plundered not only of ornaments but of heavy articles of furniture. Costly sofas and chairs were cut and injured. Exquisite lace curtains were torn into rags, and carried off in pieces. While all this was going on below, Mrs. Lincoln, shut up in her apartments, refused to see any one but servants, while, day after day, immense boxes, containing her personal effects, were leaving the White House for her newly-chosen abode in the West. The size and number of these boxes, with the fact of the pillaged aspect of the White House, led to the accusation, which so roused public feeling against her, that she was robbing the Nation's House, and carrying the national property with her into retirement. This accusation was unjust. Her personal effects, in all likelihood, amounted to as much as that of nearly all other Presidents' wives put together, and the vandals who roamed at large through the length and breadth of the White House were quite sufficient to account for all its missing treasures."

Apparently any effort Mrs. Lincoln may have made to improve the White House, shabby when she entered it, was lost in the final tragedy. But she did leave behind one notable family item, the elaborately carved, oversize Lincoln bed, a remarkable relic of a remarkable President.

When at last Mrs. Lincoln moved on to Chicago—"My God, Elizabeth, I can never go back to Springfield!" she had said—Washington had by no means heard the last of her. Senator Sumner took up a long struggle to obtain a pension for her. For comfort she turned to spiritualism; for activity, to schemes for obtaining the money she felt that the Republican politicians and the nation owed her. When a public-subscription scheme fell through, in the fall of 1867, she decided to sell her costly clothing. She wrote to Lizzie Keckley in Washington, had Lizzie meet her in New York to make the arrangement. She made the attempt under an assumed name but when the clothes failed to sell she discarded the incognito role and gave her story to the newspapers.

Soon the whole country was aghast. Eighteen of Mrs. Lincoln's dresses displayed for sale on Broadway! A bolt of point lace inventoried at $4,000; a point-lace shawl at $2,000; a camel's-hair shawl, $1,500; and so on down to a point-lace parasol cover at $250 and an $80 handkerchief. Only a few articles were sold, costs were $800. Mary Todd Lincoln again was berated in the public press until she wrote: "If I had committed murder in every state in this blessed union, I could not be more traduced. An ungrateful country this." Her son Robert sadly wrote his fiancée that on one subject his mother was not responsible, adding, "You could hardly believe it possible, but my mother protests to me that she is in actual want and nothing I can do or say will convince her to the contrary."

Soon G. W. Carleton and Company, New York publishers, brought out a book, *Behind the Scenes,* by Elizabeth Keckley, whose title page identified its author as "formerly a slave, but more recently modiste, and friend to Mrs. Abraham Lincoln." This book—obviously adeptly ghost-written—not only recounted the ill fated clothing sale, but also gave an intimate account of all the Lincoln years in the White House. It caused such a furor that the publishers were forced to withdraw it after a brief burst of high sales. Friends of the Lincolns bought up and destroyed so many copies that it was, in effect, suppressed.

Contemporary Washington accepted its incidents as authentic, and later historians leaned heavily on them. There was much public discussion over who actually wrote the book. Gossips said it was Jane Grey Swisshelm.

A relative of James Hamilton Busbey, a Kentucky newspaperman of the time who went to New York and became editor of the magazine *Turf, Field, and Stream*, later said it was well known in his family that Busbey wrote the book. He stated that Busbey had simply heard that Mrs. Keckley owned a large collection of letters from Mrs. Lincoln and had interviewed her and written the book at his home, 14 Carrol Place, New York City, the address given by Mrs. Keckley in her introduction.

There was still a final reverberation concerning Mrs. Lincoln's finery. When Rose Gouverneur Hoes gathered the collection of dresses of the mistresses of the White House for the Smithsonian Museum she reported that the descendants of Mrs. Lincoln "displayed no interest." The royal-purple velvet gown representing Mrs. Lincoln had to be purchased from "someone in Springfield." Robert Todd Lincoln, who by his will sealed the Lincoln papers for 25 years, had long since had his fill of the subject of his mother's dresses. But he and Mary Harlan Lincoln were by no means insensible to history. The White House owes to them an authentic and incomparable treasure, the Healy portrait of Lincoln, painted in the White House during the Civil War, which was accepted by the government and hung during the Franklin D. Roosevelt administration over the fireplace in the State Dining Room.

IO | *Man of Courage*

...JOHNSON

WHEN President Andrew Johnson and his family at last took posession of the White House they had to face the bitter years of the reconstruction of the defeated, devastated and destitute South. The very titles of the books about this period following the Civil War reflect its agony—*The Tragic Era, The Years of Hate.* Had Lincoln lived, he might have compelled a policy of temperance and tolerance. President Johnson, with the same policy, found he had to face the fact that he was fundamentally a Southern Democrat unequally pitted against the triumphant radical Northern Republicans of his own administration. Some of them were Shylocks for revenge, and some were avid for the Presidency. Public excitement was kept at fever pitch by the pursuit and killing of Booth, the trial and execution of the other conspirators, the implications against "higher-ups."

President Johnson himself did not escape accusation. Mrs. Keckley said that Mrs. Lincoln believed Andrew Johnson was in the plot which elevated him to the Presidency. Others did not hesitate to make this preposterous allegation in speeches on the floors of Congress. While this was soon cleared away, Republican leaders continued to go to any length to wash their hands of Johnson forever.

Many years later Speaker of the House Champ Clark of Missouri, made this analysis:

"The people of the North have never realized, and probably never will realize, the courage that was required for a man to stand up for the Union in Tennessee, Kentucky, West Virginia, or Maryland. The truth is that there really was no Civil War anywhere to any considerable extent outside of these 'border states.' So far as the extreme Northern States or the extreme Southern States were concerned what we term Civil War was to all intents and purposes a war between two countries foreign to each other. But in the 'border states' it was not only neighborhood against neighborhood, but family against family, father against son, husband against wife, slave against master. That Johnson or any other man had the moral and physical courage to stand up against an overwhelming sentiment in his own state in that critical era is one of the marvels of history."

Because of Johnson's leadership his section of Tennessee had furnished 40,000 soldiers to the Union cause. For this, the Southern forces penalized his family. When Johnson was made military governor of Tennessee the Confederates would not let his wife through the lines to join him at Nashville. His son-in-law, Colonel Daniel Stover, was a leader of the Union men of East Tennessee, a saboteur harried by the Confederates. Stover's organization was known as "The Bridge-Burners." His wife and Mrs. Johnson put out food for him in mountain hide-outs, as for a hunted animal. Because his health was broken by this type of life, he died at the age of thirty-five.

The President's wife, Eliza McArdle Johnson, was only fifty-eight when her husband became Chief Executive, but her strength was so depleted by tuberculosis and war hardships that she could not assume official duties. Yet she had a sturdy spirit which kept pace with the large and cheerful White House family. It included: two sons, Robert, his father's secretary, and Andrew, Jr., a teen-ager at school in Georgetown; a married daughter, Martha Johnson Patterson, with her husband, Tennessee Senator D. T. Patterson, and two children; and the widowed daughter, Mary Johnson Stover, and her three children. The Johnson's eldest son, an army surgeon, had been killed while on duty in the war, having been thrown from a "high-mettled" horse. Robert also rated eventually as a war casualty—he came out of it an alcoholic and had to be put in an institution.

Mrs. Johnson was given her first choice of White House bedrooms. She picked one of the small ones in the northwest corner. There she sat and sewed and read, played with her grandchildren and gave her husband the same sustaining counsel which had shaped his career from the day they met. Mrs. Johnson had taught her husband to read and write after their very early marriage.

Her one public appearance during her almost four years' White

House residence was at a party for her grandchildren. "At that time," reported Mary Clemmer Ames, "she was seated in one of the republican court-chairs of satin and ebony. She did not rise when the children or guests were presented, but simply said, 'My dears, I am an invalid,' and her sad, pale face and sunken eyes proved the expression." Mary Ames also described Mrs. Johnson as "a lady of benign countenance and sweet and winning manners."

All the First Lady duties devolved on her capable elder daughter Martha, no stranger to the White House. As a schoolgirl she had spent holidays from the Georgetown convent with Mrs. Polk. Mrs. Patterson now disarmed criticism by announcing, "We are plain people from the mountains of Tennessee, called here for a short time by a national calamity. I trust too much will not be expected of us."

Martha Patterson had her task of reconstruction too—the making over of the vandalized White House. This remarkable renovation was realistically recorded by Mary Clemmer Ames, who approved of Mrs. Patterson as heartily as she had disapproved of Mrs. Lincoln.

"The family of the new President arrived in June. The house looked anything but inviting. Soldiers had wandered unchallenged through the entire suites of parlors. The East Room, dirty and soiled, was filled with vermin. Guards had slept upon the sofas and carpets till they were ruined, and the immense crowds who, during the preceding years of war, filled the President's house continually had worn out the already ancient furniture. To put aside all ceremony and work incessantly was the portion of Mrs. Patterson from the beginning. It was her practice to rise very early, don a calico dress and spotless apron, and then descend to skim the milk and attend the dairy before breakfast.

"At the first reception of President Johnson, held January 1, 1866, the White House had not been renovated, and was dingy and destitute of ornament. Martha Patterson had by dint of covering its old carpets with pure linen and hiding its wounds with fresh flowers, and letting her beautiful children loose in its rooms, given it an aspect of purity, beauty and cheer to which it had long been a stranger.

"In the spring, Congress appropriated thirty thousand dollars to the renovation of the White House. After consulting various firms, Mrs. Patterson found that it would take the whole amount to furnish simply the parlors. Feeling a personal responsibility to the government for the expenditure of the money, unlike her predecessor, she determined not to surpass it. She made herself its agent, and superintended the purchases for the dismantled house herself, instead of seeking pleasure by the sea, or ease in her own mountain home. The hot summer waxed and waned only to leave the brave woman where it found her, wrestling with rags and ruins that were to be reset, repolished, 'made over good as new.' For herself? No for her country; and all this in addition to caring for husband, children, and invalid mother. The result of this ceaseless industry and self-denial was the President's house in perfect order and thoroughly renovated from top to bottom. When it was opened for the winter season, the change was apparent and obvious, even to the dullest eyes, but very few knew that the fresh, bright face of the historic house was all due to the energy, industry, taste and tact of one woman, the President's daughter."

Mary Johnson Stover, as in the old Biblical tale, apparently did not bestir herself so busily as her sister Martha. The "Olivia" letters termed her "a dignified, statuesque blonde, with a few very fine points which a fashionable butterfly once said would make any woman a belle if she knew how to make the most of them." The Johnson sisters definitely did not follow the current ultraelaborate trend in dress. They wore high necklines at a time when the gowns of their distinguished guests were cut to show the neck and shoulders.

The redecorated White House, with the exception of the East Room still under renovation, was reopened for the New Year's reception of 1867. Guests found Blue, Red and Green Parlors brightly repapered. They did not see the rich velvet carpets in these rooms— Martha Patterson had covered them to prevent their getting soiled. In making their exit, they "after quitting the Green Parlor passed through the hall to a bridge constructed at the hall window, and thus to the front grounds."

Later that month Martha Patterson's masterpiece of redecoration narrowly escaped destruction by fire, caused by the bursting of a flue. The flames raged through the conservatory, causing damages estimated at $20,000. Worse in the view of a nature-loving age, they destroyed about one third of the White House collection of rare plants, including "a Sago palm, prized not only for its rarity, but because it had been imported by George Washington." Four crews with fire engines worked for several hours, and a White House guard was overcome by smoke.

President Johnson soon split with the Republican radicals who were demanding a punitive policy toward the South. Two more formidable foes than Senator Charles Sumner of Massachusetts and Representative Thaddeus Stevens of Pennsylvania would be hard to find in American history. Sumner was the New Englander whose opinion was the last word on current art and literature. He had shown the rare political gift of being able to hold close friendships with women as diverse in viewpoints as Mary Lincoln and Kate Chase Sprague. A master tactician was Sumner.

Thad Stevens was thunder and lightning always ready to strike. His racial-equality views were based on convictions so deep that he had an intelligent Negro woman at the head of his household. It was contemporaneously published, and he made no denial, that she was his common-law wife. He was an old man, chiseled like a rock, almost six feet tall and with a crippled foot. He was, before his fight with President Johnson was over, a visibly dying man, and therefore the more dramatic. He was humorous as well as vindictive, and therefore the more dangerous.

The social spearhead of the radicals was Kate Chase Sprague. To political intelligence sharpened from earliest childhood and to beauty beyond compare Kate had added by her marriage wealth untold. She had a house at Narragansett with 80 sumptuous rooms; she had her father's estate, Edgewood, near Washington, with 40 servants; and her town house in Washington, a salon thronged with the famous. Only the dingy old White House eluded her.

Among the leading radicals was Lincoln's Secretary of War, Edwin M. Stanton, who was retained by Johnson. The assassination of Lincoln gave Stanton his opportunity to move into the national political situation with radical policies.

Under such pressure from many sources the war-tired Johnson at last took on a bitter-end fight, this time for his own honor and the prestige of the Presidency of the United States.

The first plan of the radicals was simply to draw up a formal accusation which would automatically cause the suspension of the President from office. The trial would then be prolonged until his term expired. Benjamin Franklin Wade, the president pro tempore of the Senate, that stalwart abolitionist who had been chairman of the Committee on the Conduct of the War and who with Henry Winter Davis had issued the "Wade-Davis Manifesto" condemning President Johnson's reconstruction policy, "would be called upon to replace Mr. Johnson."

Georges Clemenceau, then a young French newspaperman describing the American scene for a Paris journal wrote, "I find it hard to believe, however, that the Americans with their practical sense and love of legality, will take such extreme measures, whose legality is very doubtful." He was correct.

However, from the very month that the Johnsons threw open to the public the doors of the painstakingly redecorated White House, President Johnson and the Congress were deadlocked. The Capitol Hill view was thus given by Clemenceau: "Congress naturally feels that this is a decisive moment, and that weakness now will endanger the results of thirty years' struggle capped by four years of terrible slaughter, and wishes to prevent the Man in the White House from precipitating the country into ruin."

Reconstruction was conducted by the voting of harsh laws by Congress, the vetoing of them by Johnson and the final enactment of them by overriding the veto.

In one head-on clash with the President, Congress passed the Tenure of Office Bill, which decreed that the President had no right to dismiss any appointee who had to be ratified by the Senate. He thus could not dismiss any member of his cabinet. Johnson vetoed the bill, quoting James Madison's opinion that the clause of the Constitution providing that the executive power shall be vested in the President included the power to remove. It had been so construed by every preceding President.

During the recess of Congress in 1867 President Johnson decided to bring a test case on the Tenure of Office Act. He dismissed his high-handed Secretary of War, Edwin M. Stanton, and appointed General Ulysses S. Grant in his place. Clemenceau at that time stated that Grant accepted this office only at the request of Mr. Stanton himself, and that Grant took part in cabinet meetings only when some military question was under discussion, "for fear of being suspected of agreement with the President's policies."

When Congress reconvened in January of the election year, 1868, the Senate voted disapproval of the dismissal of Stanton and declared the post of Secretary of War to be his still. The next day Stanton went to the War Office, which Grant handed over to him without consulting President Johnson. For this action, Clemenceau said, Grant was berated by the Democrats, but by it he "won the entire and whole-hearted confidence of the Republican party." Despite all the "intrigues" of the beautiful Kate Chase Sprague, Grant was from that day forward the next President of the United States, whose inauguration exercises would not be attended by his predecessor, Andrew Johnson.

Through the remainder of January and the first half of February, Stanton, backed by Congress, held on to his preposterous position—a cabinet officer openly insubordinate to the President. Then Johnson committed the overt act—he again removed Stanton, replacing him with Lorenzo Thomas, his former adjutant general, challenging Congress to make it a test case of the Tenure of Office Act. The Senate immediately adopted a resolution declaring that the President had no authority to remove the Secretary of War. The House, on the motion of the same Mr. Covode of Pennsylvania who had made President Buchanan's life miserable, unanimously voted impeachment, referring the impeachment resolution to the Reconstruction Committee, of which Thaddeus Stevens was chairman. From the White House Johnson replied with strong statements upholding the powers of the Presidential office.

Stanton took physical possession of the office of the Secretary of War, sleeping on its couch, having his meals sent in and posting a sentinel at the door to ward off enemies, including anyone who might be sent by the President of the United States. Behind this barricade Stanton stayed from February until almost the end of May.

In the meantime this country witnessed the most fantastic spectacle which ever enlivened a campaign year, the impeachment trial of Johnson. In its final throes it was completely divested of ideological significance and stood out stark and bare as a junglelike struggle for power. It was President against Congress; Supreme Court against Senate. Chief Justice Salmon P. Chase, presiding in his black robes over a Senate turned into a trial court, had the Presidency ever in mind as he played to a gallery which included his beautiful daughter. Chase was accused of turning against his fellow radicals and using his backstage influence for Johnson's acquittal as a check to the ambitious president pro tempore, Benjamin Wade. If Wade assumed Presidential powers before the Republican convention, it was argued, he would hold the power reins there and could bid for candidacy.

The "Olivia" letters vividly revealed the intense interest in the impeachment trial, at which the President did not appear but was represented by counsel. Olivia said that men from all parts of the country were "pleading, swearing for admittance—offering untold sums for a little insignificant bit of pasteboard." Olivia was smug about it, remarking, "in the exclusive crowd which filled the galleries, it may be said there were two grand divisions—the aristocracy and the press. The first named were elevated to their seats by their social relations; the latter by the divine right of being anointed sovereigns in the world of mind." And she added, "Conspicuous amongst the limited but strictly exclusive set might be seen the delicate, *spiritual* face of Mary Clemmer Ames, of the New York *Independent*." Among the social leaders Olivia turned her brightest limelight on "that picture of delicacy and grace, arrayed in silk tinted with the shade of a dead forest leaf with dead gold ornaments to match— the queen of fashion—the wife of a Senator, the daughter of Chief Justice Chase."

While the impeachment trial was still on, a diplomatic reception was held at the White House, the President and his daughter Martha smilingly receiving officialdom from eight o'clock until eleven. Martha's husband was in the Senate, hearing everything said against her father. No member of the household could have been unaware of any part of the proceedings.

Yet this remarkable testimony was given by a White House historian: "In a quiet, unostentatious way, the President's daughters made themselves popular and bore their part in Washington society as if the impeachment of the President had never been thought of."

That same spirit emanated from their mother, Eliza McArdle Johnson, in her little upstairs room. She would countenance no change in White House routine, no cancellation of official entertainments. She insisted on the same calmness and cheerfulness in family life as before. Hers was the quiet air of certainty of acquittal. A White House employee at last brought her that verdict—the vote, 35 for impeachment, 19 against, lacking one of being a two-thirds majority. "Tears were in her eyes, but her voice was firm and she did not tremble once as she said, 'I knew he'd be acquitted; I knew it. . . . Thank you for coming to tell me,'" the messenger reported.

Andrew Johnson wanted personal vindication. Six years later he campaigned to return to the Senate, and won.

The Senate galleries were packed the day he took the oath of office, and as he took his seat they "broke into thunderous applause." He was embarrassed to find floral offerings on his desk. Benjamin Wade was there no more, and of the 35 Senators who had voted for his conviction only 13 were still in their Senate seats.

II | *Bigger Place for the New Woman*

...GRANT, HAYES, GARFIELD

AFTER THE Civil War, as after the Mexican, a succession of generals moved into the White House. But there was one notable difference in their lives there. The wives of Generals Ulysses S. Grant, Rutherford B. Hayes and James A. Garfield were women in their prime, all of them able and willing to assume and carry forward the First Lady role.

These three Midwesterners, Julia Dent Grant, Lucy Webb Hayes and Lucretia Rudolph Garfield, shared fully in their husbands' honors as they earlier had shared in their husbands' struggles from poverty to prominence. At a time when this country was developing at a breathless pace Grant, Hayes and Garfield came up in the all-American "rags to riches" tradition.

Mesdames Grant, Hayes and Garfield had also derived stamina for the exigencies of public life by going with their husbands to the Civil War battlefields, braving the rigors of Army life and nursing the wounded.

And they were part of new thought tides sweeping through the country in the 1870s. Susan B. Anthony and her National Women's Suffrage Association were rampaging over the landscape, demanding votes and equal rights for women and holding a national convention each year in Washington for the purpose of lobbying Congress and the President. Of one of Mrs. Grant's weekly audiences it was reported: "Woman suffrage was the burning question of the hour; and in this Mrs. Grant showed great interest."

Mrs. Grant approached the White House with imagination. She

conceived the idea of using it only for public receptions, turning the rest of the building to her husband for offices and keeping the family home on I Street as a private residence. But a few soundings of public opinion showed that this would never be sanctioned, and so she plunged into a round of renovation and redecoration.

General Grant's wife also decided to rise to her new position as First Lady with a change in her personal appearance. A Southern doctor of great surgical skill had popularized an operation correcting crossed eyes which he had learned in Paris. Someone told Mrs. Grant it would be the simplest thing in the world to correct this slight physical handicap. Her husband argued her out of the operation. He said he liked the way her eyes were crossed and would not have her different.

The Grant family, as it moved from I Street into the White House, was a large and oddly assorted aggregation, and never did it become anything less. Removals by deaths and marriages were quickly filled by accessions. There were four Grant children—two grown sons, Frederick Dent and Ulysses Simpson, Jr.; a beautiful daughter, Nellie; and a small boy, Jesse.

In the household also was Mrs. Grant's father, Colonel Frederick Dent, an unreconstructed Southern Democrat, never silent on the fact that his political views differed from those of his son-in-law, the President. This piquant situation was a delight to newspaper reporters, who never tired of interviewing Grandfather Dent.

One society writer of the time recorded that at the breakfast table old Mr. Dent occupied the first seat, the President sitting at his left, Mrs. Grant at his right, Nellie at the side of the President and Jesse beside his mother. Said this commentator: "The ascendancy of the Dent above the Grant family . . . has been remarked as singular. . . . perhaps the best explanation lies in the influence of Mrs. Grant over her husband." Grant's brother-in-law, General Fred Dent, was made a sort of major-domo to usher distinguished guests into the President's private office.

A member of Grant's old Army staff, Colonel O. E. Babcock, had, as Jesse Grant phrased it, "won acceptance as a regular member of the family." Babcock, with the rank of brevet brigadier general in the United States Army, went into the White House with Grant as his private secretary. Moving in also was General Adam Badeau, described by the journalist Olivia as "the historian whose duty it was to save the sands of history, act as chief custodian of the Presidential literary preserves, and at the same time keep all poachers away." Both Babcock and Badeau would later bite the hand that fed them.

A bad risk also was Grant's new brother-in-law, Abel R. Corbin, an elderly businessman who had married Grant's sister Jenny. Instead of aspiring to public office he entered into get-rich-quick negotiations with a high-powered Wall Street financial firm, that of Jay Gould and Jim Fiske, Jr. On Corbin's representations that he had enough influence with Grant to keep the President from selling gold from the U. S. Treasury, Gould and Fiske cornered the gold market. Corbin even went so far as to tell Fiske that Mrs. Grant was in on the scheme. His frantic messages to Grant to pay no attention to Wall Street gold manipulations at last aroused Grant's suspicions, and he instructed his wife to write to his sister Jenny. "Tell your husband," this letter said, "that my husband is very much annoyed by your speculations. You must close them as quick as you can." Gould got wind of this warning and sold gold, leaving his partner Fiske to take the full impact of the resulting smash. Grant broke the gold monopoly on September 24, 1869, by instructing his Secretary of the Treasury to sell $4,000,000 worth of gold from the Treasury. Panic and pandemonium was the reaction in Wall Street. That day thereafter was known as "Black Friday."

An almost perpetual White House visitor was Grant's father, Jesse Grant, even though his son had made him postmaster at Covington, Kentucky. Jesse exerted his influence on the appointments of other postmasters. Democratic papers began to say that the first requirement for federal office was to be kin to the Dents and Grants.

Describing his small-boy years in the White House, Grant's youngest son, Jesse, gave an amusing picture of the rivalry there of Grandfather Dent and Grandfather Grant. Grandfather Dent was the "courtier, with all the savoir faire of the Old South"; Grandfather Grant "a taciturn self-contained man" who had a "curious deafness." When Grandfather Dent proffered Grandfather Grant a chair, he couldn't hear, and Grandfather Dent would tell his daughter, "He is feeble and deaf as a post. He should never be allowed out without an attendant." To which Grandfather Grant would comment to his namesake: "Did you hear him, Jesse? I hope I shall not live to become as old and infirm as your Grandfather Dent." Both died during Grant's term of office.

Fred Grant, a graduate of West Point, accompanied General William Tecumseh Sherman on his trip around the world. Ulysses went to Harvard. Nellie was absorbed in parties and beaux. That left to Jesse the run of the White House and its grounds, and he was the one who later wrote about it. He installed a telescope on its roof, and night after night his father went up there with him to look at the stars. Jesse also had a microscope, camera and darkroom in which his mother took keen interest despite the fact that her eye defect prevented her seeing what her small son saw through his microscope.

Jesse Grant revealed that President Grant talked over all his important appointments with his wife. Said Jesse:

"No one understood better than father that by each appointment he set a light or digged a pit. I know what he sought, what he believed he found. Evening after evening, he talked with mother, and I listened. . . . Always his purpose was unmistakably clear to me. 'The country needs, I must find, a good man—the best man possible.' "

Ulysses S. Grant needed all the bolstering of his confidence which his wife unstintedly gave him to face the successive tempests which his appointments caused. Since he had won the Presidency on his military fame, Grant believed that he had no cabinet commitments. Political leaders, notably the powerful Senator Charles Sumner of Massachusetts, thought otherwise.

The result was contention and confusion and a tremendous turnover in high offices. To the Treasury portfolio Grant appointed A. T. Stewart, owner of the successful New York department store where the great ladies of the day did the bulk of their shopping. The Senate, under Sumner's strategy, refused to confirm Stewart on the basis of an ancient law (1789) which forbade any person "concerned in trade or commerce" to occupy that post. Grant sent a message to the Senate asking that Stewart be exempted from the statute. Senator Sumner not only checkmated a move for exemption made by Senators friendly to the President, but also forced the substitution of a Secretary of the Treasury pleasing to the radical Senators.

Grant had lost the first round with an erstwhile ally. But he had become thoroughly aroused to the forces which had thwarted his predecessor, Andrew Johnson. Using all his Presidential prestige, he forced the decimation of the Tenure of Office Act. Only enough of it remained to embarrass him a bit when he dismissed the only appointee resulting from Sumner's recommendation, John Lothrop Motley, the U. S. Ambassador to England. Motley refused to resign and held onto his nonexistent office all summer while Grant hunted a successor for him.

The bitter-end struggle between President Grant and Senator Sumner is one of the political sagas of United States history. Grant, like many of his predecessors, had ideas of expansion. He envisaged in Santo Domingo a new source of mineral wealth and a rich agricultural area in which to settle freed Negroes. He sent to the island his trusted personal secretary, General Babcock, to make an investigation. Babcock came back all enthusiasm, loaded with tropical specimens and with a tentative treaty of annexation already negotiated with one of the two rival claimants to the presidency of Santo Domingo.

Senator Sumner, as chairman of the Senate Committee on Foreign Relations, succeeded in having the Santo Domingo treaty rejected by the Senate. Grant took up the matter again in his message to the next session of Congress—"So convinced am I of the advantages to flow from acquisition . . . that I believe the subject has only to be investigated to be approved." This time, over Sumner's bellowing opposition, Grant won a Santo Domingo fact-finding commission. In the course of this controversy Sumner became so irate that he opposed the White House on all diplomatic questions, including the appointment of a joint high commission with Great Britain to settle the controversies left over from the Civil War. The Republican Senatorial caucus organizing the Forty-second Congress on March 8, 1871, removed Senator Sumner as chairman of the Foreign Relations Committee on the grounds that he was not on speaking terms with either the President or the Secretary of State. Top dog at last, Grant went on his way to 1872 re-election over Horace Greeley. But he never did get Santo Domingo.

The fall of Charles Sumner, long the political and social czar of the Capitol, was complete. A few years earlier he had married a Washington widow, Mrs. Alice Hooper. But he moved alone into the mansion he had built for her across Lafayette Park from the White House, and they were divorced. Ben: Perley Poore called him a "Prometheus Vinctus, bound to the desolate rock of a wrecked life." He died in 1874, leaving behind a bitter screed attacking the administration.

By the time he had finished with the Sumner fight President Grant had learned his political lessons well. Now he knew that Senate and House must be dominated by his men, that each great state machine should be headed by a political friend, and that machines are built by patronage. Over a rising New York Senator, Roscoe Conkling, Grant threw the magic cloak of political power and patronage. In fact, Grant took the New York state patronage away from the other New York senator, Reuben E. Fenton, former governor, and gave it to Conkling; and with it Conkling broke the powerful Fenton political machine. Grant invested Conkling with the national leadership which had been Senator Sumner's.

An erudite contemporary, Chauncey Depew, described Conkling as physically the handsomest man of his time, mentally almost a genius, and "an orator and debater of rare powers." But he was "very autocratic and dictatorial." His curly red hair and magnificent torso, developed by amateur boxing, were known to all newspaper readers.

Grant had great personal admiration for Conkling and through him was oriented more and more to the machinations of New York state politics; and to the moneyed men of New York City. After years of privations and frustrations Grant enjoyed wining and dining with these men and joining in their playboy interest in fast horses.

In the midst of Grant's first administration the Crédit Mobilier scandal broke, shocking capital and country. George Alfred Townsend, whose detective work as a newspaper reporter aided in the exposé, gave the chronology: In 1862 a Pacific railroad enterprise was started; in 1869 the cars of the Union Pacific were running from New York to San Francisco; in 1872 "the chief builders and capitalists of the enterprise appeared like common criminals at the bar of public opinion and the highest heads in Congress were dragged down for their complicity in the crime."

The Crédit Mobilier robbery of the United States Treasury took place before Grant ever entered the White House, and few of the men involved were his supporters. But it was always linked in political psychology with his administration, itself fraught with scandals.

President Grant was a driving constructive force in the city of Washington. Nowhere was the activity more intense than in the immediate environs of the White House, where the federal government co-operated by building the ornate State, War and Navy Building. West Executive Avenue, between this building and the White House, was paved. At its Pennsylvania Avenue end, great gate posts and elaborate iron gates were installed. Grant took a tremendous interest in this architectural venture, which came to be regarded as exemplifying the heavy taste of a period later facetiously labeled "Gloomy Grant."

Grant's control of the federal improvements was direct. While still in the War Department, he had caused the Office of Public Buildings and Grounds, which had charge of all federal parks and buildings, including the White House and its grounds, moved from the Interior Department to the War Department. This was done by law on March 13, 1867, two years before he became President. The purpose was to have an Army engineer in charge. As improvements started in 1871 Grant appointed as Commissioner of Public Buildings and Grounds, General O. E. Babcock, the Army engineer of his Civil War headquarters staff and his private secretary in the White House.

Babcock held both jobs. As private secretary his desk was just outside Grant's office. General Babcock supervised all the details of improving the White House. During the first administration the Grants razed the crumbling east wing and colonnade, long used as outbuildings. They built a grapery and more greenhouses and new stables. They painted the exterior, fenced and lighted the grounds and repaired the furniture to the extent of $15,000.

In January 1873 Commissioner Babcock made a report to Congress on the state of the White House which showed Mrs. Grant had not changed her views on its inadequacies. Said this report: "It hardly seems possible to state anything in favor of the house as a residence; but if thoroughly repaired it would serve its purpose admirably as an executive office."

Included in the bill of particulars that General Babcock brought against the Mansion were these items:

"Many of the floor and roof timbers in a state of decay . . . Hardly a ceiling which has not cracked, in the majority of cases the full extent of its width or length . . . One large ceiling fell last year, fortunately when the room was unoccupied . . . First story ceilings settled several inches from the weight of the partitions in the story above . . .

Basement very damp and unhealthy; yet the only portion of the building available for kitchen, laundry, offices and sleeping apartments for the servants.

"The second floor, the only place left for the occupation of the President and his family, and for his business office . . . badly arranged and inconvenient . . . No closets or clothes-presses, which are now considered indispensable."

This report brought on a renovation of the White House interior that year which took it far from its early Georgian simplicity. A judgment on it which came many years later ran: "The simple decorations of the East Room were changed into an over-ornamented salon, loaded down with crude decorations. It resembled the main salon of that time, seen in the Long Island Sound steamers."

At the time, however, the Grant renovation was much admired, and Mrs. Grant's weekly receptions, at which she had initiated the custom of having all the cabinet wives receive with her, became even more popular. Often the President himself appeared, a high compliment to the official ladies.

Costly were the costumes and elaborate the entertainments of the Grant regime. A fashionable lady's gown and accessories often cost more than $1,000. The average cost of a Grant state dinner was put at $700.

Even during the vacation season the Grant way of life was elaborate. The very cataloguing of the trappings they annually took from the White House to their seaside cottage at Long Branch, New Jersey, showed it. One such account began:

"The President and his family arrived here by special train at fifteen minutes past five in the afternoon in a Pullman palace car. The President's baggage had been arriving all day. . . . Eight furniture wagons had been driven down Ocean Avenue to the President's cottage containing the federal baggage. Four carriages and a buggy had been towed in the train of furniture wagons, comprising a seaside phaeton for Miss Nelly, a two-seat buggy for the President and a friend, and the huge high-backed English carriage for the united family, a dog cart for the boys, a modest rockaway for Mrs. Grant's accomodation. . . ."

The Grant administration improvements forged ahead, particularly during the summer absences of President and Congress, until in his annual message in 1873 Grant said: "Washington is rapidly assuming the appearance of a capital of which the Nation may well be proud. It is now one of the most sightly cities in the country, and can boast of being the best paved." Financially, however, it proved to have been paved mostly with good intentions, as the entire District government was pulled into bankruptcy by the failure in New York of Jay Cooke and Co.

During the Congressional sessions Washington society columns were filled with the activities of Miss Nellie Grant of the piquantly beautiful face. She "was almost daily seen on the prominent thoroughfares in a light phaeton behind a span of black ponies, usually accompanied by her most intimate friend, Miss Anna Barnes, daughter of the Surgeon General of the Army." At a White House evening affair "Miss Grant and Miss Barnes were of the receiving party, while General Babcock, in his usual courteous manner, presented the visitors." Again, "Miss Barnes wore a black silk and Roman sash. Miss Grant, over a rose-colored silk, wore a Paris muslin and valenciennes lace overskirt, gracefully looped."

Nellie Grant's popularity soared to a mighty triumph when she was taken abroad by Secretary of the Navy and Mrs. Adolph E. Borie, who had been family friends of the Grants before they entered the White House. Mrs. Borie, who had gone abroad for a rest, found that instead she was chaperoning a sensation. Robert C. Schenck, U. S. Minister to England, who introduced the game of poker into British society, and Grant's historian, Adam Badeau, serving for a time as consul general in England, gave Nellie a great whirl. She was presented to Queen Victoria. On shipboard coming home she met the handsome, blond Algernon Charles Frederick Sartoris, a nephew of the famous actress, Fanny Kemble. Their romance resulted on May 21, 1874, in one of the most spectacular of White House weddings. Nellie Grant was not yet nineteen.

The invitation to that wedding, which mentioned the name of neither contracting party, the satiny white ribbon on which the dinner menu was printed, the 18-page illustrated supplement of the New York *Graphic* commemorating the event—these and many more souvenirs were saved for future generations by Nellie Grant's closest friend and ranking bridesmaid, Miss Anna Barnes.

The invitation list was limited to 150 of the highest-ranking officials and closest family friends. The wedding presents on display in the

Oval Library upstairs were valued at from $60,000 to $75,000. The Brussels point lace on Miss Nellie's white satin wedding gown cost $5,000.

Under the great floral wedding bell centering a window-darkened, gas-illuminated East Room, the couple, flanked by four bridesmaids on each side, repeated their vows. This bell swung from a "floral arch" whose intricacies included floral monograms of the bride and groom. Close at hand was a small table with a white silk cover, whereon were the ceremonial pens with which the wedding ceremony would be officially witnessed—by Secretary of State Hamilton Fish and Sir Edward Thornton, the British Ambassador.

The bridesmaids were all dressed alike in white silk. Mrs. Grant's dress was of black silk with ruffles and puffs of black illusion. The groom was in full evening dress, his best man, Colonel Frederick Grant, in full uniform. The President wore evening dress.

Bridal party and guests proceeded to the State Dining Room "wherein was spread a table that has probably never been excelled in this country for richness, artistic skill, or systematic arrangement." From the pyramid of the "pearly-white, flower-crowned" bridal cake extended a decoration of natural flowers. Gala were miniature flags blazoning: "Success to the President," "Success to the Supreme Court," "Success to the Army," "Success to the Navy" and "Hail Columbia."

To New York went the bridal couple in the "Pullman Palace Car," accompanied by the Grant relatives and Miss Barnes. The New York farewell was almost as spectacular as the Washington wedding. The *Graphic's* toast to the departing Mrs. Sartoris ended with: "America keeps fragrant memory of the maiden whom England gains as a matron." And Walt Whitman topped this with a poem, "A Kiss to the Bride," which closed:

> "O youth and health! O sweet Missouri Rose! O bonny bride!
> Yield thy red cheeks today unto a Nation's loving kiss."

Off sailed Nellie, to return for a White House visit two years later with her first baby. After a few more years of marriage she came back with three children to make America her home again, separated from Mr. Sartoris. Late in life she had her happy ending—marriage with a sweetheart of her early youth.

Another noteworthy wedding made more spectacular the gay life of the Grants. Their son Fred chose one of the beautiful Kentucky-born Honore sisters, Ida. The ceremony was staged in Chicago by Miss Honore's society-queen sister Bertha—Mrs. Potter Palmer. The Potter Palmers presented the bride with $10,000 worth of diamonds, in addition to her wedding dress of white satin covered with rose-point lace. The President and Mrs. Grant went to Chicago for the ceremony. The Palmers' infant son Honore was present on a satin pillow in a handmade dress three yards long.

Colonel Fred Grant received a Washington assignment and took his young wife to the White House to live. Mrs. Potter Palmer was often a White House guest, which added to her growing social prestige in Chicago. It was Fred Grant's ambition to have a son born in the White House to bear the name of Ulysses S. Grant. However, when the baby arrived it was named for the First Lady, Julia Dent Grant, and was christened in the East Room. Granddaughter Julia would grow up to marry a Russian nobleman, Count Cantacuzene.

From first to last the Grant administration was bedeviled by scandals. The two most dramatic were right in the Grant inner circle during their last year in the White House. One was the Belknap case, the other the Babcock case.

Secretary of War General W. W. Belknap occupied the Sumner mansion on Lafayette Square, close to the White House. Belknap's cabinet salary fell short of full support of his fashionable wife and her sister and their spectacular salon. But money miraculously materialized from the distaff side of the menage and continued to do so even after Belknap's wife Carrie died and he married her sister.

The source of these funds, testimony later brought out, was chicanery concerned with the lucrative Fort Sill trading post in Indian territory. A New Yorker, C. P. Marsh, said he had made an agreement with Mrs. Carrie Belknap whereby he was to be appointed head of the Fort Sill trading post. But the occupant of that paying position did not care to give it up and so gave Marsh $12,000 annually not to take it from him. Half this money went from Marsh to Mrs. Belknap and, after her death, to her husband and sister.

Grant accepted Belknap's resignation on the very day before his impending impeachment. The impeachment trial proceeded, but since Belknap was no longer in the cabinet, his attorneys made the legal point that he could not be impeached. Belknap was freed.

Grant was much criticized for allowing his Secretary of War to resign—indeed escape—under fire, but Grant remained serene. Many years later his son Jesse revealed that under the chivalric code of honor of that day Grant had demanded the resignation—to protect the name of a woman, the new Mrs. Belknap. According to his son's story, Grant believed that until impeachment was upon him Belknap "had performed with no faintest suspicion of the real situation."

Belknap had convinced Grant that his sister-in-law, later his wife, had been able to make the two men involved believe that the Secretary of War was in a position to dictate the appointment—a matter which concerned only the Interior Department—of post traders and was governed in such appointments by her recommendations. Jesse Grant also gave the end of the story: "Mrs. Belknap took herself to Europe and remained there. The general returned to private life, discredited and disgraced in the eyes of the world, but to father and me an upright, chivalrous man, worthy of all respect."

From what he had been told by his father, Jesse Grant also bore witness that never for a moment did his father question the honesty of that White House major-domo, O. E. Babcock. He attributed what happened to Babcock entirely to the gentleman's "passion for helpfulness" which had resulted in his being "imposed upon."

Babcock fell before the onslaught of a Presidentially ambitious reformer, Secretary of the Treasury Benjamin H. Bristow, who started an investigation of whisky rings then evading taxes. The most pernicious were in St. Louis, from whom Babcock's pickings were said to include cigar boxes in which were thousand-dollar bills, diamonds, fine liquor stocks and receipted hotel bills. It was estimated that Babcock had been given $25,000 in cash and gifts of greater value.

Confronted with the evidence against Babcock, Grant wrote across the back of an envelope, "Let no guilty man escape," meaning also, his son said, "let no innocent man suffer." This inscription cleared the way for Babcock to be brought to trial in St. Louis. Grant wanted to go there and testify for Babcock as a character witness, but was persuaded not to, and instead sent a strong deposition which cleared his right-hand man. However, when Babcock got back from the sensational revelations in St. Louis things were not the same at the

White House. Grant dropped Babcock as private secretary, and he departed from his desk just outside the executive office door. To Babcock remained only his position of Commissioner of Public Buildings and Grounds, which he held until a few days before President Hayes entered the White House. Grant also called for and received the resignation of Secretary of the Treasury Bristow, considering him nothing less than traitorous for his attack on Babcock.

Grant himself must have reluctantly reached the conclusion that some of his appointments had not been good, for in his last address to Congress he said: "It was my fortune, or misfortune, to be called to the office of Chief Executive without previous political training. Mistakes have been made, as all can see and I admit. . . . Failures have been errors of judgment not of intent."

In this apologetic atmosphere, with reform movements rampant, the solid accomplishments of Grant were somewhat lost sight of— better feeling between North and South, a sound money policy, signing of the first reciprocity treaty with Hawaii, which began the development of American interests in the Pacific, and the great Treaty of Washington, which peacefully settled all outstanding claims and controversies between the United States and Great Britain.

To the last the Grants were socially triumphant.

The nomination of Rutherford B. Hayes, governor of Ohio, by the Republicans in 1876 astounded the nation, and his election over a strong Democratic candidate, Samuel J. Tilden, was even more of a political miracle than his nomination. Tilden won in the popular vote by a half million. Hayes was elected by one vote in the electoral college—if the votes of Louisiana, South Carolina and Georgia were his. They were as cast by the electors chosen by the carpetbag governments there. The Democrats had counterclaims. However, the Republicans held that Rutherford B. Hayes had received 185 electoral votes to Tilden's 184 and was the President-elect.

Since the controversy still raged, a commission was formed by Congress to review the election. James G. Blaine proclaimed this course highly unconstitutional. The commission consisted of three Republicans and two Democrats from the Republican Senate, three Democrats and two Republicans from the Democratic House and four judges from the Supreme Court, who were to select a fifth. Since the two parties were equally represented at this point, the deciding vote presumably would be cast by the fifteenth man, who was expected to be an independent who had voted for Tilden. However, this gentleman, at the last moment, was elected by the Democratic Illinois legislature as a Democratic Senator, and a Republican was chosen in his place, which augured final triumph for Hayes.

The elaborate election review, which took the commissioners into the disputed states, continued until the very eve of the inauguration. The President-elect and Mrs. Hayes started for Washington not yet knowing whether or not they would ever enter the White House. En route they received the message that Hayes had officially been declared elected.

March 4 that year fell on Sunday. President Ulysses S. Grant was taking no chance on an "interim" in this tense situation. To the White House on Saturday night, March 3, he invited as dinner guests the President-elect and Mrs. Hayes. He made of it a very elaborate affair, with covers laid for 36, six wine glasses and a big bouquet at each plate and a pink azalea ten feet high behind the chair of Mrs. Hayes. The entire Grant cabinet attended. Present also were Nellie Grant Sartoris and her husband, Frederick Grant and his wife, U. S. Grant, Jr., Jesse Grant and Webb C. Hayes, who was coming in as his father's secretary. There, too, were the Chief Justice of the United States and Mrs. Waite. At midnight Hayes was whisked into the Red Room, next to the State Dining Room, where, unknown to most of the guests, Chief Justice Waite administered the oath of office to President-elect Hayes, with Secretary of State Hamilton Fish as witness. The signed oath was given into the custody of the Secretary of State. President Hayes took the oath with uplifted hand, did not use a Bible, repeated it on the Sacred Book at public ceremonies on Monday, March 5.

Mrs. Hayes was hailed by the press as a dress reformer, wearing at the inauguration "merely rich black silk with real lace"; at the Grant state dinner, "cameo-tinted silk, high in the neck, no jewels"; at her first reception, "a toilette remarkable for simple elegance rather than brilliancy or cost."

Mary Clemmer Ames, studying Mrs. Hayes on the inauguration stand as her husband made his address, wrote: "A fair woman between two little children looks down. She has a singularly gentle and winning face. It looks out from the bands of smooth dark hair with that tender light in the eyes which we have come to associate always with the Madonna. I have never seen such a face reign in the White House. I wonder what the world of Vanity Fair will do with it? Will it frizz that hair?—powder that face?—draw those sweet fine lines away with pride?"

Mrs. Ames, continuing to write many an admiring article, was able to let her public know that Vanity Fair didn't frizz that hair nor powder that face. And Mrs. Hayes sent Mrs. Ames bouquets from the White House conservatory, which she acknowledged with poetry.

President and Mrs. Rutherford B. Hayes were a serious-minded and cultured couple. Both had worked hard for an education. Rutherford had been an orphan boy, Lucy the daughter of a widow. For a time Lucy was the only girl student at the Ohio Wesleyan University, Delaware, Ohio. Later she was graduated from the Cincinnati Wesleyan Woman's College. Rutherford obtained his law degree at Harvard.

Their early married life had been spent in Cincinnati, a city of remarkable culture. Eight children had been born to Rutherford and Lucy Hayes, three of them dying in infancy. When they entered the White House their son Webb had just finished at Cornell University, Birchard was in Harvard Law School and Rutherford was a student at Cornell. Fanny, their only daughter, was nine years old, and her little brother Scott was six.

Mrs. Hayes brought morning worship into the White House, half-past-eight breakfast invariably being followed by prayers. Her Sunday evening hymn-singing, participated in by cabinet and Congressmen, became famous. Representative William McKinley of Ohio was among those booming out "Blest Be the Tie That Binds," the hymn which regularly closed the song fest.

Every night was reception night with Mrs. Hayes. When the day's work was over she considered herself ready to receive all who might care to drop in and see her. Said one chronicler, "These quite informal evening gatherings, where all was bright and cheerful and of good report, became the distinctive social feature of Mrs. Hayes' regime at the White House." It was a political move, too, creating good feeling among many who had been calling the Hayes election a fraud.

Mrs. Hayes belonged to the Methodist Episcopal Church, and she and her husband walked each Sunday to the nearest one, Foundry, and worshiped there.

Very early in the administration, April 19, 1877, the President and

Mrs. Hayes bowed to diplomatic usage and permitted wine to be served at the state dinner given that night to two Russian grand dukes, Alexis and Constantin. Soon after, they gave notice that no wine whatever would be the invariable future rule so long as they were in the White House. This edict resulted in Mrs. Hayes being referred to throughout the land as "Lemonade Lucy." It brought gibes at her husband also. At one time when he had scored a notable political victory a wag remarked "buttermilk will flow like water at the White House!" Ben: Perley Poore, the famous journalist of the day, claimed that, without the knowledge of Mrs. Hayes, oranges that had been filled with old Santa Croix rum were served at diplomatic dinners. Hayes, in his diary, chortled: "The joke of the Roman punch oranges was not on us but on the drinking people. My orders were to flavor them rather strongly with the same flavor that is found in Jamaica rum. This took! There was not a drop of spirits in them!"

Hayes said in his diary that the no-liquor decision was his, and that he had made it for three reasons: first, that it was right, wise and necessary; second, he owed it to the large support given him by friends of temperance; third, he believed it would strengthen the Republican party by winning to it many who otherwise would join the political temperance party.

In June 1877 the President and Mrs. Hayes and their cabinet took a swing through the Northeast. When the Hayes party reached Providence, Rhode Island, they were given a demonstration of the telephone by Professor Alexander Graham Bell and Fred A. Gower. The conversation was between Hayes and Bell. Said Bell: "Mr. President, I am duly sensible of the great honor conferred upon me in thus for the first time presenting the speaking telephone to the attention of the President of the United States. . . . I am speaking with you through thirteen miles of wire, without the use of any galvanic current on the line. . . . I shall be very glad to hear something from you in reply, if you please." Said President Hayes: "Please speak a little more slowly." However, it was also recorded that "a gradually increasing smile wreathed his lips, and wonder shone in his eyes more and more." Hayes had both telephone and telegraph installed in the White House.

The Hayeses' travels through the Northeast and South during the first White House year dispelled the coolness which had arisen from

The Family Dining Room of the White House just prior to the 1902 restoration.

The Green Room as restored by Theodore Roosevelt.

the contested election. Soon he was regarded as a capable President with a strong cabinet who could concentrate on good administration since he definitely would not run for re-election.

The year 1877 ended and the New Year began with great festivities at the White House. House guests that week end were the Ohio friends who had been present at the Hayeses' wedding, for December 30 was their silver anniversary. A clerk had written the invitations to this celebration, but President Hayes himself had inscribed across them, "I hope you will come," and had addressed them in his own hand. That Sunday afternoon in the Blue Parlor the President and Mrs. Hayes renewed their vows. Mrs. Hayes wore her wedding gown of white flowered satin, with the same bridesmaid standing by her side, the same preacher, Dr. L. D. McCabe, of Delaware, Ohio, reading the lines. Following the ceremony, Dr. McCabe baptized the two younger Hayes children, Fanny and Scott, and Lucy Hayes Herron, infant daughter of Mr. and Mrs. John W. Herron, there as members of the wedding party. This visit of the Herrons resulted in a White House invitation for their seventeen-year-old daughter Helen, many years later a First Lady, Mrs. Taft.

The next night, New Year's Eve, the public reception celebrating the silver wedding was held. At nine o'clock, to Mendelssohn's Wedding March, President and Mrs. Hayes descended the stairs, followed by the house guests, two by two, and proceeded to the East Room where they received in front of the east windows. The President was in evening dress, Mrs. Hayes "in white silk, with draperies of white brocade, the heart-shaped neck filled with tulle, and the half-sleeves ending with lace. . . . Her only ornament was a silver comb fastening back her heavy bands of glossy black hair."

And the next day came the traditional New Year's reception, when first all officialdom, and then the general public, poured through the White House.

President and Mrs. Hayes took a great interest in adding distinction to the social events of the White House. The charts for their state dinners were elaborate and heavily ornamented, with the menu of each inscribed in the central plaque, which was surrounded by the names of the guests. They introduced the White House crest, a golden American eagle, similar to the one used on coins, at the top of the engraved invitation.

Mrs. Hayes also brought to the White House the oldest, oddest and most tenacious of national capital customs, the annual Egg Rolling on Easter Monday. When Congress passed a law closing the Capitol grounds to children rolling eggs because they were ruining the grass, Mrs. Hayes opened the White House grounds to them.

In his first message to Congress, President Hayes went vigorously into the subject of Civil Service reform, urging "the public advantages of making all nominations, as nearly as possible, impersonal." He chose the New York Custom House as the place to start his attack. As it progressed President Hayes became more and more determined that an example should be made of the men at its head, Chester A. Arthur, the Grant appointee as Collector of Customs, and A. B. Cornell, Naval Officer of the Custom House. Cornell was at that time chairman of the Republican State Committee in New York; Arthur was second-high man in the Conkling political machine.

That Chester A. Arthur had made a better record than many of his predecessors and had been an able administrator was beside the point. Hayes ordered the removal of Arthur and Cornell and appointed Theodore Roosevelt, father of a future President, Collector of Customs and L. Bradford Prince Naval Officer.

Senator Roscoe A. Conkling rose in his might against the Hayes nominations. He told the Senators it was not a personal fight—he was seeking to preserve the dignity of the Senate itself. Hayes dryly wrote in his diary, "I am now in a contest on the question of the right of Senators to dictate or control nominations." The Senate responded to the Conkling call and defeated the nominations.

The next summer, when Congress was not in session, President Hayes suspended Arthur and Cornell and promoted to their places two men already in the Custom House, E. A. Merritt as Collector and S. W. Burt as Naval Officer. Theodore Roosevelt had died in the interim.

Public opinion swerved to the side of Hayes and made itself felt in petitions to Congress. The Senate, when it reconvened, put off consideration of the distasteful subject. The last day of January 1879 President Hayes sent a pressing message to Congress, in which he was able to quote General Thomas L. James, Postmaster of New York City, who had set up a model Civil Service system, as follows: "The post-office is a business institution, and should be run as such. It is my deliberate judgment that I and my subordinates can do more for the party of our choice by giving the people of this city a good and efficient postal service than by controlling primaries or dictating nominations." Conkling raged, but the Senate confirmed the Hayes Custom House appointees. The Custom House fight was more fateful than was immediately apparent.

By the time the nomination of a new Republican candidate was in order the luster of fame which Secretary of the Treasury John Sherman had rubbed up by the New York Custom House exposé paled beside the furor over General Grant, just back in this country after a triumphal around-the-world tour. He was met at San Francisco by a third-term "draft" which had its chief power in the New York machine led by Conkling and Arthur. Sherman, in need of a powerful campaign manager at the convention in Chicago, turned to the conciliatory and persuasive James A. Garfield. Garfield was doggedly true to this trust, but turned out to be the John Alden of American politics. When it was evident to all that Sherman could not muster enough votes, Garfield accepted the nomination on the demand of the delegates for a compromise candidate. The man who handed him the biggest block of delegates was James G. Blaine. No slightest yielding of Roscoe Conkling, managing for Grant, aided in this compromise selection. It was made possible by Garfield on the convention floor by breaking the unit rule, so that the count was by Congressional districts and not by states. On every ballot the count for Grant was 306, and the Conkling men who so voted were thereafter dubbed the "Stalwarts." The "reform" forces having won the nomination, the party now needed the Stalwarts' strength to win the election. Chester A. Arthur was chosen as Vice-Presidential nominee.

President Hayes was so jubilant over the nomination of Garfield that he swallowed the Arthur pill with scarcely a murmur. To him the election of Garfield, the man who had made the Hayes-Tilden election investigation in disputed Louisiana, would mean a vindication by vote of the people of his own right to the office he had held for more than three years. In his diary he wrote: "The sop thrown to Conkling in the nomination of Arthur only serves to emphasize his defeat. He was so crushed that from sheer sympathy this bone was thrown to him."

While President Hayes took no part in the Garfield campaign, he timed the longest trip of the many he made in office for August and September 1880, just preceding the October hustings. Mrs. Hayes always accompanied him on his trips, and this swing was the climax of her career. Wherever the couple appeared Hayes's motto was quoted: "He serves his party best who serves his country best." Mrs. Hayes was everywhere feted by the fast-growing Women's Christian Temperance Union for her White House total-abstinence rule. The Hayes party visited Omaha, Cheyenne, Salt Lake City, Virginia City, San Francisco, Sacramento, Portland, Seattle, Los Angeles, Tucson, Santa Fe and Denver. In California Hayes was hailed as the first President ever to visit that state during his term of office. At San Jose Mrs. Hayes was presented by the W.C.T.U. with an impressive silk banner inscribed with her name and the line from the Bible, "She hath done what she could."

As the time approached for the Hayes family to leave the White House the outpouring of appreciation of Mrs. Hayes as typifying "the new woman" resulted in her being called "the most idolized woman in America." One analyst put it this way: "She, in lending additional strength to her husband's administration, commanded increased respect for her sex. In her successful career as the first lady of the land was outlined the future possibilities of her sex in all other positions and conditions."

To Mrs. Hayes the women of Illinois gave six great volumes of personal tribute, every sheet vellum inscribed with a notable autograph, the first signature being that of a former First Lady who had also banned wines at the White House, Mrs. James K. Polk. Henry Wadsworth Longfellow, John Greenleaf Whittier and Oliver Wendell Holmes wrote their tributes in verse. Whittier's ran:

> Her presence lends its warmth and health
>   To all who come before it;
> If woman lost us Eden, such
>   As she alone restore it.

It was already well known that such mementoes of the current scene would be preserved for history. Already the President and Mrs. Hayes were making a lasting shrine of their times at their home, Speigel Grove, Fremont, Ohio. Each summer of the Hayes administration they spent several weeks there, partially for the purpose of giving it historic association. They named trees for their most famous visitors. There they gathered meaningful antiques and a large library. This collection was to be carried forward by their son Webb. He purchased for it, at auction, the desk used by all Presidents from Lincoln to Arthur. The iron gates that Grant installed on West Executive Avenue eventually found their way to Speigel Grove when it had become a historic shrine by presentation to the state of Ohio. A Daniel Huntington painting of Mrs. Hayes, with symbolic frame made in Cincinnati, was given to the White House by the W.C.T.U., Miss Frances E. Willard making the presentation to President Garfield four days after President and Mrs. Hayes had returned to their Ohio home. Her address was full of praise for Lucy Hayes.

But perhaps the greatest tribute to Mrs. Hayes came from her own husband. After reviewing her varied life he summed it up in a remarkable passage from which are culled these phrases:

"engaged in the benevolent enterprises of the time . . . a traveller, familiar with all parts of the United States . . . familiar with all sorts and descriptions of men and women, farmers, mechanics, artists, scholars, authors, clergymen, miners, ranchmen, sailors, fishermen, cowboys, soldiers, camp followers, hospital people, the very poor and the very rich; a matchless fisherwoman; delighted with all fine animals and knowing them; in love with flowers, gardening, and farming; always and everywhere at home; knowing more people, and known to more people than, perhaps, any other woman of her time."

The President and Mrs. Hayes insisted on having President Garfield's aged mother as their house guest as soon as the family arrived from Mentor, Ohio, on March 2. The elder Mrs. Garfield thus moved into the White House two days in advance of her son.

One newspaper recorded: "On Inauguration Day, after taking the oath of office in the presence of a great multitude, the President reverently kissed the Bible; then, turning about, he kissed first his mother and then his wife. We believe there was no precedent for this recognition of his family." It was also reported that this gesture of President Garfield was most pleasing to the spectators who "rent the air with huzzas."

Lucretia Garfield, always called "Crete" by her husband, was neither temperance exponent nor suffragist, but was definitely the "new woman" type. Society editors noted while her husband was in Congress she did not spend her time scattering calling cards, as did the rest of women in Washington official life, but could be found deep in studies in the Library of Congress. The Garfields lived in a literary atmosphere so intense as to be almost esoteric. Their highly intellectual circle in Ohio was a cult, in which Garfield was a major prophet. In Washington the very exclusive literary society of which they were the stars had vitality enough to survive for many a decade.

Mrs. Garfield had a sustaining philosophy, worked out some years before she became First Lady. As she was kneading one of the huge batches of bread required by a big family in those pre-bakery days, it had come to her as an inspiration that she could overcome her dislike of baking bread by taking a special interest in that task.

"The whole of life grew brighter," she wrote. "The very sunshine seemed flowing down through my spirit into the white loaves, and now I believe my table is furnished with better bread than ever before; and this truth, old as creation, seems just now to have become fully mine—that I need not be the shrinking slave of toil, but its regal master."

Though a little less positive in her ways than either Mrs. Grant or Mrs. Hayes, Mrs. Garfield was deeply involved in her husband's career. When James G. Blaine decided to become Secretary of State under Garfield, he wrote in his letter of acceptance: "I wish you would say to Mrs. Garfield that the knowledge that she desires me in your Cabinet is more valuable to me than even the desire of the President-elect himself. Indeed, I would not think of going into the Cabinet at all if Mrs. Garfield was not friendly and favorable. Please read this letter to her and to her alone."

Clara Barton, who had been blocked in the Johnson, Grant and Hayes administrations in her campaign to make this country a party to the Geneva convention establishing the international Red Cross, won approval first from Garfield, then from Blaine. She organized the National Association of the Red Cross, with the idea that President Garfield would be its head. In other countries the custom had been to have the Red Cross headed by the highest executive. Instead, President Garfield insisted that honor should be conferred on Miss Barton, and she was accorded the place.

The Garfields had a constructive plan for the White House. They intended to base what refurnishing they did on research. The President noted that early in April, during the second month of his administration, he and his wife drove out to the Library of Congress to ask the librarian to look into the history of the White House and its contents, "of which very little seems to be known."

The White House family, when all members were home, consisted of two boys, Harry, eighteen, and James, sixteen, both of whom were being tutored to enter college; a daughter, Mollie, fourteen; and two little boys, Irwin, eleven, and Abram, nine. President Garfield was said to devote his meal hours to the education of his children—"after asking questions on some interesting point of Harry or James or Mollie to draw them out, explaining it at considerable length, instructing by the Socratic method as it were."

The happier side of the first four Garfield months was almost lost sight of, then and later, in the titanic struggle taking place first within the White House walls and later on the floor of Congress. The New York machine had the impression that a pre-election conference with Garfield had resulted in his promise that the Stalwarts would be accorded all the New York patronage if they campaigned and helped win the election. Garfield's friends have always held that he would never have made such a promise. Close students of Senator Conkling and Vice President Arthur have held that they would never have settled for less. At any rate, they made every effort to collect in full.

Furious when Blaine was made Secretary of State, they demanded a Stalwart as Secretary of the Treasury. Garfield did not oblige, and his choice of a New York Civil Service reformer for the Postmaster General mollified them not at all. However, Garfield made good on his intention to consider the claims of all factions. On the invitation of the President, Senator Conkling spent two hours with him at the White House on March 20, reviewing the entire New York situation. Garfield said in his journal that he told Conkling he must recognize some of the men who had supported him in Chicago, breaking with the Conkling machine.

The President sent to the Senate nine appointments agreed upon with Conkling, and the Stalwarts were jubilant. The newspapers started calling this complete surrender to the Stalwarts, and Blaine protested to Garfield. Suddenly Garfield sent to the Senate another list apparently all his own. Grant's biographer, Badeau, was sent from London to Copenhagen, which would not be pleasing to the ex-President. Merritt, in charge of the New York Custom House, was promoted to Badeau's former spot of consul general at London. And in Merritt's place Garfield appointed Judge W. H. Robertson, who had led the revolt against Conkling. Garfield's own comment was: "This brings on the contest at once and will settle the question whether the President is registering clerk of the Senate or President of the United States. Summed up in a single sentence, this is the question: shall the principal port of entry in which more than 90% of all our customs duties are collected be under the control of the administration or under the local control of a factional senator. I think I win in this contest."

To the White House went another illustrious caller, Vice President Chester A. Arthur. He asked that Robertson's name be withdrawn to save the Republicans from defeat in the next election. On this Garfield's comment was: "Of course I deprecate war, but if it is brought to my door the bringers will find me at home." Said Arthur: "Garfield has not been square, nor honorable, nor truthful with Conkling. . . . Garfield, spurred by Blaine by whom he is easily led, has broken every pledge made to us, and not only that, but he seems to have wished to do it in the most offensive way."

Ex-President Grant wrote President Garfield an angry letter which concluded, "I ought not to be humiliated by seeing my personal friends punished for no other offence but their friendship and support." President Garfield replied with, "I am sure you will agree with me that worthy and competent men should not be excluded from recognition because they opposed your nomination at Chicago. . . . It is my purpose to be just to all."

To force action on his Custom House appointment President Garfield withdrew five of the New York appointments he had made at Conkling's behest. Even pro-Conkling Senators began to concede that Garfield would win when the Conkling appointment came to a vote. At noon on May 16 the two New York Senators, Roscoe Conkling and Thomas C. Platt, suddenly and simultaneously presented their resignations to the Senate. Opposition to Garfield was over, the Robertson nomination was confirmed on May 18 and Garfield sent back to the Senate the New York nominations he had withdrawn. Instead of being vindicated by re-election by the New York legislature as they had expected, Conkling and Platt found themselves replaced and discarded.

At the very height of this fight Mrs. Garfield had a serious attack of malaria, and when she at last was better her husband took her to Elberon, New Jersey, near Long Branch.

Garfield returned to Washington to wind up the details of the fiscal year. He intended to rejoin his convalescing wife immediately after attending graduation exercises at his alma mater, Williams College, where he planned to enter his two sons as freshmen for the next year. It was to be the twenty-fifth anniversary celebration of his graduating class of the year 1856. Along the route, entertainments were arranged. The Garfield cabinet, all packed up to go their separate summer ways, were giving him a spectacular send-off at the Pennsylvania Station. Suddenly two bullets whizzed by Secretary of State Blaine and hit their mark, President James A. Garfield. One grazed his arm, the other—and eventually fatal—shot was in the back near the spine. Shouted his maniacal assassin, Charles Guiteau, so the July 3 New York *Herald* reported, "I am a Stalwart of the Stalwarts. Arthur is President now." Other publications stated that when Guiteau was arrested there was found on his person a copy of the New York *Herald* in which he had marked an article bitterly attacking Garfield for his "double-dealing" with Conkling in the matter of the New York appointments.

By all odds the ablest account of the Garfield tragedy was written in the letters of Mrs. James G. Blaine to members of her family. She dashed to the station where Garfield was shot, and to the White House ahead of the slow cavalcade carrying him there, reporting, "I stood with Mrs. MacVeagh in the hall when a dozen men bore him above their heads, stretched on a mattress, and as he saw us and held us with his eye, he kissed his hand to us." It was to her the wounded Garfield said: "Whatever happens, I want you to promise to look out for Crete" and "Don't leave me until Crete comes." Mrs. Blaine told how the White House was running at sixes and sevens during Garfield's long, long fight for life. She noted and disapproved of the woman doctor included among the medical consultants on the Garfield case. She pictured the "frail, fatigued, desperate, but firm and quiet" Mrs. Garfield.

Mrs. Blaine, whose trunk remained ready for the trip to Maine, told of how unbearable that summer was. In August she wrote: "You can't imagine anything so vile as Washington. It seems like a weed by the wayside, covered with dust, too ugly for notice." When the heat continued into September, decision was made that the President must be taken to the cooling ocean breezes at Elberon, New Jersey. To Secretary of State James G. Blaine this posed another question: "Should Arthur be brought to the front, and how, and if this be done, how shall he be retired?" Nothing was done about it.

At Mrs. Garfield's request, Mrs. Blaine again gave up Maine and went with the Presidential party to West End Hotel, Long Branch, about a mile from the Franklyn cottage, to which Garfield was taken. Said she, "Every evening, the whole Cabinet, with its wife, drive over to see the doctors and Mrs. Garfield, but I cannot explain why everything is so unsatisfactory." Garfield died there September 19. Mrs. Blaine saw the courageous and self-controlled Mrs. Garfield through the elaborate state funeral and the trip back to Ohio. She also witnessed and chronicled the long-drawn-out and bizarre trial of the killer; and grimly and gladly made notation when he was hanged, almost a year later.

Robert Todd Lincoln, Secretary of War in the Garfield cabinet, is authority for the fact that the cabinet never once met to transact any business during the 80-odd days of Garfield's illness. Although its members and their wives met at the White House and later at Franklyn Cottage nightly, the conversation centered completely on the condition of the President.

Lucretia Garfield lived to be eighty-six years old, and to see her son, James R. Garfield, Secretary of the Interior under President Theodore Roosevelt.

I2 | *Era of Elegance*

...ARTHUR, CLEVELAND

PRESIDENT Chester Alan Arthur of elite New York inspected his new home, the Executive Mansion, and firmly said: "I will not live in a house looking this way. If Congress does not make an appropriation, I will go ahead and have it done and pay for it out of my own pocket. I will not live in a house like this."

Just how it did look had been described by a Garfield visitor earlier that year of 1881: "The place is now full of modern abominations in upholstery and garish gilding, and all the rooms look staring, pretentious and Frenchy. The old port-wine colored mahogany sofas and chairs which were in the State Parlors in Lincoln's time were better than anything that has come in their place. At least they were quiet and dignified."

President Arthur set up a temporary White House on Capitol Hill in the granite mansion occupied by his personal friend, Senator John P. Jones of Nevada. There he conducted the business of government from September to December while he had the White House done over under the direction of an artist, Louis Comfort Tiffany, a name which in New York already connoted rare jewels and lustrous glass.

Each evening President Arthur visited the White House to give orders and inspect progress. He cleared out of the place 24 wagonloads of defunct furniture, tarnished bric-a-brac, ancient claptrap and new articles which he did not admire, all to be sold at public auction. The details of this spectacular house cleaning delighted the capital. One story had it that the clearance included the trap that caught the rat that ate the suit of clothes of President Lincoln. Colonel W. H. Crook, a member of the White House custodial staff from Lincoln to

Theodore Roosevelt, reported that night after night Arthur "would go from room to room and corridor to corridor, giving orders to change this and that according to his own taste, and in the daytime upholsterers and others were busily engaged in carrying out his wishes."

Still the mansion did not measure up to his ideals for the private lives of Presidents. He made a plan for a new official residence to be built across Lafayette Park on what later became the Hay-Adams site. Nothing concrete was ever done about it.

Included in the Arthur clearance was the elaborate frame of the Daniel Huntington portrait of Mrs. Hayes, which had so recently been ceremoniously presented to the nation's house. Apparently Arthur had no feeling for the carved oak frame nearly ten feet high with its pilaster sides, oak branches in high relief, American flag, lilies for purity, laurel for victory, acorns for power and strength, and English hawthorn and water lily for good measure. Arthur substituted a gilt frame. The original one, through the good offices of ex-President Hayes, was returned to the donors, the Cincinnati School of Design.

Tiffany himself gave the following account of the principal work done on the White House:

"In the East Room, we only did the ceiling, which was done in silver, with a design in various tones of ivory. The Blue Room, or Robin's Egg Room—as it is sometimes called—was decorated in robin's egg blue for the main color, with ornaments in handpressed paper, touched out in ivory, gradually deepening as the ceiling was approached. In the Red Room, the walls were red with a frieze in which the motif was an interlacing of a design embodying both eagles and flags. The ceiling was in old gold. The opalescent glass screen in the hall, which reached from the floor to the ceiling, had also a motif of eagles and flags, interlaced in the Arabian method."

This Tiffany glass screen, installed across the rear of the front foyer of the mansion by Arthur in order to give privacy to his family, was a distinctive feature of the White House for many years. Visitors never tired of telling how sections of this apparently unbroken opaque wall opened as doors. Arthur also put in the first elevator and the first plumbing—two baths.

So complete was the Arthur transformation that when Mrs. James

G. Blaine, wife of the Secretary of State, dined there, she somewhat bitterly reported: "The dinner was extremely elegant, hardly a trace of the old White House taint being perceptible anywhere, the flowers, the damask, the silver, the attendants, all showing the latest style and an abandon in expense and taste."

Mrs. Blaine, pithy, pungent and perceptive, had in her phrase, "the old White House taint," cut through to the real motivation of the Arthur renovation. All of Arthur's White House experiences under Garfield had been exceedingly painful to him. The place had to look different or he could not have endured it. The long weeks that Garfield lay dying had been a Gethsemane to Arthur too. In early July an official summons had brought Arthur from New York to Washington that he might be ready to take over the Presidential duties at any minute. He immediately called at the White House to see Mrs. Garfield and then meet the cabinet assembled there. When he appeared at the door of the Cabinet Room, not a member asked him to enter; all stared at him with hostile gaze. Had not another visitor there come forward with cordial greetings, Arthur would have left without a word. But the ice was broken, and perfunctory courtesies were exchanged. There had been no lifting of this coolness during Garfield's long and brave fight for life. When the President seemed to be improving, Arthur returned to New York.

At last came the midnight (September 19, 1881) when Arthur took the oath of office at his home on Lexington Avenue, New York. Said his close friend, Elihu Root:

Surely no more lonely and pathetic figure was ever seen assuming the powers of government. He had no people behind him, for Garfield, not he, was the people's choice; he had no party behind him, for the dominant faction of his party hated his name—were enraged by his advancement, and distrusted his motives. He had not even his own faction behind him, for he already knew that discharge of his duties would not accord with the ardent desires of their partisanship, and that disappointment and estrangement lay before him there.

"He was alone. He was bowed down by the weight of fearful responsibility and crushed to earth by the feeling, exaggerated but not unfounded, that he took up his heavy burden surrounded by dislike, suspicion, distrust and condemnation, as an enemy of the martyred Garfield and the beneficiary of his murder. Deep and settled melancholy possessed him; almost despair overwhelmed him. He went to power walking through the valley of the shadow of death and ascended the steps of the throne as one who is accused goes to trial."

Just before he left New York, Arthur had been so concerned about the very continuance of orderly government in this country that he met the possibility of his own sudden death by addressing a document to himself in Washington—a Presidential proclamation summoning the Senate into special session to elect a President pro Tempore. If he should be shot down on his way to Washington, the republic could go on.

When he reached Washington safely, there was a second and more ceremonious swearing in. It took place September 22 in the Vice-Presidential Room of the Capitol, with Garfield's whole cabinet and many notables present and Chief Justice Waite administering the oath.

To the amazement of everybody, Arthur declared for Civil Service reform, encouraging legislation on the subject and eventually signing the Civil Service Act. He allowed Robertson to remain as Collector of the Port of New York, making no attempt to fill the Custom House with Stalwarts. Roscoe Conkling, completely soured on Arthur, now referred to "His Accidency" in the same tones as he had earlier called Hayes "His Fraudulency." Ex-President Grant also broke with Arthur. Grant took umbrage when Arthur refused to appoint biographer Adam Badeau, still making a living by his hold on the life of Grant, to a high diplomatic post in Italy.

Slowly and carefully, in the winter of 1881-1882, Arthur assembled his own cabinet, keeping only Robert Todd Lincoln of the Garfield group.

Soon the antagonism against President Arthur faded before his demonstration of personal fairness and political ability. In his first annual message to Congress he said: "I cannot too strongly urge upon you my conviction that every consideration of National safety, economy and honor demands a thorough rehabilitation of the Navy." He convinced Congress it was no longer good sense to rebuild old Civil War battleships, and a modern Navy was begun.

Under the exorbitantly high tariffs initiated in Civil War times a surplus was piling up in the Treasury at the rate of over $80,000,000 a year, and the Democrats were making political capital of a lower-tariff move. Arthur fostered the creation of a Tariff Commission, which was set up in 1882 to consider reduction of revenue. But lobbyists for special interests blocked tariff revision. As an alternative to high or low-tariff legislation Arthur began the negotiation of reciprocal-trade treaties which were never ratified, but which pointed to a new pattern of dealings between nations.

The people liked the fact that he had the courage to veto a pork-barrel rivers-and-harbors bill, even though it was passed over his veto. They liked the easy efficiency with which national affairs were conducted. The handsome Arthur knew how to delegate authority.

President Arthur had a passion for clothes. Mrs. Blaine said that he ordered 25 new coats from his tailor early in 1882 for White House functions. And again she reported: "All his ambition seems to center in the social aspect of the situation. Flowers and wine and food, and slow pacing with a lady on his arm, and a quotation from Thackeray or Dickens, or an old Joe Miller told with an uninterfered-with particularity, for who would interrupt or refuse to laugh at a President's joke, made up his book of life, whose leaves are certainly not for the healing of the nation."

From within the White House, W. H. Crook bore out Mrs. Blaine's report on Arthur's interest in clothes, noting that, while he employed no bodyguard, he did have a valet, Aleck Powell. Said Crook: "He wanted the best of everything, and wanted it served in the best manner. He was the first President, so far as I know, to have a valet, and one was needed, for Mr. Arthur dressed fashionably, and his clothes were generally made in New York. He was always well groomed, almost faultless in his dress." To insure the excellence of his table Arthur brought in a French chef who had served New York gourmets.

Arthur drove the swankiest turnout ever boasted by a President, a dark-green landau drawn by mahogany bays with monogramed blankets. He spent large sums for flowers, often augmenting the White House conservatory supply with huge orders from New York. His personal floral bill for one state dinner was said to be $1,500.

Devotedly he placed a bouquet every day before the photograph of his dead wife, Ellen Herndon Arthur, daughter of the naval hero William Lewis Herndon. Mrs. Arthur had suddenly succumbed to pneumonia in January 1880, just five months before he was nominated for Vice-President. And ever after she remained close to his thoughts. To old St. John's Church across the square, where he worshiped as

President he gave a stained-glass window in her honor, still there to be seen by every passer-by.

Behind the Tiffany glass screen President Arthur installed his youngest sister, aristocratic Mary McElroy, with her children. There were also his two children, Alan Arthur, a Princeton student who came dashing home at unexpected moments, and Nell, a ten-year-old girl who studied with a French governess. When their father was absorbed in his official duties the young Arthurs were under the capable tutelage of their aunt. Their father took them to Annapolis to see the memorial shaft honoring their grandfather. They were also with him on a vacation trip to New York on the *U.S.S. Despatch*, a little naval vessel used by him, when he first unfurled his innovation in the customs of the highest office—the President's flag.

Mrs. McElroy was accorded high honors as a White House hostess of the extremely conservative type. Perhaps because he couldn't bear to put anybody in Ellen's place, perhaps for political reasons, President Arthur did not accord Mrs. McElroy the precedence which Buchanan earlier had given his niece and which Cleveland later gave his sister. Arthur invited 40 ladies to receive with Mrs. McElroy on New Year's Day and gave his own arm to the wife of the Speaker of the House of Representatives. Young Alan and Nell Arthur were present at many of the elaborate formal functions, but always discreetly in the background, as befitted the secluded and sedate life expected of those accepted by Old New York and fashionable Newport.

"An abode of gloom," sprightly Mrs. Blaine called the Arthur White House. Nevertheless, Mrs. McElroy's social fame mounted. Forty to 60 ladies always received with her, an honor flattering to each. She was especially gifted at seeking out those from whom fame had departed but whose very names—come to think of it—added eclat. Among them were Mrs. John Tyler—once Julia Gardiner, the Long Island Rose—and Harriet Lane Johnston, toast of the fifties. Mrs. McElroy inaugurated second-floor teas to several hundred guests following public receptions—each invitation thus a social distinction. President Arthur's sister was everywhere praised for her dignity and discretion and for her studied simplicity of gowning in a day of many fripperies. Highest White House social standards were safe in her hands.

This left President Arthur free for gay dining out. He even

attended the garish Willard's Hotel wedding of Colorado Senator H. A. W. Tabor and his beautiful Baby Doe, a pair decidedly not accepted by Washington society.

Susan B. Anthony and a hundred of her suffragists were courteously received by Arthur, but he was unimpressed by their argument that he'd stand a better chance of being President the next four years by endorsing votes for women. His record had by then become so generally praised that he thought the nomination might well be accorded to him as a matter of merit.

The Presidential family had spent their summers at Soldiers' Home, lingering one year almost until Christmas because the seclusion there was so much to their taste. However, as time for another nomination approached, President Arthur went on a personal health-seeking and political-pulse-feeling trip, first to Florida and then to the Yellowstone. Already he had the beginnings of Bright's disease, which caused him to have next to the shortest life span among Presidents, only fifty-six years. Polk died at fifty-three.

Praise of Arthur poured into the newspapers during the trips to the West. The Chicago *Daily News* filled 15 columns with such tributes; Mark Twain wrote: "I am but one in 55,000,000; still, in the opinion of this one-fifty-five-millionth of the country's population, it would be hard to better President Arthur's Administration. But don't decide till you hear from the rest."

One of those not yet heard from at that writing was James G. Blaine, of whom his wife once said: "If he cannot himself be President, no more can any other Republican without his assent." To Chester A. Arthur, Blaine had no intention of giving his assent.

Exaggerated tales of Arthur's expenditures on elegance began to go the rounds. With them circulated the falsehood that they were paid for by public, and not private, funds. The Arthur family coat of arms, used on his carriages, was said to be spurious. What happened at the Republican convention of 1884 in Chicago was dryly summarized by that rising politician Representative Joseph Gurney Cannon of Illinois in his famous sentence, "Arthur was defeated by his trousers." Thus had another fastidious New York widower, Martin Van Buren, been defeated by the White House gold spoons.

James G. Blaine was the Republican nominee, edged out in the November elections by a vigorous Democrat from Buffalo, New York— Grover Cleveland. The campaign was a particularly slimy one, the past of each candidate being as deeply excavated as had been Andrew Jackson's. In Cleveland's was found a paternity case in which he had furnished some support for a boy born out of wedlock but whom he had never accepted as his. The remarkably happy marriage of Blaine was said to have got off to a shotgun start in the remote past. On this Blaine brought a libel suit against an Indiana newspaper, but eventually dropped it.

Cleveland's victory was not due to his reform record as mayor of Buffalo and governor of New York, although that helped. He won because of the misadventures of his Republican opponent, Blaine. That ill-fated candidate lost New York state because his old rival, Roscoe Conkling, refused to support him. Due to the various railroad scandals against which he had been compelled to defend himself, Blaine was also deserted by the liberal wing of the party, called Mugwumps. But the immediate cause of grief at the polls was one campaign trip too many.

When he had really won his cause and should have gone to Maine and rested, he returned to doubtful New York for a final fling. It was too much of a fling, and it was indeed final. The exclusive high-price-per-plate party given in his honor at Delmonico's by New York moneyed men was dubbed "Belshazzar's Feast" by his opponents. And in a hotel lobby he let his mind wander during what he took to be a routine speech in his support by a routine delegation. The speaker, a preacher, had said that the common bond uniting the Democrats was Rum, Romanism and Rebellion—a catchy phrase if ever there was one. But Blaine did not catch it and squelch it on the spot. And so at the last minute he lost a large block of Catholic votes which had been his, personally, because of his Irish stock and his many public tributes to his Catholic mother.

Cleveland was very bitter toward Blaine, blaming him for the mudslinging trend of the campaign. He had high regard for Arthur and considered the Republicans less than intelligent not to have chosen him instead of Blaine as a candidate. This made for good feeling between the outgoing Republican and the incoming Democrat when the time came for the White House to change hands.

Mrs. McElroy's last reception was one of the greatest social triumphs any woman ever enjoyed in the White House. The crush was so great that the Marine Band was swept from its moorings and could not continue playing because of the pressure of people. So famous a hero as General Phil Sheridan got in only by being helped through a portico window by two policemen. President Arthur and his sister gave an Inauguration Day luncheon party for President Cleveland and his sister Rose Elizabeth Cleveland. All four had been reared in Protestant parsonages, Arthur's father having been a Baptist preacher, Cleveland's a Presbyterian preacher. Friends pressed the Arthurs and the McElroys into several weeks' stay, with many fetes. Throngs of women and girls gave Mrs. McElroy a triumphal farewell at the station, and Rose Cleveland sent her flowers.

President Arthur's last official gesture was to sign an act for the relief of General Grant, ruined in the crash of his Wall Street firm, by according him a general's full commission for life. One of Cleveland's first acts was to sign the commission. Grant did not soften toward either of them.

Many were the comparisons, not complimentary to Cleveland, between the outgoing and incoming Presidents. Beside the impeccable Arthur, who stood six feet two, the graying, balding Cleveland, two inches under six feet and corpulent, appeared crude. Arthur was the New York City cosmopolite. Cleveland had come up in the rough and tumble of industrial Buffalo. The new President may even have cultivated the curmudgeon role as buffer against argument. At any rate, he had been called the "Veto Mayor" and he would be called the "Veto President." A generation of children would grow up singing of him, "A fat man once sat in a President's chair, singing Ve-to, Ve-to, With never a thought of trouble or care, singing Ve-to, Ve-to. . . ." But he came from a family of culture as well as courage. This fact was soon shown by his sister Rose Elizabeth Cleveland, whom he installed as temporary White House mistress. She also was chaperone in his successful courtship of his ward, Miss Frances Folsom, when Miss Folsom and her mother made their first White House visit immediately after the inauguration.

Cleveland was almost as much a guiding factor in the life of the girl he married as Buchanan in the life of his niece. He was closest friend and law partner of Frances Folsom's father, Oscar Folsom. From Mr. Cleveland came her first baby carriage. When Folsom was suddenly killed by being thrown from a buggy by a runaway horse, Cleveland was executor of the estate. He amused Frances by letting her copy legal papers about her father's affairs. All through her college career he sent her flowers. He invited her and her mother to occupy the governor's box with him at official affairs in Albany. They were guests at the governor's mansion for the notification cere- monies when he ran for President. It was he who arranged her trip abroad after her graduation from Wells College and who carefully planned the White House wedding that was her welcome home. He always called her "Frank."

Rose Elizabeth Cleveland was probably the most erudite woman who ever lived in the White House. She kept her calm, while being eyed by the multitudes at the inauguration, by concentrating on the conjugation of a difficult Greek verb. Rose had taught in exclusive schools for young ladies until, irked by routine and needed at home be- cause of her mother's failing health, she figured out a new field—giving lectures to advanced classes in several such schools—sometimes, one account said, "in racy rhyme." After her mother's death she had lived alone in the old home in Holland Patent, near Utica, New York, be- cause she liked living alone. Out of her quiet hours came strong, scholarly essays of individual inspiration. "We can do no better or braver thing than to bring our best thoughts to the everyday market; they will yield us usurious interest" was a typical Rose Cleveland tenet. She used the Rose design as a sort of trade-mark in her books, but her brother called her "Libbie." And when he called her she came, even though to her the White House meant sacrifice of personal prefer- ences and a well-launched career.

There she deliberately used her high position as a challenge to thought and a prod toward better education and deeper culture for womankind. "To my countrywomen" she dedicated a volume of her essays, bought by thousands because it came from the White House. Between its covers lay a feminism deeper than the suffragists were talking, based on the great historic characters of the ages. To Moham- med's wife, Kadijah, Rose gave credit for his greatness because Kadijah "believed in him when all men despised him." She also said that Jane Welch, wife of Carlyle, deserved a high historic place because she saw through the foibles of her husband and knew what to encourage in him.

Rose Elizabeth Cleveland wrote a preface for a book titled *You and I, or Moral, Intellectual and Social Culture* and allowed her photo- graph with that of the White House to be used as its frontispiece.

"Culture," defined Miss Cleveland, "is a symmetrical development of all those faculties with which a human nature is endowed for the purpose of living a human life worthily and well." She held that social culture ran "all the way from theology to etiquette"—and that was the broad field this weighty tome covered, including how to write a letter and how to behave in public places.

Because she advocated temperance Miss Cleveland was criticized for not protesting use of wine on the President's table, even though she served lemonade at her own luncheons. Protests came on her wearing a décolleté gown. "To all her critics she replied with good-natured independence," wrote a contemporary.

With plenty of verve Miss Cleveland carried the White House through one complete social season. How could it be otherwise, considering her vast interest in people and subjects? And America itself was on the march. Those were the days when John Philip Sousa, leader of the Marine Band, was striking up an original march on many a gala White House occasion. With the marriage of her brother on June 2, 1886, Miss Cleveland gracefully bowed out of the White House and went back to her home.

Cleveland was a hard worker. He regarded public office as "a business engagement between the people and myself." He regularly kept at his desk until two or three o'clock in the morning. That former Presidential candidate Tilden once humorously said of Cleveland: "He is the kind of man who would rather do something badly for himself than to have somebody else do it well."

Nowhere was the Cleveland character better shown than in his letters to his sister Mary, Mrs. H. E. Hoyt, on his marriage plans, published in their entirety in Allan Nevins' biography. The engagement had been kept a closely guarded secret while Frances Folsom finished college and took her postgraduation trip abroad with her mother. The first intention had been to have the ceremony at the home of her grandfather, John Folsom, near Buffalo. However, he died while Frances was abroad. This posed to Cleveland the problem of making the plans himself, keeping her informed by letter. He decided that he could best protect her from a prying press within the White House walls, and to this she assented.

To his sister the President wrote:

"I want my marriage to be a quiet one and am determined that the American Sovereigns shall not interfere with a thing so purely personal to me. And yet I don't want to be churlish or mean or peculiar for the sake of being peculiar. But if the example of the President is worth anything I want in this matter to be in the direction of sense and proper decency. I have thought of having no one but the family, hers and mine, present at the ceremony. . . . Then I have thought it might be well to have the Cabinet people. . . ."

Again he confided:

"I believe I shall buy or rent a house near here where I can go and be away from this cursed, constant grind. . . . I suppose my bridal present for my new wife is in process of manufacture. I am almost afraid I shall make a mistake there and have something too expensive. I have my heart set upon making Frank a sensible, domestic American wife and would be pleased not to hear her spoken of as 'The First Lady of the Land' or 'The Mistress of the White House.' I want her to be happy and to possess all she can reasonably desire, but I should feel very much afflicted if she gets many notions in her head. But I think she is pretty level-headed."

The President himself wrote the invitations to his official family as follows:

> Executive Mansion,
> May 29, 1886

My dear Mr. ———:
I am to be married on Wednesday evening, at seven o'clock, at the White House, to Miss Folsom. It will be a very quiet affair, and I will be extremely gratified at your attendance on the occasion.
> Yours sincerely,
> GROVER CLEVELAND

The President also revised and condensed his own marriage ceremony, omitting from it the word "obey." While he may have visualized an ideal for his young wife, he had no intention of forcing her into anything.

Cleveland's plans for a quiet wedding were not a complete success. The secret of the engagement was inadvertently revealed by a friend of Miss Folsom before she landed in New York. When the President went there to meet her, the newspapers went wild and headlined every move of the President and his fiancée. While he was reviewing a Memorial Day parade the bands broke into "Come Where My Love

Lies Dreaming" and "He's Going to Marry Yum-Yum"; and Mendelssohn's Wedding March was heard the clock around.

The wedding, the only marriage of a President ever to take place within the White House walls, was limited to less than 40 witnesses. But at the seven-o'clock moment signaling the ceremony in the Blue Room, the cannons at the Navy Yard boomed out, and all the bells in the capital began to ring.

The many news columns on the subject told of floral national shields on every East Room column; of fireplaces in all the state chambers being solidly filled with flowers; of mirrors wreathed and mantels banked with floral monograms of the happy pair. Some accounts said the bride's veil was 15 feet long and some made it a full six yards. Her dress of corded satin was said to be stiff enough to stand alone.

The additional columns printed on the honeymoon in what had been chosen as a sequestered spot in the Maryland mountains at Deer Park mounted far beyond the Presidential boiling point. Reporters even used powerful field glasses to spy on the honeymoon cottage. A 38-page booklet, *Bride of the White House,* was published. Cleveland wrote scathing letters to the newspapers on the "colossal impertinence" of their reporters, and on one occasion shortly after his marriage he lashed out at them in a public address. At a dinner in Memorial Hall at Harvard, when he saw reporters staring at Mrs. Cleveland, the President interrupted his opening remarks of felicitation with: "O, those ghouls of the press!"

Cleveland had delayed any renovation of the White House, then in a very cramped and disheveled state, until his marriage. He had an executive staff of less than a dozen persons, yet they could scarcely be contained in the office quarters over the East Room. His secretaries lived and ate at the White House. Robert Lincoln O'Brien, a member of the Cleveland office staff, later told what a sorry state the White House was in at that time. He said that the Clevelands' private quarters were kept up well, but that the Office of Public Buildings and Grounds was spectacularly lax in the upkeep of the rest of the building. The attic, he said, was "a terrible mess of junk," the basement floor "a place of rubble and overturned ash cans. . . . I didn't know there were so many species of cockroaches as I got acquainted with while at my daily work," he said.

"The White House then operated a vehicle known as 'the office buggy' in which Octavius L. Pruden, the assistant secretary to the President, carried to the Capitol all the messages and papers that he had occasion to transmit to Congress.

"One day one of the men of the staff, much of an automaton, came into our second-floor offices and intoned: 'The office buggy is downstairs.' To which Benjamin F. Montgomery, telegraph operator, responded, 'And the buggy office is up here.'"

In the year of his marriage President Cleveland partially met the problem in two ways. He bought a private home as he had suggested in his letter to his sister—a farm really, named "Oak View," but dubbed "Red Top" by the press because of the color of its roof. It was a comfortable, old-fashioned, wooded place with a wonderful view near those famous old Georgetown Heights estates, Woodley, Rosedale and Grasslands. There during the rest of his first term the Clevelands lived an ordinary life except in the social season when official entertaining necessitated White House residence.

During the summer and early fall the White House had its renovation, not sweeping enough to end the reign of the roaches, but at least temporarily decimating their numbers. A change for the better was obvious to every passer-by. All the spears on the tops of the fence pickets were gilded. The exterior was painted. The interior was repainted upstairs and "touched up" in the state rooms downstairs. A newspaper assured its readers that the fancy ceilings done by Tiffany had not been renovated, nor had Tiffany's robin's-egg blue been turned to indigo as some alarmist had reported.

When Mrs. Cleveland's own official social program started spinning with the New Year's reception of 1887 she made innovations all up and down the annual line-up. She had new invitation forms, new designs for place cards. White House Thursday-evening receptions were all-inclusive, taking in the whole of Congress as a matter of course at each. The engraved invitations read:

"The President and Mrs. Cleveland
request the pleasure of the company of
The Senators and Representatives in Congress
and the ladies of their families
On Thursday evening, Jan. 13 and 27 and Feb. 10
and Tuesday evening, Feb. 22
from 9 to 11 o'clock, 1887.

Jan. 13—To meet the Diplomatic Corps.
Jan. 27—Reception to Congress and the Judiciary.
Feb. 10—To meet the officers of the Army and Navy.
Feb. 22—The public reception.

Interspersed between those reception dates the Clevelands gave a cabinet dinner on January 20, at which the central decoration was a big boat of red and white camellias; and a dinner to the Justices of the Supreme Court on February 18, the table being centered by two open books fashioned of white immortelles labeled in purple "Book of the Law."

Considering receptions and dinners together, the annual "social calendar" of the Executive Mansion, to stand until the house itself threatened to crumble, had taken shape and form. Thereafter, a set series of such events was announced at the start of each season.

The White House bride also had levees, luncheons and teas. She held Saturday-afternoon receptions, which made it possible even for shop girls, employed all the rest of the week, to shake her hand and see the White House. These affairs became increasingly popular until during the last season of the administration average attendance at a card reception was 2,000 and at a public reception 6,000. At one of Mrs. Cleveland's own "afternoons" the line waiting to be received stretched from the White House entrance to the Treasury Building. Nine thousand persons passed through the Blue Room and shook hands with her. She had to have both arms massaged, as the left set up a "sympathetic" ache.

Cleveland cleared up the old question of the independence of the Executive in matters of removals from office, getting rid of the last remnants of the Tenure of Office Act, which had plagued every President from Johnson's time.

In the autumn of 1887 the President and Mrs. Cleveland made a tour through the West and South. It was a great success. Cleveland informally addressed the people at each stop in a companionable manner. He and his wife shook innumerable hands at great receptions in each large city visited. Notable was their visit to the Nashville, Tennessee, home of Mrs. James K. Polk, and to the near-by tomb of her husband.

President Cleveland seemed headed for an easy re-election in 1888. But he had failed to reckon with a political trap cunningly set by his rivals; with a whispering-campaign canard scurrilously spread far and wide; and with pay-envelope instructions to vote against him put out by some industrialists.

Grover Cleveland felt it to be his duty to inform Congress that it was his intention to seek revision of the tariff downward. From France, James G. Blaine, who did not choose to run on the Republican ticket that year of 1888, cabled an interview calling Cleveland's message "Free Trade." On this the New York *Tribune* commented: "Mr. Blaine in Europe speaks as an American. Mr. Cleveland in America speaks as a British manufacturer, anxious to be admitted without any charge to a share of the best and largest market in the world." This gave the political tricksters a bright idea. They had a British-American in California write the British minister in Washington, Sir Lionel Sackville-West, asking him whom to vote for. Sackville-West fell for this ill-begotten bid to get mixed up in American politics and advised his unknown correspondent to vote for Cleveland because of his lower-tariff message. Cleveland demanded the British minister's recall, but the damage was done.

The campaign canard of 1888 was that Cleveland mistreated his wife, drove her out of the White House in the middle of the night, with variations which included getting drunk and beating her. These lies were vigorously disseminated until they literally had reached almost every voter in the land. Credulous ministers spread them through their congregations. In response to a woman in Worcester, Massachusetts, Maggie Nicodemus, Mrs. Cleveland authorized publication of a denial in which she said: "I can wish the women of our Country no greater blessing than that their homes and lives may be as happy, and their husbands may be as kind, attentive, considerate and affectionate as mine."

This brave open answer to an undercover campaign did not save the day, and Cleveland lost the election to Benjamin Harrison, grandson of the earlier President, William Henry Harrison. It was obviously due to this rumor that when Cleveland again ran for President Mrs. Cleveland's picture was put on the campaign posters slightly above and between the two candidates. No other woman ever had this honor of apparently actually running for office. However, when a group of women tried to start a "Frances Cleveland Influence Club" Cleveland squelched the idea.

On February 27, 1889, President-elect and Mrs. Harrison were entertained at dinner at the White House. But Mrs. Cleveland's last social gesture was made to the former and not to the succeeding administration. On February 28 she gave a "pink luncheon" in honor of Mrs. McElroy, who had been hostess for the late ex-President Arthur.

Colonel Crook of the White House staff said that Mrs. Cleveland left with the admonition: "I want you to take good care of all the furniture and ornaments in the house and not let any of them get lost or broken, for I want to find everything just as it is now when we come back again. We are coming back just four years from today."

President Cleveland sold for $140,000 the suburban estate which he had purchased for about $21,500. Immediately it became an urban development, the Cleveland Park section of the capital city. With all his improvement costs subtracted, his profit was almost $100,000. Cleveland thus set an unusual record—he was a President who actually made money while in the White House.

I3 | *Not So Gay Nineties*

...BENJAMIN HARRISON,
CLEVELAND, McKINLEY

BENJAMIN HARRISON was picked as Presidential timber by the Republicans as a Senator from a doubtful state, Indiana, with a name sufficiently well known to capture votes. He had been an able officer in the Civil War. He was a lawyer of renown, a real digger into documents. He worked with great concentration when getting in hand some tough subject to be put into his own terse prose. This habit gave him a reputation for aloofness. People told how cold he was. "If you pricked him he would bleed ice water."

Mrs. Harrison brought to her task as First Lady a sturdy Midwestern mixture of culture and practical experience. She was the daughter of a Presbyterian preacher, founder and president of Oxford (Ohio) Female Seminary, Dr. John Witherspoon Scott. There she was educated and there she met Harrison, one of her father's pupils at Miami University, also in Oxford. She and Harrison were married shortly after the latter's graduation and went off to make their way in Cincinnati and later in Indianapolis. During the Civil War she had proved a stanch soldier's wife, visiting her husband in camp, nursing and distributing food, clothing and medicine to his men. With peace she resumed community leadership. Mrs. Harrison's infant class in the First Presbyterian Church at Indianapolis was almost as famous as her husband's Bible class for men. She was a leader in the Indianapolis Women's Club. She taught china painting gratis to young ladies in her studio.

Six years as a Senator's wife had given her the experience necessary to handle her husband's "front porch" campaign, and after that the White House held no terrors for her. She could run its whole machinery—a four-generation home—with part of her day and still find time for fine needlework, literature, china painting and orchid culture.

Benjamin Harrison also combined able administration with a well-rounded personal life. Not only did he choose for his cabinet such outstanding men as James G. Blaine, Secretary of State, and John Wanamaker, Postmaster General; he also selected outstanding younger men for subcabinet positions. He brought in the crusading Theodore Roosevelt as Civil Service Commissioner and refused to fire him when John Wanamaker, whose Post Office Department was the entrenched center of the political spoils system, quite naturally demanded Roosevelt's dismissal. Under Theodore Roosevelt, Civil Service reform became an actuality and not merely an argument. He added 11,000 public positions to the "classified list." Harrison brought in a young legal prodigy, William Howard Taft, as Solicitor General.

Harrison's habit was to put in intensive hours on his executive task, but to leave many leisure hours for billiards, long walks alone or with the young people in his house, and drives about Washington.

Post-inauguration newspapers told of how the White House had been filled to overflowing by the Harrison clan. The President had taken the "Prince of Wales" Room, next to the Library on the second floor, Mrs. Harrison the southwest corner room. Their daughter Mrs. J. R. McKee and her husband had the suite opposite Mrs. Harrison; their son Russell Harrison and his wife, the daughter of Senator Alvin Saunders of Nebraska, were in the suite opposite the President. Nellie Grant's room had been turned into a nursery for the Harrison grandchildren: the much-publicized "Baby" McKee, named Benjamin for his grandfather; his infant sister Mary, who was christened in the White House by Dr. Scott with water from the Jordan River in the Holy Land; and Marthena Harrison, who later caused the White House to be quarantined for scarlet fever, although her ailment in future years probably would have been diagnosed as poliomyelitis. Also a member of the family was Mrs. Harrison's aged father, Dr. Scott. Joining it for most of the Harrison stay in the White House was her niece Mrs. Mary Scott Lord Dimmick, a charming young widow of thirty. All three of the young women were named Mary. To avoid confusion, Mrs. McKee was "Mamie"; Mrs. Russell Harrison "May"; Mrs. Dimmick was "Mame."

The advent of Mrs. Dimmick was to have consequences then unforeseen. After her aunt's death she married the ex-President, causing a split in the close-knit Harrison family.

The President and Mrs. Harrison brought back daily family prayers in the White House. Their administration was noted as going forward in an atmosphere of piety. The many young people in the household brought dancing back as a regular part of public receptions—for the first time after its banning by Mrs. Polk, according to one account. The Harrison administration was marked as having an air of genteel gayety.

But the real fame of the Harrison stay in the White House lay in Mrs. Harrison's campaign for a new White House. Mrs. Harrison had the Office of Public Buildings and Grounds prepare at least three plans for enlarging the Presidential menage. Fred D. Owen was the architect who drew up these elaborate designs. One was for a separate private residence to be built out Sixteenth Street, then being developed as the capital's most elite thoroughfare. Another, by all odds the most interesting, contemplated the development of the entire White House grounds as a hollow square, enclosing a "Private Court" with an "Allegorical Fountain" in its center. The Pennsylvania Avenue side of this square would consist of "Present (1792) Mansion" with round pavilions at either end joined to it by connecting corridors. The side across from the Treasury would be the "Historical Art Wing"; that across from the State, War and Navy Building the "Official Wing." The base would consist of conservatories—palm gardens at each corner connected by greenhouses for foliage plants and flowers and a lily pond. The semicircular frontage to the south would be devoted to a "Fountain and Cataract" and landscaping. A third plan, on which was imprinted twin slogans—"Economy, Efficiency, Emergency, Harmony" and "Past, Present, Future Art"—provided for addition of only two round buildings at either end, the east one next to the Treasury to be used as executive offices, the west one to be an entertainment suite for official guests. This third plan got the farthest—a scale model was built of it.

While all this planning was going on backstage, Mrs. Harrison gave an interview to the press. She was quoted as saying: "We are here for four years: I do not look beyond that, as many things may occur in that time, but I am very anxious to see the family of the President provided for properly, and while I am here I hope to get the present building put into good condition. Very few people understand to what straits the President's family has been put at times for lack of accommodations. Really there are only five sleeping apartments and there is no feeling of privacy."

Mrs. Harrison lost her campaign, but she won a fairly sizable compromise—$35,000 with which to fix up the old White House. How this got under way without general public knowledge was shown in official records in a rather peculiar fashion. Mr. Joseph B. Tiffany, whose New York firm had done the previous full-scale redecoration, wrote on September 11, 1890, a letter to the Public Buildings Commissioner to which he attached a newspaper clipping. Mr. Tiffany said he hoped the enclosed announcement was unauthorized and premature, adding that his firm was still awaiting the Harrisons' pleasure to receive Mr. Joseph B. Tiffany. The gossipy clipping which had disturbed Mr. Tiffany read:

"I met E. S. Yergason of Hartford at Fifth Avenue Hotel yesterday on his way to Washington to complete the arrangements for redecorating the White House for which Congress has just made an appropriation of $35,000. The White House has been in a state of dilapidation for several years, and Mrs. Harrison bravely called the attention of Congressmen to the poor furniture and poorer furnishings in the various apartments, with the result of securing the appropriation.

"Mr. Yergason is a member of the firm of W. H. Post and Co. of Hartford, which makes a specialty of interior decorations. He has spent many months of each year in Washington and was the first person to whom Mrs. Harrison turned for assistance in selecting material for refurnishing after it became certain that Congress would grant her request. He had his plan so far completed when it was certain the appropriation would be made he had a force of men ready to put to work, and they are already engaged in making the repairs, which will be completed before the President and his family get back from Cresson. The improvements to be made will include the kitchen, state and private dining rooms, the parlors, the sleeping apartments and the offices. The greatest improvement which will be noticeable to the public will be the famous Blue Room which has been untouched since it was redecorated by Tiffany and Co. of New York during President Arthur's administration.

"The designs for the Blue Room, Mr. Yergason told me, include the creation of a deep frieze, extending from the ceiling to the window tops, in fine figured work in relief, with a high wainscoting, also of raised work and similar character. The main body of the walls between the frieze and the wainscoting will be of rich American silk figured to correspond with the relief in the work above and below. New silk curtains will hang from window tops of carved wood and exquisite filigree work, and electric lights are to be put into the entire work as well as the Blue Room."

The Cresson referred to was apparently the summer resort at the summit of the Allegheny Mountains in Pennsylvania which was then fashionable.

Two months earlier, July 29, 1890, National Archives records revealed, the Hartford firm had presented its second and successful bid of $5,370.75 for decorating, painting, carpet, draperies, laces and covering furniture in the Blue Parlor. The total had been reduced from $6,988.50 by omitting gas brackets—electricity was substituted as a separate contract—and by using domestic instead of imported silk. Among the more sizable items were: decorating ceiling in relief and fresco, $950; redecorating wainscot and frieze in relief, $650; 58 yards of silk for walls, $435; 190 yards of Wilton carpet, $380; overdrapery fringes, $337.50; repairing gilding on furniture, $150.

Ike Hoover—who went into the White House as an electrician to install the new lighting system and remained there for 42 years, many of them spent as Chief Usher—left in his posthumously published memoirs a graphic account of the really thorough house-cleaning job done under Mrs. Harrison's direction. From the ground floor, he said, five layers of flooring were taken out, like geological strata, and slimy old bricks removed. A wooden heating trough, the length of the long corridor ceiling, was removed. Mr. Hoover took out the mechanical call-bell system, kept it as a souvenir for 40 years and then turned it over to Henry Ford's Early American village at Dearborn. Other records show that mantels were taken out and doors cut to make the baths private. An aspiring Pied Piper made a bid to rid the place of rats.

When Mrs. Harrison had the old china closet pulled out and a new one put in, she became historically interested. She herself had designed the Harrison set ordered for the White House. She started the White House collection of the china of past Presidents which thereafter had a great fascination for tourists inspecting the public rooms of the mansion.

Harris and Ewing Photo

Mrs. Hoover gathered furniture of the period around the 7-foot Lincoln bed, for which Mrs. Coolidge crocheted the spread.

The Red Room as redecorated by President Franklin D. Roosevelt.

The Blue Parlor, with its electric lights, was ready for the New Year's reception of 1891, and there the "reception proper" was held, the East Room being used merely for a promenade. All cabinet members and their wives, with the exception of Mrs. Blaine, wife of the Secretary of State, followed the President and Mrs. Harrison downstairs to the reception room. Each room had its great floral devices, among them the American flag and the national coat of arms.

Mrs. Harrison, who introduced a fad for orchids, set a pace even for that elegant era in the use of a staggering plethora of plants and flowers. They came from the far-spreading White House conservatories, from the federal propagating gardens in heated vans, from New York and Philadelphia. A reporter who took a statistical interest in this matter set forth that for the East Room alone in the Harrison administration 5,000 decorative plants were regularly used, and "about a mile of smilax" for chandelier festoons. On mantels and window seats the florists somehow found space for "2,000 azalea blossoms, 800 carnations, 300 roses, 300 tulips, 900 hyacinths, 400 lilies of the valley, 200 bouvardias, 100 sprays of asparagus ferns, 40 heads of poinsettia, and 200 small ferns."

The year 1891, thus auspiciously opening in the new Blue Room with Mrs. Harrison in blue-and-gold brocade, Mrs. McKee in pink-striped silk and satin and Mrs. Dimmick in black silk trimmed with jet, brought social zenith for the Harrisons. Mrs. Harrison was elected first President-General of the newly formed Daughters of the American Revolution, addressing its First Continental Congress in this vein: "We have within ourselves the only element of destruction; our foes are from within, not from without. Our hope is in unity and self-sacrifice." The young Harrisons went abroad, Mrs. McKee and Mrs. Russell Harrison being presented to Queen Victoria at the Court of St. James's.

The life of the large Harrison family in the White House was from the first complicated by a strong undercurrent of rivalry with the large family of that elder statesman, Secretary of State James G. Blaine, and that elder stateswoman, Mrs. James G. Blaine. Not quite trusting the ever-spectacular Blaine, Harrison had held off from offering him the top portfolio until Blaine was offended. Then Harrison refused to appoint Blaine's son Walker, on whom Blaine depended heavily due to his numerous illnesses, as Assistant Secretary of State. Instead, Walker Blaine was made solicitor in that department. This rankled with Blaine, who also took umbrage at editorials hitting at him in *Leslie's Weekly* and *Judge*, both in part owned and managed by Harrison's son Russell.

Mrs. Blaine in her letters referred to Mrs. Harrison as "Her American Majesty," and said, "She is too much given, as am I, to making everybody comfortable" and "The wheels of the new administration go slowly forward and creak as they go." A White House invitation was no command to Mrs. Blaine, who set down: "Last night we were all asked to the White House, but as M and I were going to Dr. Eaton's lecture on the Coaching Trip, only Mr. Blaine went."

The Blaines bought and remodeled that mansion of ill fortune, the house in which Secretary of State Seward had been attacked by assassins, close to the White House on Lafayette Park. What should have been near-neighborliness somehow got off to a sensational start as a social breach. A White House invitation got lost in the confused Blaine household. The result was that all the rest of the cabinet and their wives marched down the stairs at the first Harrison reception to receive with the Presidential pair. The Secretary of State and Mrs. Blaine arrived late, obviously took offense, and withdrew to one side of the room in open indignation. When Mrs. McKee told them they were expected in the receiving line, Mrs. Blaine replied she had not been invited. Later Mrs. Blaine made her apologies to the President's private secretary, writing, "As you may suppose, I found myself somewhat embarrassed at my unique position and I am glad to find that it was the fault of my crippled household." After such a start, Mrs. Blaine's absence at any White House function was always noted in the newspapers.

As the time drew near for another nominating convention, three paragraphs by a New York *World* political writer on Saturday, May 7, 1892, brought an open breach between President Harrison and his Secretary of State. This item, clipped by Blaine and sent to Harrison, read:

"The revival of the Blaine boom has started the political gossip in his direction. Speculation concerning Mr. Blaine's health and general condition is rife. Prince Russell a few days ago in the Fifth Avenue Hotel made a valuable and important contribution to this line of inquiry.

" 'Mr. Blaine's condition,' he said, 'is such that all talk of his nomination, even if he should become a candidate, is out of the question.

He is completely broken down both mentally and physically. He cannot remember the simplest things, and all of the work of the State Department has been on my father's shoulders for over two years. . . . He is almost as helpless as a child and it is downright cruelty to be continually bringing him to the front as Presidential candidate.'"

Denials were rushed into print by Russell Harrison. President Harrison sent a letter to Blaine discrediting the story. But the damage was done. On June 4, 1892, just before the nominating convention, Blaine resigned "effective immediately"—an announcement that his support for the re-election of his chief was withdrawn.

Personal blows now came thick and fast upon the Harrison family. Mrs. Harrison that summer became hopelessly ill of cancer. She begged to be taken back to Washington from the summer resort in the Adirondacks chosen by the family. She died in the White House on October 24. Her funeral was held in the East Room. The burial was in Indianapolis. In November, President Harrison was defeated for re-election. Late that same month Mrs. Harrison's father died in the White House, and there was another East Room funeral.

The Blaines also were dogged by disaster. While Blaine was still in the cabinet his son Walker and a married daughter, Alice, died. Shortly after his resignation he lost his son Emmons.

On New Year's Day, 1893, the White House was darkened by double mourning. On January 23 official entertaining was resumed with Mrs. McKee taking over as official hostess. The last Harrison reception was held on March 1. Friends and officialdom also thronged the place in farewell on March 3. President Harrison, glad to return to private life, was as courteous to the incoming Cleveland as President Cleveland had been to him four years before.

Back into the White House moved the Clevelands to resume their pattern of life, which had now become broader. In the interim between the Cleveland terms they had bought a new summer home, "Gray Gables" on Monument Point at Buzzards Bay, Massachusetts, close to the home of Cleveland's fishing crony, the actor Joe Jefferson. Fishing and hunting were passions to which these two gave sharpened gifts of concentration. It was against the rules to utter a word when the fish were biting.

The Clevelands now had a little daughter Ruth, born in their Madison Avenue house in New York in October 1891. When Mrs.

Cleveland sent Ruth out with her nurse for an airing on the White House south grounds, people almost smothered the child with kisses. Mrs. Cleveland had the gates closed. An utterly false rumor then was spread that the baby was deaf and dumb and had malformed ears. Their "Red Top" retreat having been sold, the Clevelands rented that fine old estate, Woodley, and openly led a private family life while in the White House—the only Presidential pair who ever took for themselves this privilege.

The second Cleveland administration began with social brilliancy, due to unusual events. A great fanfare was made of the opening of the World's Fair in Chicago in May 1893 with the President and cabinet and their ladies in attendance. This trip was made by way of New York, where a great naval review was staged on the Hudson. Infanta Eulalia, a member of the reigning family in Spain, visited Washington and was entertained at the White House early in June. Then the Clevelands were off until September to their summer home at Buzzards Bay.

Celebrations that year had a hollow ring, for the great panic of 1893 already was upon the country. Cleveland called an extra session of Congress for August 7 for the purpose of repealing the Silver Purchase Act, which was being blamed for a continued loss of gold to Europe.

The nation thus was in a crisis situation when a personal crisis hit Cleveland. He discovered that he had a cancer, a carcinoma as big as a quarter of a dollar, on the roof of his mouth. The magnificent manner in which he met this life hazard was not known until 25 years later. For President Cleveland, so as not to add to the public panic, chalked up what may well have been an all-time record for eluding the ever-pursuing press. On June 26 Cleveland boarded the yacht of his close personal friend E. C. Benedict in New York harbor, with three outstanding medical men aboard. The yacht put to sea, and Cleveland was operated on the next day. He was under anesthetics, propped up in a chair against the mast because the doctors feared apoplexy due to his corpulence. The entire left upper jaw was removed. On July 5, when the yacht put in at the Cleveland home in Buzzards Bay, the President walked from the wharf to Gray Gables.

Except for one vague rumor, which was quickly and convincingly denied, the secret of this operation was kept for more than 25 years, although it was described in meticulous detail for medical history.

Cleveland's determination to survive this operation lay not only in his deep love for his family—a second child was on its way to being born—but also in his conviction that his Vice President, Adlai E. Stevenson, would, if President, bring the nation to a silver standard.

Mrs. Cleveland did an adroit job of helping her husband "cover up" his physical condition. To Governor William E. Russell of Massachusetts she wrote on July 21 the thank-you letter for a gift of salmon, explaining that the President was not writing at all—"He came up here completely worn out and with an unusually bad attack of rheumatism besides. We have made him give up entirely to resting —and he is already another man."

All the rest of that summer President Cleveland's facial contour was preserved by dental packings. Charles S. Hamlin, Assistant Secretary of the Treasury, visited him to deliver some silver statistics late in July and jotted down in his diary: "Cleveland appeared not well at all. Had his mouth packed with some kind of bandage. Could not speak distinctly." That autumn Dr. Kasson C. Gibson, a New York City dentist, fitted Cleveland with a rubber replica of the removed portion of his jaw. The President wrote to Dr. Gibson, "I hasten to announce that you have scored another dental victory. . . . The new plate came last night. . . . I have worn it all day with the utmost ease and comfort without a shred of packing of any kind."

No note of Presidential illness even slightly disturbed public confidence as this country weathered the 1893 panic and Cleveland's special session repealed the Silver Act. It remained for a much later generation to wonder how much medical practice might have been advanced by the example of a President of the United States successfully undergoing a drastic cancer operation in the year 1893. He survived it by 15 years, living past the age of seventy, when he succumbed to a gastrointestinal ailment.

On September 9, 1893, the Cleveland's second daughter was born in the White House, only child of a President ever to have that honor.

The course of political events during the next few years showed that, in spite of Cleveland's high courage, the operation had taken its toll. President Cleveland's streak of irascibility became more marked. Those who had an opportunity to observe him at close range said that Mrs. Cleveland's role became more valuable in that her soothing influence on her husband had the effect of helping him meet irritating problems and pressuring personalities. The observant Ike Hoover said: "She would watch over him as though he were one of the children" and "Cleveland idolized Mrs. Cleveland, thought of her as a child, was tender and considerate with her always." A third Cleveland daughter, Marion, was born at Buzzards Bay before the second administration ended, and two sons, Richard and Francis, were born after the Clevelands left the White House.

Cleveland's last months in the White House were spent as "a President without a party." The leaders were furious over Cleveland's veto of a tariff bill. William Jennings Bryan had won the 1896 nomination and had taken over the rank and file. The hinterlands resounded with talk of Bryan's Cross of Gold speech and his Free Silver platform. Cleveland dropped from his cabinet Secretary of the Interior Hoke Smith because Smith came out for Bryan. It was no secret that Cleveland hoped that Bryan's Republican opponent, William McKinley, despite his high tariff platform, would win. Cleveland put sound money well above moderate tariff in his scheme of things.

The Cleveland regime in the White House ended on a note of personal harmony. President Cleveland himself wrote Hoke Smith, whom he had so recently rejected, saying that he wished the entire cabinets of his two administrations to come to the White House for a farewell dinner on January 7, 1897. The Clevelands purchased a home in Princeton, New Jersey, for their retirement.

On the night before his inauguration President-elect McKinley had dinner at the White House. In deference to Mrs. McKinley's invalidism—she had epilepsy—only the McKinleys were invited. At the last minute she was unable to come. This made it possible for an outgoing Democratic President and an incoming Republican President to hold that night a serious private conversation on the state of the nation. Cleveland's account of it later was:

"The one question on Mr. McKinley's mind was the threatened war with Spain. He went over with me, carefully, the steps that I had taken to avert this catastrophe, emphasized his agreement with the policy adopted, and expressed his determination to carry it out so far as it lay in his power."

Cleveland also said of his exchange of views with McKinley:

"Of all the interviews I have ever held during the whole of my career, none ever impressed me as being so full of settled sadness and sincerity, and no man ever gave me a stronger idea of his unyielding determination to do his duty when thus confronted by a great crisis."

Inauguration Day fell as heavily on Mrs. Cleveland and Mrs. McKinley as the night before had on their husbands. Frances Cleveland wept as she departed from the White House by a south door as her husband and the President-elect were leaving for the Capitol ceremonies by the North Portico. Mrs. McKinley had a seizure of her malady at the Inaugural Ball that night. The Smithsonian costume collector who later obtained her inaugural gown noted, "on one side of her dress is a mark or stain on the satin where she fell." That gown is one of the most exquisite in the collection of the dresses of Presidents' wives.

The McKinley marriage 27 years before had given every promise of normal happiness. Ida Saxton was the well-educated and beautiful daughter of a banker in Canton, Ohio. She had toured Europe with her sister. Her father believed a woman should be able to earn a living. While serving as a cashier in his bank she met McKinley, a lawyer of that city. A series of calamities when she was a young bride were blamed for the shattering of her nervous system. She lost her mother and two baby daughters, Kate and Ida, by death within three years. Wrote H. H. Kohlsaat, a close friend:

"After the birth of baby Ida, Mrs. McKinley suffered from epilepsy. . . . With the persistence that was part of her disease, she insisted on going everywhere with her husband. He apparently never crossed her wishes. At state dinners and receptions in the White House she was always present unless too ill to leave her room. Frequently the excitement was too much for her, and she fainted. She did not fall out of her chair, but became rigid."

President McKinley had protocol changed so that his wife always sat next to him at official dinners. When she became unconscious for a few minutes, he threw a silk handkerchief over her face until she regained normalcy.

William McKinley undoubtedly was one of the most tactful Presidents this country ever had. A saying of the nineties was that President McKinley could refuse a request as though he were granting a favor, whereas President Harrison had granted a favor as though he were refusing a request. White House usher Ike Hoover spoke of "that kind, gentle, fatherly way of Mr. McKinley's which made all comers feel that he was their friend, but left doubt in their minds as to the substantial result that they had come to accomplish."

Because of Mrs. McKinley's invalidism and the President's devotion to her, Ike Hoover said, the White House practically ran itself. "Everybody in a sense was his own boss, yet things went along well for we were all old hands at the game." Nor did the McKinleys concern themselves with their own personal business affairs which had earlier been taken over in a remarkable way by friends.

While governor of Ohio, McKinley had endorsed notes for a friend who was in financial trouble, Robert L. Walker of Youngstown, Ohio. McKinley thought he was assuming partial responsibility for $17,000. He found himself suddenly presented with liabilities totaling $130,-000. McKinley conferred with his closest friends, Mark A. Hanna and Myron Herrick of Cleveland and H. H. Kohlsaat, publisher of the Chicago *Inter-Ocean*. McKinley said to them, "I can hardly believe this, but it appears to be true. I don't know what my liabilities are, but whatever I owe shall be paid, dollar for dollar." His friends formed a trusteeship, and both McKinley and Mrs. McKinley turned over all their property to be used without preference for the equal benefit of their creditors. When McKinley said he was going to retire from politics and return to private law practice so as to pay his debts, these friends and others determined to raise a fund by public subscription to pay off. There were more than 5,000 subscribers, all debts were paid, and McKinley was enabled to go forward to the Presidency. Myron T. Herrick was treasurer of this fund. Each pay check McKinley got as President was turned over to Herrick, who continued to manage his private affairs, made fortunate investments and finally was able to turn over an estate of more than $200,000.

The entire four years of the first McKinley administration consisted of intensive concentration on crises. Immediately he called the Congress into special session for the purpose of swinging the country out of the depression by the passage of the Dingley tariff and sound money laws. A more powerful pressure was already at work to accomplish this same purpose. This country was on its way to becoming a world power. Hawaii was at last annexed. The Cuban insurrection against Spain broke out, and the nation soon found itself plunged into a war economy.

Ike Hoover later recalled that the business of waging the Spanish-

American War from the White House was carried on in a very methodical way, once McKinley decided to do what that hotheaded Theodore Roosevelt, Assistant Secretary of the Navy, had been urging. Hoover said that Roosevelt came in one night and strode up and down the length of the White House corridor, talking at the top of his voice, and tempestuously departed with the exclamation, "Mr. President, I would order the whole American Navy to Cuba tonight if I had my way." Later "T.R." got his chance to organize his "Rough Riders," and President McKinley spent his days and nights in his map room following land and sea campaigns, punching in little flags to denote the positions of battleships and regiments.

By the time McKinley delivered his second message to Congress this war, waged in spots continents apart—Cuba and the Philippines— was over. In that message McKinley told its whole story in his own words. This country, after every effort to persuade Spain to give Cuba a better government, had intervened in the war for independence there to check the hopeless sacrifice of life. This had not happened until there had been extreme provocation, notably the blowing up of the battleship *Maine* "while rightfully lying in the harbor of Havana on a mission of international courtesy and goodwill." War had been declared in April 1898. McKinley reviewed its triumphant progress to the peace protocols signed in August 1898 which made this country the bigger by Puerto Rico and the other islands under Spanish sovereignty in the West Indies; and also granted the United States occupation of the city and harbor of Manila pending conclusion of the peace treaty. The treaty was completed on Christmas Eve 1898.

Hardly was the Spanish War over when McKinley was deep in the Boxer Rebellion in China, sending in a military relief expedition to rescue from the antiforeign Chinese warriors (called Boxers) the U. S. nationals who had taken refuge in our legation. After winning both the Spanish War and indemnity from China, McKinley easily won in 1900 a second nomination and re-election over William Jennings Bryan, again the Democratic candidate.

For two years prior to 1900 the nation's capital was planning its Centennial Celebration. McKinley in his 1898 message to Congress called for some "handsome permanent memorial." Chiefly talked about were two projects, an enlarged White House and a memorial bridge across the Potomac. Colonel Theodore A. Bingham, McKinley's Superintendent of Public Buildings and Grounds, decided to add to his own fame by enlarging the White House. Glenn Brown, Secretary of the American Institute of Architects, who had once worked under Bingham and hated him, conceived a bigger and better idea—the revival of the original plan of Major Pierre Charles L'Enfant for the federal city and also restoring the White House to its original plan. Brown, great-grandson of Peter Lenox, who was "clerk of works" of the original White House construction from 1793 to 1830, had just completed a thorough research on L'Enfant's great scheme, disregarded since the administration of Madison.

Colonel Bingham, having the inside track as a White House habitué, set up a great East Room celebration, starring himself and his model of the proposed "enlarged White House," to be held as the opening event of the Centennial fete, December 12, 1900. Glenn Brown called a national convention of the American Institute of Architects for the next day.

Colonel Bingham's triumph came off exactly as he had planned— a heady show for any man. He displayed his dazzlingly white model, an adaptation of one of Mrs. Harrison's discarded plans, on a red-draped platform, palm-banked, before the President, Mrs. McKinley, Admiral Dewey, the cabinet, the Supreme Court and 22 governors including New York's Theodore Roosevelt, now also Vice-President-elect.

Glenn Brown's triumph, too, came off exactly as planned. The next day the nation's architects, in convention assembled, called Bingham's plan "a mongrel," "a monstrosity," "an unrecognizable contraption out of harmony with and destroying the individuality of the old building." They voted two resolutions. One said that since the White House was one of the best examples of American architecture, a commission of architects should be appointed to consider any contemplated changes. The other said that the city should immediately go back to the L'Enfant plan and Congress should set up a commission to accomplish that end. Congress did—the famous McMillan Commission of 1901, with the backing of Theodore Roosevelt and the nation's most outstanding architects and sculptors. Colonel Bingham's model descended ignominiously from the East Room into the basement of the Corcoran Art Gallery.

Because of his devotion to his wife President McKinley was regarded by the American people as a sort of saint. Particularly was this true when he attempted a transcontinental trip with Mrs. Mc-

Kinley in the spring of 1901. She collapsed in El Paso, hovered between life and death for two weeks in San Francisco and necessitated a nonstop transcontinental rush back to the White House, causing the cancellation of an appearance at the Buffalo Exposition scheduled for June 2, 1901.

President McKinley made his postponed Buffalo appearance in September. Mrs. McKinley, who accompanied him, was tired from the trip and was sleeping at the home of the exposition president during the late-afternoon reception of September 6, 1901. The crowd in and around the Music Hall was estimated at 40,000. An organ played the national anthem as the President and his party entered the hall, and a handshaking line was formed. In that line an intelligent-looking young man with a handkerchief tied about his right hand offered his left, and, when the President was shaking it, pulled the trigger of the gun that was hidden in the handkerchief. He was Leon Czolgosz, an anarchist, said to be a pupil of Emma Goldman and a follower of Karl Marx. He himself said nothing, proceeding to death sentence without explanation. President McKinley was fatally wounded.

"My wife—be careful, Cortelyou, how you tell her—oh, be careful!" McKinley gasped to his secretary.

Then came a new and surprising picture of Mrs. McKinley: "The invalid of years became the comforter and nurse." William McKinley died in the early morning of September 14, 1901. Mrs. McKinley's strength sufficed for the sorrowful trip to Washington with the President's body, Kohlsaat noting: "During the entire day, in the last coach a little, frail figure in black kept tender watch over her beloved dead." The body lay in state in White House and Capitol, and Col. W. H. Crook wrote: "To the amazement of her physician and other attendants, Mrs. McKinley bore up surprisingly during all the days and nights of this ordeal, and her physical condition occasioned little anxiety when the funeral train left Washington." Final services for McKinley and his burial took place at his old home in Canton, Ohio.

One of McKinley's biographers quoted an outspoken "cabinet wife" as saying: "He lived in close, stuffy rooms, for she was afraid of taking cold. He rode in closed carriages. He did not take sufficient exercise because all his leisure time was given to her. When he was shot, he had not sufficient vitality to recover." The diagnosis of McKinley's physicians bore out this view.

Mrs. McKinley outlived her husband by six years.

14 | Square Deal and Square Peg

...THEODORE ROOSEVELT, TAFT

ON A JUNE midnight in the year 1900 a political reporter crouched on a fire escape outside a smoke-filled hotel room in Philadelphia, his eyes riveted on a dramatic scene. Well-known top figures of the Republican party were pouring arguments into Governor Theodore Roosevelt of New York, who sat grasping with clenched hands an empty chair in front of him. Suddenly Roosevelt rose in rage, lifted the chair high above his head and smashed it to the floor. His anger vented, he made a gesture of resignation and acceptance. The reporter scrambled down the fire escape at record speed and made his morning paper with the news that Theodore Roosevelt had agreed to run for Vice President.

For weeks Roosevelt had been conducting an active campaign against himself for that post. He had written all the powerful Republicans whom he counted as his friends. These letters, varying from person to person in their phrasing, were all in the same tenor. One said: "Many corporations have served notice on the Republican leaders that they won't contribute if I am nominated for Governor and that they will do their best to beat me. This is mainly on account of the franchise tax. They would like to get me out of politics for good. But at the moment they think the best thing to do is to put me into the Vice Presidency."

Roosevelt even made a trip to Washington to see President McKin-

ley and Senator Mark Hanna of Ohio. Hanna was universally regarded as the political boss who motivated McKinley, and presumably the two of them could write the ticket. Secretary of State John
Hay jocosely reported this remarkable political pilgrimage. Roosevelt,
with "a sombre resolution" on his "strenuous brow," had let McKinley and Hanna "know once and for all that he would not be Vice
President" and had found "to his stupefaction" that nobody except
Platt (Senator Tom C. Platt, then regarded as the New York political boss) "had dreamed of such a thing."

Nevertheless, Roosevelt was crammed down the throats of Mc-
Kinley and Hanna for second place on the McKinley ticket by a
combination of New York's Platt plus Pennsylvania's two political
bosses, Matthew S. Quay and Boies Penrose. It was a victory of the
other politicians over Hanna, who made dramatic protest: "Don't
any of you realize that there's only one life between this madman and
the White House?" For Roosevelt the choice was between the Vice
Presidency and the political outer darkness—and he was far too young
a man for the latter. When he took over the Presidency on the death
of McKinley, having presided over the Senate as Vice President only
during a special session of one week, he was the youngest man ever
to be chief executive, forty-three years old.

Characteristically, Theodore Roosevelt was off hunting when Mc-
Kinley died. Guides had to be sent to sleuth him out. He became
immediately absorbed in pressing state affairs; in the swearing-in ceremony, held at the home of a friend, Ansley Wilcox, in Buffalo; and in
the details of the McKinley state funeral. It was Mrs. Roosevelt who
first appeared at the White House, looked the place over and managed the moving in.

Edith Carow Roosevelt had known her husband from early childhood. Her parents lived near the Fourteenth Street mansion of Theodore Roosevelt's grandfather in New York City and were of the same
high social strata. The two children played together and faithfully
wrote letters to each other when Theodore went abroad. Edith Carow
visited Theodore Roosevelt at Harvard University when he was a
student. At Harvard, however, Theodore Roosevelt fell in love with
a Bostonian, Alice Hathaway Lee, with whom he spent three blissful
married years. She died giving birth to another Alice within a few
hours of the death of Theodore's mother.

This double grief caused Theodore Roosevelt to turn to ranch life in the Dakotas for physical and mental rehabilitation. Again he wrote letters to his old friend Edith Carow and traveled all the way to London to marry her on December 2, 1886. Thereafter she recompensed for his twofold loss. She was mother as well as wife to him. Mrs. Bellamy Storer, an aunt of Nicholas Longworth who clashed in print with President Roosevelt, gave a glimpse of the early Roosevelt home life in a description as delightful as it was spiteful.

"Mrs. Roosevelt, like the rest of us, looked upon Theodore as a child. When Archie was a few weeks old, she left Washington with the five children and all the servants to go to Sagamore and open the house for the summer.
" 'Will Mr. Roosevelt let you go alone?' I asked.
" 'For Heaven's sake,' she answered, 'don't put it into Theodore's head to go too; I should have another child to take care of.' "

Something doing every second was the Roosevelt rule in the White House. Theodore Roosevelt was a President who played tennis, wrestled, took lessons in ju-jitsu. He was tagged by his own pithy phrases, "The Strenuous Life" and "Speak softly and carry a big stick; you will go far." His personal appearance aided in initiating a cartoonists' paradise—the "square deal" phrase, distinctive eyeglasses, the exclamation "Bully!," the gleaming teeth which said "De-lighted!" The Roosevelt children—Theodore, Jr., Ethel, Kermit, Archibald, Quentin—had parties, collected menageries, walked on tall stilts over White House stairways and upper halls.

As for Alice Lee Roosevelt, who made her debut in the White House soon after the family moved in, Ike Hoover later testified: "It can reasonably be asserted that no one within the recollection of the oldest inhabitant was ever entertained so much as she was. For at least two years before her marriage, there was never an evening when there was not some party being given in her honor."

The Theodore Roosevelt regime was termed by Ike Hoover "the wildest scramble in the history of the White House." Yet for all its strenuosity, this was no haphazard household. It ran serenely, smoothly, daily making happy memories for all the years to come. The reason for such a felicitous situation was Edith Carow Roosevelt, who joined in the family hiking, horseback riding and reading aloud. Yet somehow she managed to oversee every housekeeping detail—sensibly employing a caterer for official functions—and to keep a gentle but very firm hand on official society.

Mrs. Roosevelt called the wives of cabinet members to the White House for meetings each week. This was for the purpose of instructing them so as to make social events run more smoothly, to keep down rivalries between them and to decree social standing. No Senator's son, whatever the number of his millions, could marry a chorus girl and expect her to move in official society of that day. Her lot and his would be the well-bred "cut direct." Once Mrs. Roosevelt sent word to the wife of a high official that her White House invitations would be canceled if she did not end her love affair with a secretary of an Embassy. The international romance ceased.

As President, Theodore Roosevelt got off to an aggressive start with his first individualistic message to Congress, in which he did not hesitate to reiterate the same tough policy toward the trusts which had characterized his administration as governor of New York:

"Great corporations exist only because they are created and safeguarded by our institutions; and it is therefore our right and duty to see that they work in harmony with these institutions. . . . The nation should, without interfering with the power of the States in the matter itself, also assume power of supervision and regulation over all corporations doing an interstate business."

After a few weeks in office Theodore Roosevelt got from Congress the $475,445 appropriation for repairs and refurnishing which enabled him to make such sweeping changes in that noble old shell, the Executive Mansion, that it was called "The New White House." The name "The White House" then was proudly embossed on its social stationery.

Of equal importance, President Roosevelt obtained an additional appropriation of $65,196 for erection of an executive office as a west wing which enabled him to move the official business of the President outside the main mansion. The site for this office and the colonnade connecting it with the mansion was obtained by clearing away the conservatory and the mushroom growth of greenhouses clustering about it.

Theodore Roosevelt made his White House plans an integral part of the "back-to-L'Enfant" restoration project of the McMillan Commission of 1901 earlier set up by Congress. He placed in charge the outstanding architect of that day, Charles F. McKim, then president of the American Institute of Architects, with Glenn Brown, secretary of that body, in constant supervision.

The order to start the work was given late in June 1902 with the understanding that the White House was to be ready for entertaining by the first of November. The Roosevelts moved to a temporary White House on the west side of Lafayette Square.

Summarizing the condition of the Executive Mansion when the workmen started on it, Glenn Brown said it was a "source of wonder how the decorations and furnishing reached such a stage of bad art." Alice Roosevelt Longworth in her memoirs put it this way: "The furniture and decorations were all that we mean when we say 'late General Grant and early Pullman.' There was much plush and gilt and heavy upholstery, and the ceilings were frescoed with acres of oilcloth patterns."

Excavations revealed the outlines of the gracious wings planned by President Jefferson, and they were restored, the east wing as a ceremonial entrance, the west as the office. Down from the attic came some original mantels which had been discarded and pieces of fine old furniture. But where the original plans offended McKim's sense of proportion, he made changes. The four great chimney breasts in the East Room, projecting two and a half feet into the room and cutting it into three parts, annoyed him. The contractor said it was nearly impossible to change them. Said McKim: "It would be worth five thousand dollars to the appearance of this room to get them out of the way." The flues were "cut back into the brick walls which were found ample to carry them."

McKim was willing to go to any amount of trouble for architectural effects. After the three great East Room chandeliers were all hung, he had them taken down and taken apart to reduce them each by six inches in diameter. In order to achieve a gray of the exact shade to suit his taste McKim had seven coats of paint put over the entire ceiling of the State Dining Room. But when McKim put lions' heads into the State Dining Room mantelpiece instead of bison heads as Theodore Roosevelt had wanted, his triumph was not permanent. Roosevelt decided he had let the architect outargue him as to that all-American motif. Just before leaving the White House in 1909 Roosevelt had the mantel recarved, taking out the lions and putting in his bison.

In this hasty, high-pressured remodeling of 1902 the sagging old second floor was left as it was and a new and level floor superimposed above it. (Only after 46 years was it learned that shavings were left between, enhancing an astounding fire hazard.) The East Room ceiling was raised and embellished by frescoes of fruits and reclining female figures. (Tons of plaster were secured only by nails driven straight up, it was learned in the investigations of the Truman administration.) The State Dining Room was enlarged by taking out the west staircase and including part of the central corridor. (Architects of 1948 could scarcely believe their eyes when they saw how little support had been given the superstructure in this change.) The main staircase off the north front foyer, no longer to be the path of office seekers, was rebuilt so that it opened for ceremonial purposes upon the long hall close to the East Room. (This staircase was found to be poorly supported by secondhand bricks and inferior mortar.) The entire job was done within the time and appropriation limits— too much, too soon, on too little. But at the time it all appeared to be a dazzling part of the general triumph of Theodore Roosevelt.

One very sour note was struck, however. It came from Colonel Theodore A. Bingham, the Commissioner of Public Buildings and Grounds whose plan for an elaborately enlarged White House adapted from one of Mrs. Harrison's models had been nipped in the bud by Glenn Brown. Colonel Bingham had been charged by the new President, Theodore Roosevelt, himself a historian, with the task of keeping a continuing record of official White House social events. Bingham started this White House social history with the first function held after the remodeling, the cabinet dinner of December 18, 1902. This account was, to put it mildly, fault-finding.

Outside the White House east entrance the Electric Carriage Call Co., 1402 Broadway, New York, installed a newfangled punch-card system to flash out numbers which would summon the coachmen in proper sequence following White House affairs. Had this system been a signal for calling up all the old precedence controversies, it couldn't have worked better. Protocol which would last for a long, long time was in the making. Statesmen felt a great surge of patriotic priority, not for themselves, but for their offices. President Theodore Roosevelt took this assault head on, instructing that these disputed matters be entered in the White House social record, together with the decision reached in each case, as a guide to future administrations.

Most prickly of the disputed points was the place of Speaker of the House Joseph Cannon and the head of his household, his daughter Helen Cannon. Precedence had been a sore point with Speakers ever since the law of 1866 had thrown that office out of the line of succession to the Presidency. Into the White House social record went this notation: "By decision of the President, the daughter of the Speaker of the House (Miss Cannon) was given a position after the married women of the House of Representatives."

A few pages later, this entry was added: "Miss Cannon was not pleased with this arrangement, and stated that in future she would send regrets if not assured of the same consideration as would be accorded the wife of the Speaker."

Along came the New Year's reception of 1903 with Colonel Theodore Bingham protesting that the State Department had made a mistake in putting the chargé of France ahead of the chargé of Switzerland. Wrote Colonel Bingham: "This was incorrect because the chargé of an Embassy has no rights exceeding those of a chargé of a Legation. The Dean of the Diplomatic Corps, the German Ambassador, maintains the above statement and he made a complaint to the State Department of the error."

When Secretary of State John Hay upheld the precedence of the French chargé d'affaires, Colonel Bingham, who in 1900 had made out a precedence list under his own byline for the White House, set down, "While I must bow to this decision, I still do not regard it as correct."

Little did Theodore Bingham know that Theodore Roosevelt was at that moment playing a fast diplomatic game with the German Ambassador, dean of the corps, Herr von Holleben. According to Roosevelt's own story of this incident many years later—disputed, however, by other historians—the Kaiser was planning to land an occupation force in Venezuela, and Roosevelt had Admiral Dewey and his fleet of 50 vessels all steamed up at Puerto Rico and ready to sail for Venezuela at an hour's notice to prevent this breach of the Monroe Doctrine. Roosevelt then called Holleben in and issued an ultimatum—any German move would be met by an American move. Obviously the Caribbean area would be the poorest possible place for Germany to fight the United States. At the same time that Herr Holleben was complaining to the State Department in behalf of precedence for the Swiss chargé, he was reporting to his government that Theodore Roosevelt was bluffing about Venezuela.

Suddenly, however, he sensed iron in the President's attitude. He decided he'd better consult his intimate friend Dr. Buenz, German consul general in New York. Dr. Buenz earnestly assured him he could count on Roosevelt doing exactly as he had threatened. Holleben had to send a cable taking back what he'd said earlier. He was immediately recalled and dismissed from the diplomatic corps, and the Kaiser abandoned his Venezuelan adventure. Only Buenz dared to bid Herr von Holleben good-by when he left America.

The entire interchange between Roosevelt and Holleben was kept secret for years, but its results showed up immediately in the White House social record. At the diplomatic reception on January 8 there were two chargés of Embassy in advance of the chargés of Legation. A chargé for Germany as well as the chargé of France was there. Count Cassini of Russia had become dean of the corps in place of the departed Holleben. After the end of that season Colonel Bingham was no longer keeper of the record; that task had been turned over to Major Charles McCawley, military aide, who also took over as ceremonial officer at White House functions. He did less complaining than Bingham about the Roosevelt White House.

Well ahead of the 1904 election Roosevelt frankly stated that he wanted to be elected President in his own right. He felt that he had an ample record on which to campaign. He had fostered a great conservation movement, with Gifford Pinchot as his right-hand man, and had signed the Reclamation Act. He had secured the passage of the Isthmian Canal Act in order to have constructed across Panama that waterway which he thought would be the greatest work of his life. He had, with the cordial backing of former President Grover Cleveland, settled a coal strike. He had paid his respects to "the interests" by securing a law ending the system of railroad-rebate favoritism. And he had settled the Alaskan boundary dispute.

He accomplished that fall the greatest coup of all—recognition of the Republic of Panama, which had seceded from Colombia. Had the Panama Canal not been uppermost in the mind of President Roosevelt, the revolution might have gone unnoticed. After all, Panama is credited by historians with having had 53 revolutions in 53

Theodore Roosevelt's own report on this matter, termed an act of arrant imperialism by his enemies, ran:

"Panama declared itself independent and wanted to complete the Panama Canal, and opened negotiations with us. I might have taken the matter under advisement and put it before the Senate, in which case we should have had a number of most able speeches on the subject. . . . We would have had a half century of discussion, and perhaps the Panama Canal. I preferred we should have the Panama Canal first and the half century of discussion afterward."

Having thus assured the building of the Panama Canal in November 1903, President Roosevelt was in prime condition to meet the strenuous social season which started in December. Included in it was one of the most remarkable parties ever held in the White House—Mrs. Roosevelt's idea—for officialdom's 600 children between the ages of six and sixteen, on the day after Christmas, which was a Saturday. They were all fed supper. Mrs. Roosevelt obtained the invitation list by writing all officials and asking them to report the names and ages of children in the family. Instructions were sent out that adults should accompany only the youngest and most timid. Nurses were kept belowstairs. So it was almost an all-child assemblage, all in best clothes, which filed past Mrs. Roosevelt, being presented and paying respects and then settling down to a concert by the Roney Boys in the East Room. The young Roosevelts—Theodore, Ethel, Kermit, Archibald and Quentin—were all there, but with the distinct understanding that their mother was the hostess. They had never met most of the guests. The newspapers said there ha never before been more than 60 children at a White House childre party. Said the Washington *Post*, "The President himself dispen the creamed oysters."

The New Year started the precedence controversies all over The diplomatic dinner on January 14 was to be Admiral (Dewey's first appearance at the White House since the conf his new commission which made him "The Admiral of th The Admiral maintained that since he now rated a 17-g which was "greater by two than for a Foreign Minister," take precedence right after the Ambassadors and ahead isters. The Admiral lost this battle.

At the Republican convention in Chicago, June 21, 1904, Roosevelt was winner of a nomination so overwhelmingly his that it needed no dramatization.

To his son Kermit, off attending school, Roosevelt wrote how satisfied he was with his first-term accomplishments:

"From Panama down I have been able to accomplish certain things which will be of lasting importance in our history. Incidentally, I don't think any family has ever enjoyed the White House more than we have. I was thinking about it just this morning when Mother and I took breakfast on the portico and afterwards walked about the lovely grounds and looked at the stately historic old house. It is a wonderful privilege to have been here and to have been given the chance to do this work, and I should regard myself as having a small and mean mind if in the event of defeat I felt soured at not having had more instead of being thankful to have had so much."

But it wasn't defeat. To Kermit he later wrote an account of the family celebration at the White House on election night. The President had voted early in the morning at Oyster Bay, then had dashed back to Washington. Ted met him with the news that Buffalo and Rochester had sent in their returns already and that they showed enormous Roosevelt gains. Within the next 20 minutes enough returns were received from the big cities to make it evident that there was a tremendous pro-Roosevelt drift. By the time the family sat down to dinner at half-past seven election was assured. Right after dinner members of the cabinet and friends began to come in, and there was a spontaneous celebration, with Archie—"fairly plastered with badges"—running in the telegrams as fast as they hit the White House telegraphers. The President read them aloud and said when it was all over: "This was the day of greatest triumph I ever had or ever could have." But he still voted that the "really important thing" was "the lovely life I have with Mother and with you children."

Roosevelt's inauguration was filled with old associations and pleasant auguries. The Rough Riders galloped into Washington in force and had a hip-hurrah reunion with their old leader. Secretary of State John Hay, who had been ill for months, sent Roosevelt a ring fashioned from a lock of Abraham Lincoln's hair to wear on Inauguration Day. No symbol could have pleased the President more. He wrote several of his friends about it. He had many times fancied that

Lincoln's spirit still pervaded the White House. It had been Roosevelt's custom to drop into Hay's home on Lafayette Square each Sunday after church, as much to enjoy his living link with Lincoln as to converse with that famous pair, John Hay and his double-house neighbor Henry Adams.

Mrs. Roosevelt sent Aide McCawley a list of 25 Roosevelts to be looked after, provided with seats in the Senate gallery and given tickets to the Inaugural Ball. Thirteenth on the list, arranged alphabetically by first names, was Mr. Franklin Roosevelt and fourteenth was his fiancée, Miss Eleanor Roosevelt. Later that same month the President wrote Kermit he had made a scuttling visit to New York to "give away Eleanor on her marriage" and also to make a St. Patrick's Day speech.

Almost as spectacular as the career of her father was that of Alice Roosevelt. She christened the Kaiser's yacht *Meteor* when he sent his brother, Prince Henry of Prussia, to this country to take over this craft of American manufacture. She visited General and Mrs. Leonard Wood in the Governor's Palace at Havana, Cuba. That brief trip was to console her when it was decided she could not go to England for the coronation of King Edward due to the great amount of newspaper discussion as to what her "rank" might be. She also visited in historic La Fortaleza, the Governor's Palace in Puerto Rico. She was starred at the New Orleans Mardi Gras, at the Chicago Horse Show and at the St. Louis World's Fair. At the end of June 1905, three months after her father's second-term inauguration, she topped it all off with a trip to the Orient with the William Howard Taft mission of 1905.

Secretary of War Taft was the cabinet officer whom Roosevelt sent far and wide on special missions with many and varied objectives. Roosevelt had called him back from his duties as first civil governor of the Philippines, a post given him by President McKinley, to become Secretary of War when Elihu Root left that post to return to private practice of law. When John Hay died in the summer of 1905 Roosevelt called Root back as Secretary of State. Roosevelt, Taft and Root were then called "The Three Musketeers."

When Taft had left the Filipinos, whom he called his "little brown brothers," it was with the promise that he would return with a delegation of American Congressmen to see the legislative body which they had set up. The Japanese-Russian War was on. Roosevelt felt it would be a very good time for the large, strong and peaceful personage of his Secretary of War to show up in the Far East. Among the large delegation of Senators, Representatives and their wives whom Taft took with him was a gay young bachelor, his fellow Cincinnatian, Representative Nicholas Longworth from Ohio. Soon rumors of a romance between "Nick" Longworth and the President's daughter were being wafted back to the States along with stories of how Alice jumped fully dressed into the ship's swimming pool. Each day had its news grist from the tour. Alice Roosevelt was presented to the royal family of Japan and to the old Empress Dowager of China.

That summer, writing to the heads of all the great nations of earth, Theodore Roosevelt pulled the diplomatic strings which brought about peace between Russia and Japan. On September 5 the Russo-Japanese Treaty was signed in Washington, tremendously enhancing Roosevelt's reputation as a statesman. His comment was: "If I had not brought about peace I should have been laughed at and condemned. Now I am over-praised."

When Alice Roosevelt returned from her Oriental trip, laden with gifts for the family, the newspapers took turns rumoring her engagement to Longworth, Miss Winifred Mallon, long-time capital correspondent, recalled. This went on for weeks. At last the Chicago *Tribune* sent its Washington bureau an ultimatum by wire: "Is Alice Roosevelt engaged or is she not?" To which a hectored Bureau chief wired back: "She went out driving with Nick Longworth this afternoon without a chaperon. If they are not engaged, they ought to be." The *Tribune* announced the engagement in the morning paper. The President and Mrs. Roosevelt announced it that afternoon.

There never was a wedding in the White House like Alice Roosevelt's on February 17, 1906. There were a thousand guests, and all the elaborate details of their handling were set down for all time in Charlie McCawley's White House social scrapbooks.

No maid of honor or bridesmaid shared the spotlight with Alice in that formal noon wedding. She was accompanied only by her father, the President, who made no audible answer to the question of who was giving her away, but placed her hand in that of her husband. The groom, however, had a best man and eight ushers.

Rich wedding gifts were showered on "Princess Alice." A necklace of 63 matched pearls with diamond clasp was given her by the Republic of Cuba. The 1906 estimate on their value was $25,000.

The Empress Dowager of China sent a dower chest filled with silks, embroideries and ivory carvings. Rolls of rare fabrics dating far back into Chinese history, in designs which can never be duplicated, were a lifetime gift in that chest. There was a tapestry from the President of France, embroideries and two chased silver vases from the Emperor of Japan, a diamond-and-pearl pendant from the Emperor of Austria, a mosaic table from the King of Italy, a mosaic of a Vatican painting from the Pope and antique jewelry from the King of Spain.

The social reign of "Princess Alice" continued throughout her father's administration and on and on in Washington.

Theodore Roosevelt's second administration was as dramatic as his first. In November 1906 he and Mrs. Roosevelt went to Panama to see the canal so dear to his heart. This trip was touted as the first time a President of the United States had ever left its main boundaries during his term of office. In December 1907 he sent the fleet around the world, by way of emphasizing the fact that this country had indeed become a world power. He continued his domestic reforms against "the interests," vigorously signing forestry acts and homestead acts. Worthy of special mention was his backing of Dr. Harvey Wiley of the Department of Agriculture in his fight for pure food and drugs, which resulted in a Theodore Roosevelt signature on the first Food and Drug Act. It was also on the act establishing the federal Children's Bureau.

As the 1908 election year approached, his mind was ever on a successor who would carry out his policies. William Howard Taft and Charles Evans Hughes were the two most frequently mentioned. Many are the eyewitnesses who testified that Taft would never have been President had it not been for Mrs. Taft. H. H. Kohlsaat, Chicago publisher and politician, recalled an after-dinner hour in which Theodore Roosevelt, taking the role of "seventh son of a seventh daughter," saw something hanging over Taft's head, but couldn't tell whether it was the Presidency or the Chief Justiceship.

"Make it the Presidency!" said Mrs. Taft.

"Make it the Chief Justiceship," said Taft.

Ike Hoover posthumously gave written testimony. "I can remember the exact hour of the famous visit when Mrs. Taft, in the face of the opposition of both the President and her husband, carried her point."

In her autobiography Mrs. Taft gave this analysis of her role in her husband's life:

"I am not trying to pose as a woman endowed with an especial comprehension of such problems as men alone have been trained to deal with. I confess only to a lively interest in my husband's work, which I experienced from the beginning of our association, and which nothing in our long life together, neither monotony nor illness nor misfortune, has served to lessen."

Taft's concept of his wife's role was more concrete. He was quoted as having sized up the situation as follows:

"If I were presiding in the Supreme Court of the United States as chief justice, I should feel entirely at home, but with the troubles of selecting a Cabinet and the difficulties in respect to the revision of the tariff, I feel just a bit like a fish out of water. However, as my wife is the politician and she will be able to meet all these issues, perhaps we can keep a stiff upper lip and overcome the obstacles which just at present seem formidable."

On the thirteenth of May 1908 two historically significant events took place simultaneously in the White House. One was the opening of the three-day Conference on the Conservation of Natural Resources. Working sessions were held in an East Room decorated with great maps that stretched from floor to ceiling. Present were 45 governors, plus William Jennings Bryan as leader of the opposition party; Andrew Carnegie, presumably being approached to give some of his millions to conservation; James Hill, railroad magnate representing capital; and John Mitchell, labor leader.

This meeting marked the first national co-operation between governors, many of whom up to that time had never met one another. It gave a terrific impetus to the conservation movement. And Theodore Roosevelt brought out into the open the problem of the "twilight land of vague boundaries between the State and Federal governments," declaring, "If the matter is such that the State itself cannot act, then I wish, on behalf of all the States, that the national government should act."

Bryan countered: "There is no twilight zone between the nation and the state in which exploiting interests can take refuge from both." He urged that the Congress should take cognizance and make appropriations for conservation of human resources as well as natural resources. Thus in the White House East Room two great leaders of the early twentieth century tossed out two great principles which would dominate many of its later laws—those operating in the field of interstate commerce and those dealing with federal grants-in-aid to states for human-welfare purposes.

Of equal historical importance, into the White House walked that day, for a stay of several years an unforgettable character with rare attributes for a unique contribution to his times—Captain Archie Butt, military aide. Physically he was a striking figure—tall, red-headed, freckle-faced, with a close-cropped military mustache and one of the swankest uniforms ever photographed. He had been educated in the University of the South, where his widowed mother was librarian, and there had started the college newspaper. He had first come to the capital as correspondent for a string of Southern papers. He had then gone to Mexico as secretary of the United States Embassy. With the outbreak of the Spanish-American War, he had been sent to the Philippines as Assistant Quartermaster of Volunteers in charge of 557 horses and mules. On this trip he made a great reputation by proving—in disregard of orders—that animals properly cared for on board could survive the long ocean voyage in fine shape with no Hawaiian Island stopover.

Captain Butt was a born showman with diplomatic experience, thus an ideal Master of Ceremonies at the White House. He was a trained officer with expert knowledge of horseflesh, the perfect aide to a President taking daily exercise. And he was an able journalist with political intuition and a sharp sense of history in the making. More important, he was daily driven to set it down in writing, with all its human-interest sidelights.

"I find that McCawley has left the most wonderful records of all White House functions," Archie Butt enthusiastically wrote. "Every entertainment, no matter how insignificant, has been recorded and precedents laid down as decided."

Soon Archie Butt was both staging the ceremony and packing it neatly away for history. Never were there such source records as he kept. When the President took a trip, into the record went all the printed souvenirs picked up along the way. Butt nightly dictated the summary of each day.

In addition, he was impelled to write political and social history as it happened, and this he did in letters to his mother and, when she died, to his sister-in-law, so that he could truthfully say that he did not keep a diary. These women were less his correspondents than the custodians of his output. Young men must cease to be military aides at the White House when they marry. That's why Colonel Charles McCawley had ceased to keep the White House social record. It would never happen to Archie Butt, a gregarious bachelor with a mother complex so ingrained that even her death could not destroy it.

Archie Butt chronicled only the last 11 months of the Theodore Roosevelt administration, but it was with a close-up vividness unequaled by any other author. His letters of less than a year made a book of almost 400 pages. In it was pictured the delightful home life of the Roosevelt family at Oyster Bay, including the history hobby of the President, the boating and kite-flying of the boys, the Coney Island party given by Ethel and the perfect housekeeping of Mrs. Roosevelt, whom he described as "a sort of feminine luminiferous ether, pervading everybody and everything." He put onto paper the adventurous "roughing it" expeditions to Rock Creek Park in which Theodore Roosevelt led some party—he didn't care whether it was from his "Tennis Cabinet" or his own boys and those of Secretary of the Interior Garfield—in a follow-the-leader scramble across cliffs and through the water. It was a poor Rock Creek ramble in which all participants did not arrive home covered with mud. On one such jaunt Roosevelt found the leading officers of Army and Navy were short of wind. He issued orders for more exercise in the Armed Services.

Archie Butt also described in detail the terrific success of Ethel Roosevelt's debut dance, which he staged, clearing all State Parlors for dancing by serving supper in the rooms on the ground floor.

Butt confessed that he belonged to the "Incense Swingers," the group who looked on Roosevelt almost as a high priest. "His departure from the Presidency is certainly in a blaze of glory," Butt wrote. "Little did anyone think among the last things he would do would be to call a Congress of the world to meet at The Hague on the conservation of the world's energies. Really the scope of his mind is masterful." He pictured the President at Hampton Roads in February, watching the fleet come in from its trip around the world, and quoted him as saying, "I could not ask a finer concluding scene to my administration." And still Butt topped it all with the tale of

Roosevelt's leave-taking luncheon to his "Tennis Cabinet" of 30 men, whom he got together on March 1 for the first and only time and seated according to their precedence in his heart, a French Ambassador on one side, a Wild West character on the other. These strong men could not speak as they bade T. R. good-by. Butt explained that not nearly all had actually played tennis with the President—the term was used as a symbol of belonging to his gang, furthering his programs. Being included in that March 1 luncheon meant to Archie Butt that he had made the grade.

Being included for Archie Butt meant being delegated by Theodore Roosevelt to destroy a bad portrait of himself which had been commissioned and also paid for by Congress; and to break up the chipped Roosevelt china so that it couldn't be sold at auction, a custom Mrs. Roosevelt thought undignified. It also included preparing for all the changes the Tafts wanted the minute they took over. Mrs. Taft called Captain Butt into conference many times between election day in November 1908 and Inauguration Day in March 1909. Said he: "I am getting too deep into the 'twilight zones' of these two administrations to suit me, but if I am perfectly frank with both I do not see how I can offend either."

Helen Herron Taft had been no small factor in her husband's career. They had grown up in the same city, but didn't happen to meet until both were adult. It was at a bobsled party. Soon Helen Herron had steered their companionship into serious political channels by organizing, with two of her intimate friends, an exclusive "salon" which included Taft. They were married in 1886. Salon discussion continued, centering on the Cincinnati political boss, against whom Taft was waging a crusade which won for him a state-supreme-court judgeship at the astonishingly early age of twenty-nine.

Luckily Mrs. Taft liked travel, for no politician of any time ever saw more clearly than Taft how much could be done with a trip. Before her youngest son was eight years old, her husband's official career had taken Mrs. Taft twice around the world. When opportunity opened, the Tafts and their three children had gone gaily off to Manila, paying no attention to dire tales of the disease dangers in that far-off city. Their children were Robert, born in 1889; Helen, in 1891; and Charles, in 1897.

Mrs. Taft had loved Manila and its Luneta, an oval drive with a grandstand at either end where everybody greeted everybody else in the cool of the evening. She had adored being mistress of the beautiful old Malacañan Palace, where her thrift in growing an American garden, keeping a cow and raising chickens had cut down expenses so as to permit brilliant weekly receptions and many a gay garden party. When Theodore Roosevelt called Taft back to this country, Mrs. Taft saw no comparable glamour in being a "cabinet wife." "I thought what a curious and peculiarly American sort of promotion it was which carried with it such diminished advantages," she said.

President Taft dined on Inauguration Night with the Yale Class of '78, then picked up Mrs. Taft for the Inaugural Ball in the Pension Building, where they greeted a thousand people before going into their box. Butt noted that in future years greetings should be limited to diplomats who should be invited three weeks in advance and told to wear official dress. He described in the official record every detail of Mrs. Taft's Empire-style inaugural gown of white chiffon over white satin, heavily embroidered in silver in goldenrod motif.

That very month President Taft started on the travels which mounted to 114,559 miles during the four years of his term. E. W. Smithers, communications chief at the White House, who kept a mileage log of Presidential travels for 33 years starting with Roosevelt's second term, said of him, "There was the traveller! He went to Panama twice and made two or three Pacific Coast swings. Facilities were sometimes poor on the routes he had to take. Often his car had to wait five or six hours on a siding until some other train picked him up. He didn't mind as long as he slept well at night, and he saw to that. He had a special mattress made for himself. It lay in Union Station all the time, ready to go."

Taft had been elected on a platform of moderate downward revision of the tariff. Calling a special session of Congress on March 15, 1909, he went to work on that toughest of problems, in which every rate schedule is supported by a special interest and any change is sweated out in compromise. Taft, in the role of White House host, set about securing these gentlemen's agreements. He set up a series of White House dinners strictly on tariff lines, chuckling to himself at the social mixture he was stirring up. As Archie Butt phrased it, "He used the White House as a great political adjunct in the battle." At the last minute he forced a reduction on shoes. He won also, at that special session, a bill for free trade with the Philippine Islands, signing both bills on the day that the session adjourned and then going home to a "Harmony Dinner" which included all the principals in the tariff fight. He ordered the best of wines for this fete.

Archie Butt wrote that he had thought it "perfect nonsense to serve vintage wine to most of those people" and so bought only four bottles of the very finest vintage he could get at the Metropolitan Club and had it served to "Senator Root, Senator Hale, the Speaker, the Attorney General and several others who are bon vivants in their way and great connoisseurs of champagne." To his horror, he said, Nick Longworth, who sat next to him, "fired an arrow in the sky in the shape of a remark that I was serving two kinds of wines and possibly palmed off inferior brands on the unsuspecting." Said Butt, "I laughed at his suspicions and said we were serving a vintage wine and ordered the waiter to keep Nick's glass filled."

Early that summer Mrs. Taft was reveling in the success of her idea "to convert Potomac Park into a glorified Luneta where all Washington could meet, either on foot or in vehicles, at five o'clock on certain evenings." She called in Archie Butt, who put this idea into operation, with a bandstand at either end of Potomac Drive, later called the "Speedway." Taft attended these open-air band concerts on horseback. Archie Butt said that by inviting certain Senators to join him he won tariff votes, sometimes in exchange for minor appointments.

Mrs. Taft had been in the White House only two and a half months when she had a slight stroke of paralysis which hampered all the rest of her stay there. Only the week before, President Taft had told Archie Butt how proud he was of Nellie, in that she had been able to give individuality to all her entertainments. This had been a difficult thing to do, Taft said, "following so close on the Roosevelt administration which was so particularly brilliant." The day she was stricken, Mrs. Taft had gone to the hospital to see her son Charles safely through a tonsillectomy in a short recess between heavy social duties which included an afternoon party on the yacht *Mayflower* and a formal dinner. The *Mayflower* had not reached Alexandria when Mrs. Taft lost consciousness. Taft still had to go through with a dinner party that evening. It was too late to call it off. That night Archie Butt wrote: "Mrs. Taft has done too much. The last of six dinners was given tonight. Every Senator and most of the important members of the House have been entertained during the past two months. In addition to this she had planned and carried through two big garden parties and innumerable smaller affairs, besides inaugurating the driveway and realizing splendid success from the venture."

The disease had made a facial attack. Mrs. Taft had to learn again how to enunciate clearly. But her keen mind was not affected. Four of her sisters successively came to serve in her stead as hostess and to help carry out the plans which she continued to formulate.

Mrs. Taft envisaged a Japanese-cherry-blossom season, such as the Tafts had once enjoyed in Tokyo, in Potomac Park. "Both the soil and climate encouraged such ambition," she said. To make her wish come true, that famous Japanese liberal leader, the Honorable Yukio Ozaki, then mayor of Tokyo, secured the gift of 3,000 cherry trees from the Municipality of Tokyo to the City of Washington. On reaching America they were found to be infected with scale and were destroyed. When the U. S. Secretary of Embassy had to report the unfortunate fate of the cherry trees Ozaki smiled and said: "Oh, I believe your first President set the example of destroying cherry trees, didn't he?" Undaunted, the Tokyo mayor had 3,000 more cherry saplings raised on disinfected soil. It took two years to produce them, but this time the transplanting was successful. They encircled the Tidal Basin, surrounded Hains Point and eventually spread to Capitol grounds and to Washington suburbs. Mrs. Taft, who recovered remarkably from her illness and survived her husband by some years, lived to enjoy the fairyland created by her idea for many a springtime. And the far longer-lived Yukio Ozaki, after Japan had lost the war which Theodore Roosevelt had direly predicted would one day be fought, visited the Tidal Basin trees in 1950. His age at that time was ninety-two.

On his first transcontinental trip—September 4 to November 10, 1909—President Taft met President Porfirio Diaz of Mexico at the Texas border, and each was entertained in the land of the other. Taft in his speech at the banquet across the border said: "This is the first time so far as I know that a President of the United States has stepped beyond the border of the United States, either on the North or to the South, and I esteem it a great privilege to be President at the time when that event has happened." There must have been some unfavorable reaction to this gesture, for when the Tafts took a trip to Eastport, Maine, on the *Mayflower* the next summer, all the party but Taft accepted an invitation to tour Campobello Island in Canada.

Mrs. Taft reported that Mr. Taft had decided not to break the unwritten law which "decrees that a President may not set foot outside United States territory." Reported Mrs. Taft, "We had a jolly, jolting ride which ended at the summer home of Mrs. Franklin Roosevelt."

Long before Theodore Roosevelt returned from Africa, where he went shortly after Taft's inauguration, Archie Butt had been chronicling the tactics of the "Back from Elba" forces. They wanted Roosevelt back in the White House, and their every political move was toward that end. At the other extreme of the Republican party the men whom Roosevelt had always termed "the interests" and "the enemy"—Aldrich, Wetmore, Depew—were "licking their chops and looking forward to seven fat years after the seven lean years." Butt noted that Taft was driven more and more to consorting with "the enemy," notably Senator Nelson W. Aldrich of Rhode Island.

That December Helen Taft had her debut, with a tea for 1,200 on December 1 and a ball with 300 guests on December 30. Again Archie Butt was the impresario of imagination, clearing the East Room floor completely for dancing by spiriting the Marine Band upward with a method all his own. "A room for the band was built on the East Terrace, completely surrounding the triple window on the East Side of the East Room," he said. "All the window panes and sashes were taken out." The music that night was pronounced perfect.

On June 19, 1911, the Tafts celebrated their silver wedding anniversary, Archie Butt calling it "the most brilliant function ever held" in the White House. The House of Representatives presented the Tafts with a $1,700 solid-silver service, the Senate silver compote dishes.

More and more the name of Miss Martha Bowers was appearing on White House table charts, particularly when these affairs were small and intimate. After the administration was over she would become Mrs. Robert Taft.

Looking about him at his family, Taft said "I would rather be Chief Justice of the United States; and a quieter life than that which comes at the White House is more in keeping with my temperament, but when taken into consideration that I go into history as a President, and my children and children's children are the better placed on account of that fact, I am inclined to think that to be President

The portrait of Grover Cleveland above the mantle of the Red Room as redecorated by President Franklin D. Roosevelt.

The East Room as redecorated by President Franklin D. Roosevelt.

well compensates one for all the trials and criticisms he has to bear and undergo."

Taft called his own administration dull. He did not possess Roosevelt's powers of dramatization and could make nothing which appealed to the people out of such forward steps as initiating the federal budget and setting up the tariff commission. Archie Butt helped him by such humanizing stunts as taking him to the Bowery in New York and giving out the story to the papers when he interrupted a stiff official visit to a charity ball to waltz around the floor with a pretty girl.

But more and more the chasm growing between Taft and Roosevelt filled Archie Butt's letters until it became the great underlying theme of a two-volume set titled *Taft and Roosevelt*—like his first book, posthumously published. Both the President and his military aide were daily haunted by the break. Taft began to have gout and heart symptoms. However, Butt said of him: "I am convinced he would rather be at odds with the Colonel and suffer what he does than be on terms of intimacy and subject to the charge of being dominated by the ex-President."

Archie Butt lost so much weight that Taft insisted on his going abroad for a rest ahead of the conventions. Butt said that Colonel Roosevelt had sent a warning through Alice Longworth to "get out of his present job, and not wait for convention or election." Butt's reaction had been: "It would be a cowardly thing to do. If I were ever so much more worn out than I am, I would stick it out." Again, he wrote: "My devotion to the Colonel is as strong as it was the day he left, but this man has been too fond of me for the past three years to be thrown over at this time and having it sent all over the country that another Roosevelt man reads the handwriting on the wall and gets out of the sinking ship, or some other such mixed metaphor." And again, sandwiched in between two accounts of Mrs. Ned McLean's ominous Hope Diamond, which she had just introduced to Washington society, these words: "The clash which must follow between these two men is tragic. It is now moving from day to day with the irresistible force of the Greek Drama."

Archie Butt did not get out of the sinking ship. He went down with it, and thus never had to make the awful choice between the two men he had loved and served. The name of the ship was the *Titanic*, and Butt with his housemate, the artist Francis Davis Millet, were passengers whose names were not listed among the survivors. Those who did live to tell the story later said that Archie Butt took ceremonial charge of the sinking and had the passengers bravely singing "Nearer My God to Thee" as they went down. President Taft and Secretary of War Henry Stimson delivered eulogies at the memorial services for Archie Butt, and ex-President Roosevelt sent a tribute. Newspaper clippings on this service and a full-length portrait of Archie Butt were entered in the official White House record which he had so faithfully kept. And a fountain in honor of him and his friend Millet was erected just south of the White House grounds on the executive-office side.

On came the Taft-Roosevelt split with full momentum. It resulted in the organization of the "Bull Moose" Progressive Republican party—and the election of a Democrat, Woodrow Wilson.

15 | *A War Won and a League Lost*

...WILSON

WOODROW WILSON'S youngest daughter, Eleanor Randolph Wilson, wrote in her memoirs that on March 3, 1913, the day before her father's inauguration, she locked her door and crawled under the bed at the Shoreham Hotel, where the family was staying, and there lay pounding on the floor and crying "It will kill them—it will kill them both" until overcome by exhaustion.

A young girl usually the gayest of the family had suddenly been hit with the enormity of the office of the Presidency, not only for the man but for his wife. That day her mother, Ellen Axson Wilson, had burst into a flood of tears just before going to the White House to have tea with the Tafts. Mrs. Wilson's health probably was already being undermined by the Bright's disease and tuberculosis of the kidneys which claimed her a year and five months after her husband took office.

Wilson's welcome from President Taft was more than kindly. On Inauguration Day he not only went up to the Capitol with the incoming President, but also returned and stayed for lunch, helping to introduce the new family to the old mansion. Taft said to them, "I'm glad to be going—this is the lonesomest place in the world."

Yet the Wilsons immediately loved the White House and were happy there. Eleanor Wilson testified that the place became home to all of them that day when her mother drew her daughters to a south window overlooking the Ellipse and Washington Monument and said, "Isn't it lovely, children?" Thus had Ellen Axson Wilson been

287

able to create home in big old places which came with her husband's positions—privacy-lacking "Prospect," the president's house at Princeton University; and the summer residence of New Jersey's governor at Sea Girt, disturbed by the thunder of trains. Whatever the surroundings, she was able to keep the same close-knit spirit that had been wrought into "Library Place House" at Princeton, for which the brilliant young professor Woodrow Wilson had drawn architectural designs usable to the last detail and for which his artist wife had made the scale model.

The Oval Sitting Room on the family floor seemed bare and cheerless after Mrs. Taft had taken out her Oriental screens and teakwood furniture acquired in the Philippines. Mrs. Wilson, who always spent every possible moment at her easel, brought in the fine paintings and statuary which she and her husband had managed to buy on a college president's salary. She brought in the family piano and filled the bookcases with favorite books. A big Victrola was already part of its furnishing. "Almost as homelike as any room we had ever lived in," the Wilson family voted. There they resumed their routine of listening to their father read aloud and joining him in his mood of the moment—whether serious discussions or family charades. Woodrow Wilson, who attended the theater oftener than any other President, whimsically held that he might have made a living as a vaudeville actor. When a gay mood was on him he could do impersonations, cakewalk, dance a jig.

For her husband's study, the cabinet room of the old days when the Presidential offices had been in the White House, Mrs. Wilson had Watts's painting *Love and Life* brought back from the Corcoran Gallery to hang over the mantelpiece. Mrs. Wilson had known that this picture of two beautiful naked figures had been given by its artist to the government, presumably for the White House, and she had been disappointed at not finding it there. She learned that it had made many trips back and forth between the White House and the gallery.

To each of the three Wilson daughters, as different in character and temperament as three young women could possibly be, went a room according to her taste. Margaret Woodrow Wilson, the eldest, was a small, intense person determined to become a great singer. She loved solitude and chose as her own the room in which Lincoln had signed the Emancipation Proclamation, at the other end of the White

House from the rest of the family. Jessie Woodrow Wilson, the second daughter, deeply religious and very beautiful, was accorded the large room in the northeast suite when the youngest sister, Eleanor, declared for the small bed in the little dressing room adjoining. Eleanor was gay and frivolous and loved dancing. Jessie and Eleanor had much to talk over, each being engaged, a close family secret. Jessie was engaged to Francis P. Sayre, whom she later married in the White House. Eleanor's troth was not so lasting—she soon broke it to follow her sister in another White House wedding to Secretary of the Treasury William G. McAdoo.

At the east end of the long upstairs corridor between the suites of the younger girls and their parents stood the desk of Isabelle Hagner, who had been secretary to Mrs. Theodore Roosevelt. She introduced the women of the Wilson family to the intricacies of Washington society and routed each of the three girls to a different dance nightly where each could be a star and so spread the Wilson popularity. In the daytime they were swept into a whirl of worthy works—child-welfare exhibitions, benefit bazaars. Margaret was the real crusader, taking a leading national role in the movement for community centers. She believed machine politics could be ended by educating the American public politically in such centers. Once, under Margaret's leadership, they all disguised themselves and went on a sightseeing tour of Washington and the White House. They were good enough in dramatics to evade discovery.

To each of his three daughters Woodrow Wilson was a god, just as he was to their mother. Ike Hoover, White House chief usher, observed, "They pampered him and petted him and looked up to him as their lord and master." Wilson's cousin Helen Bones, called in to take care of Mrs. Wilson's private correspondence and accounts, joined in this adulation, as did all others who came within the family circle. Woodrow Wilson chose few men friends. Two of the closest were his wife's brother Stockton Axson, a professor of English poetry at Princeton; and, after he entered the White House, Dr. Cary T. Grayson, White House physician and in daily companionship with the Presidential family, for Mrs. Wilson was increasingly ill.

The closeness of the Wilson family relationship was the more remarkable to observers in that Mrs. Wilson apparently had been able to divest herself completely of the very human emotion of jealousy. She seemed to be completely content with her own intimate sharing in her husband's life and was quite willing for him to have a large number of other close women friends. One Princeton friend compared Wilson to Disraeli in that he was dependent on women in an extraordinary degree. Their companionship, admiration, attentiveness, adoration brought out his original thought and scintillating conversation. Mrs. Wilson was capable of serenely keeping a large party engaged in after-dinner conversation while her husband was deep in tête-à-tête in the adjoining library with some newly discovered beauty.

Wilson was long a regular teatime visitor of Mrs. John Grier Hibben, wife of a Princeton faculty member. Often he took Mrs. Hibben walking, obviously absorbed in her conversation. Mrs. Wilson remained Mrs. Hibben's close friend, and Woodrow Wilson was deeply hurt and simply could not understand it when Professor Hibben went over to his enemies in a faculty row.

Another friend whom Wilson met during a vacation in Bermuda was Mrs. Mary Hulbert Peck. She visited in the Wilson home, and the Wilson family visited in her Bermuda home. Over a period of seven years Wilson wrote her some 200 letters, which became the basis of a whispering campaign in the 1912 election. Scholars who have gone over them carefully have said that no one could read them and believe there was anything compromising in Wilson's association with Mrs. Peck. They were the letters of a very happy man expressing himself intellectually to an appreciative audience.

It remained for Eleanor Wilson to reveal later that Mrs. Wilson disapproved of Mrs. Peck's smoking, and that the Wilson daughters resented her efforts to have them dress in a more sophisticated fashion.

Woodrow Wilson once described his wife as "tactfully persuasive, not coercive," "receptive not aggressive," adding, "A man could read her a treatise or a long essay and she would never interrupt until the end—she had what I call a speaking silence." Mrs. Peck said of her own role in Woodrow Wilson's life, "In a sense I was an opportunity for a 'pedagogue' to walk down new lanes of thought, to hear an unacademic, fresh vocabulary."

Eleanor Wilson summed up a discussion of her father's deep and lasting friendships with many attractive and witty women in a wide age range by saying that all were shared with her mother. Said Mrs. Wilson to Woodrow, "Since you have married someone who is not gay, I must provide for you friends who are." Eleanor said her father thought women had deeper sensibilities and finer understanding than most men. She added: "Father used to say that no man had ever become a great success without having been constantly surrounded by admiring females, and that obviously he had no escape from extraordinary renown by that rule."

Wilson and his wife had similar family backgrounds. He was a Virginian, she from the deeper South, Georgia. He was a Presbyterian preacher's son, she a Presbyterian preacher's daughter. He saw her first in church while visiting a Georgia cousin, and the night he made his first call he made up his mind to marry her. They both remained close to Presbyterian tenets, even though the Irish in Wilson sufficiently balanced the Scotch to cause him to enjoy the theater and to teach all three of his daughters to play an excellent game of billiards. While in the White House he became an elder of the Presbyterian church where he worshiped with great regularity, even attending Wednesday-night prayer meetings.

Woodrow Wilson was a rare type of statesman in that he first worked out academically a philosophy of government and then went into politics to put his theories into practice. Outlined in his campaign speeches, this philosophy was entitled "The New Freedom." Said Wilson, "What I am interested in is having the government of the United States more concerned about human rights than about property rights." To that end he called a special session of Congress soon after taking office for the purpose of revising the tariff downward so as to limit special privilege; and to create the Federal Reserve System, which would make available to the country a reserve of capital to lessen the strictures of depressions.

The country was electrified when Wilson chose to present these matters to Congress in person. Not since the elder Adams had a President addressed Congress. To a joint session he gave one of the short, pithy addresses, pounded out on his own typewriter, which were to become classics as Presidential papers. On his way back to the White House after he had received a thunderous ovation, Mrs. Wilson said to her husband, "That's the sort of thing Roosevelt would have loved to do, if he had thought of it." And Wilson replied, "Yes, I think I have put one over on Teddy."

The Wilson family spent that summer in the New Hampshire hills at Harlakenden, the estate of the American author Winston

Churchill, but the President stuck to humid Washington and the tariff and fiscal bills. The artists' colony around the estate put on a Bird Masque with Eleanor Wilson playing the Bird Spirit and her sister Margaret singing offstage in the woodland amphitheater. Woodrow Wilson came up from Washington for this event. The New York feather trade rushed into print with a protest that the Bird Masque was unfair to their business. As a result of this publicity a request came that the Masque be repeated in New York the next winter. By that time the Wilson family had to do some adroit planning to fit it in, they were so busy with weddings. Jessie was married in the East Room in November 1913 and Eleanor in the Blue Room in May 1914.

Mrs. Wilson was thoroughly familiar with all her husband's democratic tenets and polished speeches. Of his political appointments she knew nothing. This was more than evident in a letter she once wrote to Joseph Tumulty, her husband's secretary, reminding him how anxious she and her daughters were that a close family friend, Dudley Field Malone, should be appointed Collector of the Port of New York. She asked Tumulty to write her if he found out anything about Malone's chances. The appointment was made, but turned out to be a boomerang. Malone resigned the collectorship with a blare of publicity in protest to Wilson's deafness to the militant suffragettes, with one of whom, Doris Stevens, Malone had fallen in love and whom he later married.

Previous Presidents had been permitted to take an interest in suffrage or let it alone. Theodore Roosevelt said he believed in it, but that other reforms were more important. Taft saw no sense in adding more voters to the electorate. But Woodrow Wilson had no respite from the "Votes for Women" clamor from the day he reached Washington until the suffrage amendment was at last added to the Constitution in 1920. A quiet but determined Quakeress, Alice Paul, had returned from England, where women were hunger-striking for the vote, and she set her suffragettes on Wilson and his White House.

For months on end the suffragettes picketed with banners, throwing words from Wilson's speeches back in his face. They kept a "perpetual fire" going in the park across the street to burn up every sentence he said about "liberty" or "democracy." They burned him in effigy. When sent to jail, they went on a hunger strike—and came out with exposés of conditions in that federally owned institution.

Of the suffragettes Edmund W. Starling, the Secret Service man who guarded Wilson, said, "Sometimes they were a joke; sometimes they were a nuisance; always they were determined and a little frightening to us men."

Ellen Axson Wilson, Georgia gentlewoman, died in the White House on August 6, 1914, without knowing that a world war had already begun, Austria and Germany against the other great powers of Europe. Her last words, her last thought, was for her husband. To her physician, Dr. Cary Grayson, she gave her charge: "Promise me that when I go you will take care of Woodrow." Fate had ended her life span with that of the old order to which she belonged. Her life in the White House was peace, and the ways of peace—a smoothly running home, hours spent enjoying indoor art and the outdoor beauty of the garden she had created. She also had had one consuming civic interest—the cleaning up of the sordid alleys, teeming with slum life, which were hidden away in the heart of the capital's handsome business and residence blocks. Congress hurried up and passed her bill so that she could know the success of her crusade before she died.

President Wilson himself laid out on a couch his beloved dead and sat by her body two long nights. For weeks after her passing he was a lost and lonely man, wandering disconsolately through the White House. His unmarried daughter Margaret was absorbed in her musical career and did not like formal social affairs. His cousin Helen Bones helped all she could. And Cary Grayson took him out to a golf course and taught him the game.

Never did a man keep a deathbed promise more completely than Cary Grayson did his vow to Ellen Axson Wilson. Into Woodrow Wilson's life, through his friendship with Grayson, came beautiful, brunette Edith Bolling Galt, widow of a Washington jeweler. She was the closest friend and, indeed, the guardian of the young lady with whom Grayson was in love and whom he later married, Alice Gertrude Gordon, called Altrude.

Grayson had first introduced Mrs. Galt to lonely Helen Bones and Margaret Wilson, not dreaming that she would soon become to the President all women in one. The fiction was long preserved that she was the friend of the women in the family, as Wilson conducted his eager courtship within the White House walls and in the summer solitude of Harlakenden. When she accepted him in September

1915 Wilson confided the fact to his two closest political advisers, Colonel Edward M. House and his son-in-law William G. McAdoo.

If in later years Edith Bolling Wilson turned against these two, she had cause. She told the story in her memoirs. President Wilson sent Dr. Grayson to tell her something which he could not bear to tell himself, nor would he put it on paper. Colonel House had told Wilson that he and McAdoo had been sounding out a few newspapermen and had learned that if the gossip as to their engagement proved true, Mrs. Peck was going to come out against the President with a statement that she had letters from him that would be compromising. Wilson felt that he could not put her through the backstairs gossip and whisperings of the 1912 campaign and so was releasing her from her promise. Wilson then took to his bed, but Mrs. Galt was equal to the emergency.

In a night-long vigil she reached the conclusion that not politics, not scandal, but "our lives" were what mattered. She went to the White House, where she and the President decided to announce their engagement on October 7. The reaction of the country was favorable, and not a word was heard from Mrs. Peck. Years afterward Mrs. Wilson pinned Colonel House down to an admission that neither he nor McAdoo had ever heard any threat or rumor of a threat from Mrs. Peck. Their concern was lest a second marriage of the President might cause unfavorable public sentiment and prevent his re-election.

President Woodrow Wilson and Edith Bolling Galt were married in her modest Twentieth Street home on December 10, 1915, but with all the dash and distinction that could be poured out by a devoted White House staff. Usher Ike Hoover was the impresario, and was proudest of his magnificent background of maidenhair fern behind the bridal pair. They were unattended, and they announced their own nuptials. Colonel Starling of the Secret Service became the best raconteur of the wild automobile chase by which they evaded the newspaper reporters, entraining for their Hot Springs, Virginia, honeymoon at Alexandria, Virginia, instead of the Washington terminal. In an intimate circle Starling could also give a wonderful impersonation of Bridegroom Wilson dancing a jig the length of the honeymoon car to his own whistled tune, "Oh, You Beautiful Doll!"

The Wilson honeymoon was somewhat shortened by a Mexican crisis. It became necessary for the President to send troops across the border in pursuit of bandits—excellent training, as it turned out, for U. S. military men who would soon be fighting a bigger war.

Mrs. Wilson brought into the White House only a few favorite pieces of furniture—a mahogany rolltop desk, the furnishings of her own room, a sewing machine, her own piano and books. There were many gibes about the sewing machine, but it became the whirring center of a Red Cross production circle in the war years that followed.

Belle Hagner's social desk by the big east window in the upper hall had been taken over by Edith Benham. Reception lists had so swelled that more than 6,000 were invited to each one. Mrs. Wilson aided by Miss Benham reduced the lists to a reasonable size for general enjoyment. And Mrs. Wilson stopped the custom of inviting favored guests "behind the lines" at these receptions, a source of social jealousy.

Woodrow Wilson made his campaign for re-election on his domestic record—his entire "New Freedom" program enacted into law. This included, in addition to his banking and tariff laws, creation of the Federal Trade Commission to curb unfair competition; a farm-loan act which reduced interest rates to finance farms and agricultural operations; and an eight-hour-day law for railroad workers. Wilson's supporters supplied the clinching argument of the campaign, "He kept us out of war." Still his re-election over the Republican candidate, Charles Evans Hughes, was by such a narrow margin that the decision was in doubt for three days. It took that long to establish that the Republicans really had lost California—due, the political analysts said, to the snubbing of Senator Hiram Johnson by Candidate Hughes.

No President ever hated war worse than Woodrow Wilson. Not even when Germany had carried her economic battle against Great Britain and France well within our shores did he ask belligerent action. The British passenger ship *Lusitania* was sunk in 1915 with our citizens aboard. Wilson made a speech in which he used the phrase "too proud to fight." A German brief case revealing a nation-wide network of espionage and sabotage conducted from the German Embassy was picked up and turned over to Secretary of the Treasury McAdoo. Wilson merely broke diplomatic relations, sending the German Ambassador and other chief plotters back home.

Not until Wilson conceived the idea of "a war to end war" which would terminate in a "League of Peace," subsequently elaborated by him into his League of Nations plan, was he ready to battle. Already he had well mapped in his mind the highly specific "Fourteen Points" which he would make the basis of any peace to which his name would be affixed. It must be "peace without victory." It must bring real freedom of the seas. Poland must be liberated and have a corridor to the sea—the great pianist Paderewski of Poland had appeared at a White House musicale and while a guest there had imbued the President with his fire for Polish freedom. Wilson's interest spread to all the little nations struggling for self-determination.

When Wilson finally moved, his action was dramatic. He called a special session of Congress for April 16, 1917, to hear his war message, and when more overt acts of German aggression hit the headlines he advanced the convening date to April 4. That eerie night in a Capitol swept by rain, with his adoring wife and daughter Margaret looking down from the first row in the balcony, Woodrow Wilson made a speech called by his enemies as well as his friends one of the greatest orations of all time. Its final sentence was "We will not choose the path of submission." There was silence, then pandemonium. The Chief Justice of the United States let out his old Confederate war whoop.

Now the White House was the center for the political and military conduct of the war. The grounds were closed and guarded. Routine entertaining ended, but important military and economic missions were accorded White House hospitality. The British, French, Italian, Belgian, Russian and Japanese missions came in that order. Theodore Roosevelt came calling and was denied his request to go overseas at the head of troops. General Leonard Wood also was kept on this side of the ocean. A new military genius, John J. Pershing, had declared for scientific warfare rather than campaigns under personal leadership.

Edith Bolling Wilson learned to decode the confidential messages sent by her husband's roving ambassador in Europe, Colonel House. She took her place beside her husband's desk in his White House study. When he was engrossed in tasks she could not share she knitted for the soldiers or patiently pursued her task of naming U. S. merchant vessels. She gave them all Indian names, in keeping with the fact that she herself stemmed in a straight genealogical line from the Indian princess Pocahontas. In her memoirs Mrs. Wilson printed the table of descent attesting that fact.

Sometimes she took her husband to Red Cross canteen duty in the railroad yards. There they both gave a great lift to carloads of American youth bound for the French battlefields.

Mrs. Wilson and the ladies of the cabinet together took the pledge "to reduce living to its simplest form" so as to free American workers for war production. The wheatless and meatless days decreed by Food Administrator Herbert Hoover were rigorously observed in the White House. On a "gasless Sunday" the Wilsons went to church in an old White House victoria. A flock of sheep were procured to crop the White House lawn, and Mrs. Wilson had the wool auctioned off for the benefit of the Red Cross. Ninety-eight pounds of "White House wool" netted nearly $100,000. Her secretary, Miss Benham, put in a highly successful war garden on the White House grounds. There were a few unwarlike interludes. Mrs. Wilson learned to bicycle in the long corridor of the White House ground floor. The President staged a White House wedding for his niece Alice Wilson.

The President's daughter Margaret also insisted on doing her part. She toured the camps in this country, singing to the soldiers and giving the proceeds to the Red Cross. By giving other paid concerts en route she earned her traveling expenses. On November 6, 1918, she arrived in France, booked for a solid year in the camp-and-trench circuit under Y.M.C.A. auspices. The very next day the entire United States with the exception of Woodrow Wilson in the White House celebrated the "false armistice." He knew it wasn't true and withheld his jubilation until the document was actually signed on November 11.

Eager to conclude the peace, President Wilson went abroad with Mrs. Wilson, her secretary and a shipload of experts in January 1919. He was swept instead into the most triumphant tour ever experienced by a President of the United States and his wife. Ovation followed ovation in spectacular crescendo. In Paris they lived at the Prince Murat Palace. In London they were guests at Buckingham Palace, dining in state with the King and Queen from an all-gold table service. One day they rode on the special trains of three heads of states— the King of England's from London to Dover; the President of France's from Calais to Paris; the King of Italy's on to Rome. Mrs. Wilson later termed the Roman triumph the most brilliant of all. It had included the old custom of bringing in golden sand from the

Mediterranean Sea to cover the streets along the line of march. They visited the King and Queen of the Belgians.

Margaret Wilson went with them on their visits to royal palaces and was, once or twice, the subject of social incidents. The Queen of the Belgians refused to let Margaret ride between herself and Mrs. Wilson in the royal automobile. However, she enjoyed the greatest triumph of her life when she sang on Christmas Day at Gondercourt in the Meuse Department of the occupation army, with her father as the guest of the occasion. Margaret Wilson had a mezzo-soprano voice and specialized in the ballads beloved by World War I soldiers— "My Laddie," "Deep River," "Old Irish," "My Old Kentucky Home."

Of Wilson's peace plan, a political writer observed: "The desirability of the abstract was embarrassed by the impracticability of the concrete." His idea of "peace without vengeance" met all the harbored venom of European statesmen who had been fighting the enemy at close hand. His "self-determination for the little peoples" ran into all known maneuvers of European power politics. Some observers held that Wilson compromised on the treaty particularly in regard to heavy reparations, in the hope of making corrections later through the League. Mrs. Wilson said that the really damaging compromises were made by Colonel House in the short while that Woodrow Wilson had to be away from the peace table on a trip to this country just after he had won his fight to incorporate the League of Nations in the peace treaty. The Assistant Secretary of the Navy and Mrs. Franklin D. Roosevelt were on the *George Washington* with them on that return trip. Governor and Mrs. Calvin Coolidge of Massachusetts met them at the dock in Boston.

Back in Paris, Wilson forced Clemenceau, Lloyd George and Orlando to accept his treaty only by making all preparations to leave without signing. Returning to this country, he had less luck in getting a Republican Senate to ratify the League, even though ex-President Taft was campaigning on his side. Against the warnings of Dr. Grayson, he carried the fight to the nation.

Making impassioned pleas for the League at every train stop, as well as in mass meetings in great auditoriums, Woodrow Wilson made a "swing around the circle" from Washington to the West Coast in September 1919. In Los Angeles Mrs. Peck, divorced and again calling herself by the name of her first husband Hulbert, came to call on the Wilsons. Mrs. Wilson described Mrs. Peck as a "faded, sweet-looking woman," but intimated that she had overstayed her welcome from a very weary man. Mrs. Peck termed Mrs. Wilson "junoesque" and said of her: "She played well the most difficult role of being the third party to the reunion of two old friends endeavoring to relive the incidents of years in a single afternoon." At Wichita, Kansas, on the return trip, the President collapsed and was rushed back to Washington. The White House was converted into a hospital, with a panel of doctors and nurses in constant attendance as Woodrow Wilson suffered and survived a long series of maladies including paralysis of his left side, a kidney stoppage and glandular ailments.

The King and Queen of the Belgians came to visit him while he was flat on his back. So did the young Prince of Wales. There also came an unfriendly committee of Congress, headed by Senator Albert Fall, intending to rule him incapacitated. But when Fall unctuously said "I am praying for you" and Wilson wise-cracked "Which way?"— in the presence of witness—Fall could hardly report that the President had lost his faculties. When Secretary of State Lansing called cabinet meetings, Wilson dismissed him.

Margaret Wilson had a breakdown too. After months of trying to recuperate, she went to Grove Park Inn, Asheville, North Carolina, for a real rest. General John J. Pershing and his staff arrived there and persuaded her to attend a public dinner. All present called on her to sing. Instead, she rose and explained her ailment—she had lost her singing voice. It had been impaired by constant use at outdoor concerts in France. General Pershing rose and paid her high tribute— Miss Wilson, he said, was as much a victim of war service as were the soldiers who filled this country's hospitals.

For 17 months in the White House Dr. Cary T. Grayson and Edith Bolling Wilson were "taking care of Woodrow." Some said that together they ran the country. More held that Mrs. Wilson did it alone. Charles Willis Thompson, long-time White House correspondent, called this White House period "the Mrs. Wilson regency." Dolly Gann, sister of Senator Charles Curtis and herself a keen political observer, commented, "All the more credit to her! I am glad there was a woman in the White House who knew how to take the reins and use authority when it was pressed upon her."

Mrs. Wilson, saying that she was writing as though she had taken a solemn oath to tell the truth and the whole truth, called her own role "my stewardship." She was told by the physicians that Wilson could still do more for the country with his maimed body than anyone else, and that if he resigned in favor of the Vice President his greatest incentive to recovery would be gone. She said that Woodrow Wilson remained the active head of the state, and that she studied, digested and presented in tabloid form the things which had to be decided by him. She said that she herself had never made a single decision regarding the disposition of public affairs, other than "the very important decision of when to present matters to my husband." Only once did she have the courage to present a suggestion for a compromise with the Republican Senators on the treaty and its Fourteen Points. Said Wilson, "Better a thousand times to go down fighting than to dip your colours to dishonorable compromise."

An instance of how Mrs. Wilson's stewardship worked was given by David F. Huston, eight years in Wilson's cabinet, first as Secretary of Agriculture and for a few months as Secretary of the Treasury. He told of a phone call from Mrs. Wilson, who asked him to tea. When he'd had that White House hospitality, she said: "Of course, you know I did not ask you to take the trouble to come merely to drink tea. The President asked me to tell you he is very anxious for you to accept the Secretaryship of the Treasury. He thought of putting you there twice before, first, when McAdoo thought of resigning, and second when he did resign—but could not make up his mind to have you leave the Department of Agriculture." When Huston indicated willingness, Mrs. Wilson sounded him out on likely candidates for the place of another cabinet officer, then rumored about to resign.

William G. McAdoo was running for the Presidential nomination, but not by the flicker of an eyelash did Woodrow Wilson aid his son-in-law. The choice in 1920 fell on James M. Cox after a long struggle and 45 ballots. Cox and the Vice-Presidential candidate, thirty-eight-year-old Franklin D. Roosevelt, declared for ratification of the treaty and the League. Wilson permitted his own partisans to help vote the League down in protest against its "emasculation" by Republican "reservations" largely written by Senator Henry Cabot Lodge. He relied on a great vote mandate from the country to sweep the Democrats back into power and bring triumph to his treaty. Quite the opposite occurred. Senator Warren Gamaliel Harding was elected, and the country was headed toward "normalcy"—and isolationism.

16 | *Era of Illusion*

...HARDING, COOLIDGE, HOOVER

WARREN G. HARDING, Ohio Senator, trotted into the Presidency as a dark horse, with a darkling colt, Calvin Coolidge, Massachusetts governor, running by his side. Five months before the Chicago convention of 1920 Harry M. Daugherty, Ohio's political boss, had told newspapermen Harding would be nominated in a "smoke-filled room" after other candidates had deadlocked. So it proved. Governor Frank Lowden of Illinois and General Leonard Wood checkmated each other. Coolidge called his own candidacy a stampede from the forces that put Harding over.

Because ambitious Florence Kling Harding had largely dominated her husband's career, she was widely credited with pushing him into the White House. However, Daugherty revealed that he forced Mrs. Harding as well as her husband into the race. "I've a presentiment against this thing. Don't ask him to run," he quoted Mrs. Harding as saying. And he told of making her pose for her first campaign photograph by threatening to use an old one of her riding a bicycle, as she had done while training carrier boys for her husband's newspaper, the Marion *Star*.

Mrs. Harding was the daughter of the leading banker of Marion, Ohio. Her first marriage, an elopement with Henry De Wolfe, a next-door neighbor, had ended in divorce. They had a son, Marshall Eugene De Wolfe. Her father had bitterly opposed her second marriage to a youth some eight years her junior, Warren Gamaliel Harding, fifth of the eight children of a country doctor. When Mrs. Harding thereafter said to all interviewers, "I have only one real hobby—

it's my husband," she was giving the key to her life motivation. For him she had broken with her past. As circulation manager, she built up the paper of which he was editor, rushing home on her bicycle a half hour ahead of her husband to broil the steak. Daugherty considered her one of the political strategists who helped make him Senator and later President. She also had a voice in his appointments to high offices.

Harding's inauguration present to his wife was a diamond sunburst to be worn on the black velvet band about her neck which she habitually affected to hide the evidence of oncreeping age. Perhaps it was because of this symbol of aristocracy that he called her "The Duchess," a nickname used by all who played poker with him while she mixed the drinks. In public she was always vivacious, handsomely dressed, smartly-coifed, devoted to the blue that matched her eyes. But those close to her knew that she was a sick woman, kept alive by following the strict diet prescribed by her home-town physician, Dr. Charles E. Sawyer. Harding made little whiskered Dr. Sawyer a brigadier general and brought him and his wife to live in the White House.

Handsome, hail-fellow-well-met Harding received as an inauguration present a Scottie, Laddie Boy, signal of the return of the human-interest story to the White House. On the south grounds he practiced golf shots with Laddie Boy as retriever. Fine days meant foursomes at the Chevy Chase Club and at the private golf course of Friendship, home of those close friends, Ned McLean, publisher of the Washington *Post*, and his wife, Evalyn Walsh McLean.

For many months it looked as though Harding were going to achieve the "normalcy" which had been his campaign battle cry. The White House, so long overshadowed by war and Wilson's illness, quickened to gayest social life again. There were huge garden parties in the spring of 1921. A peace without the League of Nations was worked out with the Central Powers, President Harding declaring the war officially ended on July 2. From Armistice Day 1921 to February 6, 1922, he was part of the apparent triumph of the Limitation of Armaments Conference held in Washington. Distinguished guests from abroad were entertained at the White House. National prohibition had become law. Wine was banned from the White House table. But hard liquor was served upstairs by President Harding to his friends. The brilliant social season included all the official state receptions and dinners which had been discontinued because of the war. The Hardings also found time for a March cruise with the Ned McLeans in Florida waters. This was soon followed by an auto trip home to Marion, where, Colonel Starling of the Secret Service said, "everyone was possessed with pride for this friend who had made good." Added Starling, "Those brief days in his home town were the happiest of President Harding's career, I think."

Back in the White House the old ailment was on Mrs. Harding again. Some said it was the criticism from organized labor of her husband's course in the railway strikes that drove her to her bed. One kidney locked. Her life was despaired of. Brigadier General Sawyer defied the great specialists, refusing permission to operate—and Mrs. Harding rallied and got well. After six months of seclusion she invited 30 women writers to tea in her upstairs sitting room, the Oval Room, to report her return to health. One of them described this room as "homelike and attractive" with "great, comfortable, chintz-covered chairs, davenports, mahogany bookcases, shaded lamps, and a fire crackling cheerily in the fireplace above which hung Laszlo's sketch of Mrs. Harding herself."

Once recuperated, Mrs. Harding was too intuitive, too alert to political situations not to realize that her husband's administration had become filled with ominous undercurrents. Chief Justice William Howard Taft wrote a friend that Mrs. Harding had been warned by a clairvoyant that her husband would not see the end of his term. Chief Usher Ike Hoover said that, unknown to her husband, she "kept in touch through private conversations with officials of the administration." The meteoric rise of the Hardings was over. Now came an even more spectacular smash.

Before Harding ever went into the White House, Alice Longworth was delegated by Republican friends to warn him not to make Harry Daugherty a cabinet officer. He disregarded the warning. Attorney General Daugherty was soon the target of organized labor. Doctor Sawyer warned Harding that "strange things were going on in the Veterans' Bureau" over which he had put his friend Colonel Charles R. Forbes. He sent Forbes abroad to escape disgrace. Soon Charles F. Cramer, legal adviser to the Bureau, committed suicide. Then Colonel Starling of the Secret Service passed on to the President a warning—which had been handed to Starling by a military friend in the form of a letter from Wyoming—against leasing scandals in western oil fields. Soon Jess Smith, companion of Harry Daugherty, committed suicide. Daugherty told Harding that Smith had "gone bad." His name had been scratched from the long list of those to go on a long-planned Alaskan trip, which Harding was taking to sort out an administrative tangle, to open the Alaskan Railroad, and as a vacation. Before starting, Mrs. Harding confided to Starling that her husband was not well, and that she wished his physicians to be billeted next to him all through the trip. He became ill in Kansas City, but proceeded with a heavy speaking schedule on to Alaska and back as far as San Francisco. Mrs. Harding there decided on a return to Washington, but the President was determined to proceed. She was reading to him an article about himself which pleased him, "A Calm View of a Calm Man" by Samuel G. Blythe—a defense against a rising tide of criticism—when suddenly he died. Colonel Starling said that the doctors explained to him that "what had happened to President Wilson partially had happened to President Harding completely, and had struck him at the base of the brain." Back across the continent through mourning crowds went the Harding funeral train. On the morning of August 7, 1923, President Harding's body was taken into the White House, where funeral services were scheduled for the next day.

Down the grand stairway at midnight went Mrs. Harding to commune with her husband as he lay in state, handsome in death as in life, in the East Room. Mrs. McLean, her guest that night, listened as she talked aloud to him—"No one can hurt you now, Warren." She went among the costly flowers sent in his honor, picked out a little garden bouquet of daisies and nasturtiums and placed it on his coffin. At 3 A.M. she finished her tearless vigil and went back to her bed. Broken Woodrow Wilson attended Harding's funeral and lived on until February 1924. Mrs. Harding died on November 21, 1924.

All that autumn of 1923 the newspapers headlined in scandalous aftermath the conspiracies of the Harding administration. Blythe, who had interviewed the President, told in his "Calm Man" article what Harding meant by "normalcy": "His father was a country doctor. Harding often observed his father giving his patients innocuous medicines in order to divert their minds and allow Nature to effect a cure. That, roughly, is the basis of his attitude toward many of his problems. He feels that many situations will compose themselves if given the opportunity." However, Harding was not working with the beneficent forces of nature. About him were the malevolent forces of human greed. He had chosen as Secretary of the Interior Albert Fall, tool of the oil interests. Fall received $100,000 from Edward Doheny in a "little black bag" and other huge donations from Harry Sinclair in exchange for the Teapot Dome oil reserve in Wyoming and other oil lands netting them millions of dollars. Fall was tried, convicted and sent to prison. Harding's Alien Property Custodian, Colonel Thomas W. Miller, in a separate conspiracy of making away with public funds met the same fate. So eventually did that spectacular liar and scamp, Gaston B. Means, who, in Daugherty's Department of Justice, had been assigned to the Federal Bureau of Investigation and thus could put a slimy finger wherever he chose. There Means prompted a scurrilous book which intimated that Mrs. Harding had poisoned her husband to prevent his disgrace, a barefaced but widely believed lie. And still the Harding scandals came on. A former resident of Marion, Ohio, named Nan Britton enjoyed a limelighted period as author of *The President's Daughter,* which stated that Harding while a Senator had fathered her child.

Curiously, President Calvin Coolidge was not embroiled in all this sensationalism. The imagination of the country had been caught by the acid individuality of his character. One and all were thoroughly enjoying as President a backhills Vermonter who on his August 1923 vacation wore a shepherd's smock to do the chores on his father's farm. No tale in modern annals so pleased the popular fancy as that of Coolidge, informed by telegram of Harding's death, being sworn in as President by his father, a notary public, by the light of a kerosene lamp. Among the titles applied to Coolidge were "Silent Cal" and "A Puritan in Babylon." His dry, laconic humor swept from coast to coast.

Grace Coolidge, who had had no chance to shine in Massachusetts, where there was no governor's mansion, blossomed out beautifully in Washington. As wife of the Vice President, much sought after socially, both Mrs. Coolidge and her clothes had become prettier as the months rolled by. Her warming, all-embracing wave and smile set street crowds to cheering, even though her husband often was staring straight ahead with a poker face. She sang and whistled at her work in the White House. She made every reception, dinner and garden party gay. She made each guest feel her smile was just for him or her, while Coolidge hurried them all along with a mechanical

"How-do-you-do." At the various summer capitals which the Coolidges successively chose, she was as winning as a stage star. Flattered indeed were visiting delegations when she took amateur movie panoramas of them. She also took kodak snaps of cute children, quaint old ladies and picturesque characters.

Said Grace Coolidge herself:

"There is a song from one of our not new musical comedies about girls, which says something about 'the short, the fat, the lean, the tall; I don't give a rap, I love them all.' This is the way I feel about people, and I have been fortunate in being placed where I had an opportunity to gratify my taste by meeting great numbers of them."

Chief Usher Ike Hoover commented on Mrs. Coolidge: "Members of the household said that she was ninety per cent of the Administration." Yet she put no feminine finger into state affairs, made no speeches, gave no interviews. She was not even allowed to run her own side of the White House. An amazed housekeeper found herself sending menus each morning to the President as well as the President's wife, and buying "a peck of wheat and a peck of rye" to make a breakfast food of whole cooked grains to suit the President's taste. "Never before has a President taken such keen and active interest in small domestic affairs . . . never has a President saved so much money!" exclaimed Mrs. Elizabeth Jaffray. Perhaps Coolidge was collecting the evidence on which to dismiss this antiquated victoria-driving employee brought in by Mrs. Taft. At any rate, that is what he did, and the next housekeeper did her shopping by automobile. Mrs. Coolidge later told of checking menus herself, but added that the President carefully went over all household accounts. It was Coolidge who chose the luncheon menu for Edward Prince of Wales—later the Duke of Windsor—who again visited the capital, choosing pretty dancing partners.

To a couple accustomed to a simple New England manner of living the White House salary spelled sumptuousness. Furthermore, it was for the first time augmented by an official entertainment fund, a law put through by President Harding. This provided that the government would pay the bills if the entertainment were "official" and members of both parties were present. Thus were financed the famous "Coolidge Breakfasts" which brought all the political leaders on

Capitol Hill to the White House at an hour too early to please them.

At his press conferences Coolidge intoned with a nasal twang little litanies of prosperity. Business was in a satisfactory condition, even though nobody's business was ever as good as he'd like to have it. The Department of Labor reported employment plentiful. The Post Office Department reported monthly increase in the sale of stamps. There was a large movement of freight on the railways. Some net earnings were not so large as last year due to increase in wages. Prices of farm products had increased—cotton, corn and wheat. Cattle prices in general were higher than a year ago.

Coolidge, a regular church attendant, had never joined until, after he became President, the First Congregational Church of Washington, D. C., simply voted him into membership. This pleased him greatly. "Had I been approached in the usual way to join the church after I became President, I would have feared such action might appear to be a pose," he said in his autobiography.

In the Coolidge years skirts were short, colors bright. Bands were jazzy, flappers smoked cigarettes and their escorts carried hip flasks. Grandmothers had their hair bobbed like their granddaughters. Dark-haired, gray-eyed Mrs. Coolidge was a part of her times, wearing with an air modish gowns of moderately short skirts and much white touched up with bright red. She stood out in any crowd and made a superb picture when accompanied by those two decorative dogs, Prudence Prim and Rob Roy, white collies.

One deep grief marred the Coolidge stay in the White House. They had two sons of college age, John and young Calvin, who spent their vacations with their parents. Calvin died on July 7, 1924, after his father's nomination to succeed himself, but before his election. "If I had not been President," his father wrote in his memoirs, "he would not have raised a blister on his toe, which resulted in blood poisoning, playing lawn tennis in the South Grounds. . . . I do not know why such a price was exacted for occupying the White House."

Coolidge made an all-time record in the simplicity and economy of the inauguration ceremonies. He did not even provide a lunch for cabinet members and other high-ranking officials who came down from the Capitol in his entourage to watch the afternoon parade from the Presidential grandstand. The White House military aide on his own initiative, however, had provided plenty of food for all on duty.

He invited the officials to this picnic, and they all arrived late for the parade.

Somewhat against his will, because he did not like the publicity attending her American trip, President Coolidge held a state dinner in October 1926 for Queen Marie of Rumania and her two grown children, Prince Nicholas and Princess Ileana. Not once did he unbend to the wiles of the beautiful queen. However, Mrs. Coolidge made of it what Ike Hoover called "a pretty party, a successful party, a party that any American could feel pride in."

Soon after Coolidge entered the White House he was told that the roof was unsafe. He received this message skeptically, observing that many another would like to live under it. He decided against any alterations until he knew whether he'd be re-elected. It was not until early 1927 that the plans to remodel the White House by raising its roof were finally put into effect. The Coolidges moved to their temporary White House, the home of Mrs. Eleanor Patterson on Dupont Circle, on March 2, 1927. There they entertained Colonel Charles Lindbergh, back from his solo flight across the Atlantic, and his mother. There Colonel Lindbergh met his future father-in-law, Dwight Morrow, Ambassador to Mexico.

That summer, the White House still being under repair, the Coolidges chose their farthest-away Summer White House, Game Lodge in the Black Hills of South Dakota. Never before had a President spent the summer west of the Mississippi River. Coolidge told his new neighbors that the place reminded him of his native hills of Vermont and the people reminded him of Vermonters. Said he: "Some of the fish here don't look quite natural. They are larger than the trout in the streams I fished as a boy. There are more cattle here, more brood mares followed by young colts, more sheep—but of the same type and variety—and that makes me feel at home." He responded to the Black Hills atmosphere like a wrinkled prune plopped into a glass of water. Soon he was sitting on the Game Lodge front porch wearing a cowboy hat and, what is more, taking it off to wave it to passers-by on a main highway to the West Coast. Perhaps he there became reconverted to the blessings of a private life. At any rate, on the fourth anniversary of taking office, he made one of his triweekly trips to his office in the Rapid City high school, 35 miles away, and there distributed to the press his famous ten-word statement: "I do not choose to run for President in 1928." Never was Coolidge economy bet-

Details of the grand piano designed for the East Room by President Franklin D. Roosevelt.

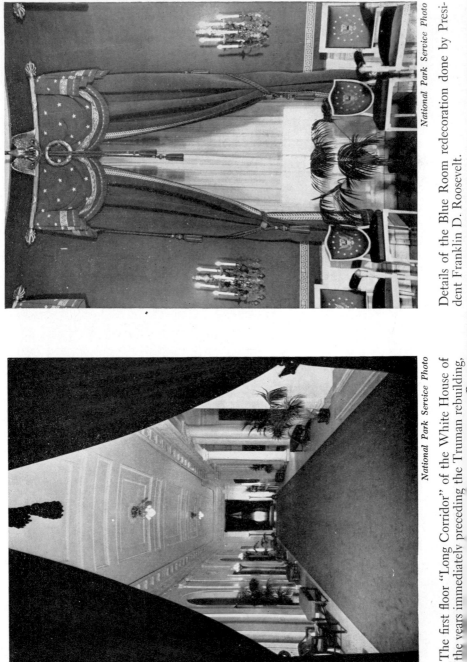

The first floor "Long Corridor" of the White House of the years immediately preceding the Truman rebuilding,

Details of the Blue Room redecoration done by President Franklin D. Roosevelt.

ter illustrated. The sentence was typed again and again on the same sheet of paper. Then the lines were scissored almost apart, to be torn off at the ends, as Bible references are distributed to a Sunday-school class.

Mrs. Coolidge later revealed that she did not even know this statement had been issued until it was mentioned to her by a Senator who called at Game Lodge later in the day. Said she, "I am rather proud of the fact that after nearly a quarter of a century of marriage my husband feels free to make his decisions and act on them without consulting me or giving me advance information concerning them." She considered that her own best value was as a wifely safety valve, declaring: "I have scant patience with the man of whom his wife says, 'He never gave me a cross word in his life.' It seems to me he must be a feckless creature. If a man amounts to much in this world, he must encounter many and varied annoyances whose number mounts as his effectiveness increases. Inevitably comes a point beyond which human endurance breaks down, and an explosion is bound to follow." Always she was a maternally indulgent onlooker at her husband's idiosyncracies.

Coolidge's closest friend, Frank Stearns, who with his wife spent long periods at the White House, also was a safety valve and not an adviser.

When the Coolidges went back to Washington that fall, it was to a much improved White House. Old wooden beams had been replaced by steel girders, and more rooms added at the top level. A badly needed second-floor replacement was recommended, but was not provided. In the later White House studies of the Truman administration it was learned that the heavy steel of the top floor pressing on the wooden story just below greatly increased the structural hazards. However, Mrs. Coolidge reveled in luxuries unknown to any previous First Lady. There was a sewing room, a pressing room, a cedar room. There was a room with wardrobes, cupboards and drawers for out-of-season clothing. There were three storage rooms lighted by overhead windows over the North Portico. There were linen closets. There were servants' rooms and other chambers, some with connecting baths. Best of all, above the South Portico there was a "Sky Parlor," a sunroom with glass on three sides, equipped with a couch, porch furniture and radio, where the White House family could enjoy the out-of-doors in privacy. Some years later a White House mistress of a different political party, Mrs. Franklin D. Roosevelt, said that she would never cease to thank Mrs. Coolidge for creating that hide-away with a sky view.

Mrs. Coolidge searched government storehouses for furniture of the period of the White House architecture, but found little of any worth. She did find an interesting mahogany center table, which seemed to her to symbolize the thirteen states, and a lovely old mahogany dining table, which she put back into use. She also discovered a chair of simple construction labeled "Andrew Jackson's Chair" which she had scraped, rubbed and recovered for the President's study. This chair was often mentioned by William O. Stoddard of the Lincoln secretariat as part of the office furniture of that administration.

Believing that many Americans who owned pieces of beautiful Early American furniture would rather have them placed in the White House than in museums, Mrs. Coolidge got a resolution through Congress authorizing acceptance of such gifts. Her supposition was wrong. Few were offered. However, she did succeed in refurnishing the Green Room with fine period pieces just before the Coolidge term closed. With her own hands Mrs. Coolidge crocheted a spread for the Lincoln bed, her gift to the White House.

As soon as Calvin Coolidge had declared himself out of the 1928 race the nomination of Herbert Hoover as Republican candidate was a foregone conclusion. As Secretary of Commerce in both the Harding and Coolidge cabinets Hoover had built up a national non-machine political following. To the leaders of this movement he was the "Great Engineer," and they called him "the Chief." They could also build on his earlier record as World War I Food Administrator, and earlier as director of Belgian relief. Teamed with him as Vice-Presidential candidate was Senator Charles Curtis of Kansas. They easily defeated Democratic candidate Alfred E. Smith, whose chief platform plank was repeal of the Prohibition Amendment to the Constitution, and his running mate, Senator Joe Robinson of Arkansas.

Herbert Hoover and his wife, Lou Henry Hoover, were a learned and cosmopolitan couple. Mrs. Taft had thought it worthy of note that her son Charles had been twice around the world before he was eight years old. Lou Henry Hoover's son, Herbert, Jr., had been three times around the world before he was three. Mrs. Hoover was the companion of her globe-trotting mining-engineer husband. There was once a time when he had office suites in San Francisco, New

York, London, Melbourne, Shanghai, St. Petersburg (later Leningrad) and Mandalay. Among the Hoover homes at various times were bungalows in Mandalay and Tokyo, a small house in Leningrad, their well-known Red House in London, the house on S Street in Washington, and always a place in Palo Alto, California, where their sons Herbert, Jr., and Allan went to school. They planned an impressive Palo Alto home on the Leland Stanford University campus eight years before they got a chance to build it, due to the leading part played by Herbert Hoover in the First World War. It was later given to the university which was so much a part of their life, along with the Hoover war records.

Herbert Hoover was a senior, Lou Henry a freshman, when they met in the geology department of the then young Stanford University. On a field trip, she vaulted a fence while he puzzled how to get her over it—and he soon saw she had just the right spirit for pioneering with a young engineer. While she finished her college course, he dashed off to Australia. He came back to take her as a bride to China, where he had been made director general of mines. She went with him into the provinces by canal boat and by pack mule. She became ill, and he had to rush her to a doctor in Tientsin—which probably saved their lives, as at that very moment the Boxer Rebellion broke out. Under fire for three weeks, the Hoovers bicycled briskly about, Hoover directing the defense, Mrs. Hoover nursing the wounded.

A natural linguist, Mrs. Hoover even picked up Chinese in her travels. For the five years prior to 1912 the Hoovers collaborated on the translation from Latin to English of Agricola's *De Re Metallica*, first great treatise on mining. Herbert Hoover resigned between 20 and 30 directorates to take over Belgian relief. His mining concerns then employed about 175,000 men in many countries. From that time on he devoted his efforts to vast enterprises for the public welfare.

Where the Coolidges had practiced stringent economy in the White House, the self-made, very wealthy and philanthropic Hoovers were lavish. According to one biographer, Herbert Hoover even turned his Presidential salary back to the U. S. Treasury. White House expenses were high, for their hospitality was prodigious. They brought in as housekeeper Mrs. Ava Long, who had formerly run the various homes of H. H. Rogers. Said Chief Usher Ike Hoover, "They set the best table that was ever set in the White House."

Mrs. Hoover's chief concern was to make the White House more comfortable—for the President and for his visitors. Her secretary throughout the four years, Mildred Hall—later Mrs. Allen Campbell of Pasadena, California—recalled that when the Hoovers moved into the mansion very little usable furniture was found in the family living quarters. She described Mrs. Hoover's redecoration as follows:

"She brought sofas and her grand piano from the house on S Street for the Oval sitting room. She had two unused doorways converted into charming cupboards which added greatly to the room. She went to a great deal of trouble to get just the right shade of green taffeta for drapes at the windows.

"The long hallway running the length of the White House was simply a passageway to get from one room to the other. Mrs. Hoover had bookcases built on each side. These housed the library which was given the President when the Booksellers of America found out there wasn't a book in the White House on Inauguration Night, 1929! On top of these bookcases, which were about five feet high, she placed various objects which she had gathered from all over the world. Then she put down the rugs which were given her on the South American tour [taken between the Hoover election and Inauguration], found sofas and comfortable chairs for conversational groupings, and changed the dismal hall into a charming gathering place. It was here that in due course a moving picture machine was installed. Mrs. Hoover even found some doll furniture and fixed up a corner for her small visitors."

The west end of this hallway, blocked off with palms, became an aviary with songsters trilling in a huge cage which matched the lines of the large west window, fan-shaped at the top. Other bird cages on tall standards stood among the palms. The furniture was of bamboo, and the floor rugs were of grass. Altogether, it was a bit of California atmosphere transplanted to the White House. It was also a room which became for feminine callers a "conversation piece," a purpose served for masculine visitors by the small room adjoining President Hoover's study, which he filled with all the varied portraits of himself sent in by amateur artists.

President Hoover chose as his study the room in which President Lincoln had signed the Emancipation Proclamation. Mrs. Hoover's secretary remembered that it was the First Lady who discovered and brought down from the storeroom for the Hoover study the chairs which were pictured in the painting of that famous Lincoln scene. Four of these chairs still remained in the possession of the White House.

Immediately Mrs. Hoover launched a White House historical project. She had her friend Dare Stark McMullin research through the scanty and ill-kept records and write a history of White House furnishings. Pictures were taken as future identification. Among the "finds" of this project were a bust of Van Buren and the desk that President Lincoln used at Soldiers' Home. Returned to the White House in the Hoover administration was a small mirror which a British soldier had looted at the time of the 1814 burning. It was hung on the wall of President Hoover's study.

Mrs. Hoover's masterpiece in interior decoration was the Rose Drawing Room to the north of the upstairs Oval Room, which had been used by Calvin Coolidge as a study. Because the Monroe furniture was probably the most beautiful and appropriate ever used in the White House, Mrs. Hoover paid a personal visit to the Monroe law office in Fredericksburg to have the remaining pieces treasured there duplicated for this room by an expert craftsman. Among them was the desk on which the Monroe Doctrine was signed. A copy of the portrait of Mrs. Monroe which hung in the White House while her husband was President also was placed in this room, and other paintings of about that period completed the *décor*. This suite of drawing-room furniture in duplication of the Monroe pieces, purchased from her own funds, was Mrs. Hoover's gift to the White House when she left it.

The state rooms and the official functions held in them benefited from her gift for making a home artistic and comfortable. The portraits of George and Martha Washington, which had overpowered the Red Room, were moved to the East Room, where they added much warmth and color and could be seen by the touring public as well as by invited guests. Mrs. Hoover bought for the mansion a half-hundred beautiful and comfortable chairs so that ranking guests at White House musicales would not have to perch for an entire evening on the small and spindly gilt chairs then used at state functions in order to get more people in.

Before the first Hoover social season started, the Gann-Longworth controversy was seething through the newspapers. Pictured as a precedence rivalry between Dolly Gann, sister and official hostess of Vice

President Curtis, and Alice Roosevelt Longworth, wife of Nicholas Longworth, Speaker of the House, this controversy was really a test of respective social prerogatives between the Vice President and Speaker. So far as the White House was concerned, it was settled as the Speaker Cannon controversy eventually was settled—by the addition of another function to the White House list, this time the dinner to the Vice President. By this method Mrs. Gann was accorded first rank as honor guest without conflict with the wives of officialdom. Mrs. Hoover also added a separate reception to the Senate, over which Curtis presided. With two functions added to the list, White House receptions and dinners were less crowded. Mrs. Hoover spent hours with her staff—she had three secretaries—working out plans to add to the pleasure of her guests at large functions. More democratic customs were worked out. The cabinet members were urged to mingle with the guests throughout the state rooms after the line had passed the President and his wife, instead of remaining clustered in the Blue Room. All guests were allowed to flow through that parlor formerly reserved for the high-ranking.

Herbert Hoover was a President with a great genius for organization who saw national problems as a challenge to immediate solution by commissions of experts. He caused telegraph wires to teem with names of important men appointed to such commissions, chiefly financed by foundations and private contributions, in keeping with his belief that the conduct of public affairs should spring from the citizenry. For the White House Conference on Child Care and Protection, a decennial custom from the time of Theodore Roosevelt, President Hoover had 100 committees of 12 experts each working for a year. His Committee on Social Trends worked all through his administration, bringing out at its close reports on taxation, social security, rural life, national resources, education, crime and labor-management problems. He staged a conference on better housing, a subject with which his name had become prominently identified while he was Secretary of Commerce. And he set the Wickersham Commission to work on the problems of prohibition, under which this country was becoming more and more restive. The findings of this important group were informally dubbed by the capital press the "Liquor-sham Report" because, while more than a majority of the members in their individual reports were against continuing the Prohibition law, the committee as a whole recommended against repeal.

What practical administrative reforms might have resulted from all these expert studies must forever remain in doubt, for soon after their prodigious work was started the country was suddenly struck by a depression unprecedented in intensity and duration. It started with the stock-market crash of October 1929 and continued with increasing intensity throughout the Hoover years. The cities of this country had their soup lines and the selling of apples on the streets became a nationally recognized symbol of dire straits. Shacktowns of down-and-outers sprang up near city dumps, called "Hoovervilles"—unfairly, since the crash would have come no matter who was President. However, the Republican party lost control of the House in the 1930 Congressional elections.

A grim and silent Herbert Hoover wrestled with the economic problem month in, month out, the year around. During his first White House summer he had ruled out the "Summer White House" type of vacation in order to grapple with the tariff bill. Instead, he set up his Rapidan Camp in the Virginia mountains about 100 miles from the capital, where he could spend week ends. As the depression deepened, this camp provided his only respite, except for one Florida vacation taken after he had failed of re-election. For recreation at Rapidan he and his distinguished guests lugged large stones to build dams and cast flies for trout. He did not enjoy trips down the the Potomac. The yacht *Mayflower* was dismantled.

The Rapidan Camp was an expression of Mrs. Hoover's seasoned scoutcraft as well as of her husband's choice in outdoor living. She herself designed much of the substantial and ingenious furniture used in the camp. She had continued in the White House her constructive interest in the Girl Scout movement. National leaders of the Girl Scouts held many conferences in the White House and at Rapidan Camp.

Prime Minister Ramsay MacDonald of Great Britain and his daughter Ishbel were guests both at the White House and at Camp Rapidan. Premier Pierre Laval (of later unsavory fame) and his daughter Josée came from France, and Signor Dino Grandi and his wife from Italy. Three Hoover grandchildren came and lived at the White House while their father, Herbert Hoover, Jr., recuperated from tuberculosis in Asheville, North Carolina. Colonel Charles Lindbergh and his wife, the former Anne Morrow, helped build Rapidan dams before flying off to the Orient. And the King and Queen of

Siam were visitors en route to Baltimore, where the king underwent an eye operation.

The depression continued—with millions added to the ranks of the jobless—climaxed by the Bonus March of the late spring and summer of 1932. Hoover sternly refused to allow the federal government to go into the business of relief. The veterans of World War I had compensation, voted by Congress, coming to them at a later date. They decided that the time when they most needed it was at that impoverished moment. By hundreds they started from the West Coast, picking up hundreds more in their broken-down jalopies, to stage, when they reached the capital, a parade of 7,000 men who marched under "Bonus Expeditionary Forces" banners.

They were allowed to build their shacktowns along Pennsylvania Avenue just below the Capitol on a site being demolished to build the Federal Triangle, and over the Anacostia flats. They also occupied condemned buildings west of the White House and on the Mall. There they stayed, demonstrating daily for the bonus, until they were driven out with tear gas by Fort Myer troops headed by General Douglas MacArthur on July 28. The burning of their Anacostia shacks lasted far into the night.

Hoover and Curtis were renominated that June, with the dramatic Franklin D. Roosevelt, New York governor, and Speaker John N. Garner, picturesque Texan, as opposition.

In one of his campaign speeches Hoover told how he had fought the depression without publicity lest he cause further panic. His hardest fight had been to prevent devaluation of the currency. "It was as if a great battle in war should be fought without public knowledge of any incident except the stream of dead and wounded from the front," he said. He defended his principles of local self-help and the "trickle-down" principle embodied in his Reconstruction Finance Corporation—stimulation of the economy through federal loans to big business. At last Hoover, who had ignored Al Smith in his 1928 campaign speeches, was goaded into mentioning the name of his 1932 opponent. It was during a denunciation of the Roosevelt plan to provide employment with public works. President Hoover called this Roosevelt plan "a hope held out to the ten million men and women now unemployed and suffering that they will be given jobs by the government." And he added, "It is a promise no government could fulfill. I ask you whether or not such frivolous promises and dreams should be held out to suffering unemployed people. Is this the 'New Deal'?"

When the election returns were in they showed that Hoover had been snowed under. It was indeed the "New Deal" and as described—the unemployed given jobs by the government on public works of a scope and variety never before conceived.

17 | *New Deal and World War II*

... FRANKLIN DELANO ROOSEVELT

THE NEW DEAL rolled into Washington from New York on March 2, 1933, by special train. It was peaceful revolution. Old ways, if it so suited the remarkable man who took over the White House on March 4, could be overturned at the flip of his long-stemmed cigarette holder. Franklin D. Roosevelt had as his chief tenet that the federal government was responsible for the welfare of the citizenry.

Commanding on Capitol Hill the Democratic votes accruing from his landslide, Roosevelt sent "must" legislation flying through the special session of Congress which he immediately called. Unemployed young men from country pool halls and city streets were put to work in his Civilian Conservation Corps. Other youth, girls as well as boys, went to college while working part-time on his National Youth Administration projects. The flow of building materials began again through the federal, state and municipal projects launched by his Public Works Administration. And the remaining reservoir of unemployed, including even artists, musicians and writers, were put to work on his relief-administration projects according to their skills. The New Deal agencies set up by Congress eventually numbered more than a score, most of them functioning under the already established principle of federal aid through matching funds with the states.

To end the epidemic of bank failures in all the states President Franklin D. Roosevelt simply closed the banks, reopening them under a system which guaranteed individual savings deposits up to $5,000. In a few weeks he blithely took the country off the gold standard which Herbert Hoover had struggled so hard to save. As a result of his long fight with the electric-power interests in New York state, he launched the Tennessee Valley Authority to demonstrate the blessings of cheap electricity, and, the next year, the Rural Electrification Administration to push power lines to farm homes all over the country. One thing led to another, until he was even feeding the farm surpluses to city families on relief.

For these measures and many others Roosevelt, a scion of Old New York aristocracy, from a family having a New York City town house and an estate on the Hudson at Hyde Park, was called a "traitor to his class." This caused him to toss back his head and laugh gaily. He had begun taking an interest in "the underdog" while at Harvard University. This trend was intensified during the time he spent in the New York legislature and as governor. It was conceded that he had the "common touch."

In the international field, however, he held his head as high as any ruler. President Roosevelt immediately set up a system of person-to-person conversations with the heads of other governments. He had three prime ministers in Washington at once—Ramsay MacDonald of Great Britain, who again brought with him his daughter Ishbel; Edouard Herriot of France; and Richard Bedford Bennett of Canada. Within a month after he took office he also had arranged conferences with the shapers of international policy in Italy, Japan, China, Mexico, Brazil and Chile. He recognized Soviet Russia, sent Secretary of State Cordell Hull to the Pan American Conference in Montevideo, and shaped that year the "Good Neighbor Policy" which was to build up hemispheric solidarity as Hitler's power increased in central Europe.

Two Roosevelt characteristics instantly struck a popular chord that opposition politicians were never able to outshout. One was his sympathetic speaking voice, which enabled him to enlist popular backing at any time through a "fireside chat." The other was his crippled condition, a paralysis of the lower limbs due to poliomyelitis. Each year he visited Warm Springs, Georgia, where he had partially conquered the paralysis. The American people never finished marveling at how much a President could accomplish from a wheel chair. For every step he took, for every address, President Franklin D. Roosevelt had to be bolstered by locked leg braces. And still he traveled from coast to coast, making speeches every time the train stopped. Eventually he toured the globe.

Into the White House as First Lady of the New Deal came Anna Eleanor Roosevelt, as astounding as her husband. She was born a Roosevelt, the daughter of President Theodore Roosevelt's brother Elliott. She included representatives of the Republican Roosevelt family—Alice Roosevelt Longworth, Mr. and Mrs. Archie Roosevelt and Mrs. Kermit Roosevelt—in the dinner of Inauguration Night, thus paying back a bit of White House hospitality accorded to her and to her then fiancé, Democrat Franklin D. Roosevelt, at the time of the Theodore Roosevelt inaugural.

True to the speedy tempo of her clan, Eleanor Roosevelt had the entire White House family quarters resettled—and with sweeping changes—in three days; and her husband's vast collection of ship's prints all hung there within a week. Then she dashed off over the country, serving as "eyes and ears" for her husband. She traveled 38,000 miles her first White House year, 42,000 the second, 35,000 the third—and after that she went to so many places unannounced that reporters had to give up the project of adding up her mileage.

Mrs. Hoover's palm-shaded California nook by the west window in the upper hall was converted by Mrs. Roosevelt into a chintzy Roosevelt sitting room, looking like a corner of the library at Hyde Park and used like it for regular five-o'clock family tea. The Monroe replicas which Mrs. Hoover had made, and which had given the room at the head of the stairs the title of "Monroe Room," were moved out into the hall or into the President's Oval Study. Mrs. Roosevelt used the Monroe Room for her regular weekly press conferences at which she took up the New Deal projects which most interested her—subsistence homesteads, work camps for single women, National Youth Administration projects, the mattress making and sewing of the women on relief, the paintings of WPA artists and the guidebooks of WPA writers. Always beside her were Malvina Thompson, her personal secretary, and Mrs. James M. Helm—the former Edith Benham—again the social secretary.

Leaders of public-welfare projects held conference after conference in the East Room. Sometimes Mrs. Roosevelt was called on to preside. Sometimes she merely listened, knitting. So, year after year, mounted her output of baby blankets for her mounting number of grandchildren and for the children of her friends.

There was no question but that she was setting a new record for the mistress of the White House. Like Abigail Adams, she was a feminist with dozens of original ideas for a larger woman-contribution to citizenship. She could achieve political results with a well-directed White House invitation as adroitly as Dolley Madison, and her parties were as popular. Like Lucy Webb Hayes, she already had a following among organized women. Like Rose Cleveland, she was an educator, a classroom teacher with theories reaching into many avenues on how to raise the level of human understanding. And she had an advantage that none of them had ever had—a practical working knowledge of the new political power brought to women by the vote. She acquired that while running campaigns for Alfred E. Smith and for her husband. As First Lady she made speeches, talked over radio, went on lecture tours, wrote for newspapers and magazines, and finally settled down to a daily column, "My Day," which would continue long after she left the White House.

When Grace Coolidge adventurously stole out to Fort Myer and took her first horseback-riding lesson and it somehow got into the papers, President Coolidge had squelched the whole idea with a dry: "I think you will find you will get along on this job fully as well if you do not try anything new." Eleanor Roosevelt, who sometimes appeared at her press conferences in a riding habit, tried one new thing after another. She rode over both Boulder Dam and Norris Dam in a bucket. As time and Roosevelt terms went on she flew the global trail. Moreover, wherever she went, she could match Grace Coolidge as a winner of crowds. She also from time to time aroused storms of criticism.

Despite all this public activity, Mrs. Roosevelt sacrificed few of the traditional home-and-mother duties for which she had been meticulously trained by a grandmother of old-school aristocracy, Mrs. Valentine Hall. After being rigorously drilled from childhood in sewing a fine seam and darning a stocking just so, in the right way to iron good linens and to polish good furniture, supervision of such details—and doing them when the need arose—had become second nature. Order prevailed among all objects around her. Her speaking schedules always dovetailed neatly into seeing members of the family off on trips. She always arrived at the summer home in Campobello in time to stock the refrigerators and make the beds for the rest of the family.

All the Roosevelt traditions into which she was born and into which she married—winters in the city and summers in the country, educational travels and broadening conversation, gala birthdays and

Christmases and Thanksgivings—were so well organized that they almost ran of their own momentum. So she found time for companionship with her husband, never forgetting to share with him at afternoon tea the most amusing happening of the day. And into the basket beside his bed she put her keen and varied reports on what she had seen and heard out over the country.

Mrs. Franklin D. Roosevelt was in the White House when it was officially important for her to be there. Each social season, running from mid-November to Lent, she stood beside her husband in the Blue Room, shaking hands with the long lines attending the five official receptions—diplomatic, judicial, Congressional, departmental and Army and Navy. She sat across from her husband at the official state dinners—the cabinet dinner, the dinner to the Chief Justice and the Supreme Court, the diplomatic dinner, the Vice President's dinner and the Speaker's dinner. To this heavy load of official entertaining were added the formal dinners and luncheons to the increasing number of visiting heads of states.

And still Mrs. Roosevelt added other informal annual functions. There was the Gridiron Widows Party, started at the White House when the President and his male cabinet officers went off to the always-stag Gridiron Club Dinner, leaving the uninvited Secretary of Labor Frances Perkins. Masquerades and lampooning skits were the entertainment for official wives, the wives of Gridiron Club members and newspaperwomen invited to this annual party. There was the annual dinner to President Roosevelt's Cuff-Links Club, which began with the newspapermen who had reported on his activities when he was Assistant Secretary of the Navy—later other cronies were added. And there was the annual spring dance for the press corps, their wives and husbands, when gardens and terraces and the swimming-pool section along the east colonnade were thrown open to strollers; beer was served in the foyer, and the Virginia Reel was danced in the East Room.

Added to these were the myriad Roosevelt family entertainments held in the White House—children's parties, dances for young people, debutante parties for relatives and protégés, and an occasional old ladies' luncheon. Dowager head of the Hyde Park Roosevelt family was the President's mother, Sara Delano Roosevelt. She owned the family home, used as a Summer White House, until she died late in her son's long tenure of office. She often was a White House visitor.

Three of the Roosevelt children, Anna Eleanor, James and Elliott, were married before their father took office. The two younger, Franklin D., Jr., and John, were in Groton at that time. They finished preparatory school, went through college, were married and had children while the family lived in the White House. President Roosevelt had but two grandchildren at the time of his first inauguration, Curtis and Anna Eleanor Dall—called "Sistie and Buzzie"—the children of Anna. At his fourth and final inauguration, staged on the White House South Portico, he had 13 grandchildren, all present and photographed.

Of the Roosevelt children Anna and James had the closest connection with the White House. Anna lived and carried on her writing and radio-broadcasting career there in the interval between her separation and divorce from Curtis Dall and her marriage to John Boettiger. She later served as a special assistant to her father during the Second World War. James was for a time on the White House staff as an executive assistant.

Inevitably the old White House itself, strained at the seams by the activities of the large and gregarious Roosevelt family and burgeoning with the business of the New Deal, was improved by a series of construction projects such as were in progress in public buildings all over the land. First came a new and deftly enlarged office building, part of it underground so as not to disturb the architectural lines created by McKim in the Theodore Roosevelt administration. This new office plant included a sunken courtyard in the rear, a hollow square of glass-walled offices; a third-floor tier of new offices created by a not noticeable raising of the roof, similar to the Coolidge remodeling of the White House proper; and the creation of a new cabinet room by the filling in of a space used as a clothes-drying yard until the Hoover administration, when the White House started sending its laundry out. While this work was being done in the summer of 1934 President Roosevelt used the Blue Room for his public office, a use to which that highly formal parlor had never before been put.

The next summer's remodeling job, placarded "Public Works Project No. 634," gave the White House an electric kitchen with work surfaces covered with stainless steel. For the first time in history the White House got an electric dishwasher. A carpenter shop and storeroom were excavated under the front lawn, and a servants' dining room was installed, decorated by two WPA paintings—one a sea scene with sailing ships, the other a mountain lake in the Grand Tetons.

The next big White House remodeling project under the Roosevelts was for the purpose of changing the old and dangerous electric wiring from direct current to alternating current. Excavation of more storerooms under the front lawn and ratproofing was included in this project. The final Roosevelt remodeling was done under World War II censorship. The east wing was rebuilt as an office for the Assistant to the President, the White House Social Bureau and its Secret Service detail. White House Architect Lorenzo Winslow said that President Roosevelt hoped that this wing eventually would become a museum for the public as well as a ceremonial entrance for official functions. It was his thought that some significant mementoes of each past administration should be installed. In this final remodeling a subterranean bomb shelter was installed. The name of Franklin Delano Roosevelt is on the bronze tablet of the east-wing cornerstone.

And indeed, he had been a planner for the place in almost the same sense that Thomas Jefferson was—in broad lines and also in minute details. When the East Room was redecorated for the first time since the Theodore Roosevelt restoration, it was Franklin D. Roosevelt who designed the American folk-music frieze around the body of the grand piano, and who suggested the lifelike American Eagle pedestals. The new set of White House china bore his mark, the stylized Roosevelt crest of three feathers. He also added historical touches.

When President John Adams had made his first inspection of the place he had written Abigail, then still in Massachusetts: "I pray heaven to bestow the best of blessings on this house and on all that shall hereafter inhabit it. May none but honest and wise men ever rule under this roof." Roosevelt took the old mansion back to its very beginning by having that prayer carved over the fireplace in the State Dining Room.

But in spite of all the works projects improving it summer after summer while the Roosevelts were at Hyde Park, the White House was beginning to show age and strain, particularly on its second floor— the private family quarters. Strange creakings of floors and poundings of plumbing were sometimes heard. John Jacob Niles, American composer and entertainer, was invited to stay the night after entertaining Roosevelt guests with his folk ballads following a state dinner. He later told a typical tale. A courteous houseman had ushered him into his room with this kindly assurance: "You may think someone is knocking on your door in the middle of the night. But don't pay it no mind. Nobody will be there."

Roosevelt was presented with a remarkable memento of the past, the small wooden medicine chest used in the White House by James and Dolley Madison, with the ancient herbs still in it, just as they were on the day when the Madisons fled from British flames. A Canadian gentleman, descendant of the British soldier who had taken it as a souvenir, brought it back. It became eventually part of the Roosevelt historical collection at Hyde Park.

In the campaign year 1936, running on his New Deal record, President Roosevelt defeated Governor Alfred M. Landon of Kansas. He campaigned across the country to Wyoming, closing with a New England tour. That same year he went to South America and addressed the Inter-American Conference for the Maintenance of the Peace, which he had called. In 1938 he completed his New Deal legislatively with the signing of the Fair Labor Standards Act.

On September 1, 1939, Hitler invaded Poland, and on September 3 Great Britain and France declared war against Germany. Soon all western Europe was under Hitler's heel. For the next two years—until December 7, 1941, the day of the Japanese attack on Pearl Harbor, the Roosevelt role was creating and forcing through Congress "measures short of war" to bolster England and Russia.

Shortly before the European war broke out, King George and Queen Elizabeth of England visited the Roosevelts. Their White House stay, June 8 and 9, 1939, followed by a week end at Hyde Park, not only was the high spot in Roosevelt entertaining, but also had a worthwhile propaganda effect in the months and years which followed.

Revision of the Neutrality Act soon after the war started in 1939 made possible the sending of weapons to England. In a deal with Britain, Roosevelt swapped 50 overage destroyers for a 99-year lease on eight Atlantic naval bases. He issued a shoot-on-sight order, to keep our sea lanes clear of German submarines. After the Nazis trapped 400,000 British soldiers on Dunkerque's blazing beaches in May 1940 he sent, on his own responsibility, all reserve U. S. Army weapons to Britain—rifles, machine guns, field artillery, billions of rounds of ammunition. He then launched a billion-dollar emergency arms program for this country and set up a National Defense Advisory Committee.

In an address at Charlottesville, Virginia, that June he departed from a prepared speech text to brand Italy's entrance into the war a "stab in the back" to its neighbor France. Public sentiment in this country was lining up on the side of the democracies, indeed was ready for an air-production program, a shipbuilding program and the September 1940 peacetime selective-service act.

That was the campaign year in which President Franklin D. Roosevelt's personal political emissary Harry Hopkins went out to the Democratic National Convention in Chicago and put Roosevelt's third-term candidacy across over the protest of Postmaster General James Farley, who had been front man for the two previous Roosevelt campaigns. And when it seemed that Paul McNutt of Indiana had the votes to defeat Roosevelt's choice for Vice President, Secretary of Agriculture Henry Wallace, Mrs. Roosevelt flew out and saved the day for her husband by a speech from the convention platform. She did it by emphasizing the heavy responsibilities on him—"You cannot treat this as you would an ordinary nomination in an ordinary time," she said. On her way there the pilot let her fly the plane. All her White House years she had wanted to take over the controls of an airplane. It came at last as a sort of side-line reward for performing probably the toughest political task which she ever undertook for her husband.

In the November 1940 elections Franklin D. Roosevelt easily shattered the precedent of no third term, winning over Wendell Willkie. The country did not choose to change leadership in the midst of a world emergency. In 1944 the story was the same, Roosevelt—with Senator Harry S. Truman as running mate—winning a fourth term by defeating Governor Thomas E. Dewey of New York. After Roosevelt's death, however, a Constitutional amendment was adopted precluding future Presidents from seeking a third term.

After the third-term election this country's program swiftly became the vast system of "lend-lease" to England and to Russia. President Franklin D. Roosevelt and Prime Minister Winston Churchill of England staged a surprise meeting at sea in August 1941 and announced the Atlantic Charter. Then came war itself, with almost as many new emergency agencies as had sprung up under the New Deal. Under cover of censorship President Roosevelt appeared unannounced in tours of war factories.

But Franklin D. Roosevelt's heart was not in this domestic and economic phase of war as much as it was in mapping out the grand strategy. Long hours he spent in the map room, set up on the ground floor of a troop-guarded White House whose gates were barred, whose roof was set with machine guns, and whose windows were equipped with blackout curtains. President Roosevelt was largely responsible for creation of an overall military unit—the Combined Chiefs of Staff. All its strategic moves were charted in the map room. Roosevelt's commander-in-chief title was a true one. As in Lincoln's time the personality of the President permeated the White House. Roosevelt worked in closest co-operation with rotund Winston Churchill, who again and again dropped unannounced into Washington for White House conferences.

Two weeks after Pearl Harbor, Churchill came to the White House and stayed 24 days. It was decided then to throw the bulk of the military might of the United States and Britain first against Germany, and then to combine their strength against Japan. The Declaration of the United Nations was worked out at this meeting. It was ceremoniously signed by 26 nations at the White House shortly afterward.

In June 1942 Churchill came again, and with Roosevelt planned the invasion of North Africa by British and American forces as a base from which to strike at Europe's "soft underbelly." They met again at Casablanca in January 1943, and again in May at the White House, where top commanders of China and India were called in, obviously to stress the war in the Pacific.

Their Quebec meeting in August 1943 was followed by a Churchill visit to the White House, during which news came of Italy's surrender. They met at Cairo in November 1943 with Generalissimo Chiang Kai-shek, who had his United States-educated wife as interpreter, and went on to Teheran, where they had their first meeting with Marshal Stalin. The overall strategy which resulted in Germany's unconditional surrender was worked out at this meeting. They met again at the Citadel in Quebec in September 1944 and planned the shifting of armaments to the Pacific as soon as final victory came in Europe. And they met again with Stalin at Yalta in February 1945, where they decided to call a meeting at San Francisco to prepare the charter for an International Security Organization.

Always at these strategy conferences (except for the second Quebec meeting) was Harry Hopkins, who served Franklin D. Roosevelt as an emissary extraordinary, flying to England for preparatory conferences with Churchill and on to Moscow for talks with Stalin. Hopkins had conducted the relief strategy of the New Deal. Roosevelt enjoyed whetting his brains on the quick intelligence of this Iowan turned New York welfare worker. With a war economy offering jobs to everyone, unemployment no longer was a problem, and Hopkins was free for other tasks under other titles. So that he could be at hand to talk things over, Roosevelt had him move into the White House. There Hopkins was married to Louise Macy on July 30, 1942—and there these newlyweds lived for months, occupying the big bedroom where Abraham Lincoln had signed the Emancipation Proclamation. Later they moved to a Georgetown home.

As in Jefferson's time, the White House dinner table was presided over by a connoisseur of food and conversation. Roosevelt had the whole world, highlighted past and teeming present, as his subject. Mrs. Roosevelt, at her end of the table, brought in auxiliary topics galore as she stirred the Sunday-night scrambled eggs in the silver chafing dish. Those ranged around the long table in the family dining room night after night were a random sampling of American democracy, although usually a Presidential adviser or two was there for specific conference later on the subject uppermost. Authors, artists, sculptors, actresses, dancers, world travelers, old family friends talked with Ambassadors, Supreme Court justices, administrators of alphabetical agencies and brain-trusters. No matter who came, there was no question as to who dominated. If Alexander Woollcott, that famous raconteur, told a good yarn, Roosevelt topped it.

The paint on the outside of the White House peeled and peeled. Franklin D. Roosevelt refused to have a brush put to it. To him this symbolized belt-tightening—the casting in of our lot with that of Britain in her austerity program. It was a pledge for the freedom of the occupied countries. As guests to the now shabby-looking mansion came a long array of dispossessed royalty—doughty Queen Wilhelmina of Holland with her daughter Juliana, later to be Holland's queen; beautiful Princess Martha of Norway, with her husband, Olaf, and their three children; George II, King of Greece; and Peter II, young King of Yugoslavia.

Mrs. Roosevelt's great interest in the war was its fighting men. With her secretary, Malvina Thompson, she visited them in England in October 1942. On her husband's suggestion she made a good-will trip to the Pacific late in 1943, wearing a Red Cross uniform as she toured the hospitals where the wounded lay. And in the spring of

1944 she toured the lonely Caribbean and South American bases, where men could only watch and wait and never saw action. Always she gave the fighting men messages from her husband. That August Franklin D. Roosevelt made his own trip to the Pacific, meeting at Pearl Harbor the two commanders in the Pacific theater, Admiral Chester W. Nimitz and General Douglas MacArthur.

The White House was closed to tourists, but Mrs. Roosevelt herself conducted tours of the returned wounded receiving treatment in Washington hospitals. These tours ended with tea in the State Dining Room, where the men, mostly amputees on crutches and in wheel chairs, asked Eleanor Roosevelt about the President's dog Fala, about the visit of the King and Queen of England to the White House and about her return visit to Buckingham Palace. She could discourse humorously on these topics, as those who had toured tipped off those about to tour. She repeatedly called attention to the Lincoln portrait over the State Dining Room fireplace and told the young veterans that Lincoln himself willed this painting to the White House, but it arrived during the Roosevelt stay, for it was to remain with Mrs. Robert Todd Lincoln during her lifetime. She told how much she loved this portrait—"humorous, kindly, and not awkward as so many of his pictures are." And always she finished with the story of how Mary Eben, one of the White House secretaries, had been frightened by thinking that she saw Lincoln sitting on his bed, pulling on his shoes. And again she said, as she so often had, that the upstairs of the White House on a lonely night—and always for that matter—has a feel of people having lived busy lives there, pushed by mighty events. She described it as having "an atmosphere of solemn responsibility—you couldn't live up there and not feel it."

At meetings held at Dumbarton Oaks in Washington plans were laid for the San Francisco Conference which would set up a United Nations. Mrs. Roosevelt announced at her press conference of April 12, 1945, that she would go to San Francisco with the President on his return from Warm Springs, Georgia, where he had gone for a brief vacation. That afternoon, at the Little White House in Warm Springs, Franklin D. Roosevelt, in the midst of having his portrait painted, suddenly died of a brain hemorrhage.

Once more a slow-moving train, bearing the casket of a President, rolled all night long through silent village and city crowds into Washington. This time a whole world mourned. The capitals of all the

United Nations lowered their colors. In Pacific jungles and in Alaskan wastes soldiers mourned. Crowds, closely packed, some silent, others weeping, watched a Presidential funeral procession march down Pennsylvania Avenue to the White House. Again a state funeral was held in a flower-filled East Room. The whole sweep of the New Deal and of World War II was personified in the men and women who came to pay a final tribute to the President who had lived longest in the White House.

There was a full week end of ceremonial tribute—on Friday at Warm Springs, where he had started the Foundation for those who, like himself, had been stricken with infantile paralysis; on Saturday at Washington, scene of his amazing ascendancy; and on Sunday at Hyde Park, his birthplace and burial place. He himself had designed the simple but dignified marker for his grave in the rose garden. He had planned the library which would house his papers and mementoes. And he had so drafted his will that Hyde Park itself, the Summer White House of his regime, should belong to the nation.

18 New Mansion in the Old Mold

...TRUMAN

IN THE late afternoon of April 12, 1945, a short and solemn swearing-in ceremony was held in the cabinet room of the White House executive office for President Harry S. Truman of Missouri. The President's wife Bess and his daughter Margaret came in quietly with sad faces to witness this historic event. The members of the Roosevelt cabinet assembled.

As had been the precedent of past Presidents in similar circumstances, President Truman's first official act was a proclamation declaring Saturday April 14 the day of the funeral service for President Roosevelt, "a day of mourning and prayer throughout the United States." The Trumans moved into Blair House across the street while Mrs. Roosevelt moved out of the White House and while it was being redecorated.

Less than a month after Truman took office the onsweep of the allied armies brought victory in Europe. VE-Day fell on May 8, the sixty-first birthday of President Harry S. Truman. With victory in the West won, Winston Churchill lost to the new Labor government in England. When President Truman attended a high-strategy conference in Potsdam in 1945, it was with British Prime Minister Clement Attlee and Marshal Stalin of the U.S.S.R. To Truman fell the momentous decision of whether or not to use the atom bomb, developed under Roosevelt as a secret weapon. Atom bombs were used on Hiroshima and Nagasaki, hastening the victory over Japan. VJ-Day was proclaimed on September 2, 1945.

That fall the old White House again looked serene and peaceful. The Trumans had had it painted outside and in. They had even introduced soft pastel colors on the walls of the upstairs bedrooms. Official entertaining was resumed with invitation lists longer than ever before, for Washington had become a world capital. Now it took two diplomatic dinners in the State Dining Room to entertain only the highest-ranking emissaries and their wives. Reception lines in the East Room were four-deep, thinning out to a single line at a point where President and Mrs. Truman received in the Blue Room.

However, unnoticed by anyone, the old Executive Mansion creaked and cracked under the weight of its years. Thirty-one families had taken successive possession—had tried to make the place fit their hurried, harried, highlighted lives. Truman was the thirty-second President. George Washington never lived there. For a century and a half there had been changes here, changes there, never any end to the changes within those stolid outer walls of white Aquia Creek sandstone.

Patched-up plumbing in the inner walls pounded out a protest. Overnight guests talked of ghosts. But President Truman quite naturally was thinking in terms of expansion, not doing over what was already there. Architecture was one of his hobbies. As a county judge in Missouri he had taken charge of the building of two courthouses, the colonial one at Independence, which was first built around a historic old one, and a skyscraper at near-by Kansas City for which he had toured the country, seeking ideas. Before he was elected Senator from Missouri he divided his working day between these two fine buildings. At the White House, however, his official plant was crowded and inconvenient. He made plans and even had the ground broken for a $1,650,000 extension to the executive office which would include a small auditorium for press conferences and motion pictures and a lunch bar for White House employees. The Senate Appropriations Committee killed this plan in February 1946, by withholding funds. Protested President Truman in a letter to Chairman Kenneth McKellar of that committee: "I am as sensitive as anyone to the necessity for preserving the general architectural scheme of the White House, and the plans which I have specifically approved maintain its historic appearance." But McKellar stood firm on his money veto of the Truman expansion plan.

Thereupon President Harry S. Truman had a $10,000 balcony built as part of the South Portico, using funds legally at his disposal. This made it possible to dispense with ugly awnings requiring $1,500 a year for upkeep and also provided a fire escape of sorts. But a nation-wide hullabaloo resulted. President Truman came out on top, since nobody had the authority to tear down the balcony, no matter how much architectural purists might question the President's right to build it. Besides, photographs were published showing similar Georgian mansions with similar balconies. With its cooling updraft from the south grounds, this balcony was the pleasantest spot in downtown summer Washington.

But behind this balcony all was not well. The floor of the President's upstairs Oval Study creaked unduly and sometimes seemed to have an undulating motion. The plaster of the Red Room ceiling had a persistent habit of cracking. Lightning struck a tree just out-side a second-floor window close to where a relative of the President and Mrs. Truman lay slumbering. The shock of it literally knocked this gentleman out of bed. But there was an elaborate system of lightning rods which even included some of the trees. So nobody went into the matter deeply enough to discover that the second floor was sheer tinder with an underlay of shavings left by the too hasty remodeling under Theodore Roosevelt.

Actually only a strange triumph of cosmic mind over crumbling mortar kept the White House from complete collapse. It might have come with the giving-away of the precarious propping of the steel superstructure above the State Dining Room. It might have come in the fall of the massive frescoed ceiling of the East Room. Or it might have come in the collapse of the grand staircase, the foundation bricks of which had crumbled apart. Moreover, the brick pilaster supporting that stairway, much weakened by heating pipes installed in 1854, was cracking under the 90-ton strain of the steel third floor.

But the old structure still stood, and the populace as well as of-ficial guests poured through it, singly and in pairs, by twenties, by fifties, by hundreds and by thousands. They came to luncheons and to teas. They came on sightseeing tours through rooms on the ground floor and up the stairs to the East Room; if given a card by their Senator, they toured the state parlors. They came for formal little functions organized by enterprising citizens to add éclat to worthy causes. And none of them noticed that the distinguished old build-ing was about ready to fall to pieces in a dozen different places. Nor would they have believed it had they been warned. For this was the White House.

Suddenly, in the midst of the formal reception to the high officials of the federal departments in mid-January 1948, President Truman heard an unnatural tinkling of the crystal chandelier centering the Blue Room ceiling directly over the spot where he and Mrs. Truman were receiving. Thinking quickly, the President halted W. W. Reynolds, Commissioner of Public Buildings, in the oncoming line with a request that he stand by. When the final hand had been shaken, the President confided to Commissioner Reynolds his misgivings about the chandelier. Soon Reynolds was able to report to the President that the chandelier's shaking was due to an unsafe floor just above in the President's study. The President was advised to call in only a few advisers at any one time. Some steel hanging rods were introduced as a temporary lift to the study floor.

By mid-April Mr. Reynolds and his staff, aided by the White House architect, Lorenzo S. Winslow, had gathered enough alarming evidence to cause a request to the Senate Appropriations Committee for a $50,000 study of the White House as a structural hazard. Commissioner Reynolds' statement to the committee concluded with the startling opinion that "the second floor was staying up there purely from habit." The $50,000 was granted.

Luckily the Presidential family was not in residence that summer and early autumn. They were at their old home in Independence, which they used as a Summer White House each year. Then all three of them went on the Whistle Stop Campaign across the country.

The political columnists and pollsters had conceded Truman's defeat by Governor Thomas E. Dewey of New York, the Republican candidate, before the trip started. With eyes firmly fixed on their own predictions, they failed to note that the President had developed an extemporaneous brand of fighting campaign oratory which was drawing crowds of remarkable size and vociferousness. At stop after stop he was winning the farmers and he was winning the laboring men. His wife and daughter also were very pleasing to the people. There was great appeal in the gay way the family trio joined high-clasped hands in a final farewell as the train pulled out. This tour ended in Independence on the election day which will ever be remembered as the "Great Upset."

The whole country stayed up all night, listening to the returns in which Truman led in every tally. The citizenry could scarcely believe its ears. The figures soon said Truman, but many of the commentators kept saying that still the tide would turn. After sleeping soundly the whole night through, Harry S. Truman awoke to hear one of the bitter-end commentators still writing him off the next morning. He later regaled audiences with an imitation of this conservative commentary.

Harry S. Truman was returned to the White House Or was he? When President Truman returned to a capital city which had spontaneously turned out en masse to welcome him he was warned away from a White House in which the East Room ceiling was held up by a hastily improvised scaffolding. A week before the election this ceiling, weighing 70 pounds to the square inch, had been found sagging six inches.

The Truman family moved to Blair House. The White House furniture was stored in a museum, and its scanty set of gold table plate went into vaults. (After Van Buren's experience no President had ever asked for gold fish forks.) The $50,000 survey was on in earnest. By the time it was completed in February 1949 Mr. Reynolds' original estimate of $1,400,000 for repairs had been raised to $5,400,000. The only part of the original mansion found to be sound was the old outer wall, and foundations for it would have to be established for 25 feet below the building.

Chairman Clarence Cannon of the House Appropriations Committee raised a serious question as to whether the old walls were worth saving. Obviously it would be cheaper to raze and rebuild than to attempt a restoration within them. The mansion stood empty and deserted, awaiting a decision on its fate, while committees of Congress wrangled as to which of them had charge of the matter. The White House invitation, symbol of official and social eclat, was in abeyance.

Still, a strange succession of sightseeing expeditions toured the crumbling structure. Members of Congress were taken through to help them make up their minds. Newspaper reporters and photographers toured at their own insistence. Fire underwriters saw and were shocked and voted national resolutions.

But the most noteworthy tour was that taken by 179 members of the Washington Chapter of the American Institute of Architects at the invitation of their fellow member Lorenzo S. Winslow. On that tour the structural secrets of the mansion were opened to inspection, even lettered on the walls. Through a hole cut into the ground floor, they viewed the subfloor of original brick, burned in the kilns on Pennsylvania Avenue in the 1790s. On that same level they saw the old brick-vaulted 1795 kitchen which Winslow said would be restored and used as a conference and broadcasting room. Up they went to abandoned state parlors, which he told them would be stripped of French and Italian Renaissance elaborateness and restored to the simplicity of the original Georgian building.

On the family floor the utility pipes and hot-air flues had been exposed in the survey, and in a number of places the inner wall had been torn out, leaving the old outer wall exposed on its inner side. One wall legend read: "Hand-made lead pipe with zinc sheets installed in 1840"—the first water system; another, "Gas pipe installed 1848—one of the first in the city." Other wall letterings informed that hot-air heating had come in 1874; electricity in 1892; hot-water heating in 1902.

The architects saw the scientific instruments from the Bureau of Standards' laboratories which were recording stresses and strains, measuring rate of fission, even recording for posterity the noise of the cracking of the inner walls.

There was still another exhibit, most interesting of all. Where the inner walls had been entirely removed, soot stains on old stones were evidence of the British burning so many years before—August 1814. One section of this inner wall showed there had been a large cavity in the limestone, now filled with mortar, bricks and even wood. Lorenzo S. Winslow had an explanation. All the accounts of the burning told of the terrible hurricane that had struck the following day. "This severe thunderstorm drenched the hot stone and it exploded, leaving this cavity which was filled in hastily to prevent further crumbling of the wall," he said. This strange scar of resistance to enemy and to elements put up a silent sentimental argument for saving the old White House.

From New York, Mrs. Franklin D. Roosevelt spoke strongly: "No new design or new house could possibly have the historic interest of this old one." Bess Truman, who had voiced no opinion on any public question since entering the White House, sent vigorous word to the women of the press that the original walls should certainly be saved. History-loving Harry Truman, who had a balcony at stake, came out for saving the wall.

At last the bipartisan Commission on the Renovation of the Executive Mansion was set up in 1949 under Public Law No. 40—two members of the Senate, two members of the House, two members appointed by the President—who by tacit agreement were the President of the American Institute of Engineers and the President of the American Institute of Architects. This commission, empowered to make all decisions on the White House, duly decreed that the White House walls, for which the cornerstone was laid October 13, 1792, with 16 toasts at the Masonic dinner in Georgetown following the ceremony, and which in the main had survived the burning by the British in 1814, should be retained.

A new steel frame was to be constructed inside these walls, linked to them by steel rods. A new and deep foundation was to be constructed beneath them. Major General Glen E. Edgerton was made executive director of this work, and Architect Winslow was Commission Secretary. The White House had stood vacant for a solid year before rebuilding started. General Edgerton settled into a detailed task which would take another two years. The firm of John McShain, by lowest bid, was the builder. Strangest sight of the construction process was the interior excavation of a two-story basement. Three bulldozer shovels at one time were digging away inside the empty shell of the White House. Then a whole new steel framework was taken in through doors and windows.

Over in Blair-Lee House, Mrs. Truman set up miniature Red, Blue and Green rooms and a miniature State Dining Room, using some of the White House furniture, vases and silver. There she conducted the greatly curtailed social activities of the Presidency. Necessary state dinners were held at a downtown hotel.

President Truman finally got a press-conference auditorium by taking over a part of the old State Department Building across the street to the west. It was the room where James G. Blaine had held the first Latin American conference. Truman's White House years still were spent in struggling with the troubled times, left over from the Second World War. On the international front Soviet Russia took country after country by boring from within and holding with Red-trained troops until more territory than Hitler ever commanded lay behind the "Iron Curtain." The Truman administration, through its Marshall Plan, rehabilitated and strengthened Western Europe, thereby "containing" Communism somewhat. But China fell to the

Communists, spelling trouble in the Far East. Communist aggression started a war in Korea in June, 1950. United Nations forces, chiefly American youth, entered into a prolonged struggle there. Domestically, Truman pressed for his Fair Deal. He secured a broadened social-security program, but failed to obtain enactment of civil-rights legislation, compulsory health insurance and a production-payments farm plan.

The Truman times were troubled, yet Truman in the main was an even-keeled President, rising early in the morning to take brisk walks to keep himself healthy and cheerful. But once in a while when strain became great, he used unconventional expletives. At one time he expressed himself in public about a columnist, calling the gentleman of the press by a highly uncomplimentary epithet. Next day Mrs. J. Borden Harriman, former Minister to Norway, met Mrs. Truman at a luncheon and laughingly mentioned the matter. Mrs. Truman said that never in her long years of married life had she heard her husband talk like that, and so she had spoken to him about it. After a while the phone rang—a long-distance call from New York. Soon Mrs. Truman heard her husband say, "Now, see here, Margaret, I have just had two hours of that from your mother, and I'm not going to take it from you." The occasional Truman explosions were not ended by the incident.

The difficulty of guarding the President in a house without surrounding grounds, such as Blair House, was dramatically called to the nation's attention with the attempted assassination of President Truman by two fanatics on November 1, 1950. The White House security system was then strengthened.

In Blair House, as in the White House, Bess Truman remained "the Independent Lady from Independence." She refused to emulate any predecessor. She reported her engagements to the press through Mrs. James M. Helm, White House social secretary, and Reathel Odum, her private secretary. Her public appearances were many, but none of them included saying anything. She got her national politics at source, in private conversations with her husband. Aside from letting it be known that she had never really wanted to live in the White House, her reaction was "No comment." She was deeply devoted to the welfare of her husband; of her mother, Mrs. D. W. Wallace, with whom she had lived or who had lived with her during her entire married life; and of her daughter Margaret.

The President's daughter combined the highest points of official life with a career of her own. When officials from Western Europe or South America were at the family table, Margaret was there and alert for jottings in the diary she had kept from the age of ten. Most of the time, however, she was in New York studying voice and appearing in radio and television; or she was on concert tours about the country. Twice she sang before her father in a crowded Constitution Hall. Her 1951 summer was spent in a tour abroad. She dined with the King and Queen of England and met not only the two young princesses, but also the King of Norway, who was visiting there. She also visited Queen Juliana of Holland. She had an audience with the Pope at Rome, saw Paris, and visited her old friend Minister Perle Mesta in Luxembourg. Margaret Truman was conceded to be an excellent good-will ambassador for this country. Her trip was followed by announcements of return visits from Prince Philip and Princess Elizabeth of England, and from Queen Juliana of Holland.

The White House reconstruction proceeded as plans were made for a $150,000 refurnishing when actual building was done. The deeper foundation made possible two full floors of utility and storage rooms below the ground level. Still more space was excavated under the front lawn. Included, of course, was a modern air-conditioning system. A change in the lines of the roof added more space up above, including a big new bedroom at each of the four corners, a skylighted recreation room in the center—and an enlarged Sky Parlor on the roof at south center.

Most noticeable change in the state parlors, which always will be called the first floor at the White House, no matter how many stories are added beneath, was the lightening of the State Dining Room. When enlarged in the Theodore Roosevelt Administration, this room had been darkly paneled with English oak. In the 1951 remodeling the walls were painted a soft blue-green to tone in with the newly installed Georgian fireplace of light verde antique Vermont marble. Gone were Teddy Roosevelt's carved bison heads. But the stone on which John Adams' prayer was carved was saved for display in the public rooms on the ground floor.

Mrs. Coolidge's plan for anonymous donors to give their best antiques to the mansion was at last bearing fruit. To the Private Dining Room was added a fine Chippendale table, worth from $8,000 to $10,000, with chairs to match. And two very fine settees designed by Robert Adam and made by Chippendale, both of them museum pieces, were used in the decorations of a simpler East Room. Its three enormous chandeliers had again been reduced in size. The Green Room wall silk was used again, but the wall coverings of both Blue and Red rooms had so faded and frayed that they had to be redone— of course in the same colors.

The selection of color schemes for family living quarters upstairs was made by Mrs. Truman, with one of the big New York department stores doing the decoration. Most important move was the grouping of the Lincoln furniture in the room where he signed the Emancipation Proclamation. The big old Lincoln bed was finally tied to the Civil War President by documentary evidence instead of folklore. About it were grouped other established Lincoln pieces, including an elaborately carved dresser and marble-topped tables. Next door to it on the west Mrs. Hoover's Monroe Room was re-established. The East Hall was furnished as a formal sitting room. The Rose Suite, slept in by the Queen of England, retained its old-time color—but with new décor.

Built-in breakfront bookcases, rising nearly to the ceiling, together with a wood wainscot and plaster cornice, at last gave a lived-in look to the big Central Hall. The small bedrooms at the four corners were bigger by a foot and a half. That space, and closet space, too, had been taken from the larger rooms of the corner suites, with plenty of room left over.

Mrs. Truman chose plum as the predominating color in her southwest sitting room and bedroom. Margaret Truman chose green for the walls of her sitting room in the northwest suite. The President chose green for his Oval Study, which got new draperies and a new rug. And at last he was rid of an old-fashioned wardrobe as the only place to hang his clothes in the stately bedroom adjoining his study.

The West Hall, a family sitting room, had historical red and off-white draperies at its big window, much red in couch and chair coverings and a new beige rug.

The White House architect held that the new ground floor was "quite the show place of the house." Five of its rooms were paneled in fine old pine from the salvaged timber of the original White House, processed by Baltimore craftsmen, leaving the old nail holes. More of the pine was carved for the mantels in these rooms, and old stone, also from the original White House, was used for fireplaces. Among these

The Blue Room with its crystal chandelier.

A charcoal drawing of a sitting room on the family floor of the White House following the Truman rebuilding.

paneled rooms are three well known to all who take White House tours—the China Collection Room, the Oval Diplomatic Reception Room and the Library, where the White House displays the books given to the mansion by the American Booksellers. Old stone mantels were used in the original vaulted kitchen, now a conference room. That room was chosen by Mr. Winslow for display of the stones into which Masonic emblems had been cut by the original workmen. These interestingly carved stones were discovered during the White House dismantling. The ground-floor corridor was made more beautiful by Vermont marble walls and floor.

The new mansion in the old mold was ready to make its public debut. Its architects and builders said it was solid enough to stand for a couple of centuries at least. So, strengthened without and restored within, the old mansion shall remain yours forever or thereabouts—the White House.

BIBLIOGRAPHY AND INDEX

BIBLIOGRAPHY

GENERAL

Agar, Herbert, *The People's Choice, Washington to Harding*. Boston and New York: Houghton Mifflin Co., 1933.

Brown, Glenn, 1860-1930, *Memories; A Winning Crusade to Revive George Washington's Vision of a Capital City*. Washington: W. F. Roberts Co., 1931.

Bryan, Wilhelmus Bogart, A *History of the National Capital from Its Foundation Through the Period of the Adoption of the Organic Act*. New York: The Macmillan Co., 1914-1916.

Cavanah, Frances, *Children of the White House*. New York and Chicago: Rand McNally & Co., 1936.

Celebration of the One Hundredth Anniversary of the Establishment of the Seat of Government in the District of Columbia, 1800-1900. Compiled by William V. Cox, under jurisdiction of Joint Committee on Printing. Washington: Government Printing Office, 1901.

Colman, Edna M., *Seventy-five Years of White House Gossip; from Washington to Lincoln*. Garden City, N. Y.: Doubleday, Page & Co., 1926.

———, *White House Gossip, from Andrew Johnson to Calvin Coolidge*. Garden City, N.Y.: Doubleday, Page & Co., 1927.

Crook, William H., *Memories of the White House*, edited by Henry Rood. Boston: Little, Brown & Co., 1911.

Devitt, George Raymond, *The White House Gallery of Official Portraits of the Presidents*. Washington and New York: Bureau of National Literature, 1912.

Dictionary of American Biography. New York: Charles Scribner's Sons, 1928.

Ellet, Mrs. E. F., *Court Circles of the Republic*. Philadelphia: Philadelphia Publishing Company, 1872.

Goebel, Dorothy Burne, and Julius Goebel, Jr., *Generals in the White House*. Garden City, N. Y.: Doubleday, Doran & Co., Inc., 1945.

Goodwin, Katharine Calvert, "White House Invitations," *Daughters of the American Revolution Magazine*, vol. 54, June 1920, pp. 335-347.

Hoover, Irwin H., *Forty-two Years in the White House*. Boston and New York: Houghton Mifflin Co., 1934. Also, the *Saturday Evening Post* series of articles, edited by Wesley Stout, vol. 206, February-May 1934; vol. 207, August-November 1934.

Hurd, Charles, *The White House, a Biography*. New York and London: Harper & Brothers, 1940.

Jaffray, Elizabeth, *Secrets of the White House*. New York: Cosmopolitan Book Corp., 1927.

Langford, Laura Holloway, *The Ladies of the White House*. Philadelphia: Bradley & Co., 1881.

Lewis, Ethel, *The White House*. New York: Dodd, Mead & Co., 1937.

Logan, Mary S., *Thirty Years in Washington*. Hartford, Conn.: A. D. Worthington & Co., 1901.

Nesbitt, Victoria Henrietta, *White House Diary*. Garden City, N. Y.: Doubleday & Company, 1948.

Pendel, Thomas F., *Thirty-six Years in the White House; Lincoln— Roosevelt*. Washington: The Neale Publishing Co., 1902.

Poore, Ben: Perley, *Perley's Reminiscences of Sixty Years in the National Metropolis*. Tecumseh, Mich.: A. W. Mills, 1886. Also published in 1886 by Hubbard Bros., Philadelphia, and W. A. Houghton, New York.

Seaton, Josephine, *William Winston Seaton*. Boston: J. R. Osgood & Co., 1871.

Singleton, Esther, *The Story of the White House*. New York: The McClure Co., 1907.

Smith, Margaret Bayard, *The First Forty Years of Washington Society*, edited by Gaillard Hunt. New York: Charles Scribner's Sons, 1906.

———, *A Winter in Washington*. New York: E. Bliss & E. White, 1824.

Wharton, Anne Hollingsworth, *Social Life in the Early Republic*. Philadelphia and London: J. B. Lippincott Co., 1902.

Whitton, Mary Ormsbee, *First First Ladies, 1789-1865*. New York: Hastings House, 1948.

CHAPTER I. *John Adams*

Adams, Abigail, *Letters of Mrs. Adams, the Wife of John Adams*. Boston: Wilkins, Carter & Co., 1848.

———, *New Letters of Abigail Adams, 1788-1801*, edited by Stewart Mitchell. Boston: Houghton Mifflin Co., 1947.

Adams, John, *Correspondence of John Adams and Thomas Jefferson, 1812 to 1826*, selected by Paul Wilstach. Indianapolis: The Bobbs-Merrill Company, 1925.

Nicolay, John G., papers in Library of Congress contain Mrs. Adams' defense of her drawing room.

Niles' Weekly Register, Baltimore, Md., January 31, 1818, contains
Editor Niles' reply.
Whitney, Janet, *Abigail Adams*. Boston: Little, Brown & Co., 1947.

CHAPTER II. *Jefferson*

Brown, Everett Somerville, ed., *William Plumer's Memorandum of Proceedings in the United States Senate. 1803-1807*. New York: The Macmillan Co., 1923.

Foley, John P., ed., *The Jeffersonian Cyclopedia* (9,000 titles). New York and London: Funk & Wagnalls Co., 1900.

Frary, Ihna Thayer, *Thomas Jefferson, Architect and Builder*. Richmond: Garrett & Massie, 1939.

Jefferson, Thomas, *Papers*, 1809, *Feb. 2—March 2*, vol. 186. Manuscript Section, Library of Congress.

Kimball, Fiske, "The Genesis of the White House," *Century*, vol. 95, February 1918, pp. 523-528.

———, *Thomas Jefferson, Architect*. Boston: Riverside Press, 1916. Printed for private distribution.

Kimball, Marie, "The Epicure of the White House; Thomas Jefferson," *Virginia Quarterly Review*, vol. 9, January 1933, pp. 71-81.

———, "The Original Furnishings of the White House," *Antiques*, vol. 15, June 1929, pp. 481-486; and vol. 16, July 1929, pp. 33-37.

———, *Thomas Jefferson's Cook Book*. Richmond: Garrett & Massie, 1938.

Koch, Adrienne, *Jefferson and Madison, the Great Collaboration*. New York: Alfred A. Knopf, 1950.

Padover, Saul K., ed., *Thomas Jefferson and the National Capital*. Washington: Government Printing Office, 1946.

Randolph, Sarah N., *The Domestic Life of Thomas Jefferson*. Cambridge, Mass.: University Press, 1939.

Weyl, Nathaniel, *Treason, the Story of Disloyalty and Betrayal in American History*. Washington: Public Affairs Press, 1950.

CHAPTER III. *Madison*

The fact that the name White House was used prior to the burning of the mansion by the British was first proved by Wilhelmus Bogart Bryan and was recorded in a letter from him published in the *Records of the Columbia Historical Society*, vol. 33-34, pp. 306-308, published by the society in Washington, 1932. It was called to my attention by

David Mearns, Assistant Librarian of Congress. I myself discovered the connotation by going back to original sources.

Adams, Henry, "Count Edward de Crillon" (John Henry incident), *American Historical Review*, vol. 1, no. 1, October 1895, pp. 51-59.
————, ed., *Documents Relating to New England Federalism, 1800-1815.* Boston: Little, Brown & Co., 1877.
Adams, John Quincy, *The Lives of James Madison and James Monroe.* Boston: Phillips, Sampson & Co.; Buffalo: G. H. Derby & Co., 1850.
American State Papers, Foreign Relations, original papers on John Henry incident, vol. 3, pp. 545-557. Washington: Gales and Seaton, 1832.
Brant, Irving, *James Madison, Father of the Constitution, 1787-1800.* Indianapolis: The Bobbs-Merrill Company, 1950.
Clark, Allen C., *Life and Letters of Dolly Madison.* Washington: W. F. Roberts Co., 1914.
Cutts, Lucia B., ed., *Memoirs and Letters of Dolly Madison.* Boston and New York: Houghton Mifflin Co., 1886.
Hunt, Gaillard, *The Life of James Madison.* New York: Doubleday, Page & Co., 1902.
————, "Mrs. Madison's First Drawing-room," *Harper's Monthly Magazine,* vol. 121, June 1910, pp. 141-148.

Chapter IV. *Monroe—J. Q. Adams*

Adams, Charles Francis, ed., *Memoirs of John Quincy Adams.* Philadelphia: J. B. Lippincott Co., 1874-1877. Vols. IV-VIII.
Bobbé, Dorothie, *Mr. and Mrs. John Quincy Adams.* New York: Minton, Balch & Co., 1930.
Cresson, William Penn, *James Monroe.* Chapel Hill: University of North Carolina Press, 1946.
Gilman, Daniel Coit, *James Monroe.* Boston and New York: Houghton Mifflin & Co., 1898.
Lipsky, George A., *John Quincy Adams, His Theory and Ideas.* New York: Thomas Y. Crowell Co., 1950.
Morgan, George, *The Life of James Monroe.* Boston: Small, Maynard & Co., 1921.
Morse, John T., Jr., *John Quincy Adams.* Boston and New York: Houghton Mifflin Co., 1882.
Styron, Arthur, *The Last of the Cocked Hats: James Monroe and the Virginia Dynasty.* Norman, Okla.: University of Oklahoma Press, 1945.

Waldo, S. Putnam, *The Tour of James Monroe, President of the United States, through the Northern and Eastern States in 1817.* Hartford, Conn.: 1818, 1820 (2 editions).

CHAPTER V. *Jackson*

Adams, Samuel Hopkins, *The Gorgeous Hussy.* Boston and New York: Houghton Mifflin Co., 1934.

Daily Globe, Washington, D. C., 1828-1837.

Eaton, John Henry, *The Complete Memoirs of Andrew Jackson.* Philadelphia: Claxton, Remsen & Haffelfinger, 1878.

Eaton, Margaret (O'Neale) Timberlake, *The Autobiography of Peggy Eaton.* New York: Charles Scribner's Sons, 1932.

James, Marquis, *The Life of Andrew Jackson.* Indianapolis: The Bobbs-Merrill Company, 1938.

Martineau, Harriet, *Autobiography,* edited by Maria Weston Chapman. Boston: J. R. Osgood & Co., 1877.

————, *Retrospect of Western Travel.* London: Saunders & Otley, 1838.

————, *Society in America.* London: Saunders & Otley, 1837.

National Intelligencer, Washington, D. C., 1828-1837.

Nicolay, Helen, *Andrew Jackson, the Fighting President.* New York and London: The Century Co., 1929.

United States Telegraph, Washington, D. C., 1828-1837.

CHAPTER VI. *Van Buren—W. H. Harrison—Tyler*

Alexander, Holmes, *The American Talleyrand.* New York and London: Harper & Brothers, 1935.

Blair, Walter, *Horse Sense in American Humor.* Chicago: The University of Chicago Press, 1942.

Cleaves, Freeman, *Old Tippecanoe, William Henry Harrison and His Time.* New York and London: Charles Scribner's Sons, 1939.

Crockett, David, *The Life of Martin Van Buren.* Philadelphia: R. Wright, 1835. (Also attributed to A. S. Clayton.)

Frémont, Jessie Benton, *Souvenirs of My Time.* Boston: D. Lothrop & Co., 1887.

Lynch, Denis Tilden, *An Epoch and a Man, Martin Van Buren and His Times.* New York: H. Liveright, 1929.

Tyler, Lyon G., *The Letters and Times of the Tylers.* Richmond, Va.: Whittet & Shepperson, 1884-1896.

Van Buren papers (unpublished), Library of Congress.

CHAPTER VII. *Polk*

Hosmer, James Kendall, *The Last Leaf.* New York and London: G. P. Putnam's Sons, 1912.

McCormac, Eugene Irving, *James K. Polk, a Political Biography.* Berkeley, Calif.: University of California Press, 1922.

Nelson, Anson, and Fanny Nelson, *Memorials of Sarah Childress Polk.* New York: A. D. F. Randolph & Co., 1892.

Nevins, Allan, ed., *Polk, the Diary of a President, 1845-1849.* London and New York: Longmans, Green & Co., 1929.

Van der Linden, Frank, *Dark Horse.* San Antonio, Tex.: The Naylor Co., 1944.

CHAPTER VIII. *Taylor—Fillmore—Pierce—Buchanan*

Auchampaugh, Philip G., *James Buchanan and His Cabinet on the Eve of Secession.* Lancaster, Pa.: privately printed, 1926.

Buchanan, James, *Mr. Buchanan's Administration, on the Eve of the Rebellion.* London: S. Low, Son & Marston, 1865. Vol. 12 of his *Works.*

Chamberlain, Ivory, *Biography of Millard Fillmore.* Buffalo: Thomas & Lathrops, 1856.

Dyer, Brainerd, *Zachary Taylor.* Baton Rouge, La.: Louisiana State University Press, 1946.

Griffis, William E., *Millard Fillmore.* Ithaca, N. Y.: Andrus & Church, 1915.

Howard, Oliver Otis, *General Taylor.* New York: D. Appleton & Co., 1892.

King, Horatio, *Turning on the Light.* Philadelphia: J. B. Lippincott Co., 1895.

McKinley, Silas Bent, and Silas Bent, *Old Rough and Ready.* New York: The Vanguard Press, 1946.

Nichols, Roy F., *Franklin Pierce, Young Hickory of the Granite Hills.* Philadelphia: University of Pennsylvania Press; London: H. Milford, Oxford University Press, 1931.

Severance, Frank H., ed., *Millard Fillmore Papers.* Buffalo, N. Y.: The Buffalo Historical Society, 1907.

Taylor, Zachary, *Letters of Zachary Taylor,* reprinted from originals in the collection of William K. Bixby of St. Louis, Mo. Rochester, N. Y.: The Genesee Press, 1908.

Tharp, Louise Hall, *The Peabody Sisters of Salem.* Boston: Little, Brown & Co., 1950.

CHAPTER IX. *Lincoln*

Ames, Mary Clemmer, *Ten Years in Washington.* Hartford, Conn.: A. D. Worthington & Co., 1873.

Commager, Henry Steele, *The Blue and the Gray.* Indianapolis: The Bobbs-Merrill Company, 1950.

Helm, Katherine, *The True Story of Mary, Wife of Lincoln.* New York and London: Harper & Brothers, 1928.

Hendrick, Burton J., *The Lees of Virginia.* Boston: Little, Brown & Co., 1935.

Keckley, Elizabeth Hobbs, *Behind the Scenes.* New York: G. W. Carleton & Co., 1868.

Leech, Margaret, *Reveille in Washington.* New York and London: Harper & Brothers, 1941.

Liebling, A. J., "Abe Lincoln in Springfield," *The New Yorker,* vol. 26, June 24, 1950, pp. 29-32.

Lincoln, Abraham, *Abraham Lincoln's Autobiography,* with additional biographical material by Robert Dale Richardson. Boston: Beacon Press, 1947.

Monoghan, Jay, *Diplomat in Carpet Slippers.* Indianapolis: The Bobbs-Merrill Company, 1945.

Nicolay, Helen, *Lincoln's Secretary.* New York: Longmans, Green & Co., 1949.

Nicolay, John G., *A Short Life of Abraham Lincoln.* New York: The Century Co., 1902.

Pryor, Mrs. Roger A., *Reminiscences of Peace and War.* New York: The Macmillan Co., 1905.

Sandburg, Carl, *Abraham Lincoln, the War Years.* New York: Harcourt, Brace & Co., 1939.

———, *Mary Lincoln, Wife and Widow.* Part I by Carl Sandburg; Part II, letters, documents and appendix, by Paul M. Angle. New York: Harcourt, Brace & Co., 1932.

Stoddard, William O. *Inside the White House in War Times.* New York: C. L. Webster & Co., 1890.

Swisshelm, Jane Grey, *Half a Century.* Chicago: J. G. Swisshelm, 1880.

Townsend, George Alfred ("Garth"), *Washington Outside and Inside.* Hartford, Conn., and Chicago: J. Betts & Co.; Cincinnati: S. M. Betts & Co., 1873.

CHAPTER X. Johnson

Beale, Howard K., The Critical Year. New York: Harcourt, Brace & Co., 1930.
Bowers, Claude G., The Tragic Era. Cambridge: Houghton Mifflin Co., 1929.
Briggs, Emily E., The Olivia Letters. New York and Washington: The Neale Publishing Co., 1906.
Clemenceau, Georges E., American Reconstruction, 1865-1870, and the Impeachment of President Johnson. New York: L. MacVeagh, The Dial Press; Toronto: Longmans, Green & Co., 1928.
Milton, George Fort, The Age of Hate. New York: Coward-McCann, Inc., 1930.
Sterling, Ada, ed., A Belle of the Fifties, Memoirs of Mrs. Clay of Alabama. New York: Doubleday, Page & Co., 1904.

CHAPTER XI. Grant—Hayes—Garfield

Beale, Harriet S. Blaine, ed., Letters of Mrs. James G. Blaine. New York: Duffield & Co., 1898.
Grant, Jesse R., In the Days of My Father, General Grant. New York and London: Harper & Brothers, 1925.
Hasseltine, William B., Ulysses S. Grant, Politician. New York: Dodd, Mead & Co., 1935.
Martin, Edward Winslow (pseudonym of James Dabney McCabe), Behind the Scenes in Washington. New York: Continental Publishing Co., 1873.
Smith, Theodore C., The Life and Letters of James Abram Garfield, New Haven: Yale University Press, 1925.
Todd, Helen, A Man Named Grant. Boston: Houghton Mifflin Co., 1940.
The White House Porcelain Service. New York: Haviland & Co., 1879.
Williams, Charles R., The Life of Rutherford Birchard Hayes. Boston and New York: Houghton Mifflin Co., 1914.
Woodward, C. Vann, Reunion and Reaction: the Compromise of 1877 and the End of Reconstruction. Boston: Little, Brown & Co., 1951.
Woodward, William E., Meet General Grant. New York: Liveright Publishing Corp., 1946.

CHAPTER XII. Arthur—Cleveland

Depew, Chauncey M., "Leaves from My Autobiography," Scribner's, vol. 70, November 1921, pp. 515-530; December 1921, pp. 664-676.

Howe, George Frederick, *Chester A. Arthur, a Quarter-century of Machine Politics.* New York: Dodd, Mead & Co., 1934.

McElroy, Robert McN., *Grover Cleveland, the Man and the Statesman.* Authorized. New York and London: Harper & Brothers, 1923.

Nevins, Allan, *Grover Cleveland, a Study in Courage.* New York: Dodd, Mead & Co., 1933.

——, ed., *Letters of Grover Cleveland, 1850-1908.* Boston and New York: Houghton Mifflin Co., 1933.

Parker, George F., *Recollections of Grover Cleveland.* New York: The Century Co., 1909.

Root, Elihu, *Miscellaneous Addresses,* edited by Robert Bacon and James Brown Scott. Cambridge: Harvard University Press, 1917.

CHAPTER XIII. *Benjamin Harrison—McKinley*

Boyd, James P., *Life and Public Services of Benjamin Harrison.* Philadelphia: Publishers Union, 1901.

Butler, Joseph G., *Life of William McKinley and History of National McKinley Birthplace Memorial.* Cleveland, 1924.

Corning, A. Elwood, *William McKinley: a Biographical Study.* New York: Broadway Publishing Co., 1907.

Fallows, Samuel, *Life of William McKinley, Our Martyred President.* International Memorial Edition. Chicago: Regan Printing House, 1901.

Hobart, Jennie, *Second Lady.* New York: privately printed (Mt. Vernon, N. Y.: W. E. Rudge), 1933. Material included in the main portion of this book appeared under the title "Second Lady" in the *Saturday Evening Post,* vol. 201, June 29, 1929.

Johnston, Frances Benjamin, *The White House* (photographs). Washington: Gibson Bros., 1893.

Kohlsaat, Herman H., *From McKinley to Harding.* New York and London: Charles Scribner's Sons, 1923.

Morrison, J. E., and William B. Lane, *Life of Our President, Benjamin Harrison, Together with that of His Grandfather, William Henry Harrison.* Cincinnati: The Economy Printing Co., 1889.

The National McKinley Birthplace Memorial. Cleveland: Penton Press, 1918.

Olcott, Charles S., *The Life of William McKinley.* Boston and New York: Houghton Mifflin Co., 1916.

Volwiler, Albert T., ed., *The Correspondence between Benjamin Harrison and James G. Blaine, 1882-1893.* Philadelphia: The American Philosophical Society, 1940.

CHAPTER XIV. *Theodore Roosevelt—Taft*

The political reporter who watched from a fire escape Theodore Roosevelt's hotel-room acceptance of the Vice Presidency before it was proffered on the convention floor was my father-in-law, Robert B. Armstrong, at that time in charge of the eastern work of the Chicago *Record*.

Bishop, Joseph Bucklin, *Theodore Roosevelt and His Time.* Authorized. New York: Charles Scribner's Sons, 1920.

———, ed., *Theodore Roosevelt's Letters to His Children.* New York: Charles Scribner's Sons, 1919.

Butt, Archibald W., *The Letters of Archie Butt*, edited by Lawrence F. Abbott. Garden City, N. Y.: Doubleday, Page & Co., 1924.

———, *Taft and Roosevelt, the Intimate Letters of Archie Butt.* Garden City, N. Y.: Doubleday, Doran & Co., Inc., 1930.

Charnwood, Godfrey Rathbone Benson, 1st Baron, *Theodore Roosevelt.* Boston: The Atlantic Monthly Press, 1923.

Longworth, Alice Roosevelt, *Crowded Hours.* New York and London: Charles Scribner's Sons, 1933.

Pringle, Henry F., *The Life and Times of William Howard Taft.* New York and Toronto: Farrar & Rinehart, Inc., 1939.

———, *Theodore Roosevelt.* New York: Blue Ribbon Books, Inc., 1934.

Restoration of the White House. Message from the President of the United States transmitting the report of the architects. Washington: Government Printing Office, 1903. (57th Cong., 2nd sess., Senate Doc. No. 197)

Storer, Bellamy, *Letter of Bellamy Storer to the President and the Members of His Cabinet.* Cincinnati, 1906.

Storer, Maria Longworth, *In Memoriam Bellamy Storer.* Privately printed. Boston: The Merrymount Press, 1923.

Taft, Helen Herron, "My Policies in White House-keeping," *Delineator*, vol. 85, September 1914, pp. 17-18.

———, "Parties We Gave at the White House," *Delineator*, vol. 85, October 1914, pp. 18-19.

———, *Recollections of Full Years.* New York: Dodd, Mead & Co., 1914.

———, "What It Is Like to Enter the White House as First Lady of the Land," *Delineator*, vol. 84, May 1914, pp. 5-6.

———, "White House Début and a Silver Wedding," *Delineator*, vol. 85, November 1914, pp. 17-18.

White, William Allen, *The Autobiography of William Allen White.* New York: The Macmillan Co., 1946.

Wood, Frederick S., *Roosevelt as We Knew Him*. Philadelphia and Chicago: The John C. Winston Co., 1927.

CHAPTER XV. *Wilson*

Anderson, Isabel W., *Presidents and Pies*. Boston and New York: Houghton Mifflin Co., 1920.

Bolling, John Randolph, *Chronology of Woodrow Wilson*. New York: Frederick A. Stokes Co., 1927.

Daniels, Josephus, *The Life of Woodrow Wilson, 1856-1924*. Philadelphia and Chicago: The John C. Winston Co., 1924.

Dodd, William E., *Woodrow Wilson and His Work*. New York: P. Smith, 1932.

Houston, David F., *Eight Years with Wilson's Cabinet*. Garden City, N. Y.: Doubleday, Page & Co., 1926.

Hulbert, Mary Allen, *The Story of Mrs. Peck, an Autobiography*. New York: Minton, Balch & Co., 1933.

Loth, David, *The Story of Woodrow Wilson*. New York: The Woodrow Wilson Foundation, 1944.

McAdoo, Eleanor Randolph, and Margaret Y. Gaffey, *The Woodrow Wilsons*. New York: The Macmillan Co., 1937.

Patterson, A. W., *Personal Recollections of Woodrow Wilson*. Richmond, Va.: Whittet & Shepperson, 1929.

Reid, Edith Gittings, *Woodrow Wilson; the Caricature, the Myth and the Man*. London and New York: Oxford University Press, 1934.

Stevens, Doris, *Jailed for Freedom*. New York: Boni & Liveright, 1920.

Sullivan, Mark, *Over Here, 1914-1918*, vol. 5 of *Our Times: the United States, 1900-1925*. New York: Charles Scribner's Sons, 1926-1935.

Thompson, Charles W., *Presidents I've Known and Two Near Presidents*. Indianapolis: The Bobbs-Merrill Company, 1929.

Tumulty, Joseph P., *Woodrow Wilson as I Know Him*. Garden City, N. Y., and Toronto: Doubleday, Page & Co., 1921.

White, William Allen, *Woodrow Wilson, the Man, His Times and His Task*. Boston and New York: Houghton Mifflin Co., 1924.

Wilson, Edith Bolling, *My Memoir*. Indianapolis: The Bobbs-Merrill Company, 1939.

CHAPTER XVI. *Harding Coolidge—Hoover*

Blythe, Samuel G., *A Calm Review of a Calm Man*. New York: Cosmopolitan Book Corp., 1923.

Coolidge, Calvin, *The Autobiography of Calvin Coolidge*. New York: Cosmopolitan Book Corp., 1929.

Coolidge, Grace A., "Home Again!" *American Magazine*, vol. 109, January 1930, pp. 18-19.

———, "How I Spent My Days at the White House," *American Magazine*, vol. 108, October 1929, pp. 16-17.

———, "Making Ourselves at Home in the White House," *American Magazine*, vol. 108, November 1929, pp. 20-21.

———, "Our Family Pets," *American Magazine*, vol. 108, December 1929, pp. 24-25.

———, commentator, "The Real Calvin Coolidge, by Fifty People Who Knew Him Best," *Good Housekeeping*, vol. 100, February 1935, pp. 18-21; March 1935, pp. 22-25; April 1935, pp. 38-41; May 1935, pp. 38-39; June 1935, pp. 42-43.

———, "When I Became the First Lady," *American Magazine*, vol. 108, September 1929, pp. 11-13.

Corey, Herbert, *The Truth About Hoover*. Boston and New York: Houghton Mifflin Co., 1932.

Daugherty, Harry M., and Thomas Dixon, *The Inside Story of the Harding Tragedy*. New York: The Churchill Co., 1932.

Harding, Warren G., *Last Speeches of President Harding*. Compiled by James W. Murphy and privately printed. Washington, 1923.

Hoover, Herbert, "Personal Memoirs," *Collier's Magazine*, vol. 127, February 17, 1951, pp. 13-15; February 24, 1951, pp. 22-23; March 3, 1951, pp. 30-31; March 10, 1951, pp. 26-27.

Lyons, Eugene, *Our Unknown Ex-President*. Garden City, N. Y.: Doubleday & Company, 1948.

McLean, Evalyn Walsh, with Boyden Sparks, *Father Struck It Rich*. Boston: Little, Brown & Co., 1936.

Roberts, Kenneth L., *Concentrated New England*. Indianapolis: The Bobbs-Merrill Company, 1924.

Rogers, Will, "Coolidge," *American Magazine*, vol. 117, June 1929, pp. 20-21.

Stark, Dare, "Heirlooms in the White House," *Woman's Home Companion*, vol. 59, March 1932, pp. 17-18.

Starling, Edmund W., *Starling of the White House*, as told to Thomas Sugrue. New York: Simon and Schuster, 1946.

White, William Allen, *A Puritan in Babylon*. New York: The Macmillan Co., 1938.

CHAPTERS XVII and XVIII. *F. D. Roosevelt—Truman*

While I have read most of the books written about the last two Presidents in this volume, the accounts here come largely from personal knowledge.

Furman, Bess, *Washington By-line*. New York: Alfred A. Knopf, 1949.

INDEX